A Legal Primer
on Managing
Museum Collections

A
Legal Primer
on Managing
Museum
Collections

Marie C. Malaro

SMITHSONIAN INSTITUTION PRESS
Washington, D.C.
1985

Library of Congress Cataloging in Publication Data
Malaro, Marie C.
   A legal primer on managing museum collections.
   Includes bibliographical references and index,
   1. Museums—Law and legislation—United States.
I. Title.
KF4305.M35   1985   344.73′093   84-23497
ISBN 0-87474-656-6   (cloth);   0-87474-697-3   (paper)   347.30493

The paper in this book meets the guidelines for permanence
and durability of the Committee on Production Guidelines for Book
Longevity of the Council on Library Resources.

95   5   4

Contents

Preface

For a number of years, the Smithsonian Institution, with the cooperation of the American Association of Museums, has joined with the American Law Institute-American Bar Association Committee on Continuing Professional Education (ALI/ABA) to present an annual course of study entitled "Legal Problems of Museum Administration." The purpose of the course is to highlight current legal issues that have relevance for the museum community, and these issues are numerous, varied and often complex. Frequently, the more experienced professionals attending the course express dismay at the amount of material that has to be digested, so pity the novice who leaves with bulging briefcase and glazed eyes. Where to begin? How to survive?

This book draws upon the author's experience as a legal advisor for a major museum complex and as a member of the planning committee and faculty for the ALI/ABA seminar. The book was written with particular purposes in mind. First of all, it is for the "novice" whether he or she be the attorney who is called upon occasionally to advise a museum, or the new museum staff member or trustee who must wrestle with a myriad of administrative problems without benefit of constant professional advice. For the nonlawyer, issues are explained simply, without heavy reliance on legal terminology. The objective is to give sufficient background information so that intelligent decisions can be made regarding the appropriate time to call legal counsel. The information contained in the book should not be considered legal advice or relied on as such. For the lawyer, there are case citations and references to legal texts and articles that may aid in researching particular problems. Much of this legal reference material has been placed in footnotes. Footnotes are a necessary evil in any text that deals with the law. It is possible to state a legal principle or issue simply, the difficulty usually lies in applying that principle or issue to the situation at hand. Footnotes in close proximity to the text serve the lawyer, but they also remind the nonlawyer that invariably there are many "if's" and "but's" to consider when making a legal judgment.

Secondly, the book focuses on collection-related issues. "Legal Problems of Museum Administration" can cover such varied topics as employee benefit plans, postal regulations and stock loan programs, but information on these topics is available in many publications devoted to nonprofit organizations. Collections, however, are unique to museums and in order to keep this volume within reasonable limits, the emphasis is on legal problems associated with this distinctive feature.

Thirdly, the book has been written with an eye toward prevention. The best way to avoid legal entanglements is to think before acting. One must understand the obligations, the limits of authority and the possible consequences of contemplated actions. Rather than offer a first-aid manual that lists instructions on how to handle each emergency situation, this text strives to encourage a thoughtful and well-informed approach to museum administration so that the patient stays healthy. The book should be read with this in mind.

The author began the task of writing the book with every intention of being objective. It soon became evident that this standard would not be maintained. There is a bit of preaching here and there, and issues of particular interest to the author receive more expansive treatment. Read the book, therefore, as one lawyer's viewpoint on issues associated with collection management, and, by all means, feel free to disagree. Any issue of consequence deserves spirited debate.

This book would not have been possible were it not for the author's colleagues at the Smithsonian Institution, and elsewhere. All offered encouragement and many advised on the text itself. The author is indebted to them all. Special recognition is due Bonnie Morgan, a legal assistant par excellence, who contributed her skills from the very first word to the final period.

Introduction

Historically, the museum profession and the legal profession have gone their separate ways. It still is not uncommon to hear the question: But what legal problems could a museum have? The existence of such a comfortable state of affairs may be attributed to acumen on the part of the museum profession, naïveté or just good fortune. But one thing is certain, times are changing.

Over the last decade or two, museums have begun to experience the warm glow of the limelight. They have found that being on stage can be challenging, exhilarating, and all too often, frustrating. Suddenly everyone wants to participate, and what was once a rather uncomplicated and exclusive domain is becoming an administrator's nightmare.

It was rare, years ago, for anyone to question the caliber or form of governance in a museum. Not so today. As a more educated and affluent society discovers its local museums, there are numerous cries for openness, participation and change. Objects that once passed silently in and out of museum collections are now the subject of national and international debate. Artists are more vocal, and emerging groups of university-trained museum professionals are questioning traditional practices. Museums can find themselves unwitting participants in ingenious profit-making or tax-shelter schemes of investors and entrepreneurs, and even for the most cautious museum there is the temptation to explore the commercial world in order to make ends meet. Government subsidies also offer attractive avenues to financial relief, but these subsidies come with innumerable strings. What legal problems could a museum have today? Perhaps it is better to ask, Where shall one begin?

Properly used, the law provides a means for freedom, for expression and for growth. Consider, for instance, the familiar traffic light. It is a simple example of the law in action. By setting in motion a prescribed order, the traffic light permits us to proceed with assurance from point to point simply because, through the mechanism of the law, we have determined in advance who will have the right of way. It is this positive function of the law that can so benefit the museum profession. When doubt and confusion reign, it is time to learn the rules of the road. Only when the rules are known can one proceed with a measure of confidence along unfamiliar and hazardous territory.

In pursuing this positive approach to the law, one must start with some very basic issues. Legal controversies have as many shades as an artist's palette and unless certain principles are understood, there is little to guide one when a unique problem arises. Even more important, without a comfortable knowledge of the fundamental rights and obligations involved in museum administration, one is ill-equipped to take preventive measures so that legal controversies are avoided. Accordingly, the book is arranged as follows. First, the legal nature of a museum is examined as well as the various consequences that flow from this status. Discussed are the responsibilities placed on board members of a museum, privileges enjoyed by museums and obligations imposed. Next, entities that may be able to question the quality of governance in a museum are examined. These range from the state Attorney General to the local citizens' group. The balance, and major portion, of the book discusses particular collection-related problems that have legal overtones. Because the emphasis is on prevention, this portion of the text begins with a section on collection management policies. Such policies are suggested as a practical method for assuring a comprehensive approach to the many issues that bear on collection management. The format for such a policy is then used to discuss individual issues as they relate to accessions, deaccessions, loans and so forth.

Museum professionals are urged to use the text as a checklist for assessing the well-being of their organization's collection-related practices. If read from cover to cover, it highlights most issues which, if addressed early and objectively, foster good management and a dedication to excellence. For those museums that have collection management policies, the text can be a useful tool for review; for museums without collection management policies, it offers a framework on which to build.

It should be remembered that this text concerns legal aspects of collection management and does not attempt to elaborate on ethical and professional standards. A museum that strives only to satisfy the law aims low. It is the melding of sound legal concepts with thoughtfully adopted ethical and professional standards that produces policies designed to foster excellence and public confidence.

PART I

The Museum

CHAPTER I

What Is a Museum?
What Is Required of Its
Board Members?

A. Museum Defined

B. A Trust

C. A For-profit Corporation

D. The Charitable Corporation

E. The Standard of Care Imposed on Boards of Charitable Organizations

F. The Standard Applied to Museums

G. Conclusions

A. Museum Defined

A museum can be defined as "a public or private nonprofit agency or institution organized on a permanent basis for essentially educational or esthetic purposes which, utilizing a professional staff, owns or utilizes tangible objects, cares for them, and exhibits them to the public on a regular basis."[1] For the purposes of this text, the words "public" and "private" need some clarification. Each of these terms is subject to various interpretations. For example, a museum can be classified as "private" because all of its support comes from the private sector. That same museum, however, may be "public" in the sense that it is an institution open to the public and dedicated to a public purpose. Similarly,

---

For a guide to footnote abbreviations and format, see "Glossary and Explanation of Footnote Citations," pages 335-36.

1. Definition used in Museum Services Act, 20 U.S.C. § 968(4). See 45 C.F.R. pt. 1180 for amplification of the scope of this definition. An "art museum" is defined by the Association of Art Museum Directors as: "a permanent, nonprofit institution, essentially educational and aesthetic in purpose, with professional staff, which acquires or owns works of art, cares for them, interprets them, and exhibits them to the public on some regular schedule." Association of Art Museum Directors, *Professional Practices in Art Museums, Report of the Ethics and Standards Committee* (1981). The word "museum," it is claimed, first referred to the "temple of the muses," built in 2 A.D. in Alexandria by Ptolemy, where performances of music, dance and poetry took place at a site adjoining a library and collection of antiquities. See Robertson, "The Museum and the Democratic Fallacy," *Art in America* 58 (July–Aug. 1971). For the evolution of the American Association of Museum's definition of "museum" see Starr, "In Defense of Accreditation," *Museum News* 5 (Jan.–Feb. 1982). For texts that describe the history and practices of museums, see E. Alexander, *Museums in Motion* (1979) and G. Burcaw, *Introduction to Museum Work* (1975).

a museum that was established through private philanthropy but receives subsidies from the government can fall into either category, depending on the subject at issue. A museum can be chartered by the legislature of a government and yet be "private" in the sense that it is not a part of that government. (It is common to find philanthropic organizations specifically chartered by legislative enactments.) Every museum, however, is in the business of managing collection objects for the benefit of the public, and when questions concern this unique aspect of their work, all museums whether "public" or "private," share common problems.[2] The observations made in this book, therefore, should have relevance for all museums, irrespective of the "public" or "private" designation. It is recognized that museums that are not autonomous because, for example, they are part of governmental units or larger educational organizations do have more complex problems in the area of governance. Sorting out appropriate lines of authority and confirming goals presupposes, however, a grasp of principles applicable to general museum operation.[3] Also, zoos, botanical gardens and the like, may have unique problems because of the nature of their collections, but the essentials of good collection management (such as articulation of a collection philosophy, clear delegation of authority, procedures for record-keeping and accountability), are still germane.[4]

Most museums can be classified as charitable corporations.[5] A charitable corporation, true to its name, is an organization established in a corporate form

---

2. Professor Katz of Harvard Law School describes a museum as "a privately organized public institution." He explains that it is public in the sense that it devotes all its resources to educational purposes and none to the pecuniary advantage of any person (other than compensation for services rendered). It is private because it is nongovernmental and derives its resources from gifts by private donors. J. Nason, *Trustees and the Future of Foundations* 10–11 (1977).

3. *Museum News* (Jan.–Feb. 1980), has several articles on special problems of university museums: King, "University Museums Staffs: Whom Do They Serve?"; Waller, "Museums in the Grove of Academe"; and Christison, "Professional Practices in University Art Museums." The Southern Arts Federation published *Trustees' Handbook* (1977) which discusses the lines of authority in a state- or city-owned museum, and Association of Art Museum Directors, *Professional Practices in Art Museums, Report of the Ethics and Standards Committee* (1981) has a section on "University and College Museum Practices." See also Damm, "What's Your Status?," *Museum News* 45 (March 1973) for results of a survey conducted by the Maine State Museum regarding the operation of state-supported museums and their place within the state structure.

4. See, for example, Luoma, "Prison or Ark?" 84 *Audubon* 102 (Nov. 1982).

5. Usually a museum is established in a corporate form under its state's procedures for the formation of nonprofit corporations. (A nonprofit corporation can make a profit, but it cannot distribute that profit to anyone who exercises control over it. Any profit is used to further the purposes of the organization.) If a museum is not incorporated, it probably will be classified as a charitable trust. For the purposes of the subject matter of this text, observations made concerning charitable corporations usually will apply to charitable trusts. The rather tortured distinctions sometimes made by courts between charitable trusts and charitable corporations appear to be more form than substance when applied to collection-related issues. See Scott, *The Law of Trusts* § 348 (3rd ed. 1967 and Supp. 1982), hereinafter *Scott on Trusts* (3rd ed.); Blackwell, "The Charitable Corporation and the Charitable Trust," 24 *Wash. U.L.Q.* 1 (1938), Karst, "The Efficiency of the Charitable Dollars: Unfulfilled State Responsibility," 73 *Harv. L. Rev.* 433 (1960); Note, "The Charitable Corporation," 64 *Harv. L. Rev.* 1168 (1951); *Holt v. College of Osteopathic Physicians and Surgeons*, 61 Cal. 2d 750, 394 P.2d 932 (1964); *Lynch v. Spilman*, 67 Cal. 2d 25, 431 P.2d 636 (1967). In California, if an organization has a charitable purpose or if it has come to serve a charitable function, its particular labeling as a "trust," "corporation" or "association" is not deemed controlling.

for the purpose of pursuing a charitable purpose or purposes.[6] From the legal standpoint, charitable corporations are a hybrid still in the process of development. These entities have attributes of both trust organizations and business corporations. If one understands, therefore, the traditional or common law concept of a "trust" and how a traditional trust differs from a business corporation, one can begin to appreciate the present legal status of the charitable corporation.

B. A Trust

Essentially, a trust is a fiduciary relationship whereby a party (known as a trustee) holds property that must be administered for the benefit of others (known as beneficiaries). A trustee, even though he has legal title to trust property, may not use that property for his own purposes. He may use trust assets only for the benefit of the individual or group that is the beneficiary of the trust, and in accordance with the terms of the trust instrument.[7]

In its pure form, a trust relationship imposes a very high degree of responsibility on the trustee. The trustee is charged with affirmative duties to protect, preserve and increase the trust assets. At a minimum, the trustee must exercise the skill and care of a person of ordinary prudence in carrying out these functions, but if the trustee possesses a greater skill then more exacting standards are required.[8] Nor can a trustee blame personal inadequacies on the conduct of a fellow trustee:

> The principle of contributory or comparative fault or neglect as between co-trustees plays no role in measuring the proper discharge of the high duty imposed by law on each trustee. . . . [It is] incumbent upon each to comply with the fiduciary standards required of a trustee irrespective of the default of the other.[9]

---

6. The term "charity" is defined quite broadly in the law. As stated by Professor Bogert, a noted authority on the law of trusts: "to the non-legal mind the word [charity] often means 'almsgiving' or 'liberality to the poor,' or 'that which is given to relieve the needy'; whereas in the law the word has a much broader meaning and includes a large number of other acts working toward the social welfare." Bogert, *Trusts and Trustees* § 369 (1977). See also *Restatement (Second) of Trusts* § 368 (1959); *People ex rel. Scott v. George T. Harding Museum*, 58 Ill. App. 3d 408, 374 N.E.2d 756 (1978) (this case held that a museum fell within the purview of Illinois' Charitable Trust Act); 12 A.L.R.2d 849 (1950), an extensive annotation on the validity of trusts created for the dissemination and preservation of material of historic or educational interest; *Richardson v. Essex Institute*, 208 Mass. 311, 94 N.E. 262 (1911) (trust for preservation of historic house held to be a public charity).

7. The expression "terms of the trust" is usually interpreted in the broad sense: "[I]t is not limited to express provisions of the trust instrument, but includes whatever may be gathered as to the intention of the settlor [the creator of the trust] from the trust instrument as interpreted in the light of all the circumstances, and any other indication of the intention of the settlor which is admissible in evidence." *Scott on Trusts* § 186 (3rd ed.). See also *Restatement (Second) of Trusts* § 186; *Attorney General v. President and Fellows of Harvard College*, 350 Mass. 125, 213 N.E.2d 840 (1966).

8. *Scott on Trusts* §§ 174, 176, 181 (3rd ed.). See also *In Re Estate of Lohm*, 440 Pa. 268, 269 A.2d 451 (1970). *In Re Mendenhall*, 484 Pa. 77, 398 A.2d 951 (1979); *Manchester Band of Pomo Indians, Inc. v. U.S.*, 363 F. Supp. 1238 (N.D. Cal. 1973), *Zehner v. Alexander*, Vol. 89, Page 262 (Penn. 39th Jud. Dist., Franklin County, Ct. of C.P., Orphans' Ct. Div., May 25, 1979) (also known as the *Wilson College* case).

9. *Henley v. Birmingham Trust Nat'l Bank*, 295 Ala. 38, 322 S.2d 688, 693 (1975).

The trustee is also under strict responsibility not to self-deal with trust assets. In other words, he must go to great pains to see that he, as an individual, does not benefit from his role as trustee. To put it rather graphically, an individual, when acting as a trustee, must step out of his everyday role, leaving his personal ambitions aside, and step into his trustee role diligently pursuing the interests of the trust for the good of the trust beneficiaries. The responsibility not to self-deal is based on the trustee's duty of loyalty, "the most fundamental duty owed by the trustee to the beneficiaries."[10] This duty is deemed breached, for example, even where the trustee acting in good faith purchases trust property for his personal use and pays fair consideration.[11] A prudent trustee, therefore, avoids even the appearance of a conflict of interest.[12]

Trust law also imposes a duty not to delegate. This is interpreted to mean that a trustee cannot delegate to others tasks which the trustee reasonably can be required to perform himself.[13] Clearly, the trustee cannot delegate to another, even to a co-trustee, the entire administration of the trust, but under certain circumstances, the authority to perform specific acts may be delegated.[14] The following are relevant considerations when deciding on the propriety of a delegation to perform specific acts:

(1) How much discretion is involved?

(2) What is the value and character of the property involved?

(3) Is the act one that requires a special skill not possessed by the trustee himself?

Where there has been a proper delegation to a co-trustee or other person, the trustee still must exercise general supervision over the conduct of that individual.[15]

From the above, it is clear that the standard of conduct required of a traditional trustee is quite exacting. The trustee must be aggressive in pursuing the interests of the beneficiaries, he must be extremely careful to avoid conflicts of interest or even the appearance of conflicts of interests, and, as a rule, he cannot delegate his responsibilities. It bears repeating that the trustee is held

---

10. *Scott on Trusts* § 170 (3rd ed.).

11. *Restatement (Second) of Trusts* § 170 (1959). Some states have laws that specifically forbid such self-dealing. If a trustee makes a full disclosure to the beneficiaries and purchases with their consent, possibly a sale of this nature would survive challenge.

12. An interesting case on the fiduciary duty not to self-deal is *Estate of Rothko*, 43 N.Y.2d 305, 372 N.E.2d 291, 401 N.Y.S.2d 449 (1977). In this case, the executors (fiduciaries) of Mark Rothko's estate were removed and surcharged for engaging or acquiescing in estate transactions that were tainted by self-interest. One of the executors was an officer in an art gallery that was retained to dispose of estate assets. Another executor was an artist who signed with the same art gallery a favorable agency agreement of his own after the estate transaction was consummated.

13. *Winthrop v. Attorney General*, 128 Mass. 258 (1880); *President and Fellows of Harvard College v. Attorney General*, 228 Mass. 396, 117 N.E. 903 (1971).

14. Nor can a co-trustee assume joint trustee power. See *Restatement (Second) of Trusts* §§ 194, 383 (1959); *Stuart v. Continental Ill. Nat'l Bank and Trust Co. of Chicago*, 68 Ill. 2d 502, 369 N.E.2d 1262 (1977), *cert. denied* 444 U.S. 844.

15. *Restatement (Second) of Trusts* § 171 (1959). See also *Scott on Trusts* § 171 (3rd ed.); *In Re Estate of Lohm*, 440 Pa. 268, 269 A.2d 451, 47 A.L.R.2d 499 (1970). Uniform Trustees' Powers Act § 4. (1964).

to an objective standard of care. It is possible for the trustee to do his best and yet his best may not be good enough. As Professor Scott explains:

> [The trustee] is under a duty in administering the trust to exercise such care and skill as a man of ordinary prudence would exercise, and he is liable for a loss resulting from his failure to comply with this standard, even though he does the best he can.[16]

Perhaps one of the most quoted descriptions of the trustee's standard of conduct is contained in a decision by Judge Cardoza during his tenure as Chief Judge of the New York Court of Appeals. In *Meinhard v. Salmon*,[17] Cardoza said:

> Many forms of conduct permissible in a workaday world for those acting at arm's length, are forbidden to those bound by fiduciary ties. A trustee is held to something stricter than the morals of the market place. Not honesty alone, but the punctilio of an honor the most sensitive, is then the standard of behavior. As to this there has developed a tradition that is unbending and inveterate. Uncompromising rigidity has been the attitude of courts of equity when petitioned to undermine the rule of undivided loyalty by the "disintegrating erosion" of particular exceptions. . . . Only thus has the level of conduct for fiduciaries been kept at a level higher than that trodden by the crowd. It will not consciously be lowered by any judgment of this court.[18]

C. A For-profit Corporation

Compare the responsibilities of a director of a business (for-profit) corporation. The assets of the business corporation are held by the corporation ultimately for the benefit of the stockholders and those who work for the corporation. Directors of a business corporation have a great self-interest in the success of the corporation and their prime objective is a monetary one. Also, as a practical matter, directors of a business corporation are subject to continued oversight by their stockholders. If the stockholders are not satisfied with performance, they have effective methods for registering their discontent. Recognizing this, the law imposes a less demanding standard of conduct on the officers of a business corporation than it does on trustees. It permits the law of the market-place to prevail and, as a rule, it does not step in and hold officers of a business corporation personally liable for their mistakes unless there has been gross

---

16. *Scott on Trusts* § 201 at 1650 (3rd ed.), see also § 174. Uniform Trustees' Powers Act § 1(3) (1964). See also Fremont-Smith, *Foundations and Government, State and Federal Law and Supervision* (1965) for a general discussion of the role of a trustee. *Stark v. United States Trust Co.*, 445 F. Supp. 670 (S.D.N.Y. 1978) analyzes New York law on the duty of trustees. *Stuart v. Continental Ill. Nat'l Bank and Trust Co. of Chicago*, 68 Ill. 2d 502, 369 N.E.2d 1262 (1977), *cert. denied* 444 U.S. 844, a trustee is personally liable for any loss occasioned by a violation of his duties as trustee. The rule applies where the violation is the result of negligence or mere oversight as well as when the trustee is wrongfully motivated.

17. 164 N.E. 545 (1928).

18. Ibid., 546.

negligence or fraud.[19] In other words, an officer of a business corporation can be somewhat less punctilious and still stay within the law.

D. The Charitable Corporation

Floating somewhere between the concept of a traditional trust and that of a business corporation, we have the charitable corporation. The corporation shares attributes of the traditional trust inasmuch as the corporation holds property for the benefit of others. Just as the trustee of a traditional trust holds legal title to trust property but can use this property only for the good of the beneficiaries, the charitable corporation holds its property under an obligation to use that property in the pursuit of certain public benefits.[20] "[T]he assets of charitable corporations are deemed to be impressed with a charitable trust by virtue of the declaration of corporate purposes."[21] Although the beneficiary of a traditional trust is a named individual or group of individuals and the beneficiary of a charitable corporation is the public at large or a broad segment of the public, the indefinite nature of the beneficiary of a charitable corporation does not relieve those charged with the administration of the corporation (whether they be called trustees, directors or board members) of a high degree of responsibility.[22]

On the other hand, the charitable corporation is not unlike the business corporation inasmuch as it can be a fairly complicated operation that must deal with many of the realities of the business world. A common example of a

---

19. For example, in *Kamin v. American Express Co.*, 383 N.Y.S.2d 807, 811 *aff'd* 387 N.Y.S.2d 993 (1976), directors were sued under the N.Y. Business Corporation Law which permits an action against a director for "the neglect of or failure to perform, or other violation of his duties in the management and disposition of corporate assets committed to his charge." The court stated:

> This does not mean that a director is chargeable with ordinary negligence for having made an improper decision or having acted imprudently. The "neglect" referred to in the statute is neglect of duties (i.e., malfeasance or nonfeasance) and not misjudgment. To allege that a director "negligently permitted the declaration and payment" of a dividend without alleging fraud, dishonesty or nonfeasance, is to state merely that a decision was taken with which one disagrees.

20. Volumes have been written regarding the proper characterization of gifts to charitable organizations. Does such a gift vest absolute title in the organization or does it create a trust obligation? (See Blackwell, "The Charitable Corporation and the Charitable Trust," 24 *Wash. U.L.Q.* 1 (1938); "Duties of Charitable Trust Trustees and Charitable Corporation Directors," 2 *Real Property Probate and Trust Journal* 545 (1967). Today, it may be more helpful to focus on the fact that, as far as charitable organizations are concerned, form is not as important as the function, i.e., to administer conscientiously the assets for the charitable purpose. See Karst, "The Efficiency of the Charitable Dollar: Unfulfilled State Responsibility," 73 *Harv. L. Rev.* 433 (1960). Note, "The Charitable Corporation," 64 *Harv. L. Rev.* 1168 (1951). In certain cases, however, form becomes important. See, for instance, *Crane v. Morristown School Foundation*, 120 N.J. Eq. 583, 187 A. 632 (1936) where creditors tried to reach school endowment funds, and *In Re the Edwin Forrest Home*, No. 154 (Penn., Philadelphia Ct. of C.P., Orphans' Ct. Div., April 24, 1981) (Opinion of Court *en banc* 1982), where the issue was whether a nonprofit organization must account as a trustee under the State's Probate, Estates and Fiduciaries Code. It could be argued that frequently the court's reasoning is result oriented.

21. *American Center for Education Inc. v. Cavnar*, 80 Cal. App. 3d 476, 145 Cal. Rptr. 736, 742 (1978).

22. *Scott on Trusts* § 379 (3rd ed.); *St. Joseph's Hospital v. Bennett*, 281 N.Y. 115, 22 N.E.2d 305 (1939); *In Re Estate of Becker*, 270 Cal. App. 2d 31, 75 Cal. 359 (1969).

traditional trust is the situation where a fund is set up to benefit one's minor children or an incapacitated individual. The trustee of such a trust usually has a relatively limited scope of activities, and most of his duties can be managed personally with ease. He is not faced with the hiring and supervision of staff, with oversight of major programs and properties, and with the innumerable problems involved in running a service for the public. These, however, are the concerns that face a board charged with the supervision of a charitable corporation, and the magnitude of these tasks makes it unrealistic to expect that the board members can adhere to the standard for personal attention required of the traditional trustee.[23] Yet the charitable corporation has control over valuable property dedicated to the public, and it is also unrealistic to think that the public effectively can monitor the board's activity, as do stockholders in a corporation. What, then, should be the standard of conduct imposed on board members who manage charitable corporations?[24] Are such board members required to follow the strict standards imposed on trustees of traditional trusts or the more relaxed business standards?[25]

E. The Standard of Care Imposed on Boards of Charitable Organizations

Fortunately, or unfortunately, the courts are now dealing with this specific issue because the public has become very interested in the management of charitable corporations. People are much more aware that these organizations must be run for their benefit and, therefore, they feel justified in questioning

---

23. As a practical matter, it must also be borne in mind that most board members of charitable corporations serve without compensation, but as stated in *Scott on Trusts* § 174 at 1410 (3rd ed.), "The trustee is held to the standard of a man of ordinary prudence whether he receives compensation or whether he acts gratuitously."

24. Managers of charitable corporations may be called trustees, regents, supervisors, etc. When used in this text the term "board member" should be construed to cover members of whatever body actually governs the charitable corporation.

25. Any discussion of the standard of care owed by a trustee also may raise the issue of the powers of that trustee. *Scott on Trusts* § 380 (3rd ed.) states:

> The trustees of a charitable trust, like the trustees of a private trust, have such powers as are conferred upon them in specific words by the terms of the trust or are necessary or appropriate to carry out the purposes of the trust and are not forbidden by the terms of the trust . . . . [T]he fact that a charitable trust may continue for an indefinite period may have the effect of giving the trustees more extensive powers than they have in the case of a private trust which is of limited duration.

In *Midlantic Nat'l Bank v. Frank G. Thompson Fund*, 170 N. J. Super. 128, 405 A.2d 866, 869 (1979), the court stated:

> The powers of the persons who act as directors of a charitable nonprofit corporation, whether called directors or trustees, are prescribed in the statute of incorporation, in the instrument creating the corporation, and those implied powers which are necessary and proper to carry out the purposes for which the charity was created and which are not in conflict with expressions in the instrument creating the charity.

In *Shelton v. King*, 229 U.S. 90 at 94 (1913), the court stated:

> It is a settled principle that trustees having the powers to exercise discretion will not be interfered with so long as they are acting bona fide. To do so would be to substitute the discretion of the court for that of the trustee.

See also *Taylor v. Baldwin*, 247 S.W.2d 741 (Mo. 1952).

their management. There have been a rash of cases brought against board members and officers of charitable corporations in which mismanagement is alleged, and, of course, in each of these cases, the basic issue is the standard of conduct required of such individuals. A fairly recent case which merits close scrutiny involved a hospital, not a museum, but it is considered a landmark decision and is frequently cited on the issue of board member liability. The case is *Stern v. Lucy Webb Hayes National Training School for Deaconesses and Missionaries* or, as it is more commonly known, the *Sibley Hospital* case.[26] The defendant school was founded as a trust but it later was incorporated under the Nonprofit Corporation Act of the District of Columbia. Subsequently, the school established the Sibley Memorial Hospital, and over the years, the hospital became the chief function of the school. This suit was brought as a class action against certain members of the hospital's Board of Trustees, six financial institutions and the hospital itself. The main allegations were that (1) the defendant trustees conspired to enrich themselves, and certain financial institutions with which they were affiliated, by favoring those institutions in financial dealings with the hospital, and (2) the defendant trustees breached their fiduciary duties of care and loyalty in the management of Sibley's funds.[27] The financial institutions were named as co-conspirators.

At the time of the suit, the hospital, under its by-laws, was to be run by a board of from 25 to 35 "trustees" who were to meet at least twice a year. There was also an Executive Committee empowered to open bank accounts, pay mortgages and enter into contracts; a Finance Committee to review the budget; and an Investment Committee. In fact, however, for over eighteen years, the hospital had been run almost exclusively by two trustee officers, the Hospital Administrator and the Treasurer. The Finance and Investment Committees never met and the Board and Executive Committee were dominated by the Administrator and the Treasurer. The facts also demonstrated that the hospital maintained excessively large, noninterest-bearing accounts in financial institutions run by certain defendant trustees, that a substantial hospital mortgage was held by a syndicate organized by certain defendant trustees, and that the Hospital retained the investment services of a firm controlled by one of the defendant trustees. With regard to the last two arrangements, the mortgage was deemed "fair" and the fee for the investment service "equitable."

A crucial factor in the case was the standard of care assigned to the "trustees" of this charitable corporation. Under traditional trust law, trustees cannot delegate major responsibilities, they must avoid conflict of interest situations because of their duty of loyalty, and they have an affirmative duty to protect, preserve and increase trust assets, as would a "man of ordinary prudence." Under corporate law, directors, as a rule, are not held liable for their actions unless "gross negligence" or fraud has been found, and transactions between

26. 381 F. Supp. 1003 (D.D.C. 1974) and also 367 F. Supp. 536 (D.D.C. 1973) (order granting plaintiffs standing to sue). An earlier case of interest is *United States v. Mount Vernon Mortgage Corp.*, 128 F. Supp. 629 (D.D.C. 1954) *aff'd* 236 F.2d 1724 (D.C. Cir. 1956) *cert. denied* 352 U.S. 988 (1957) in which the United States, as *parens patriae*, sued trustees of a charitable foundation for improper transfer of foundation property.

27. *Sibley Hospital* case, *supra*, at 1007.

the corporation and a director are not necessarily void.[28] The court in the *Sibley Hospital* case stated:

> The applicable law is unsettled. The charitable corporation is a relatively new legal entity which does not fit neatly into the established common law categories of corporation and trust. . . . [T]he modern trend is to apply corporate rather than trust principles in determining the liability of the directors of charitable corporations, because their functions are virtually indistinguishable from those of their "pure" corporate counterparts.[29]

The "indistinguishable" feature was essentially that corporate directors and board members of large charitable corporations have many areas of responsibility, while the traditional trustee is charged mainly with the management of the trust funds.[30] The court moderated its endorsement of the corporate standard, however, by specifically noting that the management of a charitable corporation imposes "severe obligations" upon board members because such an organization is not closely regulated by any public entity, it is not subject to scrutiny by stockholders, and frequently its board is self-perpetuating.

After analyzing the facts and conflicting case law,[31] the court held as follows:

> [A] director or so-called trustee of a charitable hospital organized under the Non-Profit Corporation Act of the District of Columbia [citation omitted] is in default of his fiduciary duty to manage the financial and investment affairs of the hospital if it has been shown by a preponderance of the evidence that:
>
> (1) While assigned to a particular committee of the Board having general financial or investment responsibility under the by-laws of the corporation, he has failed to use due diligence in supervising the actions of those officers, employees or outside experts to whom the responsibility for making day-to-day financial or investment decision has been delegated; or
>
> (2) He knowingly permitted the hospital to enter into a business transaction

---

28. Usually such transactions are voidable at the option of the corporation. It is assumed that because of the profit motive, the actions of directors will be watched closely by those having a pecuniary interest in the corporation.

29. *Sibley Hospital* case, *supra*, at 1013.

30. Compare, for instance, *Blankenship v. Boyle*, 329 F. Supp. 1089 (D.D.C. 1971) *aff'd* 511 F.2d 447 (1975), which was decided by the same judge who rendered the decision in the *Sibley Hospital* case. *Blankenship* involved the management of a large union welfare fund by a group of trustees. The major charge was that excessive cash deposits were maintained in a bank account by the union trustees and that this practice benefited the union and the bank rather than the beneficiaries of the trust, the union members. Evidence in the case demonstrated that management of the trust fund was a complex operation, that the trustees did not hold regular meetings, and that there was no set procedure for deciding policy questions. Despite the complex nature of the trust, the court favored the trust standard. It held that in view of the fiduciary obligation to maximize the trust income by prudent investment, the burden of justifying their conduct fell on the trustees. The trustees could not sustain this burden. The court required the removal of two trustees and ordered major management changes in the fund's administration.

31. See, for instance, *George Pepperdine Foundation v. Pepperdine*, 126 Cal. App. 2d 154, 271 P.2d 600 (1954), a case which illustrates the view that hard cases make bad law. *Pepperdine* was overruled in part by *Holt v. College of Osteopathic Physicians and Surgeons*, 61 Cal. 2d 750, 394 P.2d 932, 40 Cal. Rptr. 244 (1964). See also *Lynch v. John M. Redfield Foundation*, 9 Cal. App. 3d 293, 88 Cal. Rptr. 86 (1970) where the court held corporate trustees to the traditional trust standard with regard to investment duties. (Note that as of 1980, California has in effect a new comprehensive nonprofit corporation law that spells out standards of conduct. Cal. Corp. Code, §§ 5000-10831).

with himself or with any corporation, partnership or association in which he then had a substantial interest or held a position as trustee, director, general manager or principal officer without having previously informed the persons charged with approving that transaction of his interest or position and of any significant reasons, unknown to or not fully appreciated by such persons, why the transaction might not be in the best interests of the hospital; or

(3) Except as required by the preceding paragraph, he actively participated in or voted in favor of a decision by the Board or any committee or subcommittee thereof to transact business with himself or with any corporation, partnership or association in which he then had a substantial interest or held a position as trustee, director, general manager or principal officer; or

(4) He otherwise failed to perform his duties honestly, in good faith, and with a reasonable amount of diligence and care.[32]

Even though this less stringent standard was used, in the *Sibley Hospital* case the trustee defendants were found guilty of breaching their fiduciary duties to supervise the management of the hospital's investments. In granting relief, however, the court was lenient because, as it pointed out, the hospital had already instituted reforms, there was no evidence that any of the trustees were involved in fraudulent practices or profited personally, and this was a case of "first impressions." This last reason deserves special attention. The court, in effect was saying, "We are giving you another chance, but now that we have clarified the nature and scope of trustee obligations in a nonprofit, nonmember charitable institution, board members in this jurisdiction, beware!"[33]

Upon reflection, the court's decision in the *Sibley Hospital* case does not appear to be a radical departure from traditional trust standards. Under the court's tests, board members may delegate day-to-day financial and investment decisions if they use diligence in supervising this delegated authority. The criteria mentioned earlier in this chapter for judging a proper delegation by a traditional trustee permit a trustee to delegate (but retain supervision) if the subject requires a special skill not possessed by the trustee himself. Also, under the court's test, a board member may not actively participate in a vote in favor of a transaction that would be a conflict of interest situation for him under the trustee test, and if he knows that the charitable organization is contemplating such a transaction, he must disclose fully his activities and any other pertinent information in his possession. Here, again, the *Sibley Hospital* standard can be reconciled with the traditional trustee standard. Neither standard permits direct participation in a conflict of interest situation, but the *Sibley* test recognizes that there are practical ways in which a board member can isolate himself from a particular decision without undermining confidence in the management of the organization. The size of and frequent division of responsibilities within a board, due to the complexities of managing a charitable organization, permit an individual member, on occasion, to defer to the informed judgment of his peers. This type of situation historically did not exist in a traditional trust and hence

---

32. *Sibley Hospital* case, *supra.*, at 1015.

33. For an analysis of the *Sibley Hospital* case, see Mace, "Standards of Care for Trustees," *Harv. Bus. Rev.* 14 (Jan.–Feb. 1976).

the very strict conflict of interest rule was deemed necessary to assure loyalty of service.[34] But perhaps the key to the *Sibley Hospital* decision can be found in the fourth and last test described in the case. Here the court said a board member would be found in default of his duty if "he otherwise failed to perform his duties honestly, *in good faith*, and with a reasonable amount of diligence and care."[35] Under the traditional trustee test, good faith will not save a trustee if he fails to perform as a man of ordinary prudence in carrying out his duties. The traditional trustee must meet this objective standard. On the other hand, the corporate standard usually requires only that a director avoid gross negligence and fraud.[36] *Sibley Hospital*, in stressing "good faith," puts forth a more subjective test which permits the court to consider the rigid traditional trustee standard in light of the realities of board membership. The test still places a formidable burden on a defendant. To support a finding of "good faith," the defendant must be able to demonstrate to the court that as a board member he pursued his "severe obligations" with a reasonable degree of diligence and intelligence and that he did not in fact breach his duty of loyalty.[37]

F. The Standard Applied to Museums

What standard of conduct would a court impose today on board members of a museum when collection-related matters are at issue?[38] It is difficult to resolve this question with certainty because several of the more interesting cases on

34. See also Welles, *Conflicts of Interest, Nonprofit Institutions, Report to the Twentieth Century Fund Steering Committee on Conflicts of Interest in Securities Market* (1977). The new nonprofit corporation law that went into effect in California in 1980 approves this concept of reasonable delegation with continued oversight. Cal. Corp. Code § 5210.

35. *Sibley Hospital* case, *supra.*, at 1015 (emphasis added).

36. There is evidence that in certain areas the corporate standard is becoming more stringent. For example, in *Diamond v. Oreamuno*, 24 N.Y.2d 494, 248 N.E.2d 910, 301 N.Y.S.2d 78 (1969), corporate directors were sued by the corporation for breach of duty and for an accounting of personal profits made because of inside information. There was no evidence that the corporation itself had been harmed by the action of the directors. The court held it was not necessary to show damage to the corporation. The purpose of imposing a fiduciary-type standard on directors was not to compensate the corporation for such wrongs but "*to prevent* them, by removing from agents and trustees all inducement to attempt dealing for their own benefit in matters which they have undertaken for others, or to which their agency or trust relates." *Idem.*, at 912.

37. Compare the decision in *Zehner v. Alexander*, Vol. 89, Page 262 (Penn. 39th Jud. Dist., Franklin County, Ct. of C. P., Orphans' Ct. Div., May 25, 1979) (known as the *Wilson College* case). Trustees of Wilson College voted to close the school because of declining enrollment. The decision was challenged in court. The closing was enjoined and two trustees were ordered removed, one for gross negligence, the other because of conflict of interest (she was the president of another college) and for failure to use her special expertise. But see *Rowan v. Pasadena Art Museum*, No. C 322817 (Cal. Sup. Ct., L. A. County, Sept. 22, 1981), which stressed the broad discretion vested in trustees. In *Mountain Top Youth Camp, Inc. v. Lyon*, 20 N.C. App. 694, 202 S.E.2d 498 (1974), the court adopted a test similar to that used in the *Sibley Hospital* case.

38. See Marsh, "Governance of Non-Profit Organizations: An Appropriate Standard of Conduct for Trustees of Museums and Other Cultural Institutions," 85 *Dick. L. Rev.* 607 (1981); Note: "The Fiduciary Duties of Loyalty and Care Associated with the Directors and Trustees of Charitable Organizations," 64 *Va. L. Rev.* 449 (April 1978); J. Nason, *Trustees and the Future of Foundations* (1977); Abbott and Kornblum, "The Jurisdiction of the Attorney General Over Corporate Fiduciaries Under the New California Nonprofit Corporation Law," 13 *U.S.F. L. Rev.* 753 (Summer 1979).

this point have been settled before final judgments were rendered by the courts. However, the charges filed in the cases alone reflect some prevailing opinions regarding proper board conduct.

In the well-known *Museum of the American Indian* case,[39] trustees and officers of that museum were sued personally by the Attorney General of the State of New York for mismanagement. Among the charges listed by the Attorney General were the following:

(1) A failure to keep complete and contemporaneous records of all collection objects;

(2) The permitting of questionable accession and deaccession practices; and

(3) Self-dealing by the trustees and the director of the museum (it was alleged, for example, that trustees obtained artifacts and other benefits from the museum and that gifts to the museum from trustees were valued at inflated figures for income tax purposes).

Essentially, the Attorney General of the State of New York was saying that under his interpretation of the law, a museum, as a charitable corporation, has certain obligations to the public (as its beneficiaries). These obligations impose a standard of conduct on the board members of the museum which requires, at a minimum, that the board members themselves establish acceptable policies concerning the acquisition of collection items, the disposal of such items and the records that must be kept of such transactions.[40]

After much negotiation with the attorneys for the defendants, the State Attorney General entered into a stipulation which held in abeyance further court action. Under the terms of the stipulation, the museum agreed to have a complete inventory of its entire collection performed by an independent party. This inventory was to be made available to the Attorney General and the public. Also, it was agreed that the director would be relieved of all administrative

---

39. *Lefkowitz v. The Museum of the American Indian; Heye Foundation*, Index No. 41416/75 (N.Y. Sup. Ct., N.Y. County, June 27, 1975).

40. When investigating the case of *Lefkowitz v. Kan*, Index No. 40082/78 (N.Y. Sup. Ct., N.Y. County, Jan. 3, 1983) (compromise agreement), the Attorney General of New York questioned the purchase by the museum of several art objects once owned by a member of the museum's board. It was the Attorney General's position that in New York such a sale amounted to "self-dealing" by a fiduciary. This particular aspect of the case was settled when the Attorney General entered into an agreement with all parties concerned which required that the following be done:

(1) All transactions between the museum and the board member were to be reconsidered after the board member made full disclosure of his interests. If the museum's board rejected any piece, the board member was to refund the full purchase price.

(2) The board members would not purchase, sell or exchange any materials from, to or with the museum without advance written disclosure to the musem's board and to the Attorney General.

(3) The museum's board would establish a committee to draft a comprehensive code of ethics. Pending the adoption of this code, the museum would not purchase, sell or exchange collection objects with board members or staff.

(Statement of Louis Lefkowitz, Attorney General of New York by Charles Brody, Assistant Attorney General, May 19, 1978).

authority and that no new administrator would be appointed without the prior consent of the Attorney General. It was specifically noted that the new administrator should not have the authority to acquire for or dispose of items from the collection. While the inventory was in progress, the Board of Trustees of the museum was reconstituted and a new administrator was hired. Shortly thereafter the museum published a comprehensive collection management policy statement.[41]

The *Museum of the American Indian* case hardly had faded from the news when some of the trustees and a former director of a museum of fine arts in Washington State were sued by the state Attorney General for mismanagement of museum assets.[42] Although the museum is a charitable corporation, the complaint by the Attorney General was couched in traditional trustee language. Among the charges in the complaint were the following:

(1) The director, without the permission of the trustees, sold assets of the museum.

(2) The director did not keep proper accounts of proceeds recovered from such sales.

(3) The director and the trustees failed to maintain the collection in proper condition.

(4) The director and the trustees failed to maintain the museum building in reasonable repair.

(5) The trustees did not exercise adequate supervision over the director with regard to acquisitions.

(6) Trustees were permitted to purchase or borrow items from the collection, or to otherwise benefit from their trustee status, and this amounted to self-dealing.

The Attorney General alleged generally that the trustees "failed to exercise the standard of care of a prudent man," and hence as trustees they were personally liable for resulting damages whether caused by them directly or by the director.[43] Reading through the list of charges, it appears that this Attorney General also believed that the standard of care applicable to board members of a museum requires that the board members set policy concerning the acquisition, disposal

---

41. The collection policy was adopted by the Board of Trustees of the Museum of the American Indian, Heye Foundation on June 29, 1977, and is published in *Indian Notes*, Vol. XII, No. 1 (1978), a publication of that museum. The collection policy provides that all accessions, except certain field collections made by staff, and all deaccessions, require the approval of the Board of Trustees. This requirement, which was part of the stipulation entered into with the Attorney General, is rather stringent for a museum of this size and type.

42. *State of Washington v. Leppaluoto*, No. 11781 (Wash. Super. Ct., Klickitat County, April 1977). It should be noted that the trustees filed a countersuit against the Attorney General alleging breach of an earlier agreement between the trustees and the Attorney General regarding reorganization of the museum.

43. If a museum director is permitted to perform actions which should be reserved for the trustees, the trustees may be held liable. If there is a proper delegation of authority to the museum director, but the trustees fail to oversee generally the exercise of their delegated power, the trustees may be held liable.

and care of collection objects, and that they demonstrate active oversight of museum operation. The case was dismissed after the Attorney General and the defendants entered into a stipulation in which the museum agreed to pursue its remedies against one individual deemed responsible in large measure for the mismanagement.

The Attorney General's Office of Illinois also is pressing the trust standard in charges brought against officials of a Chicago museum.[44] The officials are charged with various counts of mismanagement of the museum collections and funds, and with counts of self-dealing. The Attorney General has taken the position that the officials are "common law trustees" and hence must be held to a strict standard of conduct. The matter still is in litigation.[45]

Actual court decisions involving museum management also tend to require more of museum officials than the bare business standard. In the *Hill-Stead Museum* case[46] the trustees were questioned regarding responsibilities to ensure the museum's collections and to provide adequate security against fire and theft. In deciding the matter, the Connecticut court quoted the traditional trustee standard of care: "It is the duty of the trustees to exercise that care and prudence which an ordinarily prudent person would who was entrusted with the management of like property for another."[47] In *Rowan v. Pasadena Art Museum*[48] the defendant trustees were absolved from charges that they had failed to preserve and maintain the museum's collections, had failed to exhibit properly, had failed to establish certain collection management policies, and had failed to receive reasonable amounts for the sale of certain collections items. The standard of conduct applied by the court stressed "good faith":

> Members of the board of directors of the corporation [the museum] are undoubtedly fiduciaries, and as such are required to act in the highest good faith toward the beneficiary, i.e., the public. . . . Acting within their broad discretion, the trustees must assume responsibility for making decisions regarding all of the affairs of the museum. . . . So long as the trustees act in good faith and exercise reasonable care as contrasted with a clear abuse of discretion, the decisions must be left in the hands of the trustees where it has been placed by the law.[49]

---

44. *People of the State of Illinois v. Silverstein*, No. 76 CH 6446 (Ill., Cook County Cir. Ct., Oct. 1976) and 408 N.E.2d 243 (1980). See also *People ex rel. Scott v. George F. Harding Museum*, 58 Ill. App. 3d 408, 374 N.E.2d 756 (1978), and *People ex rel. Scott v. Silverstein*, 412 N.E.2d 692 (1980) and 418 N.E.2d 1087 (1981).

45. A recent case is *Hardman v. Feinstein*, No. 827127 (Cal. Sup. Ct., San Francisco County, July 1984); there several citizens filed suit against the trustees of the Fine Arts Museum of San Francisco charging mismanagement of the collections because of poor inventory methods, improper disposal of certain works and lax security.

46. *Harris v. Attorney General*, 31 Conn. Sup. 93, 324 A.2d 279 (1974).

47. Ibid., at 287.

48. No. C 322817 (Cal. Sup. Ct., L.A. County, Sept. 22, 1981).

49. Ibid., at 6.

G. Conclusions

From the foregoing cases, certain conclusions may be drawn concerning board responsibility[50] for the management of museum collections:

(1) Under prevailing case law, board members of a museum will be held at least to the standard of care imposed on directors of a business corporation, and, if the matter at issue directly concerns collection policy (the core function of the museum), a court may be inclined to exact a higher standard that requires convincing evidence of good faith.[51]

(2) For their own protection, board members of a museum should exercise good faith and reasonable diligence in pursuing their duties. Adequate management may well be construed to include the establishment of policies concerning the acquisition, care and disposal of collection objects and effective oversight of the implementation of these policies.[52]

---

50. The cases just described involve charges filed against board members and directors of museums for violations of fiduciary duties. Are staff members of museums immune from such suits? This question was raised in the case of *Lefkowitz v. Kan*, Index No. 40082/78 (N.Y. Sup. Ct., N.Y. County, Jan. 3, 1983) (compromise agreement). In this case, which was settled by a compromise agreement dated January 3, 1983, the Attorney General alleged that the defendant, a curator, violated a fiduciary responsibility owed the museum when he arranged certain deaccession sales involving a dealer with whom the curator did business personally. In the settlement agreement it is stated that while there was no museum policy requiring the disclosure of the curator's personal transactions with the dealer, the situation created "at least the appearance of an impropriety" and that "full and candid disclosure of personal transactions are required by present codes of ethics and fiduciary law."

51. The unique feature of a museum is its collection and it is reasonable to assume that board members were chosen for their expertise on collection matters. Hence, policy issues regarding the collections cannot be ignored by them or delegated away. If, for example, the matter at issue concerned the museum's investment policy (not the core purpose of the museum) a court may be inclined to quote the business corporation standard of care. See Cary and Bright, *The Developing Law of Endowment Funds: "The Law and the Lore" Revisited*, a Report to the Ford Foundation (1974) and the Uniform Management of Institutional Funds Act, Prefatory Note. See also *Midlantic Nat'l. Bank v. Frank G. Thompson Fund*. 170 N. J. Super. 128, 405 A.2d 866 (1979). But see *Attorney General v. Olson*, 346 Mass. 190, 191 N.E.2d 132 (1963) where the trust standard was applied but liberally construed in favor of the trustees. Marsh, "Governance of Non-Profit Organizations: An Appropriate Standard of Conduct for Trustees of Museums and Other Cultural Institutions," 85 *Dick. L. Rev.* 607 (1981) presents another analysis of a museum trustee's responsibilities as does S. Weil in the chapter entitled "Breach of Trust, Remedies, and Standards in the American Private Art Museum" in his book *Beauty and the Beasts* (1983). See also, A. Knoll, "Museums—A Gunslinger's Dream," *Legal Rights Guide #3*, a publication of the Bay Area Lawyers for the Arts (1975); Sherrell-Leo and Meyer, "The Buck Stops Here—and Other Trustee Responsibilities," *History News* 28 (March 1984).

52. Note the section on "Museum Governance" in American Association of Museums, *Museum Ethics: A Report to the American Association of Museums by its Committee on Ethics* (1978). This report is available from the AAM, and was printed in the 1978 March–April issue of *Museum News*. In the report, the introductory paragraph on "Museum Governance" reads:

The governing body of a museum, usually a board of trustees, serves the public interest as it relates to the museum, and must consider itself accountable to the public as well as to the institution. In most cases the board acts as the ultimate legal entity for the museum, and stands responsible for the formulation and maintenance of its general policies, standards, conditions and operational continuity.

(3) For their own protection[53] board members should be sure to disclose in advance to their fellow members any possible conflicts of interest, giving full details and then removing themselves from further discussion and voting if such matters in fact come before the board.

(4) Although museum trustees have broad discretion, museum policies and procedures regarding collection objects should be made in light of what is perceived to be the best interests of the public, the beneficiary of the museum's purposes.[54]

---

53. The *Restatement on Restitution* § 197 (1937) provides that where a fiduciary in violation of his duty to the beneficiary receives or retains any profit, he holds what he receives upon a constructive trust for the beneficiary. In other words, his profits must be turned over to the beneficiary. Under this doctrine, a museum trustee could be charged with the return of any profit he might make at the expense of the museum. See, also, *U.S. v. Kearns*, 575 F.2d 729 (D.C. Cir. 1978). It is interesting to note that in California the Attorney General's office has found self-dealing to be the "single most troublesome charitable trust enforcement problem." Abbott and Kornblum, "The Jurisdiction of the Attorney General Over Corporate Fiduciaries under the New California Nonprofit Corporation Law," 13 *U.S.F. L. Rev.* 753, 777 (Summer 1979).

54. There always can be differences of opinion as to "what is best for the public." Various examples of this can be found throughout the book. One interesting case concerns a museum that had for years stored a large, privately owned collection in its building. The museum, of course, hoped that one day all or most of this collection would be donated to it. The Attorney General of the state questioned whether the storage of this collection was in the best interest of the public. Were the board members of the museum violating their duty to manage, preserve and protect museum assets by storing this collection? If not, can they be second-guessed by the Attorney General? The museum in question received substantial support from public funds. Does the receipt of public funds restrict the area of discretion reserved to board members?

CHAPTER II

Museums Are Accountable To Whom?

A. Role of the Attorney General

B. Can Donors Sue?

C. Expanding Concept of Standing to Sue

D. Museum Cases Involving the Issue of Standing to Sue

E. Oversight by Taxing Authorities

F. As Recipients of Federal Financial Assistance

G. Miscellaneous State and Local Reporting Statutes

A. Role of the Attorney General

According to figures published by the American Association of Fund Raising Counsel, contributions to the nation's charitable organizations totaled some $64.93 billion in 1983.[1] Charities are "big business" and yet, as noted in the previous chapter, they are not "business" as this term is traditionally used. Charitable organizations occupy such a unique and prominent role in our country they are often referred to as "the third sector" after government and business. In order to keep government on course, we have elaborate systems of checks and balances, and businesses must answer to stockholders, customers, the Internal Revenue Service, and innumerable other governmental entities. The third sector has its watchdogs also, and here again there is an area of evolving law.

Traditionally, the enforcement of charitable trusts or gifts to charities has been assigned to the Attorney General of the state where the charity is located.[2]

---

1. It is not clear whether this estimate takes into consideration also the value of services donated to such organizations.

2. Most states have statutes setting forth the Attorney General's duties in this regard, but even in the absence of statutes, it is generally held that the Attorney General has the power to enforce charitable trusts as a common-law incident of his office. In some states, by statute, the power to enforce charitable trusts is vested in a state agent other than the Attorney General. See 15 Am. Jur. 2d *Charities* § 144 (1976). See also *Scott on Trusts* § 391 (3rd ed.) and *The Restatement (Second) of Trusts* § 391 (1959). The law on charitable trusts developed unevenly in the various states. Interpretations reflected local social and political views as well as efforts to assimilate English precedent. Even today when a question arises concerning the enforcement of a charitable trust, it is prudent to check carefully the law of the particular jurisdiction. Two articles which describe the growth of the various legal theories in this country are Blackwell, "The Charitable Corporation and the Charitable Trust," 24 *Wash. U.L.Q.* 1 (1938) and Note, "The Enforcement of Charitable Trusts in America: A History of Evolving Social Attitudes," 54 *Va. L. Rev.* 436 (April 1968). With regard to particular state laws, see Abbott and Kornblum, "The Jurisdiction of the Attorney General over Corporate Fiduciaries Under the New California Nonprofit Corporation Law," 13 *U.S.F. L. Rev.* 753 (Summer 1979) and *Lefkowitz v. Lebensfeld*, 51 N.Y.2d 442, 415 N.E.2d 919, 434 N.Y.S.2d 929 (1980).

This practice stems from English law, where for centuries suits were brought by the King's Attorney General to enforce charitable trusts, the King being the guardian of such trusts. The practice was adopted in this country for practical as well as historic reasons. The community has a substantial interest in the enforcement of a charitable trust because it is the beneficiary, yet, it was reasoned, it would be impractical to expect individual members of the public to police trust activity. Such a situation could result in no oversight, because few, if any, individuals would assume the financial costs of court action, or it could result in the harassment of trustees because many citizens might see fit to bring a variety of actions based on their individual theories of wrongdoing. The realistic solution, it was decided, was to look to the Attorney General of the state to oversee the management of charities.[3]

A concise statement of the customary interpretation of this rule can be found in *Dickey v. Volker*:[4]

> An individual member of the public has no vested interest in the property or funds of the [charitable] trust. In common with other members, he has an interest in the charitable use. He has no right of action for the mismanagement or misuse of the fund. Any action on this account must be taken by the Attorney General as the representative of the public. However, those with a special interest may enforce the trust, or a localized or grouped charity may be enforced by a class suit. In such suits it is proper and often necessary to make the Attorney General a party defendant.[5]

Similar instruction was given in *People ex rel. Ellert v. Cogswell*:[6]

> This action is based upon averments of a public trust. It is brought to remedy abuses in the management of this trust. It is not only the right, but the duty, of the attorney general to prosecute such an action. The state as *parens patria*, [literally, "father of the country"] superintends the management of all public charities or trusts, and, in these matters, acts through her attorney general. Generally speaking, such an action will not be entertained at all unless the attorney general is a party to it. Such was the rule at common law, and it has not been changed in this state.[7]

B. Can Donors Sue?

Based on this traditional rule that enforcement of charitable trusts is reserved to the Attorney General, donors and heirs of donors usually are denied standing

---

3. The role of the Attorney General is to see that the trustees do not abuse their discretion. It is not his role to control their discretion. *Conway v. Emeny*, 139 Conn. 612, 96 A.2d 221 (1953). In *Lefkowitz v. Lebensfeld*, 51 N.Y.2d 442, 415 N.E.2d 919, 434 N.Y.S. 929 (1980), the court discusses the history in New York of the Attorney General's authority over charities and limitations on the Attorney General regarding the enforcement of obligations owed to a charity.

4. 321 Mo. 235, 11 S.W.2d 278 (1928). The decision contains extensive annotations on the then existing interpretation of the power to enforce charitable trusts.

5. Ibid., at 246.

6. 113 Cal. 129, 45 P. 270 (1896).

7. *People ex rel. Ellert v. Cogswell*, 45 P. 270 at 271 (Cal. 1896); see also *Parker v. May*, 59 Mass. 336 (1850), *United States v. Mount Vernon Mortgage Corp.*, 128 F. Supp. 629 (D.D.C. 1954) *aff'd* 236 F.2d 724 (D.C. Cir. 1956) *cert. denied* 352 U.S. 988 (1957).

to sue for the enforcement of such trusts.[8] Having made a gift for the benefit of the public, a donor is viewed as having no stronger claim to its enforcement than any other member of the public. With regard to conditional gifts or gifts which reserve a right to revoke or terminate, there is a division of authority as to whether donors, or their representatives, can sue for enforcement. If they are permitted to sue, there is the added question whether they can sue individually in their own names or only with the Attorney General as a consenting party.[9] The *Restatement of Trusts* favors the view that the Attorney General is a necessary party in any such suit, on the theory, perhaps, that a gift to charity, even though conditional, involves a public interest that must be represented.[10]

Decisions regarding standing of donors to enforce conditional gifts turn on the particular facts of each case, and it would appear that courts have little trouble in fashioning theories to support desired results. In *Amato v. The Metropolitan Museum of Art*,[11] for instance, a restricted bequest was made to the museum. The museum had six months in which to accept the gift, otherwise the bequest passed to the donor's daughter. The museum accepted. Years later, the daughter sued claiming that the museum had not honored the restriction. The court denied relief, one of the grounds being that once the museum accepted the gift, any interest the daughter had in the property terminated. Since the daughter now had no special interest, she lacked standing to sue.

Another approach taken by the courts which inhibits donor intervention is the theory that a conditional or restricted gift does not fail just because its terms cannot be followed exactly. For instance, if it proves impractical or impossible to carry out a restricted gift, a museum may seek court approval to alter the restriction in either a *cy pres* action or a petition for deviation.[12] If the court approves the change, there is deemed to be no failure of the gift because the general charitable intent of the donor is still being effected. If there is no failure, the donor and his heirs have nothing to enforce in court.[13]

In *Abrams v. The Maryland Historical Society*[14] the heirs of a donor sued to prevent the sale of an object given to the historical society claiming that the society accepted the gift with the understanding that the object would never be sold. There was some evidence to support the claim, namely correspondence from individual members of the Society's board of trustees, and there was no

---

8. *Scott on Trusts* § 391 (3rd ed.). Compare the arguments put forth by the plaintiffs in the *Pasadena Museum* case mentioned hereafter in this chapter. See also *Gifford v. First National Bank of Menominee*, 285 Mich. 58, 280 N.W. 108 (1938).

9. 15 Am. Jur. 2d *Charities*, § 143 (1976).

10. *Restatement (Second) of Trusts* § 391 comment f (1957).

11. No. 15122/79 (N.Y. Sup. Ct., N.Y. County, Sept. 1979). See also *In Re Stuart's Estate*, 183 N.Y. Misc. 20, 46 N.Y.S.2d 911 (1944).

12. See section in Chapter IV on "Restricted Gifts" for more detailed information.

13. See *Cleveland Museum of Art v. O'Neill*, 57 Ohio Op. 250, 129 N.E.2d 669 (1955). In *O'Hara v. Grand Lodge I.O. of Good Templars*, 213 Cal. 131, 2 P.2d 21 (1931), the court indicated that *cy pres* action taken by a charity without prior court approval could be confirmed later by the court to avoid intervention of the donor.

14. Equity No. A-58791/A513/1979 (Md. Cir. Ct. for Baltimore City, June 1979).

executed deed of gift. The court ruled that the heirs had no standing to sue, stating, "Gifts cannot be presumed to be conditional. Their conditions must be clearly set forth."

C. Expanding Concept of Standing to Sue

Certainly over the years the Attorneys General have not been preoccupied with supervision of museums. With limited time and resources, their efforts naturally must focus on law enforcement matters of major public concern. But as the public becomes more interested in the administration of charitable organizations, questions are being raised as to whether there should be more effective ways to monitor charities than by relying mainly on the initiative and interest of the Attorney General.[15] One avenue being explored is possible expansion of the "standing to sue" concept.

It is still the majority view that the Attorney General is a necessary party in a suit alleging mismanagement of a charity, and that the Attorney General cannot be compelled to be a party.[16] How, then, can an individual or group force a charity into court if the Attorney General is not a willing participant? Creative arguments are being fashioned in order to convince courts that certain plaintiffs in their own right should have standing to sue for alleged mismanagement of charitable organizations.

In *Holt v. College of Osteopathic Physicians and Surgeons*,[17] minority trustees of a charitable corporation sued the corporation and majority trustees for alleged breach of a charitable trust. The corporation was planning to change the focus of its college and the Attorney General had approved the change as "not detrimental to the public interest." The plaintiffs, the minority trustees, felt that the planned change violated the trust and they joined the Attorney General as a defendant in their suit for mismanagement. The defendants challenged the plaintiffs' standing to sue. The court permitted the case to be heard, stating:

> Although the Attorney General has primary responsibility for the
> enforcement of charitable trusts, the need for adequate enforcement is not

---

15. See, for example, Karst, "The Efficiency of the Charitable Dollar, Unfulfilled State Responsibility," 73 *Harv. L. Rev.* 433 (1960). Professor Karst suggests the establishment of state boards to monitor and coordinate the activities of private charities.

16. In *Dickey v. Volker*, 11 S.W.2d 278 (1928), it was argued that the Attorney General by challenging the plaintiff's right to bring such a suit violated the plaintiff's constitutional right to due process of the law. The court struck down this argument. It pointed out that the plaintiff had established no property right in the charitable trust (i.e., no special interest) and therefore he was not entitled to any trial. In *Wiegand v. Barnes Foundation*, 394 Pa. 149, 97 A.2d 81, 83 (1953), the plaintiff, as a citizen and a reporter for a major newspaper, sued a local charitable corporation. The suit was brought with the consent of the Attorney General. When the court held that the plaintiff did not have standing to sue because he had no special interest, the plaintiff argued that he had the consent of the Attorney General to sue. The court said:

> [T]he protection of the public generally against the failure of a corporation to perform the duties required by its charter is the concern of the sovereign, and any action undertaken for such purpose must be by the Attorney General on its behalf. In the absence of statutory authority, the Attorney General may not delegate the conduct or control of the suit.

17. 61 Cal. 2d 750, 394 P.2d 932, 40 Cal. Rptr. 244 (1964).

wholly fulfilled by the authority given him. The protection of charities from
harassing litigation does not require that only the Attorney General be
permitted to bring legal actions in their behalf.[18]

The court then went on to hold that board members of a governing board of
a charitable corporation and trustees of a charitable trust could bring a suit of
this nature. In essence, then, the *Holt* case held that in California any board
member of a charitable organization could bring the organization into court on
charges of mismanagement, even against the wishes of the Attorney General.[19]

It is one thing to permit board members to so sue. They are a very limited
group and certainly they may have facts not readily available to an Attorney
General. Their status as permissible plaintiffs does not undermine substantially
the reason for adopting the traditional rule regarding standing. But should the
group of permissible plaintiffs be enlarged further? In *San Diego County Council,
Boy Scouts of America v. City of Escondido*,[20] the court had to decide whether a
parent organization of Boy Scouts (the Council) had standing to sue for enforcement of a trust which had among its beneficiaries the Boy Scouts of one of the
Council's districts. The trust agreement in question had set aside real property
for the benefit of Boy Scouts and Girl Scouts from certain areas in San Diego
County. The trustees of the trust subsequently conveyed the property for $1.00
to the City of Escondido for "park purposes and particularly for youth activities." The San Diego County Council of Boy Scouts decided to sue to protect
the interests of the Scouts mentioned in the trust agreement. The court held
that the plaintiff had standing to sue, stating:

> [T]here is no rule or policy against supplementing the Attorney General's
> power of enforcement by allowing other responsible individuals to sue in
> behalf of the charity. The administration of charitable trusts stands only to
> benefit if in addition to the Attorney General other suitable means of
> enforcement are available.[21]

The court gave its decision with knowledge that the Attorney General by then
had filed an action in his own name to enforce the trust.

Of interest also is the *Wilson College* case.[22] Wilson College is a charitable
corporation that was chartered by the State of Pennsylvania in 1869 for the
purpose of educating young women. It is managed by a Board of Trustees. In

---

18. Ibid., at 248.

19. This overruled the earlier case of *George Pepperdine Foundation v. Pepperdine*, 126 Cal. App. 2d
154, 271 P.2d 600 (1954) which did not permit board members to bring such a suit. See also a more
recent case in *Rowan v. Pasadena Art Museum*, No. C 322817 (Cal. Sup. Ct., L. A. County, Sept. 22,
1981), which interprets California's new nonprofit corporation law. In *Wickes v. Belgian American
Educational Foundation*, 266 F. Supp. 38 (S.D.N.Y. 1967), certain members and directors of a charitable
membership corporation were held to have standing to bring a derivative action against the
corporation.

20. 14 Cal. App. 3d 189, 92 Cal. Rptr. 186 (1971).

21. Ibid., at 189. (Note that as of 1980 California has a new nonprofit corporation law that expressly
states who has standing to sue.)

22. *Zehner v. Alexander*, Vol. 89, Page 262 (Penn. 39th Jud. Dist., Franklin County, Ct. of C.P.,
Orphans' Ct. Div., May 25, 1979).

1979, the trustees of the college voted to close the school because of declining enrollment. A trustee, several students, a few alumnae/donors and a faculty member sued the majority of the trustees for negligence and requested the court to enjoin the closing and to remove the defendant trustees from office. The Attorney General entered an appearance on behalf of the state. Without elaborating its reason, the court concluded that the trustee, the alumnae/donors and the faculty member had standing to sue, and that the students "while having a distinct and unique interest in the proceeding do not have legal standing to maintain it."[23]

The *Sibley Hospital* case,[24] which was discussed in Chapter I on the issue of board liability, also dealt with the issue of standing. The plaintiff in that case was the parent of a child who had been a patient at the hospital, and he brought the action on behalf of all patients who were forced to pay higher hospital fees because of the alleged mismanagement by the hospital trustees. On the issue of standing, the court said:

> Plaintiffs purporting to represent a class of users of the Hospital's services have a sufficient special interest to challenge the conduct of the trustees operating this charitable institution. This is especially so here, for neither the District of Columbia nor the hospital has taken any action to question the conduct brought into issue by the . . . complaint.[25]

Compare, however, an earlier case, *Art Institute of Chicago v. Castle.*[26] This case involved a local sculpture society's attempt to prevent an art institute trust fund, which dedicated to the "erection . . . of . . . statuary and monuments," from being used for the erection of a memorial building. The Society claimed a special interest inasmuch as its members would suffer professional and financial detriment if the funds were diverted to building construction. The court refused to recognize this financial consideration as sufficient to support a special interest, stating: "The beneficiaries of the charitable trust set up by the will are the people of the State of Illinois generally, not the sculptors who may be commissioned to erect statuary."[27]

The courts of New Jersey and Maryland have taken liberal views in decisions concerning standing to sue charities. In the case of *City of Patterson v. The*

---

23. Ibid., at 82 of decision. See also *Miller v. Alderhold*, 228 Ga. 65, 184 S.E.2d 172 (1971) where students as beneficiaries of a charitable trust were denied standing to challenge actions of school trustees. But compare *Jones v. Grant*, 344 So. 2d 1210 (Ala. 1277) where faculty, staff and students were granted standing to sue the board of directors of a college. In *Stuart v. Continental Ill. Nat'l Bank and Trust Co. of Chicago*, 68 Ill. 2d 502, 369 N.E.2d 1262 (1977), *cert. denied* 444 U.S. 844, co-trustees sued a corporate trustee for mismanagement. Under the terms of the trust, gifts could be made in the discretion of the trustees to charitable organizations. Charitable organizations that were potential beneficiaries were allowed to intervene in the suit.

24. *Stern v. Lucy Webb Hayes National Training School for Deaconesses and Missionaries*, 367 F. Supp. 536 (D.D.C. 1973) (order granting standing of plaintiffs to sue). 381 F. Supp. 1003 (D.D.C. 1974) (final decision).

25. *Stern v. Lucy Webb Hayes National Training School for Deaconesses and Missionaries*, No. 267-73 (D.D.C. June 8, 1973) (order granting standing of plaintiffs to sue).

26. 9 Ill. App. 2d 473, 133 N.E.2d 748 (Ill. 1956).

27. Ibid., at 752.

Patterson General Hospital,[28] the city and two residents of the city were permitted to sue the Patterson General Hospital, a charitable corporation, alleging a deviation from its trust purposes. The court said:

> It must be conceded that in this state, and throughout the country as a whole, supervision of the administration of charities has been neglected. Charities in this state, whether or not incorporated, are, in general, only subject to the supervision of the Attorney General. The manifold duties of this office make readily understandable the facts that such supervision is necessarily sporadic. . . . While public supervision of the administration of charities remains inadequate, a liberal rule as to the standing of a plaintiff to complain about the administration of a charitable trust or charitable corporation seems decidedly in the public interest.[29]

This view was reinforced by a similar holding in *Township of Cinnaminson v. First Camden National Bank and Trust Co.*[30] and echoed in *Gordon v. City of Baltimore.*[31] In the *Gordon* case a taxpayer was granted standing to challenge the transfer of a private charitable institution's library to another private charitable institution which received considerable money from the city for its operating expenses. The court reasoned that if the library was accepted, the city would be called upon to increase its support, and thus the taxpayer had a sufficient pecuniary interest to bring suit.

D. Museum Cases Involving the Issue of Standing to Sue

The trend to enlarge the concept of "standing to sue" should be of considerable interest to museums, and this is illustrated by two recent cases. One concerns the Carnegie Institute's attempt to deaccession two of its collections; the other, the problems encountered by the Pasadena Art Museum when it put several of its works up for auction.

In January 1979, the Carnegie Institute of Pittsburgh petitioned the Pennsylvania Court for approval to sell at public sale substantially all of its coin and stamp collections.[32] The court petition approach was taken because of the volume of material at issue.[33] In its petition, the Institute explained: (1) that the stamp and coin collections marked for sale were unrestricted gifts to the museum, (2) that the Institute had never had the funds to provide professional staff and security for the collections and thus the Institute could never make the collections truly available to the public, (3) that the Institute had determined

---

28. 97 N. J. Super. 514, 235 A.2d 487 (1967).

29. Ibid., at 495.

30. 199 N. J. Super. 115, 238 A.2d 701 (1968).

31. 258 Md. 682, 267 A.2d 98 (1970). See also *Lord v. City of Wilmington*, 332 A.2d 414 (Del. 1975), *aff'd* 378 A.2d 635 (Del. 1977).

32. *In Re Carnegie Institute*, No. 208 of 1979 (Penn. Ct. of C.P., Allegheny County, Orphans' Ct. Div., May 14, 1980). The Carnegie Institute maintains two museums in Pittsburgh: The Carnegie Museum of Natural History and the Museum of Art, Carnegie Institute. The Carnegie Museum of Natural History was the petitioner in this case.

33. See section in Chapter V entitled "The Proper Authority to Approve a Decision to Deaccession."

that retention of these collections would not effectively promote the broader purpose for which the museum was formed, and (4) that it would be in the best interests of the people of Pittsburgh for the Institute to sell substantially all of these collections.[34] The Attorney General was made a party to the proceeding and he entered a brief on behalf of the public. When it became evident to the court that there was much public sentiment both for and against the proposed sale, a six-month stay was ordered so that interested parties could offer alternative solutions. At the expiration of the six months, another hearing was held. Present at the hearing and offering testimony was a local historical society. The historical society had submitted the only offer for an alternative method of disposition, but the offer had not been accepted.[35] The record on the case was then closed, but further time was given to the Institute to effect a compromise. Several months later, an agreement was reached between the Institute and the Attorney General, and this was submitted to the court. The agreement permitted the Institute to sell the collections except for certain limited exceptions. The historical society objected to the proposed agreement as well as the sale, but the court approved the agreement stating that it would be in the interest of the public to adjust the matter by mutual concession. On the issue of the historical society's standing to be heard, the court said:

> Initially it is observed that charitable trusts are enforced by the Attorney General, not individual members of the public. In the absence of statutory authority, a person who has no special interest cannot maintain a suit for the enforcement of a charitable trust, nor may the Attorney General delegate the control of such a suit. . . . This is a necessity since if one individual person could interpose objections, any other individual person could also either raise objections or give support and as the decision on one individual objection would not be a bar to another individual objection, there would be no end to litigation. Therefore, while the position of the Historical Society is appreciated as well as the individual expressions of interest, there does not appear in the record of these proceedings sufficient evidence to deny giving effect to the agreement reached between petitioner [the Institute] and the Attorney General.[36]

The historical society filed exceptions to the court's decision. It put forth several reasons why it should have standing to participate in the proceedings. Among them were the following:

    (1) The society is a nonprofit corporation chartered for the preservation of the culture and heritage of Western Pennsylvania, which is the subject of the case. Therefore, the society has a special interest.

    (2) Many of the members of the society are stamp and coin collectors and they have a greater interest in the preservation of the collections.

    (3) The historical society's submission of an alternative plan within the

---

34. The Carnegie had offered the collections to other educational organizations in the area, but none were able to purchase and maintain the collections.

35. The historical society had offered to accept the collections as a gift.

36. *In Re Carnegie Institute, op. cit.* at 2-3.

designated six-month period gave it a special interest that should be heard.

(4) The Attorney General did not adequately represent the public in the case and therefore the society should be heard.

(5) The court should hear all available evidence on the case and should not merely accept the assertions of the Institute and the Attorney General that the proposed sale was in the best interest of the public.

(6) The court should apply the *cy pres*[37] doctrine and award the collections to the historical society as successor trustee.[38]

The issue of standing became moot when the Carnegie Institute, feeling protracted litigation would be counter-productive, amended its petition to the court. It requested permission to sell only a major portion of its stamp collection, it being understood that the fate of the coin collection would not be pressed at this time. All parties interested in the matter agreed to this amended petition, and court approval was given in December 1980 for the sale of the described stamp collection. Two years had been spent in court on the matter.

Further ramifications of the "standing to sue" concept were raised in *Rowan v. Pasadena Art Museum* where legal steps were taken to halt a scheduled sale of certain works of art from the collections of the Pasadena Art Museum.[39] The museum had deaccessioned several works and they were scheduled to be sold at a major New York auction house. Shortly before the sale, three former trustees of the museum obtained a temporary restraining order from a California court enjoining the sale. The former trustees alleged that the proposed sale would violate the trust obligations of the museum. On the issue of their "standing" to bring the action, the former trustees cited the case of *Holt v. College of Osteopathic Physicians and Surgeons, supra,* claiming that their position was "functionally equivalent" to that of the minority trustees in *Holt* and therefore the policies articulated in *Holt* should be applied in their suit. In the *Pasadena* matter, the plaintiffs urged further arguments to support their claim of standing. They cited the following "personal and private interests":

(1) They were individual contributors to the museum and thus they personally should be entitled to enforce the conditions under which their gifts were made.

37. If a charitable trust lacks a proper trustee or if the trust proves impossible or impracticable for other reasons, the court may apply the *cy pres* doctrine and approve an alternate means for carrying out the general charitable intent. See section on "Restricted Gifts" in Chapter IV for more information on *cy pres*.

38. Compare *In Re Nevil's Estate,* 414 Pa. 122, 199 A.2d 419 (1964), where a charitable organization in a position similar to the historical society in the Carnegie case, was denied standing to challenge the court's action.

39. *Rowan v. Pasadena Art Museum,* No. C322817 (Cal. Sup. Ct., L.A. County, Sept. 22, 1981). Suits of this type are becoming more prevalent. A short time after the planned art sale by the Pasadena Museum was halted by a California court order, a similar restraining order was granted by a Pennsylvania court stopping another auction sale of art works belonging to the Edwin Forrest Home for Retired Actors. The restraining order was sought because it was claimed that the proposed sale violated the terms of Mr. Forrest's trust. *In Re the Edwin Forrest Home,* No. 154 of 1981 (Penn., Philadelphia Ct. of C.P., Orphans' Ct. Div., April 24, 1981) (Opinion of Court *en banc,* 1982).

(2) As former trustees they made express representations to other contributors. They considered themselves morally responsible for these representations and possibly some might seek to hold them legally responsible. (With respect to reasons 1 and 2, the plaintiffs offer no evidence that the gifts in question were conditional. It can only be assumed that the gifts were made without express conditions and that the gist of the plaintiffs' argument was that any contributor to a museum acquires a special interest which entitles him to standing to sue.)

(3) As former trustees, they have a right to vindicate the actions they took as trustees which relate to the proposed sale.

In its decision on the jurisdictional aspects of the *Rowan* case, the court had to interpret California's new Corporation Code. Section 5142 of the Code lists the following as having standing to sue a public benefit (i.e., charitable) corporation:

(1) the charitable corporation itself

(2) an officer of the corporation

(3) a director of the corporation

(4) a person with a reversionary, contractual or property interest in the assets of the corporation

(5) the Attorney General, or any person granted relator status by the Attorney General.

The court considered this list to be an exclusive one, and it then proceeded to analyze whether the plaintiffs fell within catagories 2, 3 or 4. It determined that Section 5142 was not intended to give standing to former members, directors or officers; thus categories 2 and 3 were unavailable to the plaintiffs.[40] With regard to category 4, the court indicated that this may permit separate causes of actions by individual donors seeking relief for a failure of the museum to abide by the terms of their particular gifts, but in this case the plaintiffs had failed to frame their complaint in this manner. In other words, the relief sought must be specifically related to the violated promise, the mere fact that one is a donor does not confer standing to question generally the actions of the museum. With regard to category 5, it was conceded that the Attorney General had not granted formal relator status,[41] but the plaintiffs contended that there had been an informal grant of such status. As a practical solution, the court allowed the Attorney General a short period of time in which to determine if he wished to grant such formal status and thus secure a category 5 basis for proceeding to a trial on the merits. Subsequently, the plaintiffs did obtain formal relator status.[42]

---

40. See also *American Center for Education Inc. v. Cavnar*, 80 Cal. App. 3d 476, 145 Cal. Rptr. 736, 742 (1978).

41. Relator status essentially means that the Attorney General expressly permits the individual to sue in his stead.

42. A recently filed case involving the Fine Arts Museum of San Francisco, raises the issue of the standing of city residents to sue the museum. *Hardman v. Feinstein*, No. 827217 (Cal. Sup. Ct., San Francisco County, July 1984).

Good arguments can be made for and against the expansion of the standing to sue rule, but few would deny that under the present trend a museum may be hard put to resolve efficiently a substantial management issue. Prior approval from the Attorney General may not protect it from a lawsuit, a trustee or former trustee may be encouraged to question board decisions through court action, and dissatisfied donors and other interested groups may decide to test their ability to obtain legal relief.[43]

E. Oversight by Taxing Authorities

A museum as a charity occupies a favored position in our tax structure. "Charity" status provides a dual sustenance inasmuch as it substantially renders the museum's revenues exempt from taxation and it provides strong tax incentives for donations to the museum.[44] On the other hand, this privileged status also is a basis for oversight of museum operations by the taxing authority.[45] Just how the government should control a charity through this tax power is a subject of much debate. A general understanding of the issues involved is helpful if one wishes intelligently to respond to some of the more subtle tax-related problems which can face a museum. It is easier to illustrate in an historical setting.

Early in the 1900s when our income tax system was taking root, it was acknowledged that charitable organizations were beneficial to the country and that the tax structure should foster rather than inhibit their growth. Charities had played a dominant role in the growth of our country. True to their pioneering spirit, our forefathers looked first to their community for basic social services, not to government. Innumerable voluntary organizations sprang up to satisfy community needs, and these organizations became accepted as part of the American way of life.[46] A major study on philanthropy, commonly known as the "Filer Report," describes this phenomenon as a reflection of "a national

---

43. For a different viewpoint, see Hansmann, "Reforming Nonprofit Corporation Law," 129 *U. Pa. L. Rev.* 497, 600 (1981).

44. Outside the scope of this text is the issue of unrelated business income, income which subjects even a charity to taxation. Three articles of interest on this subject are: Gilbert, "Coming to Terms with the Tax Man" and Brown, "Keeping an Eye on Each Other: The IRS and the Museum Store"; both articles appear in *Museum News* (Sept.–Oct. 1982), and Murphy, "Minding the Store," *Museum News* (Oct. 1983). See also Galloway, *The Unrelated Business Income Tax* (1982).

45. Provisions of the federal Internal Revenue Code frequently are mirrored by a state's revenue statutes. Both federal and state authorities, therefore, may assert supervision over a charity through the tax medium. On the state and local level, charities are frequently exempt from property taxes, but not always. Much depends on the interpretation of the applicable statute. For example, in the early 1980s, New York City began refusing property tax exemptions to certain educational organizations that did not have a curriculum or a faculty, but this interpretation of the law was reversed when there was widespread protest from cultural organizations generally. See decision concerning the Asian Society as reported in the *New York Law Journal* for March 7, 1983 and *Art in America* 216 (Sept. 1983), and the case entitled, *The Symphony Space, Inc. v. Tishelman*, 16 N.Y.2d 33 (1983).

46. The *Filer Report*, referred to in the following footnote, states that even today there are in the United States many more voluntarily supported educational, cultural and social organizations than are found in other countries where state-run charitable organizations are the rule. See Note, "The Enforcement of Charitable Trusts in America: A History of Evolving Social Attitudes," 54 *Va. L. Rev.* 436 (April 1968) for a detailed description of the early development of the law concerning charitable trusts.

belief in the philosophy of pluralism and in the profound importance to society of individual initiative."[47] In order to foster these perceived public benefits of pluralism and self-help, the early tax code protected and encouraged charities by granting tax exempt status and devising the charitable contribution deduction. In effect, the early tax structure encouraged diversity and sheltered charities from direct government control. As long as an organization could meet the definition given in the tax code, that it was "organized and operated exclusively for . . . educational purposes,"[48] it was assured the favored tax exempt status.

With the rise of a more enlightened social conscience in this country, there were pressures to enlarge government's control over many phases of society that up until then had been considered "private." For example, organizations that received grants or other forms of "federal financial assistance" were required to conform to a variety of government-imposed social programs as a condition for the aid.[49] There were those who argued that the tax exemption and the tax deduction enjoyed by charities were the equivalent of direct government expenditures, that is, they were sums actually owed the government but allotted, by way of the tax structure, to the charitable organizations. Under this approach, charities were not viewed as "self-help" segments of society that respond directly to private beneficence, but were considered recipients of public funds.[50]

At first glance, these differing philosophic characterizations of a tax exemption or charitable deduction may seem sophomoric quibbling, but there is a crucial distinction in end results. If, for example, a tax exemption is considered to be just what its name implies, a decision that an entity is not subject to a tax, then the only legitimate interest of the taxing authority in that entity is to see that the exemption is legitimately obtained and maintained. Oversight requirements imposed by the taxing authority essentially amount to record-keeping and reporting requirements in order to demonstrate true charity status. On the other hand, if a tax exemption is viewed as an efficient way of returning to an entity its tax payment in the form of a government grant (that is, public largesse), the mandate of the supervising government authority is more pervasive and the charity's entitlement to privileged status is far more tenuous. Under this theory, oversight can take on the additional dimension of requiring charities to adhere to standards, programs and procedures designed to further national, social and economic goals that are deemed appropriate for recipients of public largesse.[51]

---

47. "Giving in America; Toward a Stronger Voluntary Sector," Report to the Commission on Private Philanthropy and Public Needs (Washington, D.C. 1975).

48. 26. U.S.C. § 501(c)(3).

49. See next section.

50. See Surrey, "Federal Income Tax Reform: the Varied Approaches Necessary to Replace Tax Expenditures with Direct Governmental Assistance", 84 *Harv. L. Rev.* 352 (1970).

51. Stone, "Federal Tax Support of Charities and Other Exempt Organizations: The Need for a National Policy," 20 *Cal. Tax Inst.* 27 (1968); Kurtz, "Tax Incentives: Their Use and Misuse," 20 *Cal. Tax Inst.* 1 (1968); Friendly, "The Dartmouth College Case and the Public-Private Penumbra," 12 *Tex. Q. 2d Supp. 141 (1960)*; J. Nason, *Trustees and the Future of Foundations* (1977).

In the case of *Bob Jones University v. United States*,[52] the Supreme Court reached the result favored by those who espouse the more modern theory, but it used less drastic reasoning. In its decision, the court said that tax exempt status depends on meeting certain common law standards of charity status (this is inherent in the § 501(c)(3) definition of charity). These standards require that the organization have a public purpose and not operate contrary to established public policy. Thus, there is a twofold test for tax exempt status: the organization must fall within one of the categories specifically named in § 501(c)(3) (for example, educational, religious) and it must satisfy the I.R.S. that its operations do not violate "established public policies." In the *Bob Jones* case, the school had a policy that forbade interracial dating and marriage. The Supreme Court held that this school policy was contrary to established public policy, and, hence, the university could properly be denied tax exempt status.

Espousal of the more modern theory of taxation reflects an element of disillusionment with charities which fosters government-imposed standards, rather than the traditional philosophy of pluralism and encouragement of individual initiative.[53] This disillusionment is fed by any real or apparent abuse of status by a charity, whether it involves the charity's methods of conducting business or the personal conduct of its officers. A skeptical public is more amenable to the impositions of government control. In the years to come, the extent of government supervision of charities through the taxing authority (that is, whether the traditional or the more modern theory prevails) may depend in good measure on the conduct of the charities themselves.[54] A conclusion reached in a 1982 report on academic governance states it rather well:

> In the end, the authority of boards of trustees will be sustained by the quality of those chosen as members, by the wisdom of their actions, and by their willingness to serve the general interests of the public while protecting higher education.[55]

F. As Recipients of Federal Financial Assistance

The phrase "federal financial assistance" is a term of art that should be understood by the museum community because it comes with many strings attached. The phrase is used in several major pieces of federal legislation of particular interest to museums: Title VI of the Civil Rights Act of 1964,[56] Title IX of the Education Amendments Act of 1972,[57] Section 504 of the Rehabilitation Act of

---

52. 461 U.S. 574, 103 S. Ct. 2017, 76 L. Ed. 2d 157 (1983).

53. See *Green v. Connally*, 330 F. Supp. 1150 (D.D.C. 1971), *aff'd* 404 U.S. 997; *McGlotten v. Connally*, 338 F. Supp. 448 (D.D.C. 1972); *Stewart v. New York University*, 430 F. Supp. 1305 (S.D.N.Y. 1976). For general background information on theories regarding public control of private organizations, see Note, "State Action: Theories for Applying Constitutional Restrictions to Private Activity," 74 *Colum. L. Rev.* 656 (1974).

54. For a comprehensive presentation of tax implications for museums, see Comment, "Tax Incentives for Support of the Arts: In Defense of the Charitable Deduction," 85 *Dick. L. Rev.* 663 (1981).

55. Carnegie Foundation for the Advancement of Teaching, *Report on Academic Governance* (Oct. 1982).

56. 42 U.S.C. §§ 2000d-2000d-4.

57. 20 U.S.C. §§ 1681-1686.

1973,[58] and the Age Discrimination Act of 1975.[59] A recipient of federal financial assistance at a minimum must comply with these statutes, and compliance can be monitored by various governmental bodies and by private citizens.[60]

Federal financial assistance is defined broadly to mean:

> Any grant, entitlement, loan, contract (other than a procurement contract or a contract of insurance or guaranty), or any other arrangement by which the [federal] agency provides or otherwise makes available assistance in the form of
>
> (a) funds
> (b) services of federal personnel; or
> (c) real and personal property or any interest in or use of property including:
> (1) transfers or leases of such property for less than fair market value or for reduced consideration; and
> (2) proceeds from a subsequent transfer or lease of such property if the federal share of its fair market value is not returned to the Federal Government.[61]

To be a "recipient" of federal financial assistance, one need not receive the assistance directly from a federal agency. By administrative interpretation, a "recipient" includes any successor, assignee, or transferee of the original recipient, but excludes the ultimate beneficiary of the assistance. Thus, if museum programs received federal funds dispensed by a state arts agency or if museum activities are supported by municipal funds acquired from federal revenue-sharing, such indirect support is considered federal financial assistance and the affected programs and activities must be administered in compliance with the enumerated statutes. Even if federal financial assistance provides only partial support for a program or activity, usually, it is interpreted to mean that the entire program or activity must be in compliance. Similarly, if the assistance covers any portion of overhead or general operating expenses of an organization, all the organization's programs and activities may be affected.[62]

Federal agencies dispensing federal financial assistance are required to oversee compliance with the Civil Rights Act, the Education Amendments Act, the Rehabilitation Act and the Age Discrimination Act. This is accomplished through

---

58. 29 U.S.C. § 794.

59. 42 U.S.C. §§ 6101-6107.

60. For a general discussion of the legal implications of federal financial assistance for private organizations, see "The Campus and the Courts," *Bowdoin Alumnus* 12 (Spring 1980). Consider, also, whether a museum which received substantial federal financial assistance could be deemed engaged in "government action," and, therefore, subject to constitutional restrictions. See, for example, the issues raised in *Blum v. Yaretsky*, 457 U.S. 991, 102 S. Ct. 2777, 73 L. Ed. 2d 534 (1982); *Rendell-Baker v. Kohn*, 454 U.S. 891 (1982).

61. See the appropriate federal agency regulations that implement the particular civil rights statute at issue.

62. The extent to which a program or activity is affected by partial or indirect federal financial assistance is a much debated topic. It appears that a general "overhead" grant to an organization could cause all its activities to be affected, but a grant to a specific activity, even though it might have an economic ripple effect, would bring civil rights obligations only to that activity. See *Grove City College v. Bell*, _____U.S. _____, 104 S. Ct. 1211, 79 L. Ed. 2d 516 (1984).

the issuance by each agency of detailed regulations that set forth what is expected of a recipient of such assistance with regard to nondiscrimination, the methods used to audit compliance, complaint procedures, and the penalities which can be imposed for violations.[63] Before applying for (or accepting) any form of federal financial assistance, a museum should understand all the responsibilities that flow from an award and assess its ability to meet these obligations. In the following sections, each of the aforementioned statutes and their possible legal repercussions are described briefly.

Race Discrimination

Title VI of the Civil Rights Act of 1964[64] prohibits discrimination on the basis of race, color or national origin in programs or activities that receive federal financial assistance.[65] This means that a museum that receives direct or indirect federal aid that falls within the definition of federal financial assistance is vulnerable to discrimination complaints.[66] Any individual who believes that he has been discriminated against by a recipient in violation of Title VI may file a complaint with the granting agency.[67] If the recipient fails to correct an established violation, the penalty is termination of or refusal to grant assistance for the program or activity in question.[68] It should be noted that Title VI also permits a private right of action for enforcement. This means that an aggrieved individual may elect not to file a complaint with the granting agency and instead initiate a court suit for damages and/or other relief against the recipient.[69]

---

63. Under Executive Order 12250 of November 2, 1980, the U.S. Department of Justice is responsible for coordinating agency enforcement of Title VI of the Civil Rights Act, Title IX of the Education Amendments Act and § 504 of the Rehabilitation Act. This is done through the issuance of guidelines that must be followed by federal agencies when they draft their implementing regulations. The Department of Health and Human Services is the coordinating agency for the Age Discrimination Act of 1975.

64. "No person in the United States shall, on the ground of race, color, or national origin, be excluded from participation in, be denied the benefits of, or be subjected to discrimination under any program or activity receiving Federal financial assistance." 42 U.S.C. § 2000d.

65. It should be noted that federal regulations have interpreted Title VI to prohibit the denial of access to educational programs because of a student's limited proficiency in the English language. This interpretation was affirmed by the U.S. Supreme Court in *Lau v. Nichols*, 414 U.S. 563, 94 S.Ct. 786, 39 L. Ed. 2d 1 (1974). See also *United States v. Texas*, 680 F.2d 356 (5th Cir. 1982). In 1980, the U.S. Department of Education issued comprehensive proposed rules to implement this facet of Title VI. The proposal was withdrawn in February 1981.

66. On the issue of whether emphasis in a museum program on a particular ethnic group constitutes discrimination, see *Livingston v. Ewing*, 601 F.2d 1110 (10th Cir. 1979), *cert. denied* 444 U.S. 870.

67. Normally, employment complaints do not fall under Title VI unless the primary objective of the federal financial assistance is to provide employment. 42 U.S.C. § 2000d-3. Title VI focuses on nondiscriminatory distribution of services. Title VII of the Civil Rights Act of 1964 concerns equal employment and may affect a museum employing 15 or more persons. 42 U.S.C. § 2000(e).

68. 42 U.S.C. § 2000d-1.

69. See *Bossier Parish School Board v. Lemon*, 370 F.2d 847 (5th Cir. 1967), *cert. denied* 388 U.S. 911 (1967); *Cannon v. Univ. of Chicago*, 559 F.2d 1063 (7th Cir. 1976) *rev'd* and *rem'd*; 441 U.S. 677 (1979), 648 F.2d 1104 (7th Cir. 1981) *cert. denied* 454 U.S. 1128 (1981), but note qualifying language in *Stewart v. N.Y. Univ.*, 430 F. Supp. 1305 (S.D.N.Y. 1976) requiring a certain casual connection between the federal assistance and the alleged discrimination. See also, *Guardian Ass'n of the N.Y.C. Police Dept. v. Civil Service Com'n, City of N.Y.*, _____U.S. _____, 103 S. Ct. 3221, 77 L. Ed. 2d 866 (1983), which discusses whether there is a need to prove "discriminatory intent" in a Title VI action and the remedies available to a plaintiff.

Sex Discrimination

Title IX of the Education Amendment Act of 1972[70] prohibits discrimination on the basis of sex in federally assisted education programs and activities. To date, most activity under Title IX has been centered in schools, especially with regard to extracurricular activities. Only recently has attention been given to exploring the breadth of the Act's coverage.[71] As a result, some guidance should be forthcoming from government agencies concerning the coverage of cultural and educational programs held in other than classroom settings.[72]

In *Cannon v. University of Chicago*,[73] the U.S. Supreme Court confirmed that Title IX creates a private right of action for sex discrimination in federally assisted education programs. This means that the aggrieved party may elect to sue directly the recipient of the federal assistance.[74] In *North Haven Board of Education v. Bell*,[75] the Supreme Court ruled on two questions that had been the subjects of much controversy: (1) Does Title IX cover employees of educational institutions as well as the beneficiaries of the federal assistance? (2) Is Title IX "program-specific"? With regard to the first question, the court ruled that employees of educational organizations also are covered by Title IX: the act does not protect only the beneficiaries of the funded programs or activities. Thus, the employment practices of a museum that accepts federal financial assistance are vulnerable to charges of sex discrimination. On the second question, the court ruled that Title IX is program-specific. In other words, the alleged discrimination must involve the program or activity which actually receives the federal assistance, and, if there is any cutoff of federal money because of noncompliance it affects only the program or activity found to be in violation of the law. Exactly what constituted a program or activity remained unclear, however, and courts wrestled with the problem. In *Hillsdale College v. Department of Health, Education and Welfare*,[76] the college itself accepted no federal financial

---

70. "No person in the United States shall, on the basis of sex, be excluded from participation in, be denied the benefits of, or be subjected to discrimination under any education program or activity receiving Federal financial assistance." 20 U.S.C. § 1681(a).

71. In *Piascik v. Cleveland Museum of Art*, 426 F. Supp. 779 (N.D. Ohio 1976), the court held that an art museum which received federal assistance for an education program it operated for the school system and which operated library, slide and teaching facilities for a group of university students was an "educational. . . activity" within the meaning of Title IX.

72. Check the current regulations of such funding agencies as National Endowment for the Arts and the National Endowment for the Humanities for most recent guidance. These regulations appear in Chapter XI of Title 45 of the Code of Federal Regulations.

73. 559 F.2d 1063 (7th Cir. 1976) *rev'd* and *rem'd* 441 U.S. 677 (1979), 648 F.2d 1104 (7th Cir. 1981) *cert. denied* 454 U.S. 1128 (1981). In the later rehearing of this case in the U.S. Court of Appeals on the issue of proof of discrimination, the Appeals Court ruled proof of intentional discrimination is necessary to establish a Title IX violation rather than the mere "disparate impact" test.

74. *Lieberman v. Univ. of Chicago*, 660 F.2d 1185 (7th Cir. 1981) *cert. denied* 456 U.S. 937, 102 S. Ct. 1993, 72 L. Ed. 2d 456, held, however, that Title IX permits injunctive relief but does not give plaintiff a private damage remedy.

75. 456 U.S. 572, 72 L. Ed. 2d 299, 102 S. Ct. 1912 (1982). After deciding the *North Haven* case, the Supreme Court declined to hear another case which reached an opposite conclusion. See *Carter v. Dayton Board of Education* 456 U.S. 989, 102 S. Ct. 2267, 73 L. Ed. 2d 1283 (1982).

76. 697 F.2d 418 (6th Cir. 1982), *cert. granted*, but case remanded to Court of Appeals for further consideration in light of Supreme Court's decision in *Grove City College v. Bell*.

assistance, but some of its students had federal loans or grants to pay their tuitions. The court held that the college was not subject to Title IX. Yet in *Grove City College v. Bell*[77] another court came to the opposite conclusion holding that the entire college was a "program" under Title IX because of the students' receipt of federal loans and grants. *University of Richmond v. Bell*[78] added to the confusion. There the issue was whether the school's athletic program fell under Title IX sanctions. The athletic program itself received no direct federal financial assistance, but other departments of the university received federal grants, and students at the university had federal loans and grants to pay their education expenses. The court refused to give a broad, institution-wide reading to the term "program" and rejected the claim that perceived indirect benefits to the athletic program drew the program under Title IX. Finally, the *Grove City College* case was taken to the United States Supreme Court in order to resolve the confusion.[79] The Court ruled that federal loans given directly to students did constitute federal financial assistance to the school but that the only program affected was the school's financial aid program. The court rejected the idea that the whole school should be deemed covered by Title IX only because the tuition received from students with federal loans had an economic ripple effect throughout the institution.

Handicap Discrimination

Section 504 of the Rehabilitation Act of 1973[80] prohibits discrimination on the basis of handicap in programs and activities receiving federal financial assistance. This particular statute can have major consequences for a museum seeking federal assistance because at times the handicapped require special treatment if they are to enjoy equal access. Also "handicapped" can mean many things, each impairment requiring its own considerations.

One feature of § 504 deserves special mention. The statute does not require that all facilities of a recipient of federal funds be accessible; it states that any "program" or "activity" receiving such assistance must be accessible. It may be possible, therefore, to comply with the statute by moving the location of an activity to an accessible site; or, if duplicate programs are offered, by providing at least one such program in an accessible manner. Structural changes to a facility are necessary only when other methods are ineffective in making the covered program or activity accessible.

The precise reach of § 504 is still being debated. Is it "program-specific"— that is, is its effect limited within an organization to the particular program or activity that receives the federal financial assistance? The initial position taken by the federal government favored a broad reading of the statute on the argu-

---

77. 687 F.2d 684 (3rd Cir. 1982). See also, *Haffer v. Temple Univ.*, 524 F. Supp. 531 (E.D. Penn. 1981).

78. 543 F. Supp. 321 (E. D. Va. 1982).

79. _____ U.S. _____, 104 S. Ct. 1211, 79 L. Ed. 2d 516 (1984).

80. "No otherwise qualified handicapped individual in the United States. . . shall, solely by reason of his handicap, be excluded from the participation in, be denied the benefits of, or be subjected to discrimination under any program or activity receiving Federal financial assistance." 29 U.S.C. § 794.

ment that all programs and activities of an organization benefit when grants are obtained to support specific programs and activities. This view was endorsed by a federal district court in *Wright v. Columbia University*,[81] but in light of subsequent Supreme Court decisions in *North Haven Board of Education v. Bell* and *Grove City College v. Bell*,[82] it would appear that § 504 should be interpreted as program-specific.[83] Does § 504 cover employment discrimination based on handicap regardless of whether the purpose of the federal assistance is to provide employment? The Supreme Court has answered this in the affirmative.[84]

Even though the Rehabilitation Act was amended in 1978 to clarify its enforcement procedures, several procedural issues remained in doubt.[85] Must the party first exhaust his administrative remedies with the federal granting agency before bringing a private right of action?[86] To date, lower court decisions do not impose such a requirement.[87] What remedies are available to a party in a private suit? Can he seek only to enjoin (prohibit) the continuance of the discriminatory conduct or can he obtain money damages? Once, again, court decisions are split.[88]

A more complete discussion of the scope and impact of § 504 on museums is contained in Chapter XVI on "Access to the Collections," but it should be remembered that § 504 interpretations are still very much in a state of flux. As questions arise, the most current federal agency regulations and court decisions must be reviewed.

Age Discrimination
The most recent civil rights statute to affect recipients of federal financial assistance is the Age Discrimination Act of 1975.[89] The Act prohibits age discrimination in programs and activities receiving federal financial assistance, with

---

81. 520 F. Supp. 789 (E. D. Penn. 1981). The program-specific issue was before the Supreme Court in *Univ. of Tex. v. Camenisch*, 451 U.S. 390, 68 L. Ed. 2d 175, 101 S. Ct. 1830 (1981), but the case was returned to the lower court on a procedural matter without a decision on the merits.

82. See previous section on "Sex Discrimination."

83. See also *Jones v. Metropolitan Atlanta Rapid Transit Authority*, 681 F.2d 1376 (11th Cir. 1982). *Ferris v. Univ. of Tex. at Austin*, 558 F. Supp. 536 (W. Tex. 1983).

84. *Consolidated Rail Corp. v. Darrone*, _____U.S. _____, 104 S. Ct. 1248, 49 L. Ed. 2d 568 (1984).

85. The Act now specifies that "remedies, procedures and rights set forth in Title VI of the Civil Rights Act of 1964 are available to victims of § 504 discrimination (29 U.S.C. § 794a).

86. If there is a private right of action, the person claiming discrimination can sue the grantee directly in court.

87. *Puskin v. Regents of the Univ. of Colorado*, 658 F.2d 1372 (10th Cir. 1981); *Miener v. Missouri*, 673 F.2d 969 (8th Cir. 1982).

88. *Miener v. Missouri* 673 F.2d 969 (8th Cir. 1982); *Patton v. Dumpson*, 498 F. Supp. 933 (S.D.N.Y. 1980), but see also *Lieberman v. Univ. of Chicago*, 660 F.2d 1185 (7th Cir. 1981) *cert. denied*, 456 U.S. 937, 102 S. Ct. 1993, 72 L. Ed. 456 (1982), which interpreted Title IX of the Education Amendments Act of 1972, a statute similar to § 504.

89. "[N]o person in the United States shall, on the basis of age, be excluded from participation in, be denied the benefits of, or be subjected to discrimination under any program or activity receiving Federal financial assistance." 42 U.S.C. §§ 6101–6107.

specific exceptions. It does not apply to: (1) employment practices except where the purpose of the federal assistance is to finance certain employment programs;[90] (2) age distinctions established under authority of any law;[91] (3) age distinctions necessary to the normal operation or achievement of a statutory objective of a program;[92] and (4) actions based on reasonable factors other than age which may have a disproportionate effect on age. Many government agencies are still in the process of formulating their specific regulations implementing the Age Discrimination Act.[93] All of these specific regulations, however, must be patterned after general regulations issued by the Department of Health and Human Services.[94] These general regulations require a new enforcement procedure. All complaints under the Age Discrimination Act first must be referred by the granting agency to a mediation process managed by the Federal Mediation and Conciliation Service. If the mediation process is unsuccessful after sixty days, the granting agency must then begin its own fact-finding procedures.

When the Age Discrimination Act was first enacted, it specifically stated that aggrieved individuals could not maintain private causes of action against recipients, that the exclusive remedy for enforcement of the Act was a complaint processed through the granting agency. This limitation was changed as of 1978.[95] Now an aggrieved party can sue directly the recipients of the assistance if administrative remedies have been exhausted.

G. Miscellaneous State and Local Reporting Statutes

Uniform Supervision of Trustees for Charitable Purposes Act

The Attorneys General of various states have long recognized the practical difficulties each faces in monitoring the performance of charitable trusts. A major drawback can be lack of statutory authority to require trustees to report to the Attorney General the existence and administration of property held for charitable purposes.[96] To remedy this situation, the National Association of

---

90. The Age Discrimination in Employment Act of 1967, as amended, which is administered by the Equal Opportunity Commission, is the principal statute concerned with age discrimination in employment. It concerns employment practices for persons between the ages of 40 and 70.

91. Agency regulations interpret "any law" to include Federal, state or local statutes or ordinances adopted by elected, general purpose legislative bodies.

92. Refer to granting agency's regulations implementing the Age Discrimination Act for an explanation of this exception.

93. On December 28, 1982, the Department of Health and Human Services (HHS) issued its specific regulations governing the actions of recipients of federal financial assistance from that department. The HHS specific regulations might well be used as a model by other federal agencies. See Nondiscrimination on the Basis of Age in Programs or Activities Receiving Federal Financial Assistance from HHS, 47 Fed. Reg. 57850 (1982) (codified at 45 C.F.R. pt. 91).

94. 44 Fed. Reg. 33768 (1979), now codified as 45 C.F.R. pt. 90. With the creation of the Department of Education, HEW became known as the Department of Health and Human Services (HHS).

95. Public Law 95-478, § 401(c) deleted the original subsection (e) of 42 U.S.C. § 6102 which stated that the administrative process was the sole remedy for violations of the Age Discrimination Act, substituted a new subsection (e) and a subsection (f) which provides for a private right of action.

96. See Bogert, "Proposed Legislation Regarding State Supervision of Charities," 52 *Mich. L. Rev.* 633 (1954). See also Note, "State Supervision of the Administration of Charitable Trusts," 47 *Colum. L. Rev.* 659 (1947); Comment, "Supervision of Charitable Trusts," 21 *U. Chi. L. Rev.* 118 (1953).

Attorneys General in 1951 requested a "uniform act" on the subject of reporting that could be adopted by interested states. Such an act was drafted and approved by the American Bar Association in 1954.[97]

The uniform act covers trustees, corporate and otherwise, holding property for charitable purposes, and it requires that trustees file initial and periodic reports with the Attorneys General concerning the assets under their control. The act also places on the Attorneys General, and other state agents, certain responsibilities and powers concerning the monitoring of these trust assets. It should be noted, however, that the uniform act excludes from its coverage governmental units and charitable corporations organized and operated primarily for educational purposes.

To date, the uniform act has been adopted, with various modifications, in California, Illinois, Michigan and Oregon. Similar legislation exists in other states, such as New Hampshire, Rhode Island, Ohio and Massachusetts. Each museum should check the laws of its state to see if a statute of this nature has been enacted and, if so, whether the museum falls within its scope.

State and Local Charitable Solicitation Laws

Many states and some municipalities have legislation that regulates the solicitation of charitable contributions.[98] The legislation has been prompted by various considerations such as the increase of paid professional fundraisers, instances of charity fraud, and evidence that some charities spend an inordinate amount of money for administrative and other costs and comparatively little for their declared charitable purposes.

Charitable solicitation laws can take various forms and each particular statute or ordinance must be read carefully to determine whether and when it applies to a museum's activity. For example, some apply only to professional fundraisers, others only to sales and solicitations; some exempt certain organizations, and others have minimum dollar amounts for applicability. In his comprehensive text on charitable solicitations, Bruce Hopkins notes that there are approximately twenty-four state charitable solicitation laws which can be classified as "standard" inasmuch as they share a similar format.[99] The common features are:

(1) a series of definitions;
(2) registration or licensing requirements for charitable organizations;
(3) annual report requirements for charitable organizations;
(4) exemptions from all or a portion of the statutory requirements;

---

97. Uniform Supervision of Trustees for Charitable Purposes Act (1954).

98. In most states, local regulation is not preempted by state statutes. Thus, a charity may have to comply with both state and local regulations. In recent years, there have been proposals for federal regulations of charitable solicitations, but, to date, none of these proposals have been enacted. See Troyer, "Federal Legislation on Charitable Solicitations," *Philanthropy Monthly* 30 (Oct. 1977).

99. B. Hopkins, *Charity Under Seige, Government Regulation of Fund Raising* (1980). This book describes the charitable solicitation laws in force in each state, analyzes features commonly found in such statutes, and comments on proposals to regulate charitable solicitations on the federal level.

(5) registration requirements for professional fundraisers and/or professional solicitors;

(6) record-keeping and public information requirements;

(7) percentage limitations on fundraising costs or fees;

(8) certain "prohibited acts";

(9) a reciprocal agreement authorization;

(10) registered agent requirements;

(11) other varied regulatory obligations; and/or

(12) a variety of sanctions.[100]

The term "solicitation" is frequently defined quite broadly. For example, the Maryland statute reads as follows:

> "Solicit" means to request, directly or indirectly, money, credit, property, . . . or other financial assistance in any form on the plea or representations that the money, credit, property, . . . or other financial assistance will be used for a charitable purpose.[101]

This definition is construed to include oral and written requests, media releases regarding an appeal for contributions, and the sale or attempt to sell any ticket, subscription, membership or tangible item in connection with an appeal for contributions. Questions can arise, therefore, as to whether telephone calls or mail solicitations made in conjunction with an appeal for support are covered by laws in existence at the place of origin or of receipt, or both. A museum planning to engage in any kind of fund promotion frequently may find it necessary to investigate not just the charitable solicitation laws of its own state, but also the laws of any other state that its activities may touch.

States and municipalities regulate charitable solicitations under their inherent "police power," the power to protect the health, welfare and safety of their citizens. On the other hand, charitable solicitations can be a form of free speech protected by the first amendment of the Constitution.[102] Any statute regulating charitable solicitations must be drafted with care so as not unduly to intrude on the right of free speech.[103] This is illustrated by the 1980 Supreme Court decision of *Village of Schaumberg v. Citizens for a Better Environment.*[104] The village had an ordinance that prohibited door-to-door or on-street solicitation of contributions by any charitable organization which did not devote at least 75 percent of its receipts to its charitable purposes. The statute was struck down by the Supreme Court as unconstitutional because the 75 percent rule was not reasonably related to the municipality's legitimate interest in preventing fraud. The court stated: "The Village may serve its legitimate interest, but it must do so

---

100. Ibid., at 75.

101. Md. Ann. Code art. 41, § 103A(i) (1982).

102. *Village of Schaumberg v. Citizens for a Better Environment*, 444 U.S. 620 (1980); *International Society for Krishna Consciousness of Houston, Inc. v. City of Houston*, 689 F.2d 541 (5th Cir. 1982); *Maryland Secretary of State v. Joseph H. Munson Co., Inc.*, 294 Md. 160, 448 A.2d 935 (1982), *aff'd* _____U.S. _____, 104 S. Ct. 2839, 81 L. Ed. 2d 786 (1984).

103. *Hynes v. Mayor of Oradell*, 425 U.S. 610, 96 S. Ct. 1755, 48 L. Ed. 2d 243 (1976).

104. 444 U.S. 620 (1980).

by narrowly drawn regulations designed to serve those interests without unne-cessarily interfering with First Amendment freedoms."[105] This decision may cause some states and municipalities to re-examine their charitable solicitation laws to assure precision in accomplishing legitimate ends.[106]

---

105. Ibid., at 637.

106. For a brief article on the subject of charitable solicitation laws, see Hopkins, "Regulations of Fund Raising," *Business Officer* 19 (May 1981).

PART II

The Collection

CHAPTER III

Collection Management Policies

A. Why a Collection Management Policy?
B. Guidelines for Preparing a Collection Management Policy

A. Why a Collection Management Policy?

- "Our museum has quite a few objects that we have had for years, but we aren't sure if we own them. We would like to dispose of the objects, can we?"
- "Every year, our museum ends up taking objects we don't really want. How can we control this?"
- "Frequently, staff members are asked to provide appraisals for donors. We oblige but feel uneasy about it. How should these situations be handled?"

These are common questions from the museum community and the queries themselves reflect a degree of uncertainty regarding the role of the museum and the responsibilities of its officers and staff. Without clear direction, poor decisions are bound to be made and for a museum many such "mistakes" have no easy solutions. The best approach is prevention, and a suggested technique is the adoption of a collection management policy.

A collection management policy is a detailed written statement that explains why a museum is in operation and how it goes about its business, and it articulates the museum's professional standards regarding objects left in its care. The policy serves as a guide for the staff and as a source of information for the public.

A good collection management policy covers a broad range of topics:
(1) the purpose of the museum and its collection goals;
(2) the method of acquiring objects for the collections;
(3) the method of disposing of objects from the collections;
(4) incoming and outgoing loan policies;
(5) the handling of objects left in the custody of the museum;
(6) the care and control of collection objects generally;
(7) access to collection objects;
(8) insurance procedures relating to collection objects; and
(9) the records that are to be kept of collection activities, when these records are to be made, and where they are to be maintained.

Each of the above-mentioned topics raises a host of issues that must be considered if comprehensive and practical guidance is to be offered in the policy itself. Many of these issues are listed in the "Guidelines for Preparing a Collection Management Policy," which follows this section. The very exercise of reviewing and coming to terms with these issues provides a worthwhile educational opportunity for museum officers and staff. All who participate cannot help but emerge with a better appreciation of their respective roles and with a firmer grasp of important basic principles.

The guidelines should not be viewed as a rigid format for the preparation of a collection management policy. Their purpose is to provoke thought and discussion. The form and content of any policy rests essentially with the individual museum, and it should be tailored to the needs of the museum. A collection management policy is not unlike a pair of eyeglasses; both are effective aids to perception only if individually prescribed and faithfully used.

Drafting a collection management policy is not an easy task. It requires much communication among staff members and frank discussion between staff and board members. Areas of uncertainty or disagreement must be resolved and adjustments made. The objective in drafting the policy is not to attempt to solve all possible problems, but to define areas of responsibility and to set forth guidelines for those charged with making certain decisions. The completed policy should be approved by the board or entity charged with overall governance of the museum and, once in effect, the policy should serve as a formal delegation of responsibilities.[1]

As noted in the Preface, one of the objectives of this book is to stress "prevention" and for this reason, it is urged that the book be used as a tool for drafting or perfecting a collection management policy.[2] Each chapter serves this end. Chapters I and II, on the nature of a museum and its accountability, provide essential background material for understanding the role of a museum, the duties of governing boards and the obligations owed the public. Chapter III, this chapter, introduces the general topic of collection management and provides guidelines for drafting a collection management policy. Subsequent chapters discuss specific collection-related problems, but these should not be read in isolation. They presuppose an understanding of the material in the preceding chapters.

B. Guidelines for Preparing a Collection Management Policy*

These guidelines are offered as a checklist for the museum interested in drafting or revising a collection management policy. Most of the issues raised in the guidelines are treated in detail in the following chapters. Chapters I and II,

---

*This section is based on presentations made by the author in 1979 and 1981 to the American Law Institute-American Bar Association seminars on "Legal Problems of Museum Administration." Copyright 1979 and 1981 by the American Law Institute. The substantial reprinting of these presentations are with the concurrence of the American Law Institute-American Bar Association Committee on Continuing Professional Education.

1. See Chapter I, Sections E and F.

2. As of 1984, the Accreditation Commission of the American Association of Museums considers a written collection policy an essential for a museum seeking accreditation.

which concern the legal nature of a museum and its accountability, are suggested as useful preliminaries before work on a policy is begun.

1. General Comments

A collection management policy is a comprehensive written statement that sets forth the goals of a museum and explains how these goals are pursued through collection activity. One of the main functions of the policy is to guide staff members in carrying out their responsibilities. The policy, therefore, must be detailed enough to provide useful instruction and yet avoid procedural minutiae. (The latter are subject to frequent revision and are more appropriately handled in supplementary documents.) Flexibility is essential also in order to permit prudent ad hoc decisions. These objectives can be achieved by bearing in mind the following:

- Define areas of responsibility clearly;
- Where possible, delegate final decision-making authority to one individual or group;
- Establish policy but, where appropriate, permit decision-making authorities to grant exceptions in unusual circumstances; and
- Stress the maintenance of complete, written records regarding all collection-related decisions.[3]

2. Definitions

As used in these guidelines:

- A *collection object* is an item that has been or is in the process of being accessioned into the collections.
- *Accessioning* is the formal process used to accept and record an item as a collection object.
- *Deaccessioning*[4] is the formal process used to remove permanently an object from the collections.
- *Loans* are temporary assignments of collection objects from the museum or temporary assignments of similar objects to the museum for stated museum purposes, such as exhibition and research. These assignments do not involve a change in ownership.
- *Objects placed in the custody of the museum* are items that are not owned by the museum but are left temporarily in the museum for other than loan purposes, such as for attribution, identification or examination for possible gift or purchase.

3. Drafting the Policy

a. Statement of Purpose and Description of Collections

The introductory "statement of purpose" should be written so that it sets forth such basic information as:

- the purpose of the museum;

---

3. An article, "The Future of Museum Registration" by Richard Porter, *Museum News* 5 (August 1984), discusses the growing importance to a museum of a skilled registrar.

4. The term is generally accepted in the museum community though not found in the dictionary. It is postulated that it is a corruption of "decess," but many would explain it as an amalgamation of "de" (to do the opposite of) and "accession."

- the present scope and uses of the museum's collections; and
- the more immediate goals of the museum as they relate to the collections.

Statutes and legal documents pertinent to the establishment of the museum should be explained[5] as well as the role of any museum boards or committees involved in collection procedures. If the museum maintains more than one type of collection (for example, permanent collection, study collection, school collection), the "statement of purpose" section may be a convenient place to describe each type and its rationale. When a museum lists more than one type of collection, differences in the handling of these collections, if any, then should be noted appropriately in its collections policy.

The drafting of the statement of purpose can prove to be a challenge, especially for the small organization with very limited financial resources. How focused must collecting be in order to assure sufficient depth? What portions of time and money should be allocated to collecting? to exhibits? to educational outreach? Has there been a realistic appraisal of the resources it takes to support a collection (record-keeping, storage, conservation, exhibits)? Each of these questions, and others, must be considered before a realistic statement of purpose can be produced. One article which describes a particular historical society's efforts to draft a statement of purpose puts it this way:

> What the committee was actually wrestling with was a question of finding a comfortable middle ground between the ideal and carelessness. . . . Few, if any, historical organizations have the personnel or funding to pursue the ideal. What is necessary is to have an understanding of professional standards and then to develop a plan that best approaches the ideal, based on the organization's resources.[6]

Because the statement of purpose is a very crucial element in any collection management policy, it is a prudent step to go back and thoughtfully re-examine the articulated purpose after the entire policy has been drafted. What has been learned in the drafting process should provide a basis for more critical review.

b. Acquisition of Objects

Objects may be added to collections by means of gifts, bequests, purchases, exchanges, field work acquisitions, or any other transactions by which title to the objects passes to the museum. In stating criteria for determining whether an object should be added to a collection, some basic considerations are:

- Is the object consistent with the collections goals of the museum?
- Is the object so unusual that it presents an exceptional opportunity for the museum and thus should be given preferential consideration?

---

5. Care should be taken to assure that the activities of the museum are in accord with its articles of incorporation or charter, etc. See, for example, *Queen of Angels Hospital v. Younger*, 66 Cal. App. 3rd 366, 136 Cal. Rptr. 36 (1977); *Holt v. College of Osteopathic Physicians and Surgeons*, 61 Cal. 2d 750, 394 P.2d 932, 40 Cal. Rptr. 244 (1964); *Rowan v. Pasadena Art Museum*, No. C 322817 (Cal. Sup. Ct., L.A. County, Sept. 22, 1981).

6. Broenneke & Petersen, "Planning for Change," 39 *History News* 12 at 14 (No. 8, August 1984).

- If the object is offered for sale, might it or a comparable object be obtained by gift or bequest?
- Can the proper care be given to the object?
- Is the object something which probably should be refused because it is of marginal value or interest?
- Will the object be used in the foreseeable future and is there a good faith intention to keep it in the museum's collection for the foreseeable future?
- Is the provenance of the object satisfactory and how is this decision made?
- Is the object encumbered with conditions set by the donor (for example, a requirement that it be permanently displayed)? How are decisions made on such matters and by whom?
- Is the use of the object restricted or encumbered by (1) an intellectual property (copyright, patent, trademark, or trade name) or (2) by its nature (for example, obscene,[7] defamatory, potentially an invasion of privacy, physically hazardous)? How are decisions made on matters of this nature and by whom?
- Will the acceptance of the object, in all probability, result in major future expenses for the museum (for example, for conservation, maintenance, or because it opens a new area of collecting)?

The policy should state clearly the procedures to be followed in accessioning, who makes the final decision, what records must be made of the process, when the records are to be made and by whom, and where the records are to be maintained.

In determining the procedure and the appropriate level of authority for accepting items for the collections, distinctions may have to be made on the basis of such factors as size or extent of the objects, value, cost of maintenance, restrictions on use.

As a general rule, objects should not be accepted unless they are destined for particular collections for the foreseeable future. Exceptions to this rule should be permitted only with the knowledge of the donors and with due consideration to the satisfactory disposition of unwanted objects.[8]

Advice should be given regarding the appraisal of objects by the staff in response to outside requests. As a rule, museums avoid doing formal appraisals, especially at the request of donors or prospective donors. Deviations from the museum's standard practice should require the approval of an appropriate museum official.[9]

---

7. This text does not cover the topic of obscenity. See, however, Chapter III of J. Merryman and A. Elsen, *Law, Ethics and the Visual Arts* (1979); Chapter VIIB of F. Feldman and S. Weil, *Art Works: Law, Policy, Practice* (1974) and Reisman, "The Legal Obsession with Obscenity: Why Are the Courts Still Being Challenged?," *The Journal of Arts Management and Law* 54 (Fall 1983).

8. See Chapter IV, "The Meaning of the Word Accession," and Chapter XII, "Tax Considerations Relevant to Gifts."

9. See Chapter XIII on "Appraisals and Authentications."

c. Deaccessioning

As a general rule, collection objects may be deaccessioned unless there are specific restrictions to the contrary. In stating criteria for determining whether an object should be removed from a collection, some basic considerations are:

- Are there any restrictions which may prohibit removal? What is the procedure for resolving such questions?
- Is the object no longer relevant and useful to the purposes and activities of the museum?
- Is there danger of not being able to preserve the object properly?
- Has the object deteriorated beyond usefulness?
- Is it doubtful that the object can be used in the foreseeable future?
- Is there a need to weed out redundant items?
- Is there a need to improve or strengthen another area of the collections in order to further the goals of the museum?
- Have the interests and reactions of the public been considered?

The policy should state clearly the procedures to be followed in deaccessioning, such as who makes the final decision, what records must be made of the process, when the records are to be made and by whom, and when the type and value of the object under consideration may dictate such additional precautions as a higher level of approval than ordinarily required and the need for outside appraisals.

The issue of acceptable methods of disposal also may be addressed. Some basic considerations are:

- May objects be disposed of by exchange, donation or sale?
- Will preference be given to any particular method(s) of disposal?
- Will scholarly or cultural organizations be preferred as recipients rather than private individuals or commercial entities?
- Will local or national interests be given weight in deciding on the recipient?
- If an object has seriously deteriorated, may it be designated for other uses or destroyed?
- If donors of items to be deaccessioned are alive, as a matter of courtesy are they to be notified of the intent to deaccession?
- How are funds realized from deaccession sales to be used?

d. Loans

(1) Outgoing Loans

In general, museums expect to lend objects only to similar institutions. The major reasons for this practice are to afford the loaned object adequate environmental protection, to assure adequate safety precautions, to encourage research on and public enjoyment of the object, and to avoid use of the object for private gain. In drafting loan statements, these reasons should be borne in mind. Also, it is recognized that justifiable distinctions can be made between the loan of a painting and, say, the loan of a plant specimen. Following are some of the matters which should be addressed:

- When are loans from the collection made and for what purposes? To whom will loans be made?

- Who has the authority to approve loans from the collection?
- If unusual restrictions are to be placed on a proposed outgoing loan, who must approve the loan?
- Will items be lent if there is a question whether they can withstand travel, extra handling or climate changes? How are such matters resolved?
- To ensure proper accounting, should all loans be made for specified periods of time (with options for renewal)?
- What procedures must be followed by the staff in proposing and processing a loan? What is the museum's policy regarding facilities reports on prospective borrowers? What records are necessary, when must they be made and by whom, and where are these records to be maintained?
- Who has the responsibility for monitoring a loan? What procedures are to be followed in connection with a loan whose period is about to expire or when a loan is overdue?

(2) Incoming Loans

The following questions, some of which are identical to those applying to outgoing loans, should be addressed in connection with incoming loans:

- When are objects borrowed and for what purposes? From whom may objects be borrowed?
- Who has the authority to approve an incoming loan?
- If a prospective lender places unusual restrictions on a proposed loan, who in the museum must approve the loan and assure compliance?
- How are decisions arrived at concerning the provenance of an item that may be the subject of an incoming loan? (The mere possession of an object of doubtful provenance can have ethical ramifications and/or legal consequences.)[10]
- Will items be borrowed if there is a question whether they can withstand travel, extra handling or climate changes? How are such matters to be resolved?
- What procedures must be followed by the staff in proposing and processing an incoming loan? What records are necessary, when must they be made and by whom, and where are these records to be maintained?
- Who has the responsibility for monitoring a loan? For packing and shipping the material when it is to be returned?

e. Objects Left in the Custody of the Museum

It is prudent for a museum to record in some predetermined manner and within a reasonable time every object which is placed in its care. This means there should also be a registration method for objects, other than loans, left temporarily in the custody of the museum for such purposes as attribution, examination and identification. In addition, the registration method should be designed to encourage periodic review of these objects to ensure expeditious handling. Existing museum practices should be reviewed with these considerations in mind.

---

10. See discussion in Chapter IV on "Circumstances th. Can Affect the Quality of Title."

Authority to accept objects placed in the custody of the museum should be clearly delegated to specific individuals.

f. Care of the Collections

Guidance on the topic of care of the collections should touch on a range of issues, such as the following:

(1) At all times, staff members should be aware of their responsibilities to preserve and protect collection objects. This rather obvious point might warrant repetition in the collection management policy.

(2) Are the collections, whether on exhibition or in storage, adequately protected against fire, theft, vandalism and natural disaster? Are there established procedures for handling such emergencies? Who in the museum has oversight responsibilities in these areas?

(3) Conservation of collection items is a continuing responsibility. Should there be a delegation of responsibilities to appropriate staff members to monitor conservation needs?

(4) Appropriate attention should be given to the packing and shipping of collection items moving in or out of the museum. Who bears the responsibility for monitoring this?

(5) Ideally, no collection item should ever leave its assigned collecting unit unless a written record of such movement is made and the record centrally filed.

g. Records

The following comments may be helpful in judging the adequacy of a museum's record systems:

(1) Each museum should have established systems for preservation of data on collections. Collection records may be divided into two general categories. The first includes records which are commonly associated with registration functions. These primarily document the legal status of an object within the museum or on loan from the museum, and that object's movement and care while under the control of the museum. The second category includes records associated with curatorial functions. These provide a broad body of information about an object which establishes the object's proper place and importance within its cultural or scientific sphere.

(2) Good registration records normally include a descriptive catalog record as well as evidence of legal ownership or possession of all objects. These record systems should relate to objects by a unique museum number (for example, accession number, loan number) and should provide for easy retrieval of object information as well as current object locations. Records of accessioned objects should further reflect the prior history of ownership of each object and all activity of such object (loan, exhibit, restoration, deaccession). Records of objects on loan to the museum should reflect all activity of such objects while under the control of the museum.

(3) Collection records should be timely made, housed in secure locations and physically preserved by proper handling and storage methods.

(4) If possible, a duplicate copy of registration records (for example, microfiche) should be made and stored outside the museum as a security precaution.

h. Insurance

Some questions concerning insurance that may be addressed are:

(1) If funds are limited, what is the proper role of insurance versus, for instance, protection, conservation, packing and transportation requirements?

(2) Is insurance to be carried on the museum's collections when these collections are in the custody of the museum? If so, are collections insured at full value or at a fraction of value?

(3) Must outgoing loans be insured? If so, by whom? Who Pays?

(4) Must incoming loans be insured? If so, by whom? Who pays?

(5) Are objects left in the custody of the museum insured?

(6) What records must be kept regarding insurance and by whom?

(7) Who has authority to approve deviations from established insurance procedures?

i. Inventories

In order to police collection activities, a museum should establish inventory procedures. These procedures may address such topics as:

(1) uniform method of maintaining inventory records;

(2) periodic comprehensive inventories;

(3) spot-check inventories; and

(4) procedures to be followed if collection items appear to be missing.

j. Access to the Collections

This section may cover such topics as:

(1) Who has access to the collections? (Actual physical access as well as the obtaining of copies of collection or collection-related material.)

(2) When can access be denied and by whom?

(3) Are fees to be charged for record reproduction work? Before answering these questions, any "freedom of information" and/or "privacy" laws in effect in the locality should be reviewed. (A government-controlled museum may have more complex problems in the area of access.)

CHAPTER IV

The Acquisition of Objects— Accessioning

E. Circumstances That Can Affect the Completeness of Title
    1. Restricted Gifts
        a. The Offer of Restricted Gifts
        b. Is the Gift Restricted?
        c. Interpretation of Restrictive Language
        d. Relief from Restrictions
    2. Copyright Considerations
        a. What Is Copyright?
        b. Effect of the New Copyright Law on Museum Acquisitions
        c. Copyright Considerations When Acquiring Certain Objects
        d. Should a Museum Strive to Acquire Copyright Interests?
        e. Duration of Copyright
        f. Request for Permission to Reproduce Museum Holdings
        g. Additional Information on Copyright Issues
    3. Artist's Rights—*Droit de Suite* and *Droit Moral*
        a. *Droit de Suite*—California Royalty Act
        b. *Droit Moral*—California and New York Statutes
F. Acquisition Procedures

A. The Meaning of the Word Accession

There are numerous ways in which a museum may acquire objects, and objects may be sought for a variety of reasons. The method of acquisition or the intended purpose can raise special considerations, and, therefore, some preliminary observations are in order.

The subject of this chapter is the acquisition of objects for collections or "accessioning." Accessioning is the formal process used to accept and record an item as a collection object. It is sensible to use the term with precision.[1] A museum may maintain various types of collections. Permanent collections usually contain the choicest objects, while study collections have related objects, or those of lesser quality, which contribute to the understanding and appreciation of the permanent collection. School collections frequently consist of expendable material useful for instruction, and an exhibit or "prop" collection may be made up of objects that are used as background material for museum exhibitions. Archival or book collections that supplement the object collections are common. The word "collection" implies permanence; so should the word "accession." You accession only that which you intend to retain for the foreseeable future.[2] For instance, if a museum accepts the donation of an object for the purpose of placing that object in its annual auction sale, the object may be acquired, but it should not be accessioned. There is no requisite intent to retain. Indiscriminate

---

1. See also section on "Acquisition Procedures" in this chapter.

2. This is not to imply that once accessioned an object can never be removed from the collection. (See Chapter V on Deaccessioning.) Experience and changing circumstances may justify removal. However, if a museum wants to maintain its integrity, each decision to accession should be made thoughtfully and in good faith. If accessioning is used merely to "cool" (i.e., hold for a discrete period) gifts before disposal, a serious lack of professional ethics is evident.

accessioning can create a poor image. Most donors expect that objects given to a museum will be preserved for public use. A museum that routinely accessions all donations, whether it intends to keep them or not, may soon lose the confidence of its public. In addition, it may find itself in an awkward position with the Internal Revenue Service. An object given to a museum for its "related use" (a use which qualified the museum for its § 50l(c)(3) federal tax status) carries the most favorable tax consequences for the donor.[3] That same object given to the museum for an unrelated use has less favorable tax advantages.[4] For a museum, the Internal Revenue Service considers additions to the collections as a related use, but fundraising (even when the funds will be used to purchase objects for the collections) does not fall into this category. If all donations of objects are accepted and acknowledged by a museum in the same manner, regardless of the intended use, there can be the appearance of collusion with regard to tax consequences.[5] It is not wrong for a museum to accept donations of objects for an auction or for immediate exchange, it is only that such transfers should be carried out in a forthright manner. Donors should be apprised of the intended use, the method of recording the gift should be distinct from an accession, and acknowledgments should be phrased accordingly. Without tax incentives and generous donors, museums could not flourish. A lack of candor on the part of the museums in the handling of donations could jeopardize either or both of these benefits.

Another observation on the acquisition process deserves mention. Wherever possible, transfers of groups of objects should be culled before material is accessioned. There may be the temptation to accession everything in a large group and leave to a later time the weeding out of noncollection quality items. Technically, accessioning is a thoughtful process by which only appropriate material is added to a collection. Also, what has been accessioned should not be removed permanently from a collection unless it has gone through a carefully documented deaccession process. The expedient "accession everything for now" approach muddies the water and, in the long run, can be more time-consuming and expensive. There are, however, situations where accessioning by relatively unculled batch or lot may be prudent. For example, natural history specimens

---

3. Such gifts of capital gain property normally may be deducted at their fair market value. See Chapter XII, "Tax Considerations Relevant to Gifts."

4. The fair market value of a gift of tangible personal property that is put to an unrelated use by the charitable organization must be reduced by 40 percent of its appreciation. (Appreciation is fair market value minus donor's basis in the property.) (See I.R.S. Publication No. 526, "Income Tax Deductions for Contributions," for additional information. See also I.R.S. Code § 170(e)(1)(B) and I.R.S. Regulations § 1.170A-4(b)(2) and Chapter XII.)

5. The Internal Revenue Service takes the position that a gift of tangible personal property to a charitable organization may be treated as put to a related use if (1) the taxpayer establishes that the property is not in fact put to an unrelated use by the donee; or (2) at the time of the contribution or at the time the contribution is treated as made, it is reasonable to anticipate that the property will not be put to an unrelated use by the donee (see I.R.S. Publication No. 526 mentioned in previous footnote and I.R.S. Regulation § 1.170A-4(b)(3)(ii). See also Chapter XII, noting especially Section C, "Concept of 'Unrelated Use.'" Note also the discussion in Section B(2)(e) of Chapter V that explains I.R.S. notification requirements when certain gifts are transferred by a museum within two years of receipt.

which result from field collecting or archival material may come to the museum when there is no expert in that particular area then on the staff. Critical culling is not possible, but the material clearly may be worth preserving for later evaluation. The sensible solution may be to accession by batch with careful documentation of the source. This secures the material and places it on record for the interested scholar.[6] To avoid abuse of this practice (and the consequent storage problems), a museum is well-advised to have clear procedures regulating its use. At the other extreme is inordinate delay in culling and recording— a practice clearly at odds with the purposes of the museum. Often the obvious, but rarely popular, solution is for the museum not only to require that accessioning be accomplished promptly and precisely, but also to allocate sufficient resources so that this can be done.

Collection objects can be acquired in a variety of ways: gift, bequest, purchase, exchange, or any other method which transfers title to the museum. Once an object has been accessioned, however, obligations are imposed. The item must be properly stored, maintained, conserved, documented and made available for the benefit of the public. The best place to avoid many problems, therefore, is at the acquisition stage. Every item offered should be carefully weighed with regard to its suitability for the collections, its provenance, and the ability of the museum to care for the object and use it effectively. In reality, not even a gift is free. Each acquisition places demands on the museum's resources.[7]

These same considerations should be borne in mind with regard to bequests or potential bequests of objects.[8] It is sometimes assumed that a bequest must be accepted. This is not so. When a museum is notified that it is a beneficiary under a will, the first order of business is to determine the exact nature of the bequest and whether it is suitable for acceptance. A copy of the will, or pertinent portion thereof, should be obtained from the estate so the nature of the gift can be verified. (The will, or portion thereof, is also an important part of the accession records of any bequest which is accepted.) Where necessary, the object should be seen or pictures obtained in order to assist in deliberations concerning its suitability for the collections.[9] A museum may decide to take the object or not, or, if it is a group of objects, it may decide to take all the objects, a portion of the objects, or none of them. In any event, the executor of the estate should be notified promptly of the museum's desires.

---

6. If there has been a determination that a batch or lot accession is appropriate, museum procedures with regard to the deaccessioning of items within that batch or lot may be more relaxed. See Chapter V, the subsection "The Proper Authority to Approve a Decision to Deaccession."

7. See Chapter VII, footnote 21, on the cost of maintaining collection objects.

8. A bequest is something left or given under a will.

9. There may be instances when circumstances show that the decedent left property to the museum either for accessioning or, in the discretion of the museum, for immediate sale to benefit the museum. In estate situations the "related use" question normally does not arise (the exception concerns certain situations involving copyright, see, I.R.C. § 2055(e) (4) and Reg. § 20.2055-2 (E)), but there can be public perception problems. Each such case should be weighed carefully so that the museum is satisfied that a decision to accept and sell is prudent in light of all other considerations.

It is not unusual for a potential benefactor to mention to a museum that he intends to remember it in his will. There is no better time to discuss frankly the proposed bequest. If the intended gift is not appropriate, more suitable organizations can be suggested. If unacceptable restrictions will be imposed, there is an opportunity to explain the museum's reservations. As a rule, donors appreciate candor as well as tact. It really is the only way they can be assured that their generosity will be appreciated and put to effective use. At the same time, the intended recipient museum can anticipate a welcomed addition, not a possible problem.

B. Delegation of Authority to Accept Objects

If it is important to select carefully objects to be accessioned, it is equally important to specify who has the authority to accept objects for the collections. When it is clear that one individual or group bears responsibility for the decision, thoughtful attention is encouraged. Many an object has found its way into a collection because no one said "yes" or "no"; it just happened. This likelihood greatly decreases when someone must accept responsibility for the occurrence. Specific delegation of authority is also a protection for the staff. It permits them to proceed with confidence. For example, if an object is left with the attendant at the reception desk or is sent in by a well-intentioned friend of the museum, any staff member in a well-run organization can explain with assurance that there can be no immediate decision regarding acceptance, that certain procedures must be followed. The staff member can then issue a custody receipt if the object is to remain for evaluation, and the prospective donor is promptly and fairly informed of museum practice.

If authority to accept objects is not clearly defined, there are additional opportunities for error. An agreement to purchase an object can bind even though the signer for the museum had apparent but not real authority. A "Receipt and Release" form used by many probate courts to verify distribution of bequests must be signed by a museum official authorized to accept property on behalf of the organization. It should be clear within a museum who has authority to execute such an instrument. If a donor requests acknowledgment of a gift for tax purposes and any staff member feels free to oblige, the museum could be embarrassed by careless errors which place its credibility in doubt. When it is clear within a museum who has authority to purchase for the collections, who can accept property for the collections, and who may acknowledge gifts, many unpleasant consequences can be avoided.

C. What Is Title?

Title with regard to personal property may be defined as the possession of rights of ownership in that property. This simple definition, however, needs qualification and clarification. Title involves questions of completeness and quality.

Title for the layman invariably means the right to possess the object indefinitely but such a right to possess does not always bring with it complete control of the use of the object. Separate from the right of possession are, for example, copyright interests, trademark rights, and specific interest that the previous owner may have reserved by placing limitations on the use of an object (what a museum would call a "restricted gift"). When a museum acquires an object, therefore, attention should be given to the "completeness" of title. The museum should understand exactly what rights it is acquiring and whether there is proper documentation of these rights.

Of similar importance is the "quality" of title which passes. Quality for purposes of this discussion includes not just the assurance of "good title," in other words, the ability to enjoy undisturbed use of the rights which pass; but also the assurance that the object acquired is as represented. When acquiring an object, therefore, the museum must also consider the quality of title offered and the sufficiency of the documentation presented to support the represented quality.

Various aspects of these title considerations which are of particular interest to museums are discussed in the following sections.

D. Circumstances That Can Affect the Quality of Title

1. The Status of the Transferor

What do you do when Mr. X approaches the museum and asserts that the highly prized clock, which has been in the museum's collection for years, is in fact his? He explains that Mr. Y, who allegedly donated the piece, was his uncle but that Mr. Y did not own the clock. The clock had been left to Mr. X's father under the grandfather's will and he, Mr. X, is the sole heir of his father. He produces two family wills to support his claim.

This is not an uncommon problem for a museum, and it is difficult to resolve such a claim when parties to the original transaction are long dead. While the claiming party may have the burden of proof, the museum may find it difficult to refute even a thin claim if there is no evidence that the museum ever questioned the donor regarding ownership.[10]

It should not be assumed by a museum that every transferor is the owner of the object. As a practical matter, a museum cannot quiz every donor, but there are some precautions that can be taken. The museum's Deed of Gift form can be worded so that it requires the transferring party to affirm that he is the owner of the object in question, or that he is the owner's authorized agent for the purpose of passing title. This, at least, raises the issue, and, in signing the Deed of Gift, the donor specifically defends his ability to pass title. It is anticipated, also, that such an affirmation in the Deed of Gift will caution those uncertain of title to pause so that this matter may be aired before any documents are signed. But, certainly, the insertion of the affirmation in the gift form does not cure all problems, it merely is an attempt to avoid faulty transfers and to

---

10. The party having the burden of proof in a lawsuit must come forward with a preponderance of evidence in order to prevail. In other words, more in the way of convincing evidence is required of the one with the burden of proof.

provide some defense for the museum if title is challenged after the death of the donor.

There are no substitutes for common sense and a bit of skepticism when accepting objects for the museum, regardless of how carefully drawn your Deed of Gift may be. It is sensible to ask where and how the donor acquired the item, if this is not self-evident. Background information on any object destined for the collections is useful from a research point of view, and, in addition, such questioning may establish whether there is need to delve further into the issue of quality of title. For instance, if the donor is married might the spouse have an interest in the object, too? If there is doubt, perhaps both should sign the Deed of Gift. Is the donor a minor? If so, the gift may be void or voidable. Local statutes should be consulted and it may be sensible to have the gift confirmed after the donor reaches majority. If an object belonged to a recently deceased individual, be sure that the person offering it has full authority to pass good title. If the object was not specifically bequeathed to the transferor, there may be other heirs who share an interest in it. In some cases, it is prudent to have all appropriate heirs sign the Deed of Gift, or else request that the individual signing produce a delegation of authority from the other heirs. These are but a few of the situations that can arise, and each situation has its unique circumstances. The best protection is to educate staff members to be alert, to ask questions and to seek professional advice when in doubt.

The status of the transferor in a sale can be crucial. The following incident is an illustration. Museum X purchased a much desired picture from Dealer Y. Dealer Y enjoyed a good reputation and no one thought to ask any questions. The painting was entrusted to the museum and a simple statement was signed to the effect that the museum would pay $40,000 for the work. Before payment was made, the museum was informed by an attorney representing Mr. Z that Mr. Z owned the picture and that he had canceled his agency agreement with Dealer Y. Dealer Y's attorney then called to say that his client owned a part interest in the painting and the full sale price was not to be paid to Mr. Z. The museum was in the proverbial middle. Even if it chose to return the painting in order to avoid problems presented by payment, it did not know where to send the work without provoking a lawsuit. The museum's only alternative was to pick up the telephone and call its attorney. All because nobody asked at the proper time, "Who owns this painting?"

In the above case, after a period of time, the disputing parties were able to resolve their differences by negotiation, and the museum was instructed to make payment in accordance with mutually acceptable terms. If negotiation had not been successful, however, the museum would have faced some hard decisions. It would have to explore whether it had an enforceable sale contract and, if so, what options were available to it. Possibly, in the alternative, it could attempt to obtain the rivals' permission to place the purchase price in an escrow account pending resolution of the dispute between the two. If the facts seem to indicate that Dealer Y did not pass good title, remedies against him would have to be weighed. If the museum wished to wash its hands of the entire matter and return the painting, the merits of an action of interpleader would have to be considered. In an interpleader action, the museum, claiming no interest in the property, would entrust it to the court and name as defendants the rival parties. Each defendant would then have to argue his claimed interest to the court. The court's resolution of the dispute between the defendants would absolve the museum from further action by either defendant. No matter which way it turned, the museum would have to incur expenses for professional assistance in protecting its interests. The simple message in this tale is that prudent inquiries before entering into an agreement can offer better protection than an army of attorneys after the fact.[11]

2. Misrepresentation by the Seller

If a museum has acquired a collection object only to find that it did not receive good title or that the object is not what was bargained for, it is possible that the law may offer a remedy (provided the museum can show damages), but very often proving one's case can be a stumbling block. There is a legal cause of action called misrepresentation. Generally, it is defined to mean "any mani-festation by word or other conduct by one person to another that, under the circumstances amounts to an assertion not in accordance with the facts."[12] However, as described in the section on "Authentications" in Chapter XIII, usually the plaintiff in a misrepresentation suit must show that the defendant acted intentionally or at least that he, the plaintiff, "reasonably relied" on the information given. A careful reading of the section on "Authentications" will demonstrate why these elements of proof may be difficult to sustain when the object in question is unique and/or very old, and opinions regarding provenance and value may vary substantially. If the tort of misrepresentation does not provide an avenue for relief and the collection object in question was bought by the museum, relevant sections of the Uniform Commercial Code should be examined.[13]

3. Warranties in a Sale; the Uniform Commercial Code

When a collection object is purchased and the object itself or its title proves to be faulty, the sales contract may provide a basis for recovery against the seller. Such an action is based on contract, as distinguished from the tort of misrep-resentation, and this presents certain advantages. In the contract action, it is not necessary to establish that the seller intended to make false representations or did so negligently. It is sufficient to establish that a warranty existed and it was not met, even though the seller may have acted in good faith. Several sections of the Uniform Commercial Code (U.C.C.) are of particular interest.[14]

---

11. In the case of *Taborsky v. Bolen Gallery, Inc.* No. 83-C-296.5 (U.S.D.C. W.D. Wisc., July 11, 1983), the question of what is reasonable conduct in the commercial sale of art is discussed.

12. *Black's Law Dictionary* (4th ed. 1951). A plaintiff in such an action must also show that he suffered damages as a result of the alleged misrepresentation.

13. A tort is a legal wrong committed upon the person or property of another independent of contract.

14. The U.C.C. governs the sale of personal property. The Code has been adopted with occasional modification, by all states, except Louisiana, and by the District of Columbia.

Section 2–312 of the U.C.C. concerns warranty of title. It reads:

(1) Subject to subsection (2) there is in a contract for sale a warranty by the seller that:
(a) the title conveyed shall be good, and its transfer rightful; and
(b) the goods shall be delivered free from any security interest or other lien or encumbrance of which the buyer at the time of contracting has no knowledge.

(2) A warranty under subsection (1) will be excluded or modified only by specific language or by circumstances which give the buyer reason to know that the person selling does not claim title in himself or that he is purporting to sell only such right or title as he or a third person may have.

(3) Unless otherwise agreed a seller who is a merchant regularly dealing in goods of the kind warrants that the goods shall be delivered free of the rightful claim of any third person by way of infringement or the like, but a buyer who furnishes specifications to the seller must hold the seller harmless against any such claim which arises out of the compliance with the specifications.

Section 2-312 should provide protection for the museum in most sale situations, but cases can arise which fall into the "grey" area. For example, what if the object sold is an art piece which has a history that a professional might question? Would this be a circumstance which should give the museum/buyer "reason to know that the person selling . . . is purporting to sell only such right or title as he . . . may have"? It should be noted also that if the sale takes place at auction or at a dealer's, the actual "owner" may be a consignor. If title is later questioned, the auction house or dealer may quickly refer the disappointed museum/buyer to the consignor for resolution of the matter. Exactly who is "the seller" may become a critical issue.[15]

Two cases which deal with breach of warranty of title in the sale of art are *Menzel v. List*[16] and *Jeanneret v. Vichey*.[17] In the *Menzel* case, the defendant, List, was forced to return a painting to the plaintiff who could establish ownership. List, in turn, impleaded (that is, brought in as parties to the case) the art dealers who sold him the painting charging breach of implied warranty. List recovered from the art dealers without any need to establish bad faith or negligence on the part of the dealers (a mere showing that title, in fact, was faulty was sufficient basis for recovery). In the *Jeanneret* case, the plaintiff, an art dealer, sued the defendant who sold her a Matisse which left Italy under questionable circumstances. At the trial level, the plaintiff prevailed. On appeal the court reversed and remanded the case for a new hearing stating that the plaintiff in order to establish a breach of warranty had to do more than suggest improper export. The fact that the plaintiff, as a reputable dealer, could no longer sell

---

15. "Stolen Art Sold at Auction," 5 *Stolen Art Alert* 4 (No. 5 June 1984), is a series of letters written to a London magazine on the subject of stolen art sold at auction. The letters illustrate the complex issues that can arise and the differing opinions as to how such situations should be handled.

16. 267 N.Y.S. 2d 804, 49 Misc. 2d 300 (1966), *aff'd* 28 A.D. 2d 516, 279 N.Y.S. 2d 608, third party claim reversed on other grounds 24 N.Y.S. 2d 91, 298 N.Y.S. 2d 979, 246 N.E. 2d 742 (1969).

17. 541 F. Supp. 80, *rev'd* and remanded for new trial in 693 F.2d 259 (2d Cir. 1982).

the Matisse with a "cloud" on the title was not deemed an "encumbrance" sufficient to sustain a breach of warranty finding.

Similar problems arise when the U.C.C. is invoked to remedy the sale of a fake or forgery. Section 2-313 of the U.C.C. addresses warranties made by affirmation, promise, description or sample. The section reads:

(1) Express warranties[18] by the seller are created as follows:
    (a) Any affirmation of fact or promise made by the seller to the buyer which relates to the goods and becomes part of the basis of the bargain creates an express warranty that the goods shall conform to the affirmation or promise.
    (b) Any description of the goods which is made part of the basis of the bargain creates an express warranty that the goods shall conform to the description.
    (c) Any sample or model which is made part of the basis of the bargain creates an express warranty that the whole of the goods shall conform to the sample or model.

(2) It is not necessary to the creation of an express warranty that the seller use formal words such as "warrant" or "guarantee" or that he have a specific intention to make a warranty, but an affirmation merely of the value of the goods or a statement purporting to be merely the seller's opinion or commendation of the goods does not create a warranty.[19]

Section 2–313 is modified in part by 2-316 which concerns the exclusion or modification of warranties. Pertinent parts of § 2–316 read:

(3) . . .
    (b) When the buyer before entering into the contract has examined the goods or the sample or model as fully as he desired or has refused to examine the goods, there is no implied warranty with regard to defects which an examination ought in the circumstances to have revealed to him, and
    (c) an implied warranty can also be excluded or modified by course of dealing or course of performance or usage of trade.

These sections raise several qualifications which could negate a claim by a museum under the Code for the sale of a fake or forged object. Section 2-313 specifically notes that a seller's "opinion or commendation" does not create a warranty.[20] The value and provenance of museum quality objects frequently are matters of opinion.[21] Section 2-316 cautions that there is no implied warranty

---

18. The express warranties need not be recited in the sales contract itself. See Comment 7 on § 2-313 of U.C.C.

19. Two early English cases are still cited on the issue of what constitutes "opinion" in the sale of art: *Jendwine v. Slade*, 170 Eng. Rep. 459 (Nisi Prius 1797), *Power v. Barham*, 111 Eng. Rep. 865 (K.B. 1836). These cases are reproduced in F. Feldman and S. Weil, *Art Works: Law, Policy, Practice* (1974).

20. See discussion of fact versus opinion in Chapter XIII, "Misrepresentation."

21. In *Weisz v. Parke-Bernet Galleries, Inc.*, 67 Misc. 2d 1077, 325 N.Y.S. 2d 576, *rev'd* 77 Misc. 2d 80, 351 N.Y.S. 2d 911 (1974), a case decided under a statute similar to the U.C.C., the plaintiff failed to prevail in a suit to recover for the purchase of fake art. But see *Legum v. Harris Auction Galleries*, File No. 81-013 (Md. Consumer Protection Div., Office of the Att. Gen., April 1983). Here the seller was afforded some relief under the Maryland Consumer Protection Law.

with regard to defects which an inspection ought to have revealed. Similarly, it provides that an implied warranty can be excluded if this is customary in the trade. A museum if considered an expert buying in a speculative market may well find little relief in these portions of the U.C.C.[22]

4. Other Statutes or Remedies Affecting the Sale of Fake Collection Objects
Even a statute written specifically to cover the sale of fine arts may not afford protection to a museum. For example, New York has a law that imposes greater responsibilities on an art merchant when he sells fine art,[23] to a buyer who is not an art merchant.[24] An "art merchant" is defined to include a person (or an entity) who deals in works of fine arts or has knowledge or skill peculiar to works of fine arts. In order to seek the protection afforded by this statute, a museum would have to argue that it had no skill in fine arts; hardly a convincing or attractive position. A similar statute in Michigan makes the same distinction between the professional and the nonprofessional buyer.[25]

Several states have statutes dealing with the sale of fine prints.[26] "Fine prints" usually are defined to include engravings, etchings, woodcuts, lithographs and serigraphs. The statutes are designed to protect all purchasers and, as a rule, require the publication of all relevant information regarding the identity of the artist, the signature on the work, the process used to create the article offered for sale, and the number and kind of reproductions. Remedies are limited by the terms of the statutes.

Another avenue of possible relief when misrepresentation is suspected may be state or local consumer protections laws.[27] In an opinion issued by the Consumer Protection Division of the Office of the Attorney General of Maryland, a painting purchased at auction was held to be a "consumer good" and hence covered by the Maryland Consumer Protection Act.[28]

The Federal Trade Commission is charged with preventing unfair or decep-

---

22. On the general issue of the application of the U.C.C. to sale of art, see Note, "Uniform Commercial Code Warranty Solutions to Art Fraud and Forgery," 14 *W. and Mary L. Rev.* 409 (1972). F. Feldman and S. Weil, *Art Works: Law, Policy, Practice* (1974). If a cause of action can be maintained under the Uniform Commercial Code, relief may prove generous. Section 2-714(2) of the Code states "the measure of damages for breach of warranty is the difference at the time and place of acceptance between the value of the goods accepted and the value they would have had as warranted, unless special circumstances show proximate damages of a different amount." Consider this example. A painting is purchased for $1,000 and a number of years later it develops that title is faulty. The painting is now worth $5,000 and the seller is sued successfully under the Uniform Commercial Code. The plaintiff may be able to recover not only the $1,000 purchase price but $5,000, the present fair market value (see *Menzel v. List* discussed in section on Stolen Property, this chapter, with regard to recovery of List against Perls).

23. Fine art is defined to mean a painting, sculpture, drawing or work of graphic art.

24. N.Y. Gen. Bus. Law, Article 12-D.

25. Mich. Stat. Ann. §§ 19-410 (1)—19-410(14).

26. Cal. Civil Code §§ 1740-45; Hawaii Code, Title 26, Chapter 481F; Ill. Sales Code §§ 361, *et seq.*; Md. C.L. 14-501, *et seq.*; N.Y. Gen. Bus. Law Article 12-H.

27. See, for example, New York City Consumer Protection Law, Reg. 30.

28. *Legum v. Harris Auction Galleries*, File No. 81-013 (Md. Consumer Protection Div., Office of the Att. Gen., April 1983).

tive acts or practices in or affecting commerce.[29] Its general jurisdiction should be investigated as another possible means of relief. The Commission also administers the Hobby Protection Act, which requires the dating of imitation political items and the marking of imitation numismatic items.[30] Covered under the Hobby Protection Act are such objects as coins, tokens, paper money, and commemorative medals, and political buttons, posters, literature, stickers or advertisements produced for use in any political cause. If the mails or interstate wire communications have been used in an alleged deceptive sale, the federal statutes relating to mail fraud should be consulted.[31]

In addition to the common law and statutory remedies already suggested, a museum may be able to set aside a fraudulent sale contract in an action in equity or in an action for restitution. Professor William L. Prosser in § 85 of Chapter 16 of his *Law on Torts* detailed distinctions in these forms of actions.[32]

5. Stolen Property

If a museum acquires an object for its collection and subsequently it is established that the object is stolen property, what are the rights of the parties involved? The general rule in the United States is that a thief cannot convey good title. Therefore, if the party transferring the object to the museum is a thief or innocently passes stolen property, the museum does not receive good title. Title probably still remains in the party who suffered the theft, and, upon demand, the object, or its value, would have to be returned to the true owner.[33]

This rather simple explanation requires modification because of the doctrine of adverse possession and the existence of statutes of limitations. The law recognizes that title to property should not remain in an indefinite state for too long a period of time.[34] Such extended periods of uncertainty frequently make it more difficult ultimately to determine true ownership because evidence has faded, and long intervals increase the likelihood that innocent parties who acquire the stolen property in the interim may suffer. To prevent such undesirable consequences, time periods have been established by statute within which a victim of a theft must press his claim (these are called statutes of limitations) and a procedure is recognized whereby a possessor of property can acquire title if certain steps are not taken by the owner (this is called the doctrine of adverse possession).

---

29. 15 U.S.C. §§ 41, *et seq.*

30. 15 U.S.C. §§ 2101–2106.

31. 18 U.S.C. §§ 1341–43.

32. For a general discussion on the problem of fake art, see Hodes, "Fake Art and the Law," 27 *Fed. Bar J.* 73 (1967). See also "Legal Problems in Art Authentication," a report of the Committee on Art of the Bar of the City of New York, 21 *Records of N.Y.C.B.A.* 96–102 (1966), and F. Feldman and S. Weil, *Art Works: Law, Policy, Practice* (1974). For problems in the print market, see Hobart, "A Giant Step Forward—New York Legislation on Sales of Fine Art Multiples," 7 *Art and the Law* 261 (1983).

33. If purchased property turns out to be stolen and has to be returned, quite possibly the museum/purchaser might have a cause of action against the seller based on the sales contract or some form of misrepresentation (see previous sections).

34. *Wood v. Carpenter*, 101 U.S. 135, 25 L. Ed. 807 (1879).

a. Statutes of Limitations

Statutes of limitations vary in length depending on the cause of action at issue and the jurisdiction. If a museum determines that it is in fact holding stolen property it could find itself a defendant in a suit for conversion[35] when it refuses to return the property upon demand. In looking to its possible defenses, the museum would want to determine the applicable statute of limitations for conversion and whether the statute had begun to run.[36] This second determination, when such a statute begins to run, can be complex, and, here again, the law of the particular jurisdiction must be studied.

The traditional rule is that the statute of limitations begins to run from the time of the theft, but frequently this rule is not invoked if the property is concealed. It is recognized that the owner cannot assert his remedies if he cannot identify the wrongdoer. If the thief sells to an innocent purchaser, the statute of limitations may be construed to run from the date of purchase, but, at times, this rule is not applied if it is still unlikely that the owner could know the whereabouts of the property. More recent decisions appear to focus on the ability of the victim to press his claim. In other words, the statute of limitations is viewed as commencing when the victim discovers, or with the exercise of reasonable diligence should have discovered, facts which form the basis of his cause of action.[37]

Two cases which illustrate the complexities that can arise in this area and the different approaches which can be taken by courts are *Menzel v. List*[38] and *O'Keeffe v. Snyder*.[39] In *Menzel v. List*, the Menzels purchased a Marc Chagall painting in 1932 for about $150 at an auction in Brussels, Belgium. In 1941, when the Germans invaded Belgium, the Menzels were forced to flee the country and the painting was left behind in their apartment. Upon their return six years later, the painting was gone, having been taken by the Germans. In 1955, Klaus Perls and his wife, proprietors of a New York art gallery, bought the painting from a Parisian art gallery for $2800. The Perls knew nothing of the painting's history and did not question the Paris gallery. Mr. Perls testified that it would be an "insult" to question a reputable dealer as to his title.[40] Several months later, the Perls sold the painting to Albert List for $4,000. In

---

35. Conversion is a civil action for money damages based on the unlawful withholding of property. If the plaintiff seeks the return of the property itself, rather than its value, the action may be called replevin.

36. In *State of North Carolina v. West*, 293 N.C. 18, 235 S.E.2d 150 (1977), North Carolina was demanding the return of certain historic documents that were once the property of the state. The Court held that in North Carolina the statute of limitations would not be applied against the state. Individual state law should be checked on this point.

37. This interpretation frequently is referred to as the "discovery rule." See 51 Am. Jur. 2d, *Limitation of Actions* § 146 at 716 (1970). See also Comment, "The Recovery of Stolen Art: Of Paintings, Statues and Statutes of Limitations," 27 *U.C.L.A. L. Rev.* 1122 (1980).

38. 267 N.Y.S. 2d 804, 49 Misc. 2d 300 (1966), *aff'd* 28 A.D.2d 516, 279 N.Y.S.2d 608; third party case *rev'd* on other grounds 24 N.Y.2d 91, 298 N.Y.S.2d 979, 246 N.E.2d 742 (1969).

39. 170 N.J. Super. 75, 405 A.2d 840, 416 A.2d 862 (1980). See also Amram, "The Georgia O'Keeffe Case: New Questions About Stolen Art," *Museum News* 49 (Jan.–Feb. 1979) and Amram, "The Georgia O'Keeffe Case: Act II," *Museum News* 47 (Sept.–Oct. 1979).

40. 24 N.Y.2d 91.

1962, Mrs. Menzel noticed a reproduction of the painting in a book which gave List's name as the owner. She requested the return of the painting and List refused to surrender it. Mrs. Menzel then instituted an action for replevin[41] against List, and he, in turn, brought Mr. and Mrs. Perls into the suit alleging that they were liable to him for breach of an implied warranty of title.[42] The defendants argued, among other issues, that they were bona fide purchasers for value and that the statutes of limitations of New York and Belgium barred the action. The court disagreed stating that the plaintiff's cause of action arose upon the defendant's (List's) refusal to return the painting upon demand, and, therefore, the statutes of limitations began to run from that point. In this case, the date of the original taking and the dates of sales to innocent purchasers were not considered relevant for purposes of initiating the period of limitations. After much litigation, Mrs. Menzel was awarded her painting and the Perls were ordered to pay Mr. List the value of the painting as of the date the painting was surrendered to Mrs. Menzel. The Perls only recourse was to sue the Paris dealer.

If we apply the reasoning of the *Menzel* case to the hypothetical museum that purchases a stolen piece of art, it may be that the museum has no statute of limitations defense unless the plaintiff actually makes a demand for return and then fails to take legal action within the required time. The museum's only recourse might be a breach of contract or warranty suit against the seller, hoping that the seller is able to pay any judgment awarded. If the museum received the stolen object as a gift, it may have little, if anything, on which to base any cause of action against the donor for loss of the work.

The case of *O'Keeffe v. Snyder* further highlights the difficulties involved in cases of this nature, and it illustrates a different solution. In 1946, the artist Georgia O'Keeffe noticed three of her paintings, valued at about $150 each, had disappeared from her husband's New York City art gallery. She suspected that a man named Estrich may have taken them, but she never investigated because "It wouldn't have been my way!" She did mention the loss to several acquaintances in the art profession. Sometime before 1955, the paintings came into the possession of a Dr. Frank of Concord, New Hampshire, and, in 1965, Dr. Frank gave the paintings to his son, Ulrich Frank, as a gift. Dr. Frank died in 1968, and it is unknown how he acquired the works. The Franks displayed the pictures in their homes and for a single day in 1968, they were displayed at a community center in Trenton, New Jersey.

In November 1972, O'Keeffe, through her secretary, reported the paintings missing to the Art Dealers Association of America. In 1973, Ulrich Frank consigned the paintings to a New York City gallery for sale. When they did not sell, they were consigned to the Princeton Gallery of Fine Art owned by Barry Snyder. In 1975, Snyder bought the pictures for $35,000.

O'Keeffe learned the whereabouts of the paintings in 1976, and she demanded their return. Snyder refused and O'Keeffe immediately instituted a replevin action against him. Snyder's first defense was that the statute of limitations

---

41. Replevin is an action seeking the return of misappropriated property.

42. Note previous section on warranties in a sale.

had run. In New Jersey, an action for replevin is barred if not brought within six years of the time the action accrued. O'Keeffe argued that her cause of action did not accrue until she knew the whereabouts of her property, but the trial court found for Snyder, stating:

> The Court will not countenance the application of a rule of law which will remove the repose granted by the Statute of Limitations to allow this plaintiff to advance a claim based on her recitations of facts not to seek or confront a thief at the time of the alleged theft and to institute suit thirty years later when the defendants are incapable of presenting contrary evidence to either refute the plaintiff's claim or establish the validity of their own title.
>
> The Statute of Limitations . . . bars the plaintiff's recovery. The cause of action accrued in March, 1946.[43]

O'Keeffe appealed the decision and was upheld by the appellate court. The members of the court differed in their reasoning, but it was the majority view that the defendant, Snyder, had not proven that the paintings had been held openly and adversely, and such open and adverse possession was necessary in order to start the statute of limitations running. The appellate court did not stress O'Keeffe's failure to report the theft, but instead focused on Snyder's failure to protect himself:

> Moreover, defendant Snyder was not without means of self-protection. He was not a novice in dealing with art work. He purchased the paintings without provenance. He was thus aware of the uncertain history of the paintings' ownership. The artist, however, is alive and it was always open to him to check with her as to their authenticity and the legitimacy of his purchase. He elected to take his chance with this result.[44]

Essentially, the appellate court put the burden of proving a right to possession on the defendant, Snyder.

The case was appealed to the Supreme Court of New Jersey and in July 1980, the court issued a detailed opinion which reversed the appellate court and sent the case back to the trial level for the gathering of additional facts. The Supreme Court's opinion strongly endorsed the use of the discovery rule in cases of this nature. As previously noted, the discovery rule provides that a cause of action will not accrue "until the injured party discovers, or by exercise of reasonable diligence and intelligence should have discovered, facts which form the basis of a cause of action."[45] The discovery rule places the burden on the owner, as the one seeking the benefit of the rule, to establish facts that justify deferring the running of the statute of limitations. Applying this to the *O'Keeffe* situation, the Supreme Court ordered the case back to the trial court[46] so that issues such as the following could be settled:

> (1) Whether O'Keeffe used due diligence to recover the paintings at the time of the alleged theft and thereafter;

---

43. The trial court opinion is cited as *O'Keeffe v. Snyder*, Docket No. L-27517-75 (N.J. Super. Ct., Law Div., Mercer County, July 1978). It is printed in *Museum News* 50 (Jan.–Feb. 1979).

44. 405 A.2d 840, 848.

45. 416 A.2d 862, 869.

46. O'Keeffe elected not to pursue the case further and the parties entered into a private settlement.

(2) whether at the time of the alleged theft there was an effective method, other than talking to her colleagues, for O'Keeffe to alert the art world; and

(3) whether registering paintings with the Art Dealers Association of America, Inc., or any other organization would put a reasonably prudent purchaser of art on constructive notice that someone other than the possessor was the true owner.[47]

Under this test if O'Keeffe was not able to convince the court or jury that she had used due diligence in trying to recover her loss within the six years after she discovered the paintings missing, she would be barred from pursuing her claim. In effect, the court points out, at the end of the statutory period of limitations, title vests in the possessor.[48]

The *Menzel* (New York) rule and the *O'Keeffe* (New Jersey) rule offer different solutions to the same problem. The *Menzel* rule favors the owner, because it does not begin the running of a statute of limitations until the owner makes a demand for the return of the property. The *O'Keeffe* rule places a burden on the owner to establish a consistent pattern of efforts to recover the lost property. A careful reading of all opinions in the *Menzel* and *O'Keeffe* matters shows painstaking efforts by the courts to weigh the "equities" between relatively innocent parties. The prevailing party is usually one who, in the court's eye, acted more prudently in trying to protect his interest.[49] The lessons for museums may be that: care should be taken in the accession process to see that the right questions are asked about provenance; accurate records should be maintained; and acquisitions should be duly publicized.[50]

b. Adverse Possession

Closely associated with the statute of limitations defense is the doctrine of adverse possession. Adverse possession is a method used by a possessor of property to establish title to the property. In order to perfect this title, the possession of the property must be hostile (that is, clearly at odds with anyone else's assertion of title), actual, visible, exclusive and continuous for the period of time required by statute.[51] Invariably, the burden is on the person claiming

---

47. 416 A.2d 862, 870.

48. 416 A.2d 862, 874. See also *Desiderio v. D'Ambrosio*, 190 N.J. Super. 424, 463 A.2d 986 (1983).

49. In *Kunstsammlungen zu Weimar v. Elicofon*, 536 F. Supp. 829 (E.D.N.Y. 1981) *aff'd* 678 F.2d 1150 (2d Cir. 1982), the court was faced with a fact situation similar to that in *Menzel v. List*. The paintings at issue had been stolen from Germany in 1945, were purchased by Elicofon in New York in 1946 from an American serviceman and were "discovered" and claimed by the plaintiffs in 1966. One of the Elicofon's defenses was that the statute of limitations had run, and, hence, the plaintiff's suit was barred. In deciding the timeliness of the commencement of action, the court acknowledged the recent Supreme Court of New Jersey's opinion in *O'Keeffe v. Snyder* but stated that it need not decide whether it would adopt the *O'Keeffe* approach in New York because the undisputed evidence in the *Elicofon* case clearly demonstrated that the plaintiffs made diligent efforts to locate the paintings. In other words, even if the *O'Keeffe* standard were used, no unreasonable delay in making a demand could be shown. The court held in *Elicofon* that the statute of limitations began to run when the demand was made for the paintings. See also Feldman, "The Title to a Work of Art Means Much More than Just Its Name," *The Collection-Investor* 38 (Feb. 1982).

50. On the other side of the coin, if a museum suspects that one of its works has been stolen, it should notify law enforcement authorities and take other practical steps to protect its interests.

51. 54 C.J.S., *Limitations of Actions*, § 119 at 23 (1948).

title under adverse possession to prove all of these elements. Thus, if a museum wishes to take steps to perfect title to collection objects of uncertain ownership, it would have to establish evidence that it held the objects for the required period of time in a manner hostile to the true owner (that is, clearly claiming title in the museum), that this possession was actual, continuous and exclusively claimed, and that its hostile possession was readily discernible to the general public. This is a hard case to make, especially with regard to personal property. The doctrine of adverse possession is more closely associated with real property, and, in the *O'Keeffe* case, the court held that in New Jersey the doctrine of adverse possession henceforth should be confined to real property situations.[52] The doctrine has, however, a substantial history of application in personal property cases.[53]

The new Convention on Cultural Property Implementation Act contains a section which concerns the importation of stolen cultural property.[54] The section reads as follows:

> No article of cultural property documented as appertaining to the inventory of a museum or religious or secular public monument or similar institution in any . . . [nation which has accepted the UNESCO Convention] which is stolen from such institution after the effective date of this . . . [act][55] or after the date of entry into force of the Convention for the . . . [nation in question], whichever date is later, may be imported into the United States.[56]

The provisions of the Act do not apply, however, to imported cultural property if such property:

> (A) has been held in the United States for a period of not less than three consecutive years by a recognized museum or religious or secular monument or similar institution, and was purchased by that institution for value, in good faith, and without notice that such material or article was imported in violation of this title but only if—
>
>   (i) the acquisition of such material or article has been reported in a publication of such institution, any regularly published newspaper or periodical with a circulation of at least fifty thousand, or a periodical or exhibition catalog which is concerned with the type of article or materials sought to be exempted from this title,
>
>   (ii) such material or article has been exhibited to the public for a period or periods aggregating at least one year during such three-year period, or

---

52. Supreme Court Case pp. 16, *et seq*. In this regard the court overruled *Redmond v. N.J. Historical Society*, 132 N.J. Eq. 464, 28 A.2d 189 (1942), a case involving a museum's refusal to return a painting, which had been placed on loan subject to the occurrence of certain events.

53. But see *Wogan v. State of Louisiana*, No. 81-2295 (La. Civ. Dist. Ct. for Parish of Orleans, Jan. 8, 1982). *Wogan* involved a demand for the return of a painting originally placed on loan in a museum and subsequently claimed by the museum as its own. Citing the peculiarities of Louisiana law, the court would not recognize an adverse possession defense. See also discussions in Chapter VII, "Unclaimed Loans" and Chapter X, "Objects Found in the Collections."

54. See Chapter IV, Section D.6.

55. April 1983.

56. § 308 of Pub. L. 97-466.

(iii) such article or material has been cataloged and the catalog material made available upon request to the public for at least two years during such three-year period;

(B) if subparagraph (A) does not apply, has been within the United States for a period of not less than ten consecutive years and has been exhibited for not less than five years during such period in a recognized museum or religious or secular monument or similar institution in the United States open to the public; or

(C) if subparagraphs (A) and (B) do not apply, has been within the United States for a period of not less than ten consecutive years and the State Party concerned has received or should have received during such period fair notice (through such adequate and accessible publication, or other means, as the Secretary shall by regulation prescribe) of its location within the United States; and

(D) if none of the preceding subparagraphs apply, has been within the United States for a period of not less than twenty consecutive years and the claimant establishes that it purchased the material or article for value without knowledge or reason to believe that it was imported in violation of law.[57]

These enumerated exceptions clearly establish statutes of limitations applicable to the described imported cultural property stolen after the effective date of the Act. Whether these same time periods will be invoked as reasonable periods of notice in cases involving cultural objects, imported or not, stolen prior to that date remains to be seen.

6. Objects Improperly Removed from Their Countries of Origin

At the 1980 seminar on "Legal Problems of Museum Administration," sponsored by the American Law Institute–American Bar Association Committee on Continuing Professional Education and the Smithsonian Institution,[58] the theme of the program was "No Museum Is an Island." This theme is illustrated quite graphically when discussion centers on problems associated with cultural objects allegedly improperly removed from their countries of origin.

Today, when a museum is offered a piece of pre-Columbian art or when questions are raised concerning the provenance of certain African pieces in a museum's collection, there are international ripples. If an exhibition of American Indian artifacts is planned and objections are raised by Native Americans, there are international ripples. Consider, for example, the following news item:

ANKARA, Turkey, Feb. 22—The Minister of Culture has praised the work of archaeological teams in Turkey but warned that the activities of some foreign institutes may be curbed if the country's "stolen treasures" are not returned soon.

"If these works are not restored, we could revise excavation permits issued to some foreigners," the Minister, Cihat Baban, cautioned. "We prefer

---

57. Section 312 of Pub. L. 97–446. Property imported for temporary exhibit and protected by a declaration of immunity from seizure under 25 U.S.C. § 2549 is also exempt.

58. Washington, D.C., March 19–21, 1980.

to preserve our cultural assets even under the ground rather than let them slip through our hands."

Mr. Baban's warning was made during a recent week-long symposium on excavation works carried out last year at 56 sites around the country, including 18 being worked by foreign teams.

Addressing the gathering of archaeologists and students, Mr. Baban singled out the Byzantine works from the Antalya region that were said to have been smuggled out of the country to "an American museum."

. . .

United States officials here expressed concern about Mr. Baban's threats and the possible effect on the work of American archaeologists.

. . .

The officials also said they feared that any Turkish retaliation might jeopardize attempts to organize the first major showing of Turkish archaeological works at the Metropolitan Museum of Art in New York.[59]

Similarly, it was reported in the July 1982 issue of *Stolen Art Alert* that an "Open Letter" from the Egyptian Antiquities Organization was being sent to foreign museums asking their cooperation in stemming the trade of objects illegally removed from Egypt. The letter stated:

We are obliged to call your attention to a decision already taken by the Egyptian Antiquities Organization that any sort of scientific archaeological cooperation between the E.A.O. and any museum proved to be retaining or dealing with such artifacts will be terminated. Such cooperation includes scholarly exchanges, loans, and exhibitions, and archaeological excavations and surveys.[60]

In a sense, every museum in the country has an opportunity to affect the international climate regarding the import or export of cultural objects. Two justifications are offered for this statement. First, the problems raised in this area do not lend themselves to simple solutions. They are many–faceted, and they can raise legal and ethical considerations which strain the traditional avenues of redress. As a result, courts and legislatures find it difficult to offer comprehensive guidance. Often, practical considerations demand that cases of this type be decided on their individual merits with the assistance of members of the museum profession. This cannot be done effectively unless all in the museum community keep abreast of the issues and, through mutual support, create and sustain an enlightened atmosphere where these problems can be aired and resolved. Secondly, the term "international strains" can touch very close to home. In the area of repatriation or return of cultural objects, an American Indian tribe may frequently claim the status of a foreign nation.[61] An action in response to a request for return of cultural property to Mexico or Zaire may well be interpreted as precedent for a similar request from an Amer-

59. *The New York Times*, Feb. 23, 1981, at A.3, Col.1. Copyright © 1981 by the New York Times Co. Reprinted by permission.

60. at 1.

61. See section on "American Indian Religious Freedom Act," this chapter.

ican Indian tribe. Conversely, if a museum is approached for the return of a
Zuni war god or Houdanessee mask, its reply may well be construed as the
museum community's views on the propriety of returning important cultural
property to other countries of origin.

Every museum, whether it is a large natural history museum, a major art
gallery or a small historical society, shares in this common problem. Each has
an obligation to see the whole picture and to weigh its attitudes and actions
in light of all relevant considerations. If the museum community fails to step
forward with constructive assistance, it can hardly complain when economic
and political considerations alone determine the fate of cultural objects.[62]

Problems arise in the international movement of cultural property because
of the different perspectives of what might be called the "art rich" nations and
the "art poor" nations. Essentially, the former comprise those countries that
now see much of their cultural properties located outside their borders, or in
danger of being exported, and the latter are composed of countries that house
or seek these cultural properties.[63] Some of these properties have left their
countries of origin because of war, or through licit or illicit trade, and the
countries themselves have varied histories regarding the effectiveness of internal export controls. Today, in our more enlightened atmosphere, there is a
greater sympathy for general proposals to return major cultural properties to
their countries of origin or to halt improper export of such properties. It is
recognized that countries of origin have unique claims and that some works
of art have an integrity which transcends conventional concepts of ownership.[64]

Closely allied are the concerns of the scholarly community over the pillage
of archaeological sites by organized entrepreneurs or the more amateur pot
hunter. For the anthropologist, the archaeologist and the art historian, the
original context of an artifact is as important as the object itself, and an artifact
unscientifically removed from its site is, at most, a vapid beauty:

> What help are those looted "floating" artifacts for answering questions about
> the forces behind the emergence or decay of civilization, social
> heterogeneity, population pressures on available resources, political or
> technical intensification? . . . [In this regard,] the artifact with no context or
> provenance is virtually worthless, despite the irony of a fat price tag.[65]

---

62. For detailed description of practices in the international art market, see B. Burnham, *The Art
Crisis* (1975); K. Meyer, *The Plundered Past* (1973).

63. The term "cultural properties" generally is defined to mean properties which, on religious or
secular grounds, are designated by a nation as being of unique importance to the nation for reasons
relating to archaeology, prehistory, history, literature, art or science. The term has been refined
further by UNESCO action. See the section on "Post-UNESCO Convention Activity." See also the
"Convention on Cultural Property Implementation Act," hereinafter described, which defines the
term.

64. Burcaw in "A Museological View of the Repatriation of Museum Objects," *Museum Studies
Journal* 8 (Spring 1983), argues against repatriation of most museum objects.

65. Sheets, "The Pillage of Prehistory," 38 *Am. Antiquity* 317, 319 (1973). See also Coggins, "Illicit
Traffic of Pre-Columbian Antiquities," 29 *Art J.* 94 (1969). Coggins, "Archeology and the Art
Market," 175 *Science* 263 (1972); Robertson, "Monument Thievery in Mesoamerica," 37 *Am. Antiquity*
147 (1972); "International Protection of Cultural Property," 1 *Art Research News* (No. 2 1981).

Frequently, such despoliation is outlawed by the country of origin, but these statutes do little to deter those bent on financial gain and urged on by an ever-growing market for such artifacts.[66]

While, in the abstract, there may be much sympathy for claims of countries of origin and despoliation of archaeological sites may be roundly condemned, the search for acceptable methods of repatriation and control is an arduous one.[67] Central to any discussion on the international movement of cultural property is the Convention on the Means of Prohibiting and Preventing the Illicit Import, Export, and Transfer of Ownership of Cultural Property, which was adopted by the General Conference on the United Nations Educational, Scientific and Cultural Organizations (UNESCO) on November 14, 1970,[68] and subsequent actions of the United States to implement the Convention. Also of significance is the Treaty of Cooperation Between the United States of America and the United Mexican States Providing for the Recovery and Return of Stolen Archaeological, Historical, and Cultural Property; the U.S. statute regulating the importation of certain monumental-type pre-Columbian art; the case of *United States v. McClain*, and the American Indian Religious Freedom Act.[69] An explanation of each follows.

---

66. See Hamblin, "The Billion Dollar Illegal Art Traffic—How It Works and How to Stop It," *Smithsonian* 16 (March 1972).

67. Merryman and Elsen in "Hot Art: A Reexamination of the Illegal International Trade in Cultural Objects," 12 *J. of Arts Management and L.* 5 (Fall 1982), set forth a detailed "interest analysis" as a mechanism for resolving claims of exporting nations which may not be adequately served by the traditional legal remedies available in the United States. L. Prott and P. O'Keefe, *Law and the Cultural Heritage* (1984) is an "in progress" five-volume series by two University of Sydney, Australia, law professors. It is described as a major study of all aspects of legal protection afforded a cultural heritage.

68. See Appendix for a copy of the Convention. A comprehensive study of the history of the UNESCO convention is found in Bator, "An Essay on the International Trade in Art," 34 *Stan. L. Rev.* 275 (1982).

69. Another federal statute should be kept in mind when American Indian objects are at issue. 18 U.S.C. § 1163 makes it a crime to embezzle or steal property from an Indian tribal organization. The statute reads as follows:

> Whoever embezzles, steals, knowingly converts to his use or the use of another, willfully misapplies, or willfully permits to be misapplied, any of the moneys, funds, credits, goods, assets, or other property belonging to any Indian tribal organization or intrusted to the custody or care of any officer, employee, or agent of an Indian tribal organization; or
> Whoever, knowing any such moneys, funds, credits, goods, assets, or other property to have been so embezzled, stolen, converted, misapplied or permitted to be misapplied, receives, conceals, or retains the same with intent to convert it to his use or the use of another—
> Shall be fined not more than $5,000, or imprisoned not more than five years, or both; but if the value of such property does not exceed the sum of $100, he shall be fined not more than $1,000, or imprisoned not more than one year, or both.
> As used in this section, the term "Indian tribal organization" means any tribe, band, or community of Indians which is subject to the laws of the United States relating to Indian affairs or any corporation, association, or group which is organized under any of such laws.

The statute became law in 1956 and can be invoked only for violations occurring on or after that date. If a museum is considering acquiring Indian material located in Canada, it may be prudent to become familiar with Canada's Cultural Property Export and Import Act of 1977. (Chapter 50.23–24 Elizabeth II, Vol. 1, No. 9, Canada Gazette Part III.)

a. UNESCO Convention

The purpose of the Convention on the Means of Prohibiting and Preventing the Illicit Import, Export, and Transfer of Ownership of Cultural Property (the UNESCO Convention) is to provide a common framework among nations for alleviating abuses in the international trade of cultural property.[70] Nations were asked to join in the Convention by ratifying, accepting or acceding to its terms in accordance with procedures required by their respective constitutions.

Before the Convention could be effected in the United States, it first had to be approved by the U.S. Senate and then implemented by federal legislation which would establish internal methods of enforcement. The State Department in urging Senate ratification described the Convention as follows:

> The convention responds to the growing concern of the world community at the illegal removal of the national art treasures from their countries of origin. In recent years there appears to be an increase in the theft of art objects and the despoliation of national monuments and archaeological sites in all parts of the world. Churches and temples are frequently looted and some ceremonial centers of ancient civilizations have been virtually dismantled. One of the most serious problems is the clandestine excavation of archaeological sites which can destroy the scientific value of the objects removed and of the site itself.
>
> The situation is a problem for each country to deal with at home, but it is also a matter of international concern and responsibility. Every country has an interest in the preservation of the cultural patrimony of mankind. Moreover, the flourishing international art market provides a major inducement of these illegal operations. The appearance in the United States of important foreign art treasures of suspicious origin gives rise to problems in our relations with other countries and makes it more difficult for American archaeologists and scholars to work in these lands. It also stimulates over-restrictive export controls by the countries concerned which sometimes compound the problem.
>
> The UNESCO convention deals with these issues by recognizing the primary responsibility of each state to protect its own cultural heritage and by establishing a framework for international cooperation that should be of significant assistance in a number of areas.
>
> . . . [T]hree of the most important provisions [are as follows]. First, the states parties undertake in article 7(b) to prohibit the import of cultural property stolen from museums, religious or secular public monuments, or similar institutions in other states parties and to take appropriate steps, upon request, to recover and return such property to the country of origin. This provision, like the other provisions of the convention, is not retroactive.
>
> Second, the parties agree in article 7(a) to take the necessary measures, consistent with national legislation, to prevent museums and similar institutions within their territory from acquiring cultural property illegally removed from another state party after entry into force of this convention. In

---

70. For a brief account of the history of the Convention and reactions to it, see Zelle, "Acquisitions: Saving Whose Heritage?" *Museum News* 19 (April 1971). See also, *ICOM News* for September, 1969; March, June, September 1970; Craven, "Patrimony, Museums and the Law," *Southeastern Museums Conference Journal* 23 (Nov. 1978).

the United States this provision applies primarily to institutions controlled by the Federal Government; it does not require enactment of new legislation to control the acquisition policy of other institutions. However, it does create a standard for private and local institutions, and it is expected they will develop their own code of ethics in the spirit of this provision.

Third, the convention includes a specific provision relating to materials of archaeological and ethnological importance. Article 9 provides that a state party whose cultural patrimony is in jeopardy from pillage of archaeological or ethnological materials may call upon other state parties to participate in a concentrated international effort to determine and to carry out the necessary concrete measures including appropriate controls of imports, exports, and international commerce in these materials. The Congress will be asked to enact appropriate legislation to implement this provision and the import controls required by article 7(a).

These are the highlights of the convention. It is by no means a panacea, but it is a significant effort to deal with a complex problem that does not yield easily to legal solutions.[71]

The Convention was ratified by the Senate in 1972 with certain reservations and with the understanding that any federal legislation implementing the agreement would have to conform to U.S. constitutional and legal standards. The task of framing and passing such implementing legislation, however, proved to be far more difficult than ratification of the Convention itself. For the next ten years, a variety of bills were introduced to effect the Convention's objectives and each evoked comment from groups and individuals representing museums, private collectors, art dealers, anthropologists, and so on.[72] Some argued for very strong, comprehensive legislation to demonstrate that we are a "moral nation." Others contended that art objects of ancient and primitive cultures belonged to everyone, and there was no fundamental obligation to return them to countries of origin which may have done little to preserve them. Archaeologists stressed the irreparable damage done when objects are unscientifically excavated. Some dealers and collectors feared that strong U.S. legislation would only divert treasures to other importing nations which failed to implement the Convention. Practical problems were raised concerning statutes of limitations, methods of enforcement and compensation of innocent holders. Each new version of the proposed legislation became more complex in order to accom-

---

71. Statement by Mark B. Feldman, then Assistant Legal Advisor for Inter-American Affairs, Department of State, before the Senate Committee on Foreign Relations.

72. An excellent overview of the divergent views expressed can be found in the legislative histories of the bills proposed to implement the Convention, for example: H.R. 5643 of the 95th Congress, H.R. 3403 of the 96th Congress, S. 1723 of the 97th Congress, lst Session, and H.R. 4566 of the 97th Congress, 2nd Session, the bill which eventually became law. See also "Proceedings of the Panel on the U.S. Enabling Legislation of the UNESCO Convention on the Means of Prohibiting and Preventing the Illicit Import, Export and Transfer of Ownership of Cultural Property," 4 *Syracuse J. Int'l L. & Com.* 97 (1976) and Wisner, "Implementing the Convention on Illicit Traffic in Antiquities: Proposals, Past and Prospective," 2 *Art Research News* 3 (No. 1 1983). The definitive work may be Bator, "An Essay on the International Trade in Art," 34 *Stan. L. Rev.* 275 (1982), also published in book form under the title *The International Trade in Art* by the University of Chicago Press (1983).

modate the concerns of commentators, and, at times, the protracted debate appeared to hinder rather than encourage resolution.

In December 1982, in the waning hours of the 97th Congress, implementing legislation finally was passed without fanfare. The Convention on Cultural Property Implementation Act[73] contains the following major provisions:

1. Procedures by which the President of the United States can, upon request, impose temporary import restrictions in order to deter a serious situation of pillage of archaeological or ethnological materials of a state which has acceded to the Convention. As a rule, such action cannot be taken unless the application of import restrictions will be applied in concert with similar restrictions imposed by other nations having significant import trade in such materials. There are also procedures for unilateral action in emergency situations.

2. The creation of a Cultural Property Advisory Committee to assist the Government in implementing and evaluating the effectiveness of such temporary import restrictions.

3. Restrictions on the importation of cultural property appertaining to the inventory of a museum or public institution of a party to the Convention if such property was stolen from the institution after a prescribed date.

4. Procedures for seizing and disposing of cultural property illegally imported into this country.

5. Exemption of certain cultural properties from coverage such as: those imported for temporary exhibit or display and rendered immune from seizure under 25 U.S.C. § 2459;[74] those purchased in good faith by a museum or similar institution and held by it for at least three consecutive years under certain conditions; those held in the United States for at least ten consecutive years and displayed during that time at least five years in a museum or similar institution; those held in the United States for at least ten consecutive years with evidence of actual or constructive notice to the foreign nation concerned of the location of such cultural properties; and

---

73. Title II of Pub. L. 97–466 (a copy of the Act is included in the Appendix). It is of interest also that in September, 1977, Canada adopted a Cultural Property Export and Import Act (Chapter 50.23-24, Elizabeth II, Vol. 1, No. 9, Canada Gazette, Part III), a portion of which is designed to implement the UNESCO Convention. The Canadian Act provides a relatively simple format whereby the Attorney General of Canada is charged with instituting legal proceedings necessary to resolve claims of countries of origin. For a discussion of the Canadian Act, see Clark, "The Cultural Property Export and Import Act: Legislation to Encourage Co-operation" 2 *Art Research News* 8 (No. 1 1983). One of the first cases arising under the Act has attracted international interest. In 1981, the New York art dealer Ben Heller brought into Canada for authentication by the Glenbow Museum in Calgary, and possible sale, a Nigerian Nok sculpture. While in Canada, Heller and the owner of the sculpture, a Mr. Zango, were arrested by the Canadian government when they could not produce a Nigerian export license. A major issue in the case is what "illegal export" means under the Canadian statute: Does it mean illegal export from the country of origin only after the effective date of the Canadian statute (1977) and/or Canada's acceding to the UNESCO Convention (1978), or does it mean illegal export at any time, even years prior to these dates? As of 1984, the matter is still in litigation. (See, *Between Her Majesty The Queen and Heller, Zango and Kassam*, In the Court of Queen's Bench of Alberta, Judicial District of Calgary (Canada) 2/21/83 (*sic*, 84). See also *Stolen Art Alert* (Jan.–Feb. 1982 and Oct. 1983).

74. See Chapter VIII, "International Loans."

those held for a period of not less than twenty consecutive years with evidence of good faith purchase.

It was specifically noted by the Senate in its confirmation of the UNESCO Convention that it was not the intention of Congress to enact legislation to control the acquisition policies of museums generally. This "reservation" was directed to Article 7(a) of the Convention, which reads as follows:

> The State parties to the Convention undertake:
> (a) to take the necessary measures, consistent with national legislation, to prevent museums and similar institutions within their territories from acquiring cultural property originating in another State Party which has been illegally exported after entry into force of this Convention, in the States concerned. Whenever possible, to inform a State of origin Party to this Convention of an offer of such cultural property illegally removed from that State after the entry into force of this Convention in both States.

In the opinion of Congress, museums voluntarily would conform their policies to meet standards expressed in the Convention.[75] Many institutions have done so already.[76] The policy statement approved by Harvard College in 1972 and the prefatory explanation that follow represent the work of a variety of collecting disciplines.[77]

HARVARD UNIVERSITY
CAMBRIDGE, MASS.
617-495-1585

RELEASE: IMMEDIATE   UNIVERSITY NEWS OFFICE
                                                Tuesday, January 18, 1972

The President and Fellows of Harvard College have approved a policy aimed at countering illicit international trade in objects of art.

So far as is known, Harvard is the first university to establish such a policy for an entire university, although institutions within other universities have taken similar measures. The Harvard policy governs not only acquisitions but also loans and exhibitions.

The policy, proposed by a committee that included directors of the major

---

75. See the "Report of the Special Policy Committee of the American Association of Museums," as reported in *Museum News* 22 (May 1971). The Committee submitted recommendations on the then proposed UNESCO Convention to the Council of the American Association of Museums.

76. Policies adopted prior to the 1982 enactment of the "Convention on Cultural Property Implementation Act" were drafted without benefit of this national legislation. Passage of the Act should not materially affect most policies, which generally express a commitment to consider carefully relevant legal and ethical issues. As a practical matter, the Act should assist in implementing such policies by providing guidance on the issue of legality.

77. Another area of museum activity, sales in museum shops, also can affect the illegal movement of cultural properties. The Code of Ethics promulgated by the Museum Store Association, Inc., contains the following statement: "Sale of illicitly acquired antiquities is offensive to the affected cultures and destructive to archaeological sites. The Museum Store Association fully supports existing laws and recognizes the need for their rigid enforcement in order to preserve and protect our dwindling cultural . . . resources from wanton commercial exploitation." *Museum News* 51 at 51 (Jan.–Feb. 1982).

Harvard collections of art and antiquities, requires that officers of the University—curators, directors of libraries and museums or others—responsible for acquisitions should assure themselves that the University can acquire valid title to the object in question. They must assure themselves that the object was not recently exported illegally from the country where it originated or where it was last legally owned.

In any doubtful case, the responsible officer must consult widely with others within, and perhaps outside of, the University.

If Harvard should in the future acquire an object exported in violation of the laws of another country, it should return it if it can legally do so.

The most important part of the policy states:

"The University will not acquire (by purchase, bequest, or gift) objects that do not meet the foregoing tests. If appropriate and feasible, the same tests should be taken into account in determining whether to accept loans for exhibition or other purposes."

The report of the committee, accepted by the Corporation, stated that "no matter how complex, badly framed, or impractical" national legislation might be, "a responsible collecting institution must abide by it."

Prof. Stephen Williams, Director of the Peabody Museum of Archaeology and Ethnology, commented: "The trade in antiquities in recent years, particularly those of Mexico and Central America, has led to great destruction of the heritage of these nations—and of all mankind. The great Maya civilization, which reached its climax about 700–800 A.D. is of particular concern. Very little is known about the language of the Maya, which is recorded in hieroglyphic carvings on stone monuments. So far only the calendar can be read. Yet vandals steal, and mutilate for easy transportation, these magnificent stone documents. Indeed, at least two murders have occurred when gangs of looters were surprised at Mayan sites."

Central America, while perhaps the largest source of illegal objects, is not the only one. The countries of the eastern Mediterranean and India have been plagued with smuggling of treasures and the consequent destruction of their archaeological history.

A UNESCO conference of 1970 proposed an international treaty—so far not yet ratified by many nations, including the United States—to regulate illicit trade. Last year, the State Department proposed to Congress legislation that would have made illegal the import of pre-Columbian objects from Central America.

The Harvard statement called for a "firm, united stand, publicly taken by leading institutional and private collectors" to try to "eliminate or at least diminish the power of the black market."

The committee had as members William H. Bond, Librarian of the Houghton Library of rare books and manuscripts, chairman; and Alfred W. Crompton, Director of the Museum of Comparative Zoology; J. David Farmer, Curator of the Busch-Reisinger Museum of Germanic Culture; Agnes Mongan, recently retired director of the Fogg Art Museum; William R. Tyler, Director of the Dumbarton Oaks Library and Research Collection of Byzantine Culture in Washington, D.C.; Stephen Williams, Director of the Peabody Museum of Archaeology and Ethnology; and Paul M. Bator, Professor of Law, who has worked with UNESCO on the problem.

The committee was appointed in the fall of 1970 by President Nathan M. Pusey. It made its report in June, 1971.

The policy statement is attached:

The collections in the museums and libraries of Harvard University have been formed and are augmented and maintained primarily to promote teaching and research. In recent years a flourishing international black market has grown up in the kinds of objects that are the proper concern of our collections, and this threatens the work of the University in various ways. For example, sites have been ravaged by thieves and vandals, to the irreparable damage and even total loss of important objects, while persons involved in this traffic either carelessly lose or deliberately conceal information about the precise origins of objects, often rendering them valueless for scientific study.

In response to this situation many countries have developed legislation designed to regulate the collection and export of antiquities, art objects, and natural specimens found within their borders. But without the cooperation of the ultimate consumer—the collecting institution or individual—such legislation has often proved inadequate to control abuses.

More and more countries attempt to regulate these matters. The resulting legislation is far from uniform and has become steadily more complex. But no matter how complex, badly framed, or impractical such legislation may appear to be, a responsible collecting institution must abide by it. The violation, real or apparent, of regulatory legislation by one branch of the University is likely to have adverse effects upon the legitimate interests of all other branches of the University who pursue activities within the countries in question; and a bad reputation, once gained, is difficult to improve.

What is needed is a firm, united stand, publicly taken, by leading institutional and private collectors against illicit commerce in these materials. We believe that Harvard has a generally good record in the policies that have been privately and independently developed by its several collecting agencies. But it is now highly desirable that our informal and private code be formalized and made public, and that Harvard join with other responsible institutions and private collectors in an effort to eliminate or at least diminish the power of the black market. Such an action will serve both the particular interests of various sectors of the University and the more general aims of teaching and research.

Regulatory legislation differs widely from country to country, and the different kinds of objects that are collected also differ widely in their method of production or appearance on the market, the channels through which they are normally procured, and the extent to which their origin and history can be reasonably documented. Certification is no guarantee; if the stakes are high enough, certificates can be bought or forged even more easily than art can be faked. On the other hand, objects from currently restricted areas may have been exported in the period before restrictions were imposed, or have come out through legal means, and they may be legitimately on the market. Because absolute criteria applicable to all cases are difficult or impossible to formulate, heavy reliance must be placed upon the knowledge and experience of the curatorial staff.

We believe that it is the business of the Curators of the several collections to master, as far as possible, these complexities in their individual fields of competence. Curators should be relied upon for judgement in such matters in their special fields, and they must assume responsibility for the decisions that they make. The integrity of Harvard's collecting policy must be firmly maintained. A Curator's basis for decision should be a matter capable of public record; whether it need actually be published will depend upon the circumstances surrounding each individual case. In doubtful cases and in unfamiliar circumstances Curators should have recourse to the advice of the General Counsel to the University, who may in turn call upon other Curators and officers of the University for assistance in reaching a decision. If a difference of opinion arises between branches of the University over a matter of acquisitions policy, and if agreement cannot be reached between the interested parties, a similar mechanism of advice and appeal should be available.

To a great extent the proposed rules reflect practices long observed by the collecting agencies of the University. It will be noted, however, that the rules are largely forward-looking. In view of the tangle of international legislation, the complications arising from trusteeship, the probability of conflicting claims, and the extreme difficulty or impossibility in many cases of establishing a clear and unbroken line of provenance for past acquisitions, something resembling a statute of limitations must apply—as, in fact, it does among museum collections throughout the world. By taking a public stand along the lines we suggest, we hope that the University will play a significant role in the attempt to curb the abuses that have aroused so much public concern.

We therefore recommend that the President and Fellows adopt the following general principles to govern the University with respect to the acquisition (whether by gift, bequest, or purchase, or through the activities of scientific or archaeological expeditions) of works of art and antiquities:

1. The museum director, librarian, curator, or other University officer (hereinafter to be referred to as "Curator") responsible for making an acquisition or who will have custody of the acquisition should assure himself that the University can acquire valid title to the object in question. This means that the circumstances of the transaction and/or his knowledge of the object's provenance must be such as to give him adequate assurance that the seller or donor has valid title to convey.

2. In making a significant acquisition, the Curator should have reasonable assurance under the circumstances that the object has not, within a recent time, been exported from its country of origin (and/or the country where it was last legally owned) in violation of that country's laws.

3. In any event, the Curator should have reasonable assurance under the circumstances that the object was not exported after July 1, 1971, in violation of the laws of the country of origin and/or the country where it was last legally owned.

4. In cases of doubt in making the relevant determinations under paragraphs 1–3, the Curator should consult as widely as possible. Particular care should be taken to consult colleagues in other parts of the University whose collecting, research, or other activities may be affected by a decision to acquire an object. The Curator should also consult the General Counsel to the University where appropriate; and, where helpful, a special panel should be created to help pass on the questions raised.

5. The University will not acquire (by purchase, bequest, or gift) objects that do not meet the foregoing tests. If appropriate and feasible, the same tests should be taken into account in determining whether to accept loans for exhibitions or other purposes.

6. Curators will be responsible to the President and Fellows for the observance of these rules. All information obtained about the provenance of an acquisition must be preserved, and unless in the opinion of the relevant Curator and the General Counsel to the University special circumstances exist in a specific instance, all such information shall be available as a public record. Prospective vendors and donors should be informed of this policy.

7. If the University should in the future come into the possession of an object that can be demonstrated to have been exported in violation of the principles expressed in Rules 1–3 above, the University should, if legally free to do so, seek to return the object to the donor or vendor. Further, if with respect to such an object, a public museum or collection or agency of a foreign country seeks its return and demonstrates that it is a part of that country's national patrimony, the University should, if legally free to do so, take responsible steps to cooperate in the return of the object to that country.

b. *Post-UNESCO Convention Activity*

When it became evident that the UNESCO treaty would not meet with prompt, widespread acceptance, the international community began to explore other alternatives.[78] UNESCO, with the assistance of the International Council of Museums (ICOM)[79] initiated work on a new approach. First, it was acknowledged that traditional legal mechanisms for deciding and adjusting questions of title worked poorly when the return of cultural objects was at issue.[80] The focus, therefore, was on devising a system whereby museums themselves could bilaterally decide issues concerning the fate of cultural objects without directly involving government action. As explained in an ICOM study report,[81] such a

---

78. As of January 1983, about 50 nations had ratified the Convention and adopted implementing legislation. Canada, Italy and the United States are the only major countries in the international art market among the adherents.

79. ICOM, The International Council of Museums, is a nongovernmental organization composed of museums and representatives of museums. It was established in 1946 and has its headquarters in Paris. For ICOM's early role in working for international restraints on the illicit international movement of cultural property, see Nafziger, "Regulation by the International Council of Museums: An Example of the Role of Non-Governmental Organizations in the Transnational Legal Process," 2 *Denver J. of Int'l L. and Policy* 231 (1972).

80. The ICOM report cited in this section addressed itself to "cultural properties" defined as follows: (a) objects and documentation of ethnological interest; (b) works of fine art and decorative art; (c) archives and documents; (d) paleontological and archaeological objects; and (e) zoological, botanical and mineralogical specimens. At its 20th session in 1978, the General Conference of UNESCO modified this list as follows: "cultural property, shall be taken to denote historical and ethnographic objects and documents including manuscripts, works of the plastic and decorative arts, paleontological and archaeological objects and zoological, botanical and mineralogical specimens."

81. "Study on the Principles, Conditions and Means for the Restitution or Return of Cultural Property in View of Reconstituting Dispersed Heritages," prepared by the Ad Hoc Committee appointed by the Executive Council of ICOM, 1978.

system would require the acceptance of certain premises:

(1) The legality of a claim is not necessarily determinative. In order to accept this premise, there must be an acknowledgment that certain important elements of a nation's cultural heritage belong with that nation, whether or not the object in question left the country or its people legally.

(2) The museum community must assist in trying to determine what constitutes an important element of a country's or people's cultural heritage, or a representative portion of that heritage, so that extravagant claims cannot be pressed.

(3) The country of origin, as the requesting nation, must establish that it can protect and preserve objects that are requested, and also that it is doing its utmost at the time to preserve similar objects already within its borders.

(4) Restitution need not always be a one-way street. At times, long-term loans, interchange of exhibits or exchange of objects are suitable alternatives.

In order to implement these ideas, the general conference of UNESCO established a new international committee in November 1979, called "The Inter-governmental Committee for Promoting the Return of Cultural Property to its Countries of Origin, or its Restitution in Case of Illicit Appropriation."[82] The group, which has a rotating membership of 20 member states, is essentially an advisory body. Its main function is to facilitate bilateral negotiations based on offers or requests by member nations of UNESCO. It is hoped that offers of return or requests will be made known to the committee so that it can use its resources as an impartial third party to assist in negotiations.

The committee also has important auxiliary tasks. It will assist in identifying objects that warrant international negotiations. This may entail working with individual nations to define and limit what constitutes an important element of cultural heritage. If an object does not meet established criteria, the committee will not lend its assistance in negotiations. Secondly, the committee will offer technical and, perhaps, financial assistance to a country of origin so that it can provide facilities to care for and protect objects which are returned. The country of origin would be expected to demonstrate that it has sensible internal measures for taking care of such objects, and that it has clear and enforced export laws. Thirdly, the committee plans to promote the international exchange of important cultural objects. It is believed that when there is a greater opportunity to borrow such objects, the question of ownership becomes less significant. Finally, the committee is charged with the task of creating a favorable international climate for the acceptance of its mission.

The committee met for the first time in May 1980, at UNESCO headquarters in Paris, and adopted a program of work. It should be noted that the committee

---

82. A distinction sometimes is made between "return" and "restitution," the former being applied to a voluntary offer to return, the latter to a situation when a claim for return is based on an alleged legal right in the property. The word "return" frequently is favored when there is no desire to suggest illegal action on the part of the holder.

does not view its role as a substitute for implementation of the UNESCO Convention. At its initial meeting, the committee urged wider application of the principles of the Convention because national-level involvement in the control of the illicit traffic is an important element in any negotiation.[83]

c. U.S. v. McClain (Simpson Case)

Once an object has been exported in contravention of the laws of a country, that country normally has limited recourse. The object and its possessor are beyond the country's jurisdiction, and, in the absence of a specific international commitment to do otherwise, the importing country frequently is reluctant to take affirmative steps to secure the return of the object.[84] For example, in the United States a foreign country may be able to bring a civil action to recover property clearly stolen from it, but, as a rule, a U.S. court will not entertain a criminal charge against the alleged thief or enforce fines and other penalties based on foreign law.[85] This means that once an illegally exported object arrives in the United States, and there is no U.S. statute specifically barring its importation, the possessor of the object rarely worries about legal action.[86] A protracted court proceeding in the late 1970s, known as the *Simpson* case or *U.S. v. McClain*,[87] threatened to upset this relatively secure situation.[88]

---

83. See Braun, "Subtle Diplomacy Solves a Custody Case" *Art News* 100 (Summer 1982).

84. An example of such an international agreement is the "Treaty of Cooperation Between the United States of America and the United Mexican States Providing for the Recovery and Return of Stolen Archaeological, Historical and Cultural Properties," July 17, 1970, United States–Mexico; 22 U.S.T. 494. The treaty, which is discussed in the following section, provides for the return through diplomatic channels of stolen archaeological, historical and cultural objects that belong to the government. In *U.S. v. McClain*, this treaty was not invoked by Mexico, possibly because the treaty applies to objects of outstanding importance to the national patrimony. Instead criminal charges were filed by U.S. federal law enforcement officials against the alleged thieves.

85. J. Story, *Commentaries on the Conflict of Laws* § 18 (8th ed. 1883); J. Moore, *A Digest of International Law* 236 (1906); Bator, "An Essay on the International Trade in Art," 34 *Stan. L. Rev.* 275 (1982), also published in book form under the title *The International Trade in Art* by University of Chicago Press (1983).

86. But note *Jeanneret v. Vichey*, discussed later, where the possessor could be subject to suit by a subsequent purchaser for breach of implied warranty of title.

87. *McClain I*, 545 F.2d 988 (5th Cir. 1977). *McClain II*, 593 F.2d 658 (5th Cir. 1979), *cert. denied* 444 U.S. 918.

88. An earlier case, *U.S. v. Hollinshead*, 495 F.2d 1154 (9th Cir. 1974), was similar in nature but did not arouse such interest. Hollinshead, a California art dealer, was arrested for violating the National Stolen Property Act when he was found in possession of a pre-Columbian stela allegedly stolen from Guatemala. The prosecution was able to prove that the stela was removed from Guatemala, that the laws of Guatemala vested title to such property in the state, and that Hollinshead was aware of such laws. Hollinshead was convicted, and his conviction sustained on appeal. Perhaps this case did not create as much controversy as *U.S. v. McClain* because *Hollinshead* involved a stela, a piece readily identified as a choice cultural object and one commonly known to be subject to control by its country of origin. In addition, the stela in question had been documented *in situ* some years earlier by the noted archaeologist Ian Graham. In *McClain v. U.S.*, the objects at issue were movable pre-Columbian artifacts, a category not so readily associated with state control. It is easier to imagine innocent possession of movable pre-Columbian material than it is innocent possession of stelae. Nevertheless, *Hollinshead* has been subject to legal criticism. See, for example, Hughes, "*U.S. v. Hollinshead*: A New Leap in Extraterritorial Application of Criminal Law," 1 *Hastings Int'l & Comp. L. Rev.* 149 (1977).

The *McClain* case concerned a group of U.S. citizens who were engaged in transporting movable pre-Columbian artifacts from Mexico into the United States. After transferring a group of such artifacts from California into Texas in order to offer them for sale, the parties were arrested and indicted for violating and conspiring to violate the National Stolen Property Act.[89] That Act makes it a federal crime knowingly to transport in interstate or foreign commerce "any goods . . . of the value of $5,000 or more," which were "stolen, converted or taken by fraud." The prosecution argued that the artifacts were considered stolen under Mexican law and that the court should give full faith and credit to the foreign law. The group was convicted and an appeal was filed. The American Association of Dealers in Ancient, Oriental and Primitive Art appeared as *amicus curiae*[90] in the appeal arguing that giving full faith and credit to the Mexican law would establish a dangerous precedent.

Mexican statutes on the subject of archaeological monuments date back to 1897, and these laws have been revised on several occasions, the latest revision occurring in 1972. A good deal of court argument centered around the translation and interpretation of these various statutes. It was important to determine, the court said, whether the laws merely imposed export requirements or whether they vested title to the artifacts in the Mexican government. If they did the latter, then, under Mexican law, a removal of the artifacts from the control of the government would constitute theft.[91] The appeals court did not agree with the trial court's opinion that Mexican law from 1897 vested title to the artifacts in the government, and it remanded the case to the lower court for a new trial on this subject. The group was convicted again and a second appeal was filed. In the second appeal the court agreed to give full faith and credit to the 1972 Mexican statute which, in its opinion, clearly claimed state ownership of all pre-Columbian antiquities. On the basis of this, the convictions of the defendants were upheld for conspiring to violate a federal law (the National Stolen Property Act). The appeals court stated that it would not enforce the pre-1972 Mexican statutes because they were not written "with sufficient clarity" to survive translation into terms understandable by and binding upon American citizens.[92]

The *McClain* decisions highlight possible difficult questions for museums. Many foreign countries have statutes regulating the movement of cultural property. Some of these statutes cover only selected materials, are carefully administered and are well-publicized. Others, however, are not widely promulgated and/or present problems of interpretation or administration. Even assuming

---

89. 18 U.S.C. §§ 2314, 2315 and on conspiracy 18 U.S.C. § 371.

90. Literally, "friend of the court." With this status, one who is not a party to a case is granted permission to advise the court on the merits of the case.

91. If Mexican law merely imposed an export tax, a U.S. court normally would not entertain a suit to enforce such a foreign tax. If the foreign law made export a theft then, as noted before, a U.S. court might entertain a foreign country's civil suit for the return of the material. Note, however, that *McClain* was a criminal action to enforce a foreign law.

92. 593 F.2d 658 at 665-6. The court was saying, in essence, that the pre-1972 Mexican statutes would not be enforced because under U.S. constitutional standards they were "void for vagueness."

knowledge of a statute, it may be difficult to determine with surety whether the statute merely imposes an export requirement or whether it vests ownership in the state with sufficient clarity to survive translation into terms understandable by and binding upon American citizens. When faced with making a decision concerning the acquisition or retention of an object which may be subject to such a foreign statute, a museum, even after obtaining competent legal advice, may not be able to determine with any degree of assurance whether the statute is enforceable in the United States.[93] The museum is then between Scylla and Charybdis. If it elects to acquire or retain the object and legal action is brought, a court may give full faith and credit to the statute. If it decides to be cautious and refuses the object, or offers to return it, it must hope that the public will understand its actions.[94]

There are other practical considerations. The objects at issue may be of minor significance to the patrimony of the country of origin, or they may be of little monetary value, yet important for a museum's collection. Efforts to establish provenance and to clarify legal and ethical considerations may entail considerable expense. At what point can a museum say it has exercised sufficient caution?

Conviction under the National Stolen Property Act requires a finding of knowledge on the part of the accused. However, if museum professionals are involved, a court or jury might be more disposed to infer knowledge, placing a higher standard of conduct on "experts." Also, there is always the possibility that a civil action could be brought by the country of origin for the return of the object. In a civil action, it normally would not be necessary for the country of origin to establish knowledge of wrongdoing on the part of the museum. That country merely would have to convince the court that it should recognize its claim of title.[95]

Museums would be well-advised to proceed with caution when making

---

93. There can even be problems regarding how a foreign law is established in a U.S. court. Is it a question of law for the judge or a fact question? See Schmertz, "A Modern Procedural Framework for Establishing the Law of a Foreign Country," 28 *The Practical Lawyer* 63 (No. 6 1982).

94. If the object in question is being imported, possibly it risks detention by the U.S. Customs Service. Since the *McClain* decision, Customs has on occasion routinely stopped suspect material and inquired of the country of origin whether it wishes to assert a claim of ownership. Under 19 U.S.C. § 482, Customs may seize material brought into the United States "in any manner contrary to law." On the basis of this authority, Customs takes the position that it can at least detain material in order to allow the country of origin an opportunity to prove title. Whether this policy will be altered in light of the new "Convention on Cultural Property Implementation Act" remains to be seen. See also footnote 97.

95. For a discussion on the use of existing American civil and criminal statutes to deter foreign archaeological plundering, see Nowell, "American Tools to Control the Illegal Movement of Foreign Origin Archaeological Materials: Criminal and Civil Approaches," 6 *Syracuse J. of Int'l Law and Commerce* 77 (1978). With the passage of the "Convention on Cultural Property Implementation Act" (see prior section on UNESCO Convention), some were of the opinion that the National Stolen Property Act should be amended to exclude from its coverage certain imported cultural property. Bills to this effect have been introduced to Congress (see, for example, S. 1559 of the 98th Congress, 1st Session) but as of June 1984, none has passed.

decisions concerning objects possibly subject to control by countries of origin.[96] When in doubt, professional advice should be sought and actions documented. If the museum is later questioned, the existence of a record of thoughtful deliberation and prudent action should weigh heavily in the museum's favor.[97]

d. Treaty of Cooperation Between the United States and Mexico for the Recovery and Return of Stolen Cultural Properties

The late 1960s saw more attention focused on the international movement of art. The UNESCO Convention was in the process of development and increased publicity was being given to the illicit traffic in pre-Columbian artifacts. The climate was right for the United States to take two significant steps. In July 1970, the United States and Mexico signed a treaty to cooperate in the recovery and return of certain cultural properties, and in October of 1972, Congress passed Public Law 92-587 which regulated the importation of monumental-type pre-Columbian artifacts.

The treaty concerns itself with the recovery and return of "archaeological, historical and cultural properties" which belong to either country.[98] Such properties are defined to be:

> (a) art objects and artifacts of the pre-Columbian cultures of the United States of America and the United Mexican States of outstanding importance to the national patrimony, including stelae and architectural features such as relief and wall art;
>
> (b) art objects and religious artifacts of the colonial periods of the United States of America and the United Mexican States of outstanding importance to the national patrimony;
>
> (c) documents from official archives for the period up to 1920 that are of outstanding historical importance;
>
> that are the property of federal, state, or municipal governments or their instrumentalities, including portions or fragments of such objects, artifacts, and archives.

---

96. Consider, also, the case of *Jeanneret v. Vichey*, 541 F. Supp. 80, *rev'd* and remanded 693 F.2d 259 (2d Cir. 1982) where the plaintiff, an art dealer, purchased a Matisse painting from the defendant in New York. Later the plaintiff learned that the picture might have left Italy in violation of Italian export laws. The plaintiff sued for breach of warranty of title and prevailed in the trial court even though the exact nature of the "cloud" on the title was not proven. On appeal, the decision was reversed and the case remanded for a new trial so that more evidence could be submitted on the nature of the "cloud." In the opinion of the appeals court, the plaintiff in order to prevail had a greater burden of proof than that required by the trial court. The case is of interest to museums that may purchase or sell imported art.

97. See "*McClain* Decision," *Aviso* 5 (June 1979); McAlee, "The *McClain* Decision: A New Legal Wrinkle for Museums," *Museum News* 37 (July–Aug. 1979); McAlee, "From the Boston Raphael to Peruvian Pots: Limitations on the Importation of Art into the United States," 85 *Dick. L. Rev.* 565 (1981); Merryman and Elsen, "Hot Art: A Reexamination of the Illegal International Trade in Cultural Objects," 12 *J. of Arts Management and L.* 5 (Fall 1982).

98. "Treaty of Cooperation Between the United States of America and the United Mexican States Providing for the Recovery and Return of Stolen Archeological, Historical and Cultural Properties," July 17, 1970, United States–Mexico; 22 U.S.T. 494.

Under the treaty, both countries undertake to encourage the proper excavation and study of archaeological sites, to deter illicit excavations and the theft of properties covered by the treaty, to encourage the exhibit in both countries of properties covered by the treaty, and to permit legitimate international commerce in art objects. Also, each country agrees to assist in the return from its territory of stolen property covered by the treaty, and, if the requesting party cannot otherwise effect recovery, the Attorney General of the country where the property is located is authorized to institute civil proceedings on behalf of the requesting party.[99] Expenses incident to a return are borne by the requesting party.[100]

e. U.S. Statute Regulating the Importation of Pre-Columbian Monumental or Architectural Sculpture or Murals

Public Law 92-587, which was enacted in October 1972 (19 U.S.C. §§ 2091, *et seq.*), establishes a method of halting the importation into the United States of certain monumental-type pre-Columbian artifacts. The statute empowers the Secretary of the Treasury to promulgate a current list of stone carvings and wall art which are pre-Columbian monumental or architectural sculpture or murals, and objects covered in the list cannot be imported into the United States without proof of a valid export permit from the country of origin. The statute is enforced at U.S. borders by U.S. Customs agents, and contraband objects are subject to forfeiture.

In 1973, the Treasury Department issued regulations detailing the implementation of the statute and defining the term "pre-Columbian monumental or architectural sculpture or mural":[101]

---

99. Apparently the first time Mexico asked for the assistance of the U.S. Attorney General in this regard was in July 1978. At issue were pre-Columbian murals bequeathed to the de Young Museum in San Francisco. See Braun, "Subtle Diplomacy Solves a Custody Case," *Art News* 100 (Summer 1982).

100. On September 15, 1981, the United States and Peru entered into an Executive Agreement (as distinct from a treaty) for the recovery and return of their respective stolen archaeological, historical and cultural properties. The Agreement was patterned after the 1970 United States–Mexico Treaty, but it lacks the provision regarding the authority of the Attorney General to institute civil proceedings on behalf of the requesting party. The Agreement does not address the issue of what may be considered "stolen" in the United States under Peruvian law, but it does provide a means for returning directly to Peru any objects forfeited in the United States. Forfeiture can occur, for example, by the strict application to suspected parties of U.S. Customs laws requiring that all entering merchandise be declared, its fair value stated, and that it comply with United States law (19 U.S.C. §§ 1481, 1484, 1485, 1497–1499, 1592 and 18 U.S.C. §§ 542, 545). Museums should note especially 18 U.S.C. § 545 which makes it a crime knowingly to receive merchandise imported contrary to law, and 19 U.S.C. § 1592 which imposes a penalty on anyone aiding or abetting in the fraudulent or negligent importation of merchandise. See also, *United States v. Pre-Columbian Artifacts, Peru and David Goldfarb,* 81–1320–Civ. (S.D. Fla. 1981). Burnham, "Peru Marks a Milestone in the Antiquities Trade," *Museum News* 7 (Feb. 1983). It is anticipated that the Executive Agreement with Peru will serve as a model for similar negotiations by the United States with other Central American countries.

101. See 19 C.F.R. §§ 12.105, *et seq.* One author questions whether these regulations accurately reflect the statutory language. See, McAlee in "From the Boston Raphael to Peruvian Pots: Limitations on the Importation of Art Into the United States," 85 *Dick. L. Rev.* 565 (1981).

(a) The term "pre-Columbian monumental or architectural sculpture or mural" means any stone carving or wall art listed in paragraph (b) of this section which is the product of a pre-Columbian Indian culture of Bolivia, British Honduras, Columbia, Costa Rica, Dominican Republic, Ecuador, El Salvador, Guatemala, Honduras, Mexico, Panama, Peru, or Venezula.

(b) The term "stone carving or wall art" includes:

(1) Such stone monuments as altars and altar bases, archways, ball court markers, basins, calendars, and calendrical markers, columns, monoliths, obelisks, statues, stelae, sarcophagi, thrones, zoomorphs;

(2) Such architectural structures as aqueducts, ball courts, buildings, bridges, causeways, courts, doorways (including lintels and jambs), forts, observatories, plazas, platforms, facades, reservoirs, retaining walls, roadways, shrines, temples, tombs, walls, walkways, wells;

(3) Architectural masks, decorated capstones, decorative beams of wood, frescoes, friezes, glyphs, graffiti, mosaics, moldings, or any other carving or decoration which has been part of or affixed to any monument or architectural structure including cave paintings or designs;

(4) Any fragment or part of any stone carving or wall art listed in the preceding subparagraphs.

Articles forfeited to the United States are first offered for return to the country of origin, but the country of origin must bear all expenses incident to the return.

f. The American Indian Religious Freedom Act

The American Indian Religious Freedom Act[102] was passed in 1978 and its central portion reads as follows:

[I]t shall be the policy of the United States to protect and preserve for American Indians their inherent right of freedom to believe, express, and exercise the traditional religions of the American Indian, Eskimo, Aleut, and Native Hawaiians, including but not limited to access to sites, use and possession of sacred objects, and the freedom to worship through ceremonials and traditional rites.

The key words for museums are "use and possession of sacred objects."[103] There are numerous museum artifacts which could be classified as Indian "sacred objects" and the question whether the American Indian Religious Freedom Act will affect their disposition is yet unanswered.

The legislative history of the Act makes it clear that the statute is not intended to alter constitutional protections guaranteed to all Americans or to

---

102. Pub. L. 95–341, 92 Stat. 469 (1978).

103. Possibly, the Act could be construed to strengthen Indian control over the excavation of certain Indian burial sites, the use of Indian remains, and other areas of particular interest to anthropologists. See, for example, the Archeological Resources Protection Act of 1979 and its specific reference to Indian concerns, and Rosen, "The Excavation of American Indian Burial Sites: A Problem in Law and Professional Responsibility," 82 *American Anthropologist* 5 (1980).

override existing laws.[104] Its purpose is to prevent those actions which would constitute a violation of the American Indian's First Amendment rights.[105] In order to have such a constitutional violation, the offending activity must be "government action" (action by a governmental entity or that of a private entity that, for the matter at issue, is closely associated with the government), and, as several federal court cases have held, it must inhibit a central or indispensable part of the religion.[106] This test can be a difficult one to apply. What constitutes "government action" is a subject worthy of a text in itself,[107] and the issue of centrality to religion can present serious problems of proof. The Indian concepts of religion are quite different from those of the Judeo-Christian tradition:

> It is deceptive to compare Western religious standards to Indian concepts of sacredness. In most native languages there is no word that translates specifically to "religion" because spiritual thoughts, values, and duties are totally integrated into the social, political, cultural, and artistic aspects of daily life. This unity of thought—the combination of individual and community life in expressing thanks to the Creator—is the Indian "religion." In American Society, there has been a clear separation between church and state that is nearly impossible in traditional Indian Society.[108]

Also, if the requested remedy is the removal from public access, and perhaps destruction in accordance with religious tenets, of unique cultural objects, are there countervailing rights in society?[109]

If the American Indian Religious Freedom Act has not changed the legal mechanisms available to Native Americans who seek the return of culturally

---

104. On the issue of whether special privileges for Indians amount to reverse discrimination, see *Livingston v. Ewing*, 601 F.2d 1110 (10th Cir. 1979) *cert. denied* 444 U.S. 870, and *Morton v. Mancari*, 417 U.S. 535 (1974), 94 S. Ct. 2474, 41 L. Ed. 2d 290.

105. 124 *Cong. Rec.* H6873 (daily ed. July 18, 1978). See also, Statement of President Carter upon signing Pub. L. 95–341, August 11, 1978, which is reprinted in the Appendix to the "American Indian Religious Freedom Act Report" cited in footnote 118 of this chapter; *Crow v. Gullet*, 706 F.2d 856 (8th Cir. 1983), *Hopi Indian Tribe v. Block* (a.k.a. *Wilson v. Block*), 708 F.2d 735 (D.C. Cir. 1983) *cert. denied* _____U.S. _____, 104 S. Ct. 371 and 104 S. Ct. 739 (1984).

106. *Sequoyah v. Tenn. Valley Authority*, 620 F.2d 1159 (6th Cir. 1980). *cert. denied* 449 U.S. 953; *Hopi Indian Tribe v. Block* (a.k.a. *Wilson v. Block*), 708 F.2d 735 (D.C. Cir. 1983) *cert. denied* _____U.S. _____, 104 S. Ct. 371 and 104 S. Ct. 739 (1984).

107. See, for example, *Burton v. Wilmington Parking Authority*, 365 U.S. 715, 81 S. Ct. 856 (1961), and *Greenya v. George Washington University*, 512 F.2d 556, *cert. denied* 423 U.S. 995 (1975); *Rendell-Baker v. Kohn*, 457 U.S. 830, 102 S. Ct. 2764 (1982); Note, "State Action: Theories for Applying Constitutional Restriction to Private Activity," 74 *Colum. L. Rev.* 656 (May 1974); See, however, the National Endowment for the Humanities "Code of Ethics for Projects Relating to Native Americans" which went into effect on October 1, 1981 (NEH Press Release of October 1, 1981). NEH cites the American Indian Religious Freedom Act as a primary authority for issuing the Code. If this implies that the acceptance of an NEH grant involves one in "government action," there is much legal authority to the contrary.

108. Hill "Indians and Museums: A Plea for Cooperation," 4 *Council for Museums Anthropology Newsletter* 22, 23 (No. 2, 1979).

109. See *Crow v. Gullet*, 706 F.2d 856 (8th Cir. 1983), *cert. denied* _____U.S. _____, 102 S. Ct. 413 (1984); *Badoni v. Higginson*, 638 F.2d 172 (10th Cir. 1980).

significant artifacts, it has focused attention on such claims.[110] Whether the Act will assist in resolving these disputes remains to be seen. The problems inherent in a UNESCO Convention-type situation frequently surface with regard to an Indian request for return of property,[111] and, if there is no clear constitutional violation at issue, the parties can find themselves mired in the debates which have plagued implementation of the UNESCO Convention.[112] For example, should full faith and credit be given to Indian law which may hold that title to an object resides in the tribe?[113] Should the traditional defenses of adverse possession and the running of statutes of limitations be available to the possessor of Indian artifacts?[114] Should an innocent holder be left without compensation if an object is returned? Who acts as the official representative of the tribe in negotiating such matters?[115] Can restrictions rightfully be placed on the

---

110. As previously noted, at least one government granting agency (the National Endowment for the Humanities) has promulgated a Code of Ethics for Native American Research. The Code, based on the American Indian Religious Freedom Act, must be followed in all NEH-supported research, publications, films, and other projects about Native Americans (NEH Press Release of October 1, 1981). Also, on November 26, 1982, the National Park Service published in the Federal Register a proposed revised management policy concerning Native American relationships. The proposed policy sets forth N.P.S.'s philosophy in dealings within the area of Native American relationships and covers such specific topics as burial and cemetery sites, archaeological sites, and the acquisition, exhibition and disposition of artifacts (Proposed Revised Native American Relationship Policy, 47 Fed. Reg. 53688 (1982) (to replace Special Directive 78-1)).

111. See preceding section on UNESCO Convention. Indian tribes have taken the position that they are covered by the UNESCO Convention because they are foreign nations. See *Santa Clara Pueblo v. Martinez*, 436 U.S. 49, 56 L. Ed. 2d 106, 98 S. Ct. 1670 (1978). See also *Rice v. Rehner*, 463 U.S. 713, 103 S. Ct. 3291, 77 L. Ed. 2d 961 (1983), *reh'g denied* 104 U.S. 299; *Worcester v. Georgia*, 31 U.S. 515, 8 L. Ed. 483 (1832); *Long v. Chemehuevi Indian Reservation*, 171 Cal. Rptr. 733 (1981); U.S. *cert. denied* 454 U.S. 831; *Johnson v. Chilkat Indian Village*, 457 F. Supp. 384 (Alaska 1978); and F. Cohen, *Handbook of Federal Indian Law* (1945). A recent text by V. Deloria and C. Lytle, *American Indians, American Justice* (1983) gives an overview of Indian systems of government and justice, and discusses the relationship between the Indian and the U.S. government.

112. See, for instance, Nason, "Finders Keepers?" *Museum News* 20 (March 1973); Blair, "American Indians v. American Museums: A Matter of Religious Freedom," *American Indian Journal of the Institute for the Development of Indian Law* (May and June 1979); Childs, "Museums and the American Indian: Legal Aspects of Repatriation," 4 *Council for Museums Anthropology Newsletter* 4 (No. 4 1980).

113. For an early case which raises this question, but does not answer it, see *Onondaga Nation v. Thatcher*, 53 A.D. 561, 65 N.Y.S. 1014 (1900), *aff'd* 169 N.Y. 584. See also *Andrews v. State of New York*, 192 N.Y. Misc. 429, 79 N.Y.S.2d 479 (1948); *New York Indians v. United States*, 40 Ct. of Claims 448 (1905); *Johnson v. Chilkat Indian Village*, 457 F. Supp. 384 (Alaska 1978). In *Santa Clara Pueblo v. Martinez*, 436 U.S. 49, 56 L. Ed. 2d 106 at 113 (1978), the U.S. Supreme Court states:

> Indian tribes are "distinct independent political communities retaining their original natural rights" in matters of local self-government. . . . Although no longer "possessed of the full attributes of sovereignty" they remain a "separate people, with the power of regulating their internal and social relations". . . . They have power to make their own substantive law in internal matters . . . and to enforce that law in their own forums.

114. See Chapter VII, "Unclaimed Loans," for explanation of adverse possession and statutes of limitation.

115. Return to the wrong party may subject the museum to a cause of action by the right claimant. See *Johnson v. Long Island Railroad*, 162 N.Y. Rep. 462, 56 N.E. 992 (1900) which discusses proper tribal representation.

use of an object if it is returned?[116] If the American Indian Religious Freedom Act is looked upon as an impetus to negotiation rather than confrontation, it could prove to be a useful vehicle. In this regard, the "Study of the Principles, Conditions and Means for Restitution or Return of Cultural Property in View of Reconstituting Dispersed Heritages," prepared under the auspices of the International Council of Museums, deserves a reading.[117]

One section of the American Indian Religious Freedom Act required the President to conduct an evaluation of federal policies and procedures which affect Native American religions and to report back to Congress in a year with the results of the study and appropriate recommendations. The President, in turn, directed the Secretary of the Interior to establish a task force comprised of various Federal agencies to prepare such a report. The report was presented to Congress in August 1979.[118] Section III.E. of the Report is entitled "Sacred Objects—Museums," and it is of interest to any museum that houses Indian artifacts.[119]

g. Conclusions

The UNESCO Convention and its implementation, the *McClain* case, and the American Indian Religious Freedom Act highlight the sensitive issues that can arise when a museum holds or seeks to obtain culturally significant property which may be claimed by its country of origin. An awareness of these issues by the museum community, the use of liberal doses of common sense in handling specific demands, and time, should assist in formulating appropriate methods of resolution.[120] Already examples exist of successful accommodations.[121] Museums have returned objects voluntarily and frequently the countries of origin have seen fit to loan the objects back. Exchanges have been negotiated whereby in return for relinquishing culturally significant material, museums have acquired access to other choice objects. Discreet inquiries made to knowledgeable persons in this country and/or in countries of origin before objects were acquired have paved the way for amicable solutions. An indis-

---

116. If title has been established in the claimant, there would appear to be little legal basis for imposing restrictions. If the object is being returned voluntarily, there should be more room for negotiation, but the question of interference with religious practice may arise. For example, some objects under Indian beliefs must be exposed to the elements and allowed to disintegrate. In some discussions these ramifications do not appear to be addressed. See, for instance, Lester, "Deaccessioning and Ethnographic Material Culture: Implications and Considerations," 164 *The Museologist* 12 (Summer 1983).

117. This study is noted in the section of the UNESCO Convention.

118. "American Indian Religious Freedom Act Report," Federal Agencies Task Force, Chairman, Cecil D. Andrus, Secretary of the Interior (August 1979).

119. It should be noted also that there is a federal statute of fairly recent vintage, 18 U.S.C. § 1163, that makes it a crime to steal or knowingly convert property belonging to an Indian Tribal organization. The statute can affect only incidents occurring after August of 1956. See footnote 69.

120. The new Convention on Cultural Property Implementation Act (see Appendix No. C) contains provisions which should alleviate some problems in this area.

121. See, Braun "Subtle Diplomacy Solves a Custody Case," *Art News* 100 (Summer 1982).

pensable ingredient in all such instances, however, has been a willingness to discuss and negotiate.

7. Laws Protecting Plants and Wildlife (and parts thereof)

There is a consistently expanding range of federal, state and foreign laws designed to protect certain types of plants and wildlife and these laws can have an immediate effect on museum collection activity field collecting and the operation of museum shops. The laws regulate the disposition, sale, trade, taking and transportation of such fish, wildlife and plants. Some of the statutes cover live as well as dead specimens, parts of specimens or products made from parts of specimens.[122] Thus, every museum, zoo or museum shop unwittingly could run afoul of these laws unless there is a sustained effort to keep abreast of current developments. This section discusses only the federal protective statutes which are of general interest to the museum community, but it should be noted that the violation of a state or foreign law can amount to a federal violation. A section of the Lacey Act, for example, makes it a federal offense to transport, receive or acquire in interstate or foreign commerce fish or wildlife, or parts thereof, taken in violation of a state or foreign law.[123] Another section of the Act makes it a federal offense to so transport, receive or acquire plants, or parts thereof, in violation of any state law.[124] It is essential, therefore, to be familiar with the laws of the jurisdiction where a specimen is obtained so that necessary precautions can be taken not only to satisfy local requirements but also to avoid subsequent federal entanglements.

There are six federal protective laws that frequently affect museum activity: the Lacey Act, the Endangered Species Act, the Marine Mammal Protection Act of 1972, the Migratory Bird Treaty Act, the Bald Eagle Protection Act, and the Antarctic Conservation Act of 1978.[125] The essential features of each are as follows:

a. *Lacey Act* (16 U.S.C.A. § 3371, *et seq.*)[126]

The Lacey Act was originally passed in 1900, and has been amended several times, most recently in 1981.[127] It prohibits the importation, exportation, transportation, sale, receipt, acquisition or purchase of any fish, wildlife or plant

---

122. Animal and plant parts, for example, can be used in native handicrafts, jewelry, wearing apparel, decorative objects, etc.

123. § 3(a)2A of Pub. L. 97–79, 16 U.S.C.A. § 3372(a)(2)(A).

124. § 3(a)2B of Pub. L. 97–79, 16 U.S.C.A. § 3372(a)(2)(B).

125. This list mentions only the statutes most likely to affect museum activity. Not mentioned, for example, are: U.S. Department of Agriculture and the Public Health Service restrictions on the importation of certain plants and animals, or parts thereof, for health and safety reasons. Information on such regulations can be obtained from U.S. Department of Agriculture (Animal and Plant Health Inspection Service, Hyattsville, Maryland 20782), and the U.S. Public Health Service (Center for Disease Control, Atlanta, Georgia 20222). No attempt is made to cover state or municipal regulation of the movement of wildlife. On the municipal level, regulations usually address live animals that may be dangerous, a health hazard or noisy.

126. Regulations implementing the Act are found in 50 C.F.R. subchapter B.

127. Lacey Act Amendments of 1981, Pub. L. 97–79, 95 Stat. 1073.

taken or possessed in violation of any law, treaty or regulation of the United States or in violation of any Indian tribal law. In addition, the Act has a provision which prohibits the transportation in interstate or foreign commerce of: (1) fish or wildlife taken, possessed, transported or sold in violation of any law or regulation of any state or in violation of any foreign law, or (2) any plant taken, possessed, transported, or sold in violation of any law or regulation of any state. This particular provision is intended to apply to fish, wildlife or plants introduced into any state or foreign country in violation of its laws, as well as to fish, wildlife or plants removed from a state or foreign country in contravention of its laws. The term "fish or wildlife" is defined to include any wild animal, dead or alive, and any part, product, egg or offspring thereof. It covers mammals, birds, reptiles, amphibians, fish, mollusks, crustacea, anthropods, collenterates or other invertebrates. The term "plant" means any wild member of the plant kingdom including roots, seeds or other parts thereof, which is indigenous to any state and which is either (a) listed as protected by the Convention on International Trade in Endangered Species of Wild Fauna and Flora (CITES) or (b) listed pursuant to any state law that provides for the conservation of species threatened with extinction.

In order to provide a mechanism for enforcement of the law, the Secretary of the Interior and the Secretary of Commerce are authorized to promulgate regulations for the marking and labeling of containers or packages containing fish or wildlife. Failure to abide by these regulations amounts to a violation of the Act:

> It is unlawful for any person to import, export, or transport in interstate commerce any container or package containing any fish or wildlife unless the container or package has previously been plainly marked, labelled, or tagged in accordance with the regulations issued pursuant to [this Act].[128]

It should be noted also that certain material can move in or out of the country only through specially designated ports.[129]

Recent amendments to the Lacey Act provide for more efficient forfeiture procedures and now all material moved in violation of the Act is subject to forfeiture without the need to establish civil or criminal liability.[130] The Act carries civil penalities of up to $10,000 per violation, and such a penalty can be imposed if a violation occurs because of lack of "due care." Criminal penalties for intentional violations can go as high as $20,000 and/or five years' imprisonment for each violation. Negligent violators also may incur criminal liability.[131]

---

128. Ibid., § 3(b). See also 50 C.F.R. pt. 14.

129. See 50 C.F.R. pt. 14.

130. See 50 C.F.R. pts. 11 and 12. See 47 Fed. Reg. 56856–61 (1982) for explanation.

131. Cases that interpret the criminal sanctions of the Lacey Act prior to its amendment in 1981 are: *United States v. Molt*, 599 F.2d 1217 (3d Cir. 1979); *United States v. Molt*, 615 F.2d 141 (3d Cir. 1980); *United States v. Jonas Brothers of Seattle, Inc.*, 368 F. Supp. 783 (D. Ala. 1974).

b. Endangered Species Act of 1973, as amended (16 U.S.C. §§ 1531, et seq.)
The Endangered Species Act prohibits the importation and exportation, and the sale, trade, or shipment in interstate and foreign commerce, of listed endangered species, their parts, and products made from them.[132] The Act also makes it illegal to harass, harm, capture or kill any such species within the United States. The prohibitions apply to threatened species as well as to endangered species.

The term "endangered species" means "any species which is in danger of extinction throughout all or a significant portion of its range." The term "threatened species" means "any species which is likely to become an endangered species within the foreseeable future throughout all or a significant portion of its range." The term "species" includes any subspecies of fish or wildlife or plants, and any distinct population segment of any species of vertebrate fish or wildlife which interbreeds when mature.[133] The current list of endangered and threatened species can be found in 50 Code of Federal Regulations, Part 17 (50 C.F.R. 17).

Permits may be granted for scientific or propagational purposes, or in other limited situations. All wildlife must be imported and exported through certain designated ports, but permits may be obtained for entry of fish and wildlife other than endangered species through nondesignated ports of entry for scientific purposes.[134]

The Endangered Species Act also implements the "Convention on International Trade in Endangered Species of Wild Fauna and Flora." The Convention establishes permit requirements for member countries for the importation and exportation of species listed in Appendices to the Convention.[135] These species are not necessarily the same as those listed under the Endangered Species Act. The requirements of the Convention are in addition to, not in lieu of, the requirements of the Endangered Species Act. Penalties under the Endangered Species Act can be substantial, ranging up to a $10,000 fine and one year's imprisonment.[136]

132. The Endangered Species Act Amendments of 1978 (Pub. L. 95–632, 92 Stat. 3751) amended the 1973 Act to permit the importation of certain antique articles (other than scrimshaw) that (1) were made before 1830; (2) are composed in whole or in part of any endangered or threatened species; (3) have not been repaired or modified with any part of any endangered or threatened species on or after Dec. 28, 1973; and (4) are entered at a designated port.

133. 16 U.S.C. § 1532.

134. Designated ports of entry are: New York, N.Y.; Miami, Fla.; Chicago, Ill.; San Francisco, Cal.; Los Angeles, Cal.; New Orleans, La.; Seattle, Wash.; Honolulu, Hawaii; Dallas/Fort Worth, Tex. See 50 C.F.R. pt. 14.

135. See 50 C.F.R. pt. 23.

136. For more comprehensive discussions of the Endangered Species Act, see Campbell, "Facing Extinction?," 24 *Environment* 6 (No. 5 1982); Rosenberg, "Federal Protection of Unique Environmental Interests: Endangered and Threatened Species," 58 *N. C. L. Rev.* 491 (1980).

c. Marine Mammal Protection Act of 1972, as amended (16 U.S.C. §§ 1361, et seq.)[137]

The Marine Mammal Protection Act establishes a moratorium on the taking of marine mammals and bans the importation of such mammals. The term "marine mammal" means "any mammal which (A) is morphologically adapted to the marine environment . . . or (B) primarily inhabits the marine environment, . . . and . . . includes any part of any such marine mammal, including its fur, skin, bones or teeth."[138] Falling within the definition are polar bears, sea lions, porpoises, whales, sea otters, walruses, seals, dugongs and manatees.[139]

An exception is made for Indians, Aleuts or Eskimos who dwell on the coast of the North Pacific Ocean or the Arctic Ocean. They are permitted to hunt for subsistence purposes and in order to obtain material for certain traditional native handicrafts to be sold in interstate commerce. Permits can also be granted for research and display and in certain cases of economic hardship. Penalties for violating the Act can range up to a fine of $20,000 and one year's imprisonment.

d. Migratory Bird Treaty Act (16 U.S.C. §§ 703, et seq.)[140]

The Migratory Bird Treaty Act was originally passed in 1918 and has been amended several times. The Act makes it unlawful to kill, capture, collect, possess, buy, sell, ship, import or export most migratory game and nongame birds, including their parts, nests or eggs, unless an appropriate Federal permit is obtained. Sport hunting of certain migratory game birds is permitted under Federal regulation, and certain commercial activities involving captive-reared birds are allowed under permit.

Violation of the Act can bring penalties of up to $20,000 and six months' imprisonment.

e. Bald Eagle Protection Act (16 U.S.C. §§ 668, et seq.)[141]

The Bald Eagle Protection Act, originally enacted in 1940 and since amended, makes it illegal to take bald or golden eagles, or to sell, purchase, or barter their parts (including feathers), or products made from them. It also prohibits the killing or harassment of any bald or golden eagle. Exceptions may be granted for scientific, exhibition or Indian religious purposes.

Penalties range up to a fine of $10,000 and two years' imprisonment.

f. Antarctic Conservation Act of 1978 (16 U.S.C. § 2401 et seq.)

The purpose of the Antarctic Conservation Act of 1978 is to conserve and protect the native mammals, native birds and native plants of Antarctica, and the

---

137. Regulations implementing the Act are found in 50 C.F.R. pts. 18 and 82. "To improve the operation of the Marine Mammal Protection Act of 1972," Pub. L. 97–58, 95 Stat. 979, signed on October 9, 1981, provides for increased Federal–State cooperation in managing marine mammals in ocean waters from 3 to 200 miles off shore. State regulations may now be adopted and enforced in federally controlled waters.

138. 16 U.S.C. § 1362(5).

139. Some of these are also protected by the Endangered Species Act.

140. Regulations implementing the Act can be found in 50 C.F.R. pts. 10 and 21.

141. Regulations implementing the Act can be found in 50 C.F.R. pt. 22.

environment upon which they depend. The Act makes it unlawful, without permit authority, for any U.S. citizen:

1) to take within Antarctica any native mammal or native bird;
2) to collect any native plant within specially protected areas;
3) to introduce into Antarctica any animal or plant that is not indigenous to Antarctica;
4) to enter any specially protected area or site of special scientific interest; or
5) to discharge or dispose of any pollutant within Antarctica.[142]

The Act makes it unlawful also for a U.S. citizen to receive, possess or ship a mammal, bird or plant improperly taken from Antarctica. While these prohibitions do not apply to any such mammal, bird or plant held in captivity on or before October 28, 1978, the effective date of the statute, the burden of proof is on the possessor to prove that this exception applies.[143]

Except with regard to specially protected species, permits usually can be obtained for the acquisition of native mammals and birds for use as specimens in museums, zoological parks, and similar organizations, and for approved scientific study.

g. Application to Museums

As noted, the above-described statutes can restrict the acquisition,[144] loan and disposal of certain collection objects, and can limit the kinds of merchandise sold in a museum's shop.[145] Because some of these statutes serve also as a basis for enforcing state and foreign laws which may apply to the objects in question, frequently it is necessary to do considerable research before one can act with any degree of certainty. It is recognized, too, that a literal reading of some of the statutes occasionally can place obstacles in the way of scientific investigations or can create seemingly impossible dilemmas for those actually attempting to further the laudatory objectives of the protective legislation.[146] The sensible approach, however, is to meet these statutes in a positive manner, prepared for some inconvenience and with an understanding of the magnitude of the problems the statutes are designed to address. In recent years, there has been a boom in the commercial wildlife trade in live animals, plants and their

---

142. 16 U.S.C. § 2403.

143. Pub. L. 95–541, 92 Stat. 2048 (1978). Regulations implementing the Act can be found in 45 C.F.R. pt. 670.

144. Even being a consignee may draw a museum within the purview of a statute. Acquisition by gift can also be affected. A prospective donor of an object possibly covered by a protective statute should be cautioned to check carefully the status of the object before any transfer is made.

145. The Code of Ethics promulgated by the Museum Store Association states: "The sale of any object or any merchandise which is manufactured from or incorporates parts of any endangered species is a grievous offense against the moral principles upon which museums are established. . . . The Museum Store Association fully supports existing laws and recognizes the need for their rigid enforcement in order to preserve and protect our dwindling. . . natural resources from wanton commercial exploitation." *Museum News* 51 (Jan.–Feb. 1982).

146. See Hart, "The Burden of Regulations," *Museum News* 23 (Jan.–Feb. 1978); "The Law Moves In," *Nature* 1 (March 1977).

products. In 1979, it is estimated that over 420,000 cage birds, 940,000 live reptiles, 200,000 amphibians and 148,000,000 tropical fish were imported into the United States for the pet business alone. In that same year, the United States clothing and leather industry imported approximately 17 million raw and 28 million processed mammal skins and hides, and 3 million raw and 8 million processed reptile skins. Also in 1979, over 2 million feather products, 3.5 million African elephant ivory trinkets, 9 million pounds of crude marine shells, 85 million manufactured shell articles and 760,000 pounds of crude coral were imported into this country.[147] With the commercial stakes so high, smuggling wildlife into the United States also has become a multimillion dollar business, and this, plus the legal trade, are placing unprecedented strains on an ever-growing number of plant and animal species. Although museums are minor consumers, they can play a vital role in encouraging cooperation in furthering regulatory objectives. The first task, however, is to keep informed.[148]

The U.S. Fish and Wildlife Service of the U.S. Department of the Interior has the major burden of implementing the Lacey Act, Endangered Species Act, Marine Mammal Protection Act, Migratory Bird Treaty Act and the Bald Eagle Protection Act. The Service publishes numerous pamphlets on various aspects of these statutes and on procedures for obtaining permits, and it maintains lists of foreign counterparts that can advise on import/export restrictions within their respective countries.[149] The National Science Foundation administers the Antarctic Conservation Act through the Division of Polar Programs.[150] The U.S. Department of Agriculture also can offer assistance if a question pertains to the importation or exportation of terrestrial plants. The Association of Systematic Collections[151] produces a current "Index to the U.S. Federal Wildlife Regulations" and a current "Directory of State Protected Species." If resources permit, the Association will try to answer inquiries from museums pertaining to wildlife

---

147. "The Wildlife Trade," *ASC Newsletter* 70 (Association of Systematics Collections, October 1981). These figures represent legitimate imports. It is estimated that there are numerous illegal takings within U.S. borders, also.

148. Bavin & Levitt, "A Hank of Hair and a Bag of Bones," *Museum News* 39 (May 1974). See also, Williams, *et al.*, *A Guide to the Management of Recent Mammal Collections*, Special Publication No. 4—Carnegie Museum of Natural History (1977); "Field Study and Collecting," a section of American Association of Museums, *Museum Ethics: A Report to the American Association of Museums by its Committee on Ethics* (1978); Zelle, "ICOM Ethics of Acquisition: A Report to the Profession," *Museum News* 31 (April 1972); Neal, *et al.*, "Evolving a Policy Manual," *Museum News* 44 (Jan.–Feb. 1978); Coggins and Pattie, "The Emerging Law of Wildlife II: A Narrative Bibliography of Federal Wildlife Law," 4 *Harv. Envt'l L. Rev.* 164 (1980); *Everything You've Wanted to Know About Federal Wildlife Permits But Were Afraid to Ask*, U.S. Fish and Wildlife Service, Washington, D.C.

149. Information on permits can be obtained from the special agent in charge of the nearest Division of Law Enforcement, U.S. Fish and Wildlife Service. Local offices are maintained in major cities throughout the country. A current listing of local offices can be obtained from the central office of the Division of Law Enforcement, U.S. Fish and Wildlife Service, Department of the Interior, Washington, D.C. 20240. See also 50 C.F.R. pt. 10 for addresses.

150. Permit Office, Division of Polar Programs, National Science Foundation, Washington, D.C. 20550.

151. The Association's mailing address is: c/o Museum of Natural History, University of Kansas, Lawrence, Kansas 66045.

regulations using information within its data management system at Lawrence, Kansas.

For years, most of the wildlife parts, wildlife products, and plants forfeited under the laws described in this section have been stored by the U.S. Fish and Wildlife Service with no formal procedures for disposal. In April 1982, the U.S. Fish and Wildlife Service remedied this situation by publishing rules for the disposal of such wildlife and plants.[152] Methods of disposal, in order of preference, are:

1) return to the wild;
2) use by the U.S. Fish and Wildlife Service or another government agency for official purposes;
3) donation or loan for noncommercial, scientific, educational or public display purposes; or
4) sale.

These procedures afford another source of collection material for museums and they should clarify how a museum might lawfully obtain wildlife and plants inadvertently collected by it in contravention of conservation statutes.

8. Laws Protecting Antiquities and Historic Properties

Cornerstones of existing limited Federal protection for antiquities and historic properties are: (1) the Antiquities Act of 1906, as strengthened by the Archaeological Resources Protection Act of 1979, and (2) the National Historic Preservation Act of 1966, as amended. These statutes can bear directly on the collection activity of a museum and the quality of title of proffered objects.[153]

a. Antiquities Act of 1906 and the Archaeological Resources Protection Act of 1979
The Antiquities Act of 1906[154] was the first federal acknowledgment of a general need to preserve domestic antiquities.[155] The portion of the original statute that

---

152. 47 Fed. Reg. 17521 (April 23, 1982). There had been some uncertainty concerning the authority of the U.S. Fish and Wildlife Service to promulgate its own disposal procedures. The authority was clarified in 1978 with the passage of the Fish and Wildlife Improvement Act of 1978. The relevant portion of the Act, 16 U.S.C. § 742(c), states:

> (c) *Disposal of Abandoned or Forfeited Property.* Notwithstanding any other provision of law, all fish, wildlife, plants, or any other item abandoned or forfeited to the United States under any laws administered by the Secretary of the Interior or the Secretary of Commerce regulating fish, wildlife, or plants, shall be disposed of by either Secretary in such manner as he deems appropriate (including, but not limited to, loan, gift, sale or destruction).

153. There are other federal statutes that encourage "in federal undertakings" the preservation of historic and cultural properties, and, indirectly, these may affect collecting activity. State statutes should also be reviewed on this subject. C. McGimsey, *Public Archaeology* (1972) offers a survey of state statutes and major federal legislation as of 1972. See also, Fowler, "Federal Historic Preservation Law," 12 *Wake Forrest L. Rev.* 31 (1976). For an international view of laws designed to protect cultural heritages see L. Prott and P. O'Keefe, *Law and the Cultural Heritage* (1984). This is a planned five-volume work by two University of Sydney, Australia law professors. As of 1984, only the first volume is in print.

154. 16 U.S.C. §§ 432, *et seq.*

155. Earlier statutes offered protection to certain national historic properties on a case by case basis.

affected museum collection activity most directly read as follows:[156]

> Any person who shall appropriate, excavate, injure, or destroy any
> historic or prehistoric ruin or monument, or any object of antiquity situated
> on lands owned or controlled by the Government of the United States
> without the permission of the Secretary of the Department of the
> Government having jurisdiction over the lands on which said antiquities are
> situated, shall, upon conviction, be fined in a sum of not more than $500.00
> or be imprisoned for a period of not more than ninety days, or shall suffer
> both fine and imprisonment, in the discretion of the court.

In essence, the statute forbade the harming or unauthorized taking of antiquities
which were located on certain government-controlled property. "Examinations,
excavations, and gatherings" on such properties by institutions were allowed
by permit, however, if these activities were carried on for educational purposes
and resulting "gatherings" were permanently preserved in museums.

This portion of the Act proved at best to be a mild deterrent. Initially, there
was scant public support for its enforcement, and, decades later when attention
began to focus on the abuses the Act was designed to correct, its penalty
structure was woefully outdated. A major blow to enforcement came in 1974
with the decision of *United States v. Diaz*,[157] the first reported federal case
interpreting the statute.

Ben Diaz was convicted of taking "objects of antiquity" from government-
controlled property in violation of the Antiquities Act. The objects at issue were
Indian ceremonial masks which had been located on an Apache Reservation
in Arizona. On appeal, Diaz argued that the masks were not "antiquities,"
because they had been made only four or five years previously. In reply the
government contended that age was not necessarily controlling, but that the
socio-religious importance of an object and its use in the culture could place
that object in antiquity status, regardless of age. The conviction was upheld
and Diaz appealed, again questioning the lower court's interpretation of "object
of antiquity." The Court of Appeals reversed the conviction finding the penalty
section of the Antiquities statute unconstitutionally vague because the Act did
not define with sufficient clarity the terms "ruin," "monument" or "object of
antiquity."[158] Considerable doubt then existed concerning the government's
ability to protect any "object of antiquity" on federal lands and there was
confusion as well concerning the title status of objects previously removed in
apparent violation of the Antiquities Act.

---

156. 16 U.S.C. § 433. Other sections of the statute permit the President to designate as national
monuments "historic landmarks, historic and prehistoric structures, and other objects of historic
or scientific interest" located on federal property.

157. 499 F.2d 113 (9th Cir. 1974) reversing 368 F. Supp. 856 (D. Ariz. 1973).

158. See Cooper, "Constitutional Law: Preserving Native American Cultural and Archeological
Artifacts," 4 *Am. Indian L. Rev.* 99 (No. 1 1976). But see *U.S. v. Smyer*, 596 F.2d 939 (10th Cir. 1979),
cert. denied 444 U.S. 843, a later case which held that the Antiquities Act was not unconstitutionally
vague when applied to the facts in that case. See also *U.S. v. Jones*, 607 F.2d 269 (9th Cir. 1979),
cert. denied 444 U.S. 1085, where the government chose not to sue under the Antiquities Act for
alleged improper removal of archaeological material but rather under more general theft and
malicious mischief statutes, 18 U.S.C. §§ 641 and 1361.

The Archaeological Resources Protection Act of 1979[159] was enacted to cure major deficiencies in the Antiquities Act. The scope of protection was clarified and penalty provisions were expanded.[160] Activities prohibited by the 1979 Act are as follows:

(a) No person may excavate, remove, damage, or otherwise alter or deface any archaeological resource located on public lands or Indian lands unless such activity is pursuant to a [duly authorized] permit.

(b) No person may sell, purchase, exchange, transport, receive or offer to sell, purchase, or exchange any archaeological resource if such resource was excavated or removed from public lands or Indian lands in violation of:

(1) the prohibition contained in subsection (a), or

(2) any provision, rule, regulation, ordinance, or permit in effect under any other provisions of Federal law.

(c) No person may sell, purchase, exchange, transport, receive, or offer to sell, purchase, or exchange, in interstate or foreign commerce, any archaeological resources excavated, removed, sold, purchased, exchanged, transported, or received in violation of any provision, rule, regulation, ordinance, or permit in effect under State or local law.[161]

The term "archaeological resources"[162] is defined to mean:

[A]ny material remains of past human life or activities which are of archaeological interest, as determined under uniform regulations promulgated pursuant to this Act. Such regulations containing such determinations shall include, but not be limited to: pottery, basketry, bottles, weapons, weapon projectiles, tools, structures or portions of structures, pit houses, rock paintings, rock carvings, entaglios, graves, human skeletal materials, or any portion or piece of any of the foregoing items. Nonfossilized and fossilized paleontological specimens, or any portion or piece thereof, shall not be considered archaeological resources, under the regulations under this paragraph, unless found in an archaeological context. No item shall be treated as an archaeological resource under regulations under this paragraph unless such item is at least 100 years of age.[163]

Criminal penalties for knowingly violating the 1979 Act are substantial. If the commercial or archaeological value of the material involved is $5,000 or less, penalties can total up to $10,000 and a year imprisonment. Violations involving material which exceed the $5,000 figure carry penalties up to $20,000

159. Pub. L. 96–95, 93 Stat. 721, 16 U.S.C. §§ 470aa–11. Department of Interior regulations implementing the Act were published in 49 Fed. Reg. 1016 (Jan. 6, 1984) and are cited as 43 C.F.R. pt. 7.

160. The Act also stresses increased communication and exchange of information among government authorities, the professional archaeological community, Native Americans, collectors, and the general public in order to further the goal of protecting and conserving domestic archaeological resources (§§ 10, 11, & 13 of Pub. L. 96–95, 93 Stat. 721 (1979).

161. § 6 (a–c) of Pub. L. 96–95, 93 Stat. 721 (1979).

162. This phrase is used instead of the Antiquities Act terminology of "ruin" or "monument" and "object of antiquity."

163. Section 3(1) of Pub. L. 96–95, 93 Stat. 721 (1979). See § 7.3 of 43 C.F.R. for Interior Department regulations that clarify this definition. (Published in 49 Fed. Reg. 1028 (Jan. 6, 1984)).

and a two-year imprisonment. Second time or more violators can be fined up to $100,000 and imprisoned for as many as five years. Under another section of the Act, civil penalties[164] can be assessed against anyone who is in violation of the Act or who does not abide by the terms and conditions of a permit.[165]

It should be noted that the 1979 Act makes several changes in the law which are of specific interest to museums. Under the Antiquities Act, permits for excavations could be obtained only by qualified institutions; under the Archaeological Resources Protection Act, such permits are available to qualified individuals as well as institutions.[166] Under the Antiquities Act, "gatherings" from such excavations had to be preserved in public museums; under the Archaeological Resources Protection Act such gatherings and associated data are to be preserved "by a suitable university, museum, or other scientific or educational institution."[167] Also, careful attention should be given to the fact that the Archaeological Resources Protection Act broadens considerably the enforcement power of the federal government. Not only can unsanctioned activity on federal and Indian land be prosecuted, but the mere holding of property unlawfully removed from such lands constitutes an offense. Thus, if a museum subsequently were to acquire such property, it could be in violation of the Archaeological Resources Protection Act.[168] The Archaeological Resources Protection Act also contains an omnibus provision, similar to that found in the Lacey Act, which makes it a crime to receive or dispose of any archaeological resource in interstate or foreign commerce if the resource was taken in violation of any state or local law.[169] A knowledge of local restrictions is essential, therefore, to judge the provenance of any archaeological resource considered for acquisition.[170]

---

164. In a civil matter it is not necessary, as a rule, to prove that one had knowledge of the law he or she is charged with violating.

165. The Act specifically notes that these penalty provisions do not apply to "any person with respect to the removal of arrowheads located on the surface of the ground" (§ 6g of Pub. L. 96–95, 93 Stat. 721 (1979)). See, however, 43 C.F.R. pt. 7 and 49 Fed. Reg. 1018 (Jan. 6, 1984) for an explanation of how arrowheads can fall within the definition of archaeological resource.

166. See definition of "person," § 3(6) and § 4 of Pub. L. 96–95, 93 Stat. 721 (1979).

167. § 4(b) of Pub. L. 96–95, 93 Stat. 721 (1979).

168. § 6(b) of Pub. L. 96–95, 93 Stat. 721 (1979). § 6(f), however, states that persons who were in lawful possession of archaeological resources prior to the date of the enactment of Pub. L. 96–95 (Oct. 31, 1979) are not deemed in violation of § 6(b)(1). The legislative history of the Act explains that this provision is aimed at protecting individuals and institutions possessing artifacts or collections of archaeological resources which had been obtained legally. See 49 Fed. Reg. 1024 (Jan. 6, 1984) for additional comments on this subject.

169. § 6(c) of Pub. L. 96–95, 93 Stat. 721 (1979).

170. For informatoin on state laws see: National Trust for Historic Preservation, *A Guide to State Programs* (1972); C. McGimsey, *Public Archeology* (1972). (These publications were compiled in 1972 and information should be checked for current status.) See also: Rosen, "The Excavation of American Indian Burial Sites: A Problem in Law and Professional Responsibility," 82 *American Anthropologist* 5 (1980). This article has an extensive listing of state statutes that concern archaeological sites.

b. National Historic Preservation Act of 1966, as amended

The National Historic Preservation Act of 1966 (NHPA), as amended,[171] provides a broad base for federal protection of domestic cultural resources. While earlier legislation had focused on federal acquisition of specific properties of national significance, NHPA recognizes a federal interest in encouraging generally the preservation of culturally significant resources through public and private efforts:[172]

> [I]t is . . . appropriate for the Federal Government to accelerate its historic preservation programs and activities, to give maximum encouragement to agencies and individuals undertaking preservation by private means, and to assist state and local governments and the National Trust for Historic Preservation in the United States to expand and accelerate their historic preservation programs and activities.[173]

Central to the accomplishment of the goals of NHPA is the National Register which is maintained by the Secretary of the Interior.[174] The National Register is a current listing of districts, sites, buildings, structures and objects deemed significant in American history, architecture, archaeology and culture. National Register status, or in some cases even eligibility for such status, triggers NHPA action. The two major forms of NHPA action are: (1) financial assistance to accomplish preservation projects, and (2) mandatory review of federal undertakings that may affect properties of National Register quality.

The majority of NHPA grant money is expended through states that have developed historic preservation programs that meet federal requirements.[175] State programs are designed to promote public and private participation in the preservation of properties of National Register quality. When an approved state program is in place, the state, in turn, may take a significant role in nominating properties for the National Register.

Section 106 of NHPA[176] provides a major source of protection for properties of National Register quality. Under Section 106, no federal agency can approve a federal undertaking or issue a federal license which may affect a district, site,

---

171. 16 U.S.C. §§ 470, *et seq.* (Pub. L. 89–665 of October 15, 1966). The National Historic Preservation Act has been amended several times, the most comprehensive amendments to date are contained in the National Historic Preservation Act Amendments of 1980 (Pub. L. 96–515 of December 12, 1980, 94 Stat. 2987).

172. For a comprehensive discussion of early federal historic preservation legislation, see Fowler, "Federal Historic Preservation Law," 12 *Wake Forest L. Rev.* 31 (1976).

173. 16 U.S.C. § 470(d).

174. The 1979 amendments to NHPA afford statutory recognition also to the National Historic Landmark Program which had evolved from the Historic Sites Act of 1935. The Historic Landmark Program identifies properties that possess exceptional value in commemorating or illustrating the history of the United States. See Fowler, "Federal Historic Preservation Law," 12 *Wake Forest L. Rev.* 31 (1976).

175. 36 C.F.R. pt. 61 sets forth procedures for federal approval of such programs. The 1980 amendments to NHPA also direct that procedures be established whereby qualified local governments can seek approval of their own historic preservation programs. On this see, 49 Fed. Reg. 14890 (April 13, 1984).

176. 15 U.S.C. § 470(f), as amended.

building, structure or object on, or eligible for, the National Register without first considering the effects of its planned action. This consideration must include consultation with the Advisory Council on Historic Preservation, a group created by NHPA to advise and encourage in the furtherance of NHPA goals.[177] In practice, Section 106 touches on a broad range of activities which can be considered federal "undertakings." The term "undertaking" is construed to include:

> . . . any Federal, federally assisted, or federally licensed action, activity or program or the approval, sanction, assistance or support of any non-Federal action, activity or program. Undertakings include new and continuing projects and program activities (or elements of such activities not previously considered under Section 106 . . . that are: (1) directly undertaken by Federal agencies; (2) supported in whole or in part through Federal contracts, grants, subsidies, loans, loan guarantees, or other forms of direct and indirect funding assistance; (3) carried out pursuant to a Federal lease, permit, license, certificate, approval or other form of entitlement or permission; or (4) proposed by a Federal agency for Congressional authorization or appropriation.[178]

Thus, before a federal agency can award a grant or issue a license, types of federal assistance more commonly sought by museums, it must go through a Section 106 proceeding with regard to any culturally significant property that may be affected by its action.[179] A museum, therefore, that seeks such type of federal assistance when acquiring collection objects should be prepared for a possible Section 106 proceeding.[180]

One area of activity that caused some confusion in this regard is of particular interest to museums. Many had contended that before a permit for archaeological research could be granted under the Antiquities Act, there had to be a Section 106 proceeding to consider any possible adverse effects on culturally significant sites. The Archaeological Resources Protection Act of 1979 settled this dilemma by stating specifically that the issuance of such a permit does not require compliance with Section 106.[181]

---

177. 16 U.S.C. §§ 470(i), et seq., as amended.

178. "Procedures for the Protection of Historic and Cultural Properties," 36 C.F.R. § 800.2(c).

179. A federally financed or licensed undertaking is considered to have an effect on a National Register listing (districts, sites, buildings, structures, and objects, including their settings) when any condition of the undertaking causes or may cause any change, beneficial or adverse, in the quality of the historical, architectural, archaeological, or cultural characteristics that qualified the property to meet the criteria of the National Register. See "Procedures for the Protection of Historic and Cultural Properties," 36 C.F.R. § 800.3.

180. At least one government granting agency (the National Endowment for the Humanities) has promulgated a Code of Ethics for Native American Research. The Code, based in part on the National Historic Preservation Act of 1980, must be followed in all NEH–supported research, publications, films and other projects about Native Americans (NEH press release of October 1, 1981).

181. Section 4(i) of Pub. L. 96–95, 93 Stat. 721 (1979).

E. Circumstances That Can Affect the Completeness of Title

1. Restricted Gifts

Every museum is confronted with the problem of the restricted gift whether it concerns an object already given or one presently being offered. If experience is the best teacher, few museums would need to be cautioned about the perils of accepting collection objects with strings attached. Unfortunately, even among those who should know better, the offer of an attractive gift, even though tightly bound, can bring on a sudden case of myopia. While there can be defensible exceptions, a good general rule is to accept only unrestricted gifts.

a. The Offer of Restricted Gifts

A reluctance to accede to the offer of a restricted gift should not be viewed as a sign of ingratitude. Rather, it is an acknowledgment by the museum of the importance of the contribution of the donor and evidence of a desire to make the best use of that contribution. As John Stuart Mill pointed out over one hundred years ago: "No reasonable man, who gave . . . when living, for the benefit of the community, would have desired that his mode of benefiting the community should be adhered to when a better could be found."[182]

Ideally, the offer and acceptance of an object for the collections represent the best contemporary judgments as to the suitability of the object and its potential for museum use, and both donor and curator naturally hope that time will prove them right. But, if time is not so accommodating, who would refuse another opportunity to reevaluate the situation? The acceptance of the restricted gift denies the donor the opportunity for reevaluation. A paragraph from *Central University of Kentucky v. Walters' Executors*[183] states the point rather well:

> The very nature of the enterprise, on the contrary, looked to improvement. It contemplated, by every reasonable implication, that new methods, new people, even new ideas, would be employed, when approved by the governing body of the Institution. A [museum] means, or ought to mean, growth; the elimination of the fake; the fostering of the true. As it is expected to be perpetual in its service, it must conform to the changed condition of each new generation, possessing an elasticity of scope and work commensurate with the changing requirements of the times which it serves. For the past to bind it to unchangeableness would be to prevent growth, applying the treatment to the head that the Chinese do to the feet.

There is an additional consideration. The beneficiaries of the material held by a museum are the members of the general public, and, therefore, the museum must use its best efforts to mold and use its collections for the good of the public. It is difficult to reconcile prudent trusteeship with the acceptance of restrictive conditions that can limit the future usefulness of collection objects or limit the exercise of good judgment by subsequent museum administrators. Consider the following: If a prospective donor approaches a university offering to give a valuable book collection with the condition that those books always

---

182. 1 *Dissertations* 36 (1864).

183. 122 Ky. 65, 83, 90 S.W. 1066 (1906).

be part of the university curriculum, the conflict with academic freedom and the pursuit of excellence would be recognized immediately.[184] That the gift must be declined would be a foregone conclusion. Is there not an analogy to be drawn when a museum is offered a valuable collection of objects on the condition that the collection always be displayed as a unit? If there is no similarity, how can a museum represent itself as an educational organization? Upon reflection, the natural desire to acquire choice objects should be tempered by an awareness of the possible needs of generations to come. A donor given the opportunity to ponder these points often is amenable to suggestions.

It is wise to have a general museum policy that prohibits the acceptance of restricted gifts. It also is wise to have a procedure for considering exceptions to the rule. At a minimum, the procedure should state who has the authority to approve exceptions and what written records are to be maintained which explain each decision. As a safeguard, museum policy should require that a deed of gift for a restricted gift should be counter-signed by a museum official authorized to approve exceptions and that evidence of the restriction should always be on file with the accession records.[185]

Whether it is prudent to accept an object with restrictions depends on the facts. What is the object involved? What is the limitation? A promise never to dispose of an object (unless it is a national treasure) may be unacceptable, but a promise to dispose of the object only to another educational organization may, considering the nature of the item, be within reason. A requirement that an object always be displayed usually is anathema, but one that requires the museum to use its best efforts to have the object on display (whether on its premises or on loan) for two months each year may merit consideration if the item is unusually significant. A promise to return an object to the donor if the museum ever decides to dispose of it can be fraught with problems. If the donor is long since dead when the disposal occurs, is the museum charged with finding his proper heirs? If the museum wishes to exchange the object with another museum, is this a "disposal" within the contemplation of the donor? What is meant by return? An offer to return that must be accepted

---

184. In *In Re Estate of Rood*, 41 Mich. App. 405, 200 N.W.2d 728 (1972), the testator established a fund so that colleges could teach certain political theories. When the validity of the trust purpose was questioned, the court stated: "No legitimate institution of higher learning could permit this kind of control of the classroom from the grave." (at 736). See also *Chapin v. Benwood Foundation, Inc.*, 402 A.2d 1205, *aff'd* 415 A.2d 1068 (Del. 1980). In *Chapin*, at issue was whether trustees of a charitable corporation could bind themselves in advance regarding the filling of vacancies on their board. The court said:

> To commit themselves in advance, perhaps years in advance, to fill a particular board vacancy with a certain named person, regardless of the circumstances that may exist at the time that the vacancy occurs, is not the type of agreement that this Court should enforce, particularly when it is an agreement made between persons who . . . owe a duty to those intended to be benefitted by the charitable corporation they are charged with managing.

Some commentators appear to lose sight of the educational function of a museum. See, for example, Gerstenblith, "The Fiduciary Duties of Museum Trustees," 8 *Art and the Law* 175 (No. 2, 1983).

185. One of the first considerations in deaccessioning is whether there is any restriction that prohibits removal. Record-keeping practices should be such that all relevant information on restrictions is maintained in the master accession file.

within a set time? A right to meet the museum's best price if the object is put up for sale? If it is determined that the museum can accept some restriction of this nature, it is prudent to have the restriction binding only for a set period of time[186] and to spell out when and how the return should be effected. It is difficult to be more specific regarding when a restriction prudently can be accepted, but these procedural suggestions are offered: (1) before each case is considered, review the reasons for the general prohibition against restricted gifts; (2) if the museum is willing to make a concession, consider carefully the wording of the restriction; (3) when in serious doubt about the advisability of accepting a restricted gift, don't accept.

Sometimes, when a donor feels strongly about limiting his largesse, alternative techniques can be discussed. The use of precatory rather than mandatory language is one such technique. If the donor states that it is his wish but not his command that an object be used in a particular way (or language of similar import), this can be interpreted as imposing a moral, but not a legal, obligation on the museum to administer the gift accordingly.[187] In other words, the museum agrees in good faith to follow the restriction, deviating from it only when such a course is dictated by good judgment in light of current circumstances.[188] Such a moral obligation should not be assumed lightly. Before the good faith of the museum is pledged, there should be a careful assessment of the museum's probable ability to carry out the wish within its overall responsibilities to the public.

A somewhat similar technique is to draft a gift document with a mandatory restriction but to state that the restriction can be lifted and an alternative course of action approved by vote of the museum's board of trustees. This procedural requirement may offer the donor needed assurance that changes in his instructions will not be made in an arbitrary manner. Here, again, this type of gift should not be accepted lightly, and it behooves the museum to demonstrate over the years to come that any internal decisions to alter such gifts are made

---

186. For example, the museum might agree to a return if the object is sold within twenty years of its acceptance. The twenty years assures the donor the acceptance is not frivolous and it is a manageable period of time if a return must be made. See also discussion of the Rule Against Perpetuities in Section B(2)(e) of Chapter V.

187. Such gifts are not without peril, as occurred in the de Groot affair at the Metropolitan Museum. Miss de Groot left a sizable collection of art to the Metropolitan with the "wish," stated in her will, that the Metropolitan give to other museums works it did not want. Some years later, thirty-two of the paintings were sold by the Metropolitan. Unfavorable publicity and an investigation by the Attorney General of New York followed. It was the museum's position, affirmed by legal counsel, that Miss de Groot's bequest was absolute and her request not to sell was not binding but merely precatory. After having considered the request and also the benefit to the museum of acquiring finer works that would bear the de Groot name, the trustees of the museum chose to sell. Many questioned the wisdom of the decision, but the Attorney General took no formal action. Shortly thereafter, the trustees of the museum published a deaccession policy that requires considerable internal review of each deaccession proposal. One self-imposed restriction states that no work of art valued at more than $10,000 and held less than twenty-five years will be disposed of if the donor or his heirs objects. "Procedures for Deaccessioning and Disposal of Works of Art," Metropolitan Museum of Art (June 20, 1973).

188. Relief from a legally binding restriction usually can be obtained only with court approval. (See later sections of this chapter.) Such a process can be time consuming and costly. A decision concerning precatory language may be made internally.

only after there has been thoughtful weighing of all relevant facts. Public confidence is at stake.

A situation with less options presents itself when the museum is faced with a restricted bequest.[189] With the donor deceased, there is no one to negotiate with, and the museum must judge the advisability of accepting the bequest as it is written in the will. Executors[190] and heirs cannot change the terms of a will, but they may prove helpful in shedding light on the interpretation of bequests. For example, if a bequest reads that an object "must be exhibited," there are several interpretations that can be given to this language. Must the object always be on exhibit? Need the object be exhibited only in accordance with the museum's internal policy which places the responsibility on a certain individual or group to determine when and where objects are exhibited? Can the object be placed on loan for exhibit? In a situation of this nature, the museum may want to explore with the executor and heirs whether there is mutual agreement regarding the interpretation of the restriction. If all are agreed that the deceased benefactor meant to give the museum flexibility, a written record should be made of this understanding. The museum may then see its way clear to accept the bequest with some confidence that these contemporaneous inquiries may put to rest any later questions which could arise concerning the donor's intent. However, if circumstances are such that the museum prudently cannot accept the restricted bequest, all may not be lost with a refusal. If heirs are put on notice that the museum would welcome the object, but for the restrictions, and the heirs are alternate beneficiaries, they may in time decide to make an unrestricted gift of the object to the museum.

b. Is the Gift Restricted?

A question can arise as to whether expressed conditions actually were imposed when the gift was made. Frequently, a gift comes to a museum after a long series of communications with the donor. Various proposals may have been discussed, and more than one staff or board member may have been involved in the exchanges. A formal deed of gift may or may not have passed.[191] Years later, a misunderstanding may arise as to whether the gift was in fact restricted. How are such matters decided?

Normally, a properly executed deed of gift will control, but if such an instrument does not state expressly that the gift is unrestricted or if, in fact, there is no formal gift instrument, there is a greater opportunity for the donor to place in doubt the completeness of the gift. A case of this nature was before a Maryland court in 1979.[192] The defendant historical society had received some

---

189. See section A of Chapter IV as it relates to the merits of discussing in advance with owners the wording of proposed bequests.

190. Executors, or administrators, are parties appointed by the courts to see that estates are properly administered.

191. A firm practice of requiring formal deeds of gift is highly desirable.

192. *Abrams v. Maryland Historical Society*, Equity No. A-58791 A-513/1979 (Md. Cir. Ct. for Baltimore City, June 20, 1979). See also *Trustees of Dartmouth College v. Quincy*, 357 Mass. 521 at 533–34, 258 N.E.2d 745 (1970).

years prior a valuable desk from a patron, but no deed of gift was executed. When the society decided to sell the desk at auction in order to obtain a much-desired native-made piece for its collections, the heirs of the donor sued claiming it was "understood" between the donor and the museum that his donations would always be retained for display by the society. The society, in turn, argued that there was no clear restriction on the gift. In deciding for the historical society, the court stated: "Gifts cannot be presumed to be conditional. Their conditions must be clearly set forth, as the memories of men do fade with time."

c. Interpretation of Restrictive Language

A related question is the interpretation of an acknowledged restriction. A museum may concede that a gift is restricted, but there may be a difference of opinion as to the actual restraints placed on the use of the gift. Court advice can be sought in a petition for instruction or what is sometimes called a "declaratory judgment."

In the case *In Re Trust of the Samuel Bancroft, Jr., Art Collection*,[193] the Delaware Art Museum petitioned for instructions concerning a valuable collection of English pre-Raphaelite paintings left to the museum by Mr. Bancroft. Under the terms of the gift the museum:

(1) . . . shall not sell, transfer, or in any manner part with the possession of the objects in said collection . . . unless said objects, or any of them, shall so irreparably deteriorate in condition, because of the passage of time, or otherwise, as to substantially impair their value as works of art.

. . .

(6) . . . shall exhibit, or make available to the public said art collection at an appropriate place in the City of Wilmington. It is the desire of the Estate of Samuel Bancroft, Jr., Incorporated, but the [museum] shall not be absolutely bound thereby, that said art collection shall be so exhibited, or made available, at least five days each week during at least 10 months annually.

The Delaware Art Museum wanted to lend the collection to an exhibition traveling throughout the country for two years and it also wanted to accommodate the request of an out-of-state museum for a loan of the collection for a three-month exhibition. The issue was whether the terms of the restriction permitted such loans. A contingent beneficiary, the City of Wilmington, took the position that such loans violated the terms of the gift because in the City's view the works always had to be held and maintained within city limits.

The court construed the gift liberally in deciding for the museum. In its view, the word "possession" does not necessarily mean physical possession, but it can also mean control over the property.[194] Looking at the intent of the donor as expressed in the entire donative instrument, the court concluded that his primary purpose was to assure the ongoing public exhibition of the collec-

---

193. An unreported opinion of the Court of Chancery of the State of Delaware, New Castle County, Civil Action No. 6601 (Oct. 28, 1981).

194. Citing *Restatement (Second) of Trusts* § 175 and *Scott on Trusts* § 175 (3rd ed.).

tion, and thus the proposed loans, with control remaining in the Delaware Art Museum, were consistent with the restrictive language.

In *Morgan Guaranty Trust Co. of New York v. The President and Fellows of Harvard College*,[195] the court was called upon to interpret the phrase "permanent exhibition." The executor of the estate of Scofield Thayer petitioned the court for instructions in connection with the distribution of certain works of art to the Fogg Art Museum and to the Metropolitan Museum of Art. Mr. Thayer's will contained the following provisions:

> I give and bequeath to the Fogg Art Museum of Cambridge, Massachusetts, all drawings of Aubrey Beardsley of which I may die possessed, the gift of which said Museum shall accept for permanent exhibition.

> I give and bequeath to the Metropolitan Museum of Art in the City of New York, all sculpture, paintings, drawings, etchings and other works of plastic or graphic art of which I may die possessed (other than those mentioned [above]) the gift of which said Museum shall accept for permanent exhibition.

At the trial, testimony was introduced with regard to routine museum practices of changing exhibitions and lending works for exhibition. Especially noted were the facts that the Thayer collections contained many works on paper and some erotic art. Under current museum practices, the former, in order to be preserved, were stored most of the time in acid-free boxes; the latter were held available for study upon request. The court's conclusions were as follows:

> "Permanent exhibition" as used in this will means readily accessible to anyone desiring to examine the art objects under such reasonable rules as the museum may make in respect thereto and not that they shall be continuously exposed to the public view on the walls or in cases in the museum.

> The word "exhibition" as used in this will includes display of the art objects in public galleries, study-display areas or in other facilities available to the public upon reasonable request.

> The term "permanent exhibition" does not prohibit loans to other museums as the decedent did not require the permanent exhibition of his collection "solely" or "only" at the Metropolitan and/or Fogg Art Museum.

> The term "permanent exhibition" does not prohibit the removal of art objects for gallery renovation, photography, preservation, cleaning, or scholarly examination.

Frick Collection v. Goldstein[196] also was a petition for instructions regarding a gift to a museum. In this instance, the donor had left his art collection to the public with instructions to his trustees to incorporate an art gallery at his residence to be known as "The Frick Collection." The donor also left a substantial endowment fund, the income from which was to be used:

> for the maintenance, care, protection and support of said gallery of art . . . and any surplus of such income to be expended from time to time as

---

195. No. E 1855 (Mass. Probate Ct. for Worcester, Dec. 20, 1983).

196. 83 N.Y.S.2d 142 (1948), *aff'd* 86 N.Y.S.2d 464.

the director, trustees or managers of said corporation may determine in the purchase of other suitable works of art to form part of such gallery. . . .[197]

Subsequently, a third party offered to the trustees of the museum additional monies and valuable works of art, both to be used to add to the donor's collection. The question in dispute was whether the terms of the gift permitted such outside additions or whether additions could be purchased only with endowment fund income. The *Frick* court also took a liberal approach in interpreting the gift instrument. Lacking clear evidence in the donative instrument of the donor's intention to impose a restriction on the acceptance of outside gifts to augment the collection, the court said it was not inclined to read such a restriction into the terms of the gift. The court refused to give weight to testimony offered by the donor's daughter to the effect that the donor intended a restrictive reading. This same reluctance to read conditions constrictively is reiterated by the Massachusetts Court in *Trustees of Dartmouth College v. Quincy*:[198]

> A donor who brings into existence a charitable institution must recognize that most institutions are likely to change with time, that they will become sterile if they remain static, and that they must be adaptable to new public considerations and unpredictable economic circumstances. For this reason, the intention to make mandatory even detailed restrictions on the conduct of such institutions is not lightly to be inferred.[199]

d. Relief from Restrictions

As a general rule, a legal restriction imposed by a donor (as distinct from a moral restriction founded on precatory language) and accepted by the museum subsequently cannot be waived by the museum of its own accord. If the museum wishes relief, it must seek court approval either in a *cy pres* action or in an action based on the doctrine of equitable deviation.[200]

Cy pres,[201] literally translated to mean "as near as may be," "designates that powers which courts of equity have evolved to correct the lack of wisdom and foresight of the benevolently inclined, permitting them to mold the charitable trust to meet the vicissitudes of a changing world."[202] In a *cy pres* action, it usually is necessary to demonstrate that the donor's purpose is impossible

---

197. Ibid., at 144.

198. 357 Mass. 521 (1970). See also *Gordon v. City of Baltimore*, 258 Md. 682, 267 A.2d 98 (1970) and *Morgan Guaranty Trust Co. of New York v. The President and Fellows of Harvard College*, No. E 1855 (Mass. Probate Ct. for Worcester, Dec. 20, 1983).

199. Ibid., at 533–34. Other cases dealing with interpretation of restrictions are: *Attorney General v. President and Fellows of Harvard College*, 350 Mass. 125, 213 N.E.2d 840 (1966); *President and Fellows of Harvard College v. Attorney General*, 228 Mass. 396, 117 N.E. 903 (1917), *Wilstach Estate*, 1 Pa. D&C2d 197 (1954); *Parkinson v. Murdock*, 183 Kan. 706, 332 P.2d 273 (1958). In *Ranken-Jordan Home v. Drury College*, 449 S.W.2d 161 (Mo. 1970), the court treated as an interpretation what other courts might consider a deviation (see next section). Peculiarities of Missouri law may explain this. See also *Taylor v. Baldwin*, 247 S.W.2d 741 (Mo. 1952).

200. See *O'Hara v. Grand Lodge I. O. of Good Templars*, 213 Cal. 131, 2 P.2d 21 (1931) and *Gordon v. City of Baltimore*, 258 Md. 682, 267 A.2d 98 (1970) regarding the ability of a court to confirm *cy pres*-type action already taken by a charity.

201. *Cy pres* is sometimes called the doctrine of approximation. See, for example, *Britton v. Killian*, 27 Conn. Sup. 483, 245 A.2d 289 (1968).

202. Blackwell, "The Charitable Corporation and the Charitable Trust," 24 *Wash. U.L.Q.* 1 (1938).

or impractical to carry out. An alternate course of action, which conforms to the donor's general charitable intention, then is offered to the court for its approval. *Cy pres* is unique to charitable trusts and charitable corporations, and it was developed in order to prevent the "dead hand" from thwarting common sense and decisions of the living.[203] *The Restatement of Trusts* explains *cy pres* as follows:

> If property is given in trust to be applied to a particular charitable purpose, and it is or becomes impossible or impracticable or illegal to carry out the particular purpose, and if the settlor [creator of the trust] manifested a more general intention to devote the property to charitable purposes, the trust will not fail but the court will direct the application of the property to some charitable purpose which falls within the general purpose of the settlor.[204]

Court interpretations of the *cy pres* doctrine vary and in part this is due to the fact that some states have statutes which specifically address situations of this nature,[205] or there may be case law in a particular state which limits the application of the doctrine to narrow circumstances.[206] As a rule, however, as long as the donor has evidenced a general charitable intention when making the original gift, a court may approve an alternate purpose which appears to be in accord with what the settlor would have wished had he had knowledge of present-day circumstances.[207]

The doctrine of equitable deviation differs from *cy pres* as follows. *Cy pres* is invoked when the purpose of a charitable trust cannot be carried out. If only a method of accomplishing the purpose is at issue, the doctrine of equitable

---

203. A much quoted treatise on the subject is Scott's "Education and the Dead Hand," 34 *Harv. L. Rev.* 1 (Nov. 1920). As Scott explains on the first page of the article:

> If a testator chooses to leave his property to definite beneficiaries, he cannot control its disposition for more than a generation or two [i.e., the Rule Against Perpetuities]. But a trust for charitable purposes may last forever. By the creation of such a trust, a specific property or the beneficial interest in specific property or in a shifting fund or mass may be rendered forever inalienable, may be forever "taken out of commerce," may be devoted in perpetuity to the accomplishment of the purposes for which the trust was created. One who happens to acquire property during the short span of his lifetime may by giving it for charitable purposes control its disposition throughout the ages.

204. *Restatement (Second) of Trusts* § 399.

205. See, for example, § 8–1.1(c) of the New York Estates, Powers and Trust Law.

206. These reasons frequently explain why the lines between *cy pres* actions, actions for equitable deviation, and petitions for declaratory judgments tend at times to blur. When issues arise concerning restrictive gift language applicable state law should be reviewed carefully.

207. In some jurisdictions, courts are reluctant to apply *cy pres* if there is an alternative charitable purpose specified in the donative instrument. See, for example, *Hartford National Bank and Trust Co. v. Oak Bluffs Baptist Church*, 116 Conn. 347, 164 A. 910 (1933); *Burr v. Brooks*, 83 Ill. 2d 488, 415 N.E.2d 231 (1981). In DiClerico, "*Cy Pres*: A Proposal for Change," 47 *B.U.L. Rev.* 153, the author discusses the weight to be given the intent of the testator v. current public need and policy. Another consideration is the Rule Against Perpetuities. If the gift over (the next party to benefit if the first gift fails) is to an individual, the Rule Against Perpetuities may prevent it from vesting. This is not necessarily so if the gift over is to another charity. See *Restatement (Second) of Property*, Donative Transfers, § 1.6, part of which is quoted in the section "Notification to Donor of Deaccession" in Chapter V. But see *Smyth v. Anderson* 238 Ga. 343, 232 S.E.2d 835 (1977).

deviation is invoked. In other words, in an action for equitable deviation, there is no request to change the purpose of the trust, only a request for permission to alter the prescribed method of accomplishing that purpose.[208] There is no need to demonstrate impossibility or impracticability of purpose, only that the prescribed method is thwarting accomplishment of the trust purpose. Defining the difference in the two doctrines is easier than applying the correct doctrine to a particular situation. For instance, a donor leaves his art collection to a museum to establish a room in his honor with all his paintings to be kept together and to be displayed as a unit. In time, the museum finds it burdensome to display everything together and seeks relief from the court. Is this properly a *cy pres* action or one for equitable deviation? If the purpose of the donor is perceived to be the maintenance of an example of a typical turn-of-the-century art collection, a *cy pres* petition would seem to be in order. If, however, the donor's purpose is interpreted to be the making of his art available to the public, all that is at issue in court is the method of accomplishing this purpose, and equitable deviation is the proper vehicle.[209] Courts have not lacked ingenuity in fashioning arguments which support the form of action which will achieve the result deemed to be best for the public.[210]

An example of such ingenuity is found in *Cleveland Museum of Art v. O'Neill*.[211] In that case, the museum petitioned the court to apply the doctrine of deviation so that certain trust funds, restricted by their donors for the purchase of art, could be used for building construction costs:

> In passing upon a request such as that prayed for . . . the Court has two general duties: to determine (1) what was the basic purpose of the settlors in establishing the respective trusts, and (2) what would the settlors now direct in view of the changed conditions which have resulted with the passing of time.[212]

The court determined that the settlors had a broad purpose—to help create and maintain an art museum that would endure indefinitely and that when the gifts were made, the need was for art for the collections. Hence, the direction

---

208. *Restatement (Second) of Trusts* § 381.

209. In *Sendak v. Trustees of Purdue University*, 279 N.E.2d 840 (Indiana 1972) and the *Toledo Museum of Art v. Bissell*, Case No. 83-2229 (Ohio C.P. Ct. of Lucas County, 1984), the courts were faced with donative language which presented similar problems of interpretation. See also *Burr v. Brooks*, 83 Ill. 2d 488, 416 N.E.2d 231 (1981).

210. See *Trustees of Dartmouth College v. Quincy*, 357 Mass. 521, 258 N.E.2d 745 (1970); *Ranken-Jordon Home v. Drury College*, 449 S.W.2d 161 (Mo. 1970); *Britton v. Killian*, 27 Conn. Sup. 483, 245 A.2d 289 (1968); "Cy Pres and Deviation: Current Trends in Application," 8 *Real Property, Probate and Trust Journal* 391 (Fall 1973).

211. 57 Ohio Op. 250, 129 N.E.2d 669 (1955). See, also, *Harris v. Attorney General*, 31 Conn. Sup. 93, 324 A.2d 279 (1974); *Moore v. City and County of Denver*, 292 P.2d 986 (Colorado 1956); *Hinkley Home Corp. v. Bracken*, 21 Conn. Sup. 222, 152 A.2d 325 (1959); *In Re Stuart's Estate*, 183 N.Y. Misc. 20, 46 N.Y.S.2d 911 (1944); *City Bank Farmers Trust Co. v. Arnold*, 283 N.Y. 184, 27 N.E.2d 984 (1940); *Olds v. Rollins College*, 173 F.2d 639 (N.C. 1949).

212. *Cleveland Museum of Art v. O'Neill*, 57 Ohio Op. 250, 129 N.E.2d 669 at 670 (1955).

that funds were to be used to purchase art was viewed as merely a means to achieve the desired end. Under the doctrine of deviation, this means could be changed to accommodate current circumstances. Applying this reasoning, the court saw its way clear to approve the use of the funds for building construction even though one of the funds at issue provided that failure to abide by its terms voided the fund. The court ruled specifically that with regard to that particular fund, the exercise of the power of deviation did not constitute a failure to abide by the terms of the trust.

As illustrated in the *Cleveland Museum* case, the mere fact that a donor has stated that property can be used "only" for a certain purpose or that it is given "upon condition" that it be applied to a certain purpose does not necessarily prevent the application of the doctrines of equitable deviation or *cy pres*.[213] Courts tend to favor the perpetuation of charities. For instance, in *In Re Stuart's Estate*,[214] the New York Public Library petitioned the court for relief from various restrictions imposed on a gift. Under the terms of the donor's will, books, manuscripts, paintings and other works of art were left to the Lenox library in 1891. These articles were to be housed separately from other library holdings and were to be exhibited to the public at all reasonable times, but never "on the Lord's Day." The will further stated that the library had ninety days in which to accept or refuse the gift, and if it did not accept, the gift would pass to residuary legatees. The library accepted. Years later, the Lenox library merged and became part of the New York Public Library. By 1944, because of changed conditions, the New York Public Library found the restrictions burdensome and it proposed to the Court that permission be granted under *cy pres* to transfer the material to the New York Historical Society with the provision that it could be displayed on Sunday, the day when many people choose to visit museums. At issue was whether the gift would be forfeited upon failure to abide by the conditions and, thus, it would have to pass to the residuary legatees. The court ruled that under the terms of the will, the residuary heirs could receive the gift only if the library refused to accept it within the stated ninety-day period. When the library accepted, any interest held by the heirs terminated. The "conditions subsequent, those regarding housing and display, were for the benefit of the public and would be enforced subject to the usual rules applicable

---

213. Comment (e) of § 351 of the *Restatement (Second) of Trusts* states:

> A charitable trust may be created although the settlor uses words of condition. If the owner of property transfers it *inter vivos* or by will "upon condition" that it be applied for a charitable purpose, a charitable trust is created if the transferor manifested an intention that the transferee should be subject to a duty so to apply it, rather than that he should be divested of his interest if he should fail so to apply it. In the absence of other evidence, a transfer of property "upon condition" that it be applied for a charitable purpose indicates an intention to create a charitable trust rather than an intention to make a transfer "upon condition."

See, however, footnote 204 regarding application of *cy pres* if there is an alternate charitable donee.

214. 183 N.Y. Misc. 20, 46 N.Y.S.2d 911 (1944).

to charities."[215] The court found a general charitable intention on the part of the donor and, applying *cy pres*, approved the library's proposed disposition of the material.[216]

A situation with a similar twist was presented in *Amato v. Metropolitan Museum of Art*,[217] a case previously noted.[218] Here, the daughter of a donor sued the museum in 1975 for the return of two paintings bequeathed in 1959. Under the donor's will, the paintings were to be displayed as gifts of the donor in memory of her parents. The museum had six months in which to accept the gift with the stipulated conditions, otherwise the paintings were to go to the daughter. The gift was accepted by the museum. Over the years, the paintings were placed on loan for display to other cultural institutions, properly labeled, but they were not displayed at the Metropolitan. The plaintiff was on notice of this practice. The court rejected the plaintiff's request for return on two grounds; one being that acceptance by the museum of the gift under the terms specified eliminated the possibility that title to the paintings might vest in the daughter at a later date. Here, as in *In Re Stuart*, once the gift was accepted by the charity, the heirs lost standing to sue. The conditions imposed were construed to be for the benefit of the public, and, if any enforcement was necessary, this was the prerogative of the Attorney General.

2. Copyright Considerations
a. What Is Copyright?
Copyright is the legal recognition of special property rights which a creator may have in his work.[219] The rights are distinct from the right to possess the work. For the nonlawyer it may be easier to visualize copyright as a bundle of rights that is carried on the back of certain objects. The object may be acquired with or without the bundle, or with one or some of the rights in the bundle. When a museum obtains an object that may carry such a bundle, it is important for the museum to know if the ability to use any or all of the rights in that bundle pass to it with the object itself.

Copyright protection exists for original works of authorship that are fixed

---

215. In other words, the Attorney General could instigate action to force the museum to comply or relief could be sought in a *cy pres* action or in one for equitable deviation. An additional reason for holding void such a gift over to individuals would be the Rule against Perpetuities. See § 1.6 of *Restatement (Second) of Property*, Donative Transfers.

216. See also *Matter of the Application of the New York Historical Society*, Index No. 17162–65 (N.Y. Sup. C., County of N.Y., June 20, 1967). In that case, the Society sought to alter the terms under which it held the Bryan Collection of paintings. Also of interest is *Abel v. Girard Trust Co.*, 365 Pa. 34, 73 A.2d 682 (1950); *In Re Estate of Rood*, 41 Mich. App. 405, 200 N.E.2d 728 (1972); *Gray v. Harriet Lane Home*, 64 A.2d 102 (Md. 1949) and *The Toledo Museum of Art v. Bissell*, Case No. 83–2229 (Ohio C. P. Ct. of Lucas County, 1984).

217. Index No. 15122/79 (N.Y. Sup. C. N.Y. County, Special Term, Sept. 1979).

218. See Chapter II, "Museums Are Accountable to Whom?"

219. Art. 1, § 8 Cl. 8 of the U.S. Constitution empowers Congress to enact legislation "to promote the progress of science and useful arts, by securing for limited times to authors and inventors the exclusive right to their respective writings and discoveries."

in a tangible medium of expression.[220] Copyright protects the tangible expression of the idea, not the idea itself. In other words, the idea to create a statue called "Supermom" is not eligible for copyright, but once the statue has been created, the owner of the copyright can control certain specific uses of the statue. Examples of types of works that may be protected by copyright are: literary works, musical and dramatic compositions, paintings, drawings, sculpture, photographs, motion pictures, stage presentations, television programs, and cartographic works. Artistic craftsmanship such as jewelry, toys, fabric designs, and even the embellishments of furniture and architecture may be protected but only to the extent that they are not utilitarian.

The owner of a copyright controls five distinct uses of the work in question. These are:

(1) the right of reproduction (the right to make copies of the work);

(2) the right of adaptation (the right to produce derivative works based on the work itself);

(3) the right of distribution (the right to distribute copies of the work for sale, rental, loan, and so on);

(4) if the work is of such nature, the right of performance (the right to perform the work publicly); and

(5) if the work is of such nature, the right of display (right to display the work publicly).[221]

If a museum acquires a work that could have copyright protection without clear evidence of its ability or inability to exercise the enumerated rights, there is a serious potential for copyright infringement.[222] In determining the status of rights to a particular object, much depends not only on the instrument conveying the right to possess the article, but also on the time when the object was conveyed. The time element is especially important because of a revision of the federal copyright law that became effective on January 1, 1978.[223]

b. Effect of the New Copyright Law on Museum Acquisitions

Prior to January 1, 1978, if a museum acquired an object subject to copyright and there was no mention of copyright interests in the conveyance, there was a presumption that the museum obtained any existing "bundle of copyrights"

---

220. 17 U.S.C. § 102. See *Original Appalachian Artworks, Inc. v. The Toy Loft*, 684 F.2d 821 (11th Cir. 1982); *Gracen v. Bradford Exchange*, 698 F.2d 300 (7th Cir. 1983); Ward, "The 'For Hire' Rule in Copyright and Related Laws," *Course of Study Materials, Legal Problems of Museum Administration* (ALI/ABA 1984). On the issue of whether copyright protection exists for oral histories, see Neuenschwander, "Oral History and Copyright: an Uncertain Relationship," 10 *J.C. & U.L.* (No. 2 1983–4), reprinted in *Course of Study Materials, Legal Problems of Museum Administration* 527 (ALI/ABA 1984).

221. 17 U.S.C. § 106.

222. Possibly there might be personal liability as well as institutional liability. In January 1983 a group of publishers filed suit against New York University and nine of its faculty members for alleged copyright infringement. While the case was settled out of court, it brought home the fact that an employee of an educational organization could find himself personally charged in such a suit.

223. Pub. L. 94-553 which now appears as Title 17 of the United States Code.

along with the right to possess the object itself.[224] This presumption frequently is referred to as the "Pushman presumption," because it was enunciated in *Pushman v. New York Graphic Society, Inc.*[225] Under the new copyright law, this presumption is reversed. As of January 1, 1978, if the conveyance to the museum does not expressly note that existing copyright interests pass, the museum does not acquire the ability to exercise such rights.[226]

Prior to January 1, 1978, if the creator of a work distributed the work without notice of a claim of copyright (the familiar ©),[227] copyright was deemed to be waived. Thus, acquisition by a museum of a work created before January 1, 1978, which lacks a copyright notice, invariably suggests that the work is in the public domain. The new law, however, emphasizes that copyright exists at the instant of creation, and neither registration with the U.S. Copyright Office nor use of the copyright notice is essential to secure copyright. This "automatic copyright" can be divested by "publication" without copyright notice, but reestablished under certain circumstances if the omission of notice is inadvertent.[228] Public display of the work and/or a gift or sale of the work itself does not necessarily constitute publication. The Copyright Act now defines publication to mean:

> The distribution of copies or phonorecords of a work to the public by sale or other transfer of ownership, or by rental, lease, or lending. The offering to

---

224. But note that since September 1, 1966, New York had a different rule governing the sale of works of fine art. Section 224 of Article 12-E of the New York General Business Law reads:

> Whenever a work of fine art is sold or otherwise transferred by or on behalf of the artist who created it, or his heirs or personal representatives, the right of reproduction thereof is reserved to the grantor until it passes into the public domain by act or operation of law unless such right is sooner expressly transferred by an instrument, note or memorandum in writing signed by the owner of the rights conveyed or his duly authorized agent. Nothing herein contained, however, shall be contrued to prohibit the fair use of such work of art.

The term "fine art" was defined to mean "a painting, sculpture, drawing or work of graphic art," and the term artist meant "the creator of a work of fine art" (§ 223). Note also that § 301(a) of the new federal copyright law preempts all common law and states' rights that are equivalent to copyright protection. Therefore, as of January 1, 1978, reproduction rights in the sale of works of fine art in New York are governed by the federal act, but the New York special statute still is applicable to works sold in New York after September 1, 1966, but not created after January 1, 1978.

225. 287 N.Y. 302, 39 N.E.2d 249 (1942).

226. 17 U.S.C. § 202 reads as follows:

> Ownership of a copyright or of any of the exclusive rights under a copyright, is distinct from ownership of any material object in which the work is embodied. Transfer of ownership of any material object, including the copy or phonorecord in which the work is first fixed, does not of itself convey any rights in the copyrighted work embodied in the object; nor, in the absence of an agreement, does transfer of ownership of a copyright or of any exclusive rights under a copyright convey property rights in any material object.

227. The copyright notice can be © or the word "copyright" or the abbreviation "copr." with the year of first publication of the work and the name of the copyright owner. See 17 U.S.C. § 401.

228. 17 U.S.C. §§ 405, 406. See *Innovative Concepts in Entertainment, Inc. v. Entertainment Enterprises, Ltd.*, 576 F. Supp. 457 (E.D.N.Y. 1983) and *Original Appalachian Artworks v. The Toy Loft, Inc.*, 684 F.2d 821 (11th Cir. 1982).

distribute copies or phonorecords to a group of persons for purposes of further distribution, public performance, or public display, constitutes publication. A public performance or display of a work does not of itself constitute publication.[229]

It is possible, therefore, that a museum can acquire a work created on or after January 1, 1978, that lacks any copyright notice and yet find that the work is subject to copyright interests held by another. In other words, the mere lack of a copyright notice on such works is no assurance that copyright has been waived, and a museum acquiring such a work without an expressed conveyance of copyright interests acts at its peril if it does more than merely display the work or exercises other than a traditional "fair use."[230]

In determining the status of acquired material, two additional points should be borne in mind. If a work is prepared by an employee in the course of his employment, copyright is presumed to vest in the employer.[231] What constitutes "work in the course of employment" however is not always crystal clear,[232] and, if there is any doubt, it is preferable to have a written agreement between the creator and the employer that spells out their understanding.[233] The written agreement can alter the presumption afforded by statute. If a work is commissioned in writing with the expressed use of the term "work made for hire," the person or organization commissioning the work is deemed to be the author and thus owns all copyright interests. However, it should be noted that 17 U.S.C. § 101 which defines "work made for hire" lists within this definition only certain types of works "specially ordered or commissioned."[234]

c. Copyright Considerations When Acquiring Certain Objects

As explained in the preceding section, the new federal copyright statute has created situations that require a museum to pay special attention to possible copyright issues when acquiring objects for its collections. In addition, there is a greater sophistication about copyright matters among those who deal in the

---

229. 17 U.S.C. § 101. See Weissman, "Can an Artist's Copyright Be Jeopardized? An Analysis of Current Marketing Practices In the Sale of Art Works," 6 *Art and the Law* 66 (1981).

230. See later section that describes "fair use."

231. 17 U.S.C. § 201(b) and 17 U.S.C. § 101 (for definition of "work made for hire").

232. See *Public Affairs Associates, Inc. v. Rickover*, 284 F.2d 262 (D.C. 1960); *Williams v. Weisser*, 273 Cal. 2d 726, 78 Cal. Rep. 542 (1969); Knoll and Drapiewski, "Knowing Your Copyrights," *Museum News* 49 (March–April 1977). In *Town of Clarkstown v. Reeder*, 566 F. Supp. 137 (S.D.N.Y. 1983), it was held that the copyright on a manual prepared by a volunteer with a town youth project belonged to the town under the "work for hire" doctrine.

233. This matter frequently arises for a museum regarding writings done or photographs taken by museum employees.

234. In this regard, 17 U.S.C. § 101 with its definition of "work made for hire" and 17 U.S.C. § 201 regarding ownership of copyright may have to be reviewed with expert assistance to determine copyright status of a particular commissioned work. See in *Course of Study Materials, Legal Problems of Museum Administration* (ALI/ABA 1984): Wolff, "Copyright Ownership: A Consideration of Works Made for Hire" and Ward, "The 'For Hire' Rule under the Copyright and Related Laws." On the question whether an "unwritten understanding" can alter the work for hire presumption, see *Arthur Retlaw and Associates, Inc. v. Travenol Labs, Inc.*, 582 F. Supp. 1010 (N.D. Ill. 1984).

art world because of the new law. A museum can no longer presume that it has certain rights. It must take reasonable steps to investigate and document.

When a museum now acquires an object that appears to be protected by copyright, it is important to establish, if possible, who holds copyright and to clarify whether any of the existing copyright interests pass to the museum with the object.[235] If the work offered was created after January 1, 1978, and it is being offered by the creator, it usually will be the case that copyright resides in the creator.[236] It is not controlling whether a copyright notice is affixed to the work because, as previously mentioned, inadvertent omission can be remedied. If the work was created before January 1, 1978, and it bears the copyright notice, inquiry should be made to ascertain whether copyright has expired.[237] If copyright still exists, or appears to exist, attempts should be made to determine who holds the copyright interests. Even if the museum is not currently interested in acquiring such interests, copyright status may become important at a later date, especially if the museum wishes to transfer the object. If the object was created before January 1, 1978, and it bears no copyright notice, it often is the case that copyright has been waived and the object is in the public domain.[238]

If copyright interests in the object exist, or appear to exist, and the object is conveyed to the museum after January 1, 1978, without reference to copyright interests, it is likely that the museum has acquired no copyright interests. As a precaution, lack of such interests should be noted on the accession records along with any information on the actual copyright holder. If copyright interests exist and the museum wishes to obtain them, or the right to exercise some or all, this must be negotiated with the copyright holder and expressly noted on the conveying instrument.[239] Such a transfer of rights is commonly called a license and the license may be exclusive or nonexclusive. The exclusive license[240]

---

235. Photographs can present even more complex problems. For example, if the photograph is a picture of an original work one can hold the copyright in the photograph, but, in using the photograph, can infringe the copyright of the creator of the original work. In dealing with photographs, the subject of the photograph must also be considered. Consider also the question of whether the photograph itself is an "original work" and hence subject to protection. On this point refer back to footnote 217.

236. Note, however, exception regarding "work made for hire," i.e., a commissioned work or work of an employee.

237. See section on "Duration of Copyright" which follows.

238. See discussion in prior section on publication of work without copyright notice before January 1, 1978.

239. 17 U.S.C. § 204(a) states:

> A transfer of copyright ownership, other than by operation of law, is not valid unless an instrument of conveyance, or a note or memorandum of the transfer, is in writing and signed by the owner of the rights conveyed or such owner's duly authorized agent.

In *Eden Toy, Inc. v. Florelee Undergarment Co., Inc.* 697 F.2d 27 (2d Cir. 1982), the U.S. Court of Appeals for the Second Circuit held that a copyright holder's later execution of a written statement confirming the terms of an informal understanding fulfills § 204(a) requirements.

240. An exclusive license can also be called a "transfer of copyright ownership," 17 U.S.C. § 101.

gives the museum the power to prevent others from exercising the right (that is, the museum can sue for infringement if there is an improper use). The nonexclusive license permits the museum to exercise the right, but the copyright holder reserves the right to grant others a similar nonexclusive right. Licenses also may be limited for use in certain geographic areas and/or may be limited as to duration.[241]

It is prudent to have a method for focusing staff attention on copyright matters before collection acquisitions are consummated. This can be done by including the copyright issue in the museum's collection management policy and requiring that informed decisions be made by staff prior to acquisitions. Deed of gift and sale contract forms, and/or instructions on their use, should call staff attention to the fact that express language concerning transfer of copyright interests must be used if such interests are desired.[242] If a museum has occasion to commission works, and/or hire photographers, expert advice may be needed to assure clear resolution of copyright issues before contracts are signed.

d. Should a Museum Strive to Acquire Copyright Interests?
There is considerable debate as to whether a museum always should strive to secure copyright interests in objects acquired for its collections. There is also debate as to the scope of the museum's power over an object that it owns when copyright interests reside in another.

With regard to the second issue, what can a museum do with an object it owns when someone else holds the copyright in the object? As previously mentioned, a copyright holder has the right to reproduce the work, the right to adapt it, the right to distribute copies of the work, the right of performance and the right to display the work publicly. Under the fair use doctrine, it would seem that copying or photographing a work for internal registrational or archival purposes would be permissible.[243] Fair use also permits copying for such purposes as criticism, comment, news reporting, teaching, scholarship or research. In determining whether a particular use is fair, the copyright statute lists these criteria for consideration:

(1) the purpose and character of the use, including whether such use is of a commercial nature or is for nonprofit educational purposes;

(2) the nature of the copyrighted work;

(3) the amount and substantiality of the portion used in relation to the copyrighted work as a whole; and

---

241. While the transferror may establish a definite termination date for a license, under the federal copyright law all licenses, other than those passing by will, may be terminated at the option of the owner or his heirs during a five-year period which commences, as a general rule, thirty-five years from the date of the execution of the license. Termination is not automatic, however, and if not enforced and the license does not specify otherwise, the license will last for the duration of the copyright. See 17 U.S.C. § 203 for more details. Just how this provision may affect museums is unclear at this time.

242. In the section entitled "Acquisition Procedures" in Chapter IV, note sample Deeds of Gifts.

243. See 17 U.S.C. § 107, 17 U.S.C. § 108(b).

(4) the effect of the use upon the potential market for or value of the copyrighted work.[244]

Any reproduction by the museum which falls outside the generally accepted interpretation of "fair use" would be in a grey area with possible liability for infringement. In such cases, it is safer to contact the holder of the copyright and secure written permission to exercise the desired uses.[245]

With regard to the right to display, the copyright statute specifically provides that the owner of an object, or any person authorized by such owner, can, without the authority of the copyright owner, display the object publicly.[246] Thus, even without copyright, it is generally conceded that a museum, if it owns the object, can display it and lend it for display elsewhere.[247]

There is no simple answer to the question whether a museum should always seek to acquire existing copyright interests in objects acquired for its collections. There are many variables, such as:

- the availability of such interests (photographers, for example, frequently do not want to part with copyright interests);
- the cost of acquiring the interests; and
- the perceived need for such interests.

In situations where the transferor is willing to convey copyright interest at little or no cost, there is no problem, and a transfer of copyright (that is, exclusive license) can be made a part of the conveyance.[248] However, if it is a matter for

---

244. 17 U.S.C. § 107. For a discussion of copyright v. the first amendment's protection of a free flow of ideas, see Goldwag, "Copyright Infringement and the First Amendment," 5 *Art and the Law* 80 (Issue 4 1980).

245. As previously noted, in 1983 New York University and some of its faculty were sued by a group of publishers for alleged copyright infringement growing out of distribution of certain course materials without the permission of the copyright owners. The publishers settled their suit against the University and faculty when the university issued a policy statement and guidelines to be followed by faculty in determining whether prior permission of copyright owners should be sought before reproduction. (See settlement agreement reached in *Addison-Wesley Publishing Co. v. New York University*, as published in *Course of of Study Materials, Legal Problems of Museum Administration* 479 (ALI/ABA 1984). It remains to be seen whether N.Y.U.'s policy will have a ripple effect on educational organizations generally. Museums should be familiar also with 17 U.S.C. § 108 which governs reproduction by libraries and archives. See also "Reproduction of Copyrighted Works by Educators and Librarians," Circular R21, Copyright Office, Library of Congress.

246. 17 U.S.C. § 109(b) reads:

Notwithstanding the provisions of section 106(5), the owner of a particular copy lawfully made under this title, or any person authorized by such owner, is entitled, without the authority of the copyright owner, to display the copy publicly, either directly or by the projection of no more than one image at a time, to viewers present at the place where the copy is located.

247. If a museum has an object on loan, normally it would not reloan it to someone else without the express approval of the owner. (See Chapter VI, "Loans, Incoming and Outgoing.") This express approval (usually in the loan agreement) should constitute a license to display.

248. In such instances, some museum professionals argue that it is better to ask the copyright holder to dedicate the work to the public. It is reasoned that once the work is in the public domain, the overall benefits outweigh any loss to the museum. Also, the work is no longer subject to a termination of assigned rights. Another practical consideration is that if a living artist transfers copyright to the museum, as distinct from dedicating the work to the public, the artist may expect the museum to take action if there is possible infringement. This burden a museum may not wish to assume.

negotiation, the museum may find that even a reluctant copyright owner is willing to consider a carefully drafted license that grants the museum limited rights frequently associated with routine museum functions. Such rights might include the following: the right to reproduce the work in catalogs for sale, both the museum's and those of a museum that borrows the work; the right to create marketable slides designed for classroom use; the right to print postcards or inexpensive posters for the museum's use in its gift shop; the right to grant permission to scholars to reproduce in educational publications, such as university press publications. Frequently, it is to the benefit of the copyright holder to have the work promulgated by the museum in such ways. Such educational endeavors can in fact increase the commercial value of the rights retained by the copyright holder. Part of such negotiations could involve a payment of royalties to the copyright holder if the requested use involves major commercial considerations. If it is uncertain whether the individuals in question have or still retain copyright interests, the museum may wish to request a conveyance of any such rights they "may be deemed to have." Such a quitclaim document can be helpful in putting to rest shadow claims which may lessen the value of the object to the museum over the years.

e. Duration of Copyright

With the revision of the copyright law effective January 1, 1978, new time periods were established for copyright protection for works created on or after that date and for works in existence prior to that date. Before the revision, under common law, "unpublished" original works were protected until they were published. Once published (with the required copyright notice), copyright protection existed for a period of twenty-eight years from the date of first publication, and this protection could be renewed for an additional twenty-eight years. Upon the effective date of the new Act (January 1, 1978), common law protection was abolished. Copyright can no longer go on indefinitely if the work remains unpublished. Any work unpublished as of January 1, 1978, is subject to the following limitations:

- if the author was alive on January 1, 1978—lifetime of the author plus fifty years; or
- if the author was dead as of January 1, 1978—fifty years from the death or December 31, 2002, whichever is later.

Copyrights still in their first term as of January 1, 1978 (that is, published works) are now renewable at the conclusion of the term for an additional forty-seven years. Copyrights in their second term as of January 1, 1978, are extended to endure for a total of seventy-five years from the date copyright was originally obtained.[249] All works created on or after January 1, 1978, whether published or not, are protected from the date of creation. Protection lasts for the life of the creator plus fifty years.[250] If the work is "made for hire," protection extends

---

249. If copyright had expired as of January 1, 1978, the new act does not revive it.

250. If jointly created, the fifty-year period begins at the death of the last survivor.

for seventy-five years from the date of first publication or one hundred years from the date of creation, whichever expires first.[251]

f. Request for Permission to Reproduce Museum Holdings

Any museum, especially one with a large archival or photograph collection may find it prudent in the long run to review with legal counsel its acquisition policies and practices as they pertain to copyright. At the same time, care should be taken to think through the museum's responsibilities when third parties request permission to reproduce material in the museum's collections. Has the museum the ability to give such permission? What, if any, cautions must be given the requestors?

Usually, a museum has a form for requesting permission to reproduce for publication objects in its collection. Similarly, a form is frequently used to process requests for permission to use museum archival material. If such a form contains a general caution that the burden of obtaining all necessary reproduction permission rests with the requesting party, the requesting party is clearly on notice that he may be required to go beyond the museum to resolve copyright issues. As individual requests are processed, the museum can then ascertain whether it has any definitive information on record regarding the copyright status of the material in question.

Examples of cautionary clauses in use follow:

Photographs

The Museum can grant the permission requested only to the extent of its ownership of the rights relating to the request. Certain works of art as well as the photographs of those works of art, may be protected by copyright, trademark, or related interests not owned by the Museum. The responsibility for ascertaining whether any such rights exist and for obtaining all other necessary permissions, remains with the applicant.

Archival Material

I understand (a) that the Museum makes no representation that it is the owner of any copyright or other literary property in the materials contained in its archives, (b) that, in providing access to or permitting the reproduction of any such materials, the Museum does not assume any responsibility for obtaining or granting any permission to publish or use the same, and (c) that the responsibility (i) for determining the nature of any rights, and the ownership or interest therein, and for obtaining the appropriate permissions to publish or use and (ii) for determining the nature of any liabilities (including liabilities for defamation and invasion of privacy) that may arise from any publication or use, rests entirely with the researcher.

g. Additional Information on Copyright Issues

The Copyright Office of the Library of Congress cannot give legal opinions on particular problems, but it does offer numerous informative booklets. Of particular interest to museums might be "Highlights of the New Copyright Law," Circular R. 99, and "Reproduction of Copyrighted Works by Educators and

---

251. See 17 U.S.C. §§ 302–305 for more details.

Librarians," Circular R. 21.[252] An article dealing specifically with museum copyright issues is "Copyright in Museum Collections: An Overview of Some of the Problems" by Nicholas Ward. The article appears in *Journal of College and University Law*, Volume 7, Number 3-4. The ALI/ABA Course of Study on "Legal Problems of Museum Administration"[253] for March 1978 contains two sections on copyright: Hilliard, "Museum Administration Under the New Copyright Law," and Lang, "Some Specific Matters of Concern to Museums Under the Revised U. S. Copyright Law." Available from the Association of American Publishers[254] are: "Photocopying by Academic, Public and Nonprofit Research Libraries" and "Agreement on Guidelines for Classroom Copying in Not-for-Profit Educational Institutions with Respect to Books and Periodicals." Chapter IV of *Law, Ethics and the Visual Arts* by John Merryman and Albert Elsen has extensive coverage of copyright issues as they apply to the artist, and the *Business of Art*, edited by Lee Caplin, has a chapter on "Safeguarding the Uniqueness of Your Work: Copyright, Trade Secret, Patent, and Trademark Law."

3. Artists' Rights: *Droit de Suite* and *Droit Moral*
a. *Droit de Suite—California Royalty Act*
Droit de suite acknowledges a property right in the artist to benefit for a certain period of time from the resale of his work, on the theory that the artist should share in the success of his creations. The concept has been embodied in statutory protections in numerous foreign countries, but it remains the subject of much debate in the United States.[255] As of January 1, 1977, California initiated such protection.

The California Royalty Act[256] applies to the sale of works of fine art[257] which takes place in the State of California after January 1, 1977, or which are sold after that date by a seller residing in California or his agent. The right survives only 20 years after the death of the artist.[258] Under the Act, in any initial sale (other than from the artist himself) or resale (subject to certain exceptions) of such art during the lifetime of the artist, 5 percent of the sale price must be withheld for the artist. If the artist cannot be located, the 5 percent is withheld

---

252. Write: Information and Publications Section, Information and Reference Division, U.S. Copyright Office, Library of Congress, Washington, D.C. 20559.

253. ALI/ABA Committee on Continuing Professional Education, 4025 Chestnut Street, Philadelphia, PA 19104.

254. 2005 Massachusetts Avenue, N.W., Washington, D. C. 20036.

255. See F. Feldman and S. Weil, *Art Works: Law, Policy, Practice* (1974); J. Merryman and A. Elsen, *Law, Ethics and the Visual Arts* (1979); Duffy, *Art Law: Representing Artists, Dealers and Collectors* (1977).

256. Cal. Civil Code § 986, as amended. At the same time, California's "Art in Public Buildings Act" went into effect (Cal. Gov't Code §§ 15813-15813.8). The Act requires the state to respect certain moral rights (see next section) of artists whose work is purchased by the state and also provides for a *droit de suite*-type payment if the parties so agree in writing.

257. Fine art is defined to mean an original painting, sculpture or drawing, or an original work of art in glass.

258. An amendment effective January 1, 1983.

for the California Arts Council. Failure to withhold exposes the seller to an action for damages. A California museum acquiring a work that may be subject to the statute should note this on its accession records. If the work is ever deaccessioned by sale (or exchange) a determination of its status under the Royalty Act will have to be made. Similarly, if a museum is purchasing a work of fine art from a California resident, organization or agent (whether by sale or exchange) or is selling (or exchanging) such a work, and the sale (or exchange) conceivably could be viewed as taking place in California, possible ramifications of the California statutes should be considered.[259]

There are many who argue that legislative attempts to implement the *droit de suite* concept create more problems than benefits. Others with equal vigor support the concept.[260] In 1978, a proposal was introduced into Congress to create a federal resale royalty, but when it became apparent that the art community was deeply divided on the merits of the legislation, the bill never reached a vote.[261] As of 1982, the California Royalty Act is the only example of state *droit de suite* legislation in this country. The act reads as follows:

California Royalty Act
§ 986 of California Civil Code

(a) Whenever a work of fine art is sold and the seller resides in California or the sale takes place in California, the seller or the seller's agent shall pay to the artist of such work of fine art or to such artist's agent 5 percent of the amount of such sale. The right of the artist to receive an amount equal to 5 percent of the amount of such sale may be waived only by a contract in writing providing for an amount in excess of 5 percent of the amount of such sale. An artist may assign the right to collect the royalty payment provided by this section to another individual or entity. However, the assignment shall not have the effect of creating a waiver prohibited by this subdivision.

(1) When a work of fine art is sold at an auction or by a gallery, dealer, broker, museum, or other person acting as the agent for the seller the agent shall withhold 5 percent of the amount of the sale, locate the artist and pay the artist.

(2) If the seller or agent is unable to locate and pay the artist within 90 days, an amount equal to 5 percent of the amount of the sale shall be transferred to the Arts Council.

(3) If a seller or the seller's agent fails to pay an artist the amount equal to 5 percent of the sale of a work of fine art by the artist or fails to transfer such amount to the Arts Council, the artist may bring an action for damages

---

259. The California statute has already weathered a court challenge to its constitutionality: *Morseburg v. Balyon*, 621 F.2d 972 (9th Cir. 1980), *cert. denied* 449 U.S. 983. See also Katz, "Copyright Preemption Under the Copyright Act of 1976: The Case of *Droit de Suite*," 27 *Geo. Wash. L. Rev.* 200 (1978).

260. For differing views, see: Soloman and Gill, "Federal and State Resale Royalty Legislation: What Hath Art Wrought?," 26 *U.C.L.A. L. Rev.* 322 (1978); Ashley, "A Critical Comment on California *Droit de Suite*," 29 *Hastings L. J.* 249 (1977); Baldwin, "Art and Money: The Artist's Royalty Problem," *Art in America* 20 (March–April 1974); S. Weil, *Beauty and the Beasts* (1983) at 210.

261. H.R. 11403, 95th Cong., 2d Sess., (introduced March 8, 1978), "The Visual Artists' Residual Rights Act," 137 *U.S. House of Representatives Bills*.

within three years after the date of sale or one year after the discovery of the sale, whichever is longer. The prevailing party in any action brought under this paragraph shall be entitled to reasonable attorney fees, in an amount as determined by the court.

(4) Moneys received by the council pursuant to this section shall be deposited in an account in the Special Deposit Fund in the State Treasury.

(5) The Arts Council shall attempt to locate any artist for whom money is received pursuant to this section. If the Council is unable to locate the artist and the artist does not file a written claim for the money received by the council within seven years of the date of sale of the work of fine art, the right of the artist terminates and such money shall be transferred to the council for use in acquiring fine art pursuant to the Art in Public Buildings program set forth in Chapter 2.1 (commencing with Section 15813) of Part 10b of Division 3 of Title 2, of the Government Code.

(6) Any amount of money held by any seller or agent for the payment of artists pursuant to this section shall be exempt from enforcement of a money judgment by the creditors of the seller or agent.

(7) Upon the death of an artist, the rights and duties created under this section shall inure to his or her heirs, legatees, or personal representative, until the 20th anniversary of the death of the artist. The provisions of this paragraph shall be applicable only with respect to an artist who dies after January 1, 1983.

(b) Subdivision (a) shall not apply to any of the following:

(1) To the initial sale of a work of fine art where legal title to such work at the time of such initial sale is vested in the artist thereof.

(2) To the resale of a work of fine art for a gross sales price of less than one thousand dollars ($1,000).

(3) Except as provided in paragraph (7) of subdivision (a), to a resale after the death of such artist.

(4) To the resale of the work of fine art for a gross sales price less than the purchase price paid by the seller.

(5) To a transfer of a work of fine art which is exchanged for one or more works of fine art or for a combination of cash, other property, and one or more works of fine art where the fair market value of the property exchanged is less than one thousand dollars ($1,000).

(6) To the resale of the work of fine art by an art dealer to a purchaser within 10 years of the initial sale of the work of fine art by the artist to an art dealer, provided all intervening resales are between art dealers.

(7) To a sale of a work of stained glass artistry where the work has been permanently attached to real property and is sold as part of the sale of the real property to which it is attached.

(c) For purposes of this section, the following terms have the following meanings:

(1) "Artist" means the person who creates a work of fine art and who, at the time of resale, is a citizen of the United States, or a resident of the state who has resided in the state for a minimum of two years.

(2) "Fine art" means an original painting, sculpture, or drawing, or an original work of art in glass.

(3) "Art dealer" means a person who is actively and principally engaged

in or conducting the business of selling works of fine art for which business such person validly holds a sales tax permit.

(d) This section shall become operative on January 1, 1977, and shall apply to works of fine art created before and after its operative date.

(e) If any provision of this section or the application thereof to any person or circumstance is held invalid for any reason, such invalidity shall not affect any other provisions or applications of this section which can be effected, without the invalid provision or application, and to this end the provisions of this section are severable.

(f) The amendments to this section enacted during the 1981-1982 Regular Session of the Legislature shall apply to transfers of works of fine art, when created before or after January 1, 1983, that occur on or after that date.

(Amended by Stats. 1982, C.1609, § 1.5.)

b. *Droit Moral—California and New York Statutes*

Like *droit de suite*, *droit moral* is a concept recognized in many foreign countries but still struggling for acceptance in this country. It embodies what are called the "moral rights" of the artist in his work, rights that are of a personal nature rather than economic. *Droit moral* assumes that every work of art carries with it the distinctive imprint of its creator, and, hence, the fate of the work and the reputation of the artist are inextricably bound. This being assumed, it is argued that the artist should have a right to prevent the misuse of his work.

Droit moral has been described to include the following:

(1) the right of the artist to insist that his name be connected with his work and only his work;

(2) the right of the artist to insist that the integrity of his work be respected;

(3) the right of the artist to have his work published only with his consent;

(4) the right of the artist to withdraw his work from sale; and

(5) the right of the artist to protection from excessive criticism.[262]

While some aspects of these rights are in fact enforceable under American law as it pertains to copyright, misrepresentation, libel, slander, contract, and so on,[263] the core concept of *droit moral*—the artist's ability to protect his integrity

---

262. Devlin, "Moral Right in the United States," 35 *Conn. Bar J.* 509, 510 (1961). See also Sarraute, "Current Theory of the Moral Right of Authors and Artists Under French Law," 16 *Am. J. Comp. L.* 465 (1968). Hoffman, "The California Art Preservation Act," 5 *Art and the Law* 53 (No. 3 1980); Merryman, "The Refrigerator of Bernard Buffet," 27 *Hastings L. J.* (No. 5 May 1976), also reprinted in J. Merryman and A. Elsen, *Law, Ethics and the Visual Arts* 4.1 (1979).

263. There is an unreported decision in Superior Court for the District of Columbia where an artist, Mirella Belshe, convinced the court that a builder who had commissioned her to create five marble sculptures for the lobby of an office building should be temporarily enjoined from altering the works. Part of Ms. Belshe's case was that she was paid $30,000 for the task, and, since her costs were $30,000, it was implicitly agreed that her true compensation was the assurance that the work would have continued public exposure in an unaltered state. The case was eventually settled by a compromise agreement with the defendant promising not to disturb the sculptures as long as the defendant owned or controlled the works. *Belshe v. Fairchild*, C.A. 16988-80 (D.C. Super. Ct., Aug. 13, 1982).

as it is embodied in his work—has, as of 1983, no legislative backing in the United States except in the States of California and New York.[264]

In 1980, California's Art Preservation Act[265] went into effect. As described by one expert:

> Where the Art Preservation Act most differs from the [foreign] moral right laws . . . is in its legal approach. It has, literally, an American accent. Rather than proclaiming a cluster of inalienable and imprescriptible rights, the act carefully defines certain conduct that, if occurring within the State of California, can serve as the basis for a legal action by the artist or the artist's heirs.[266]

Essentially, the Act serves to protect the artist from having his work intentionally defaced, mutilated, altered or destroyed,[267] and affords him a means of claiming or disclaiming his work. The Act applies only to "fine art" defined to mean "an original painting, sculpture, or drawing, or an original work of art in glass of recognized quality," but works prepared under contract for commercial use by the purchaser are excluded. The legislation affects only action taking place within the State of California.

The New York "Artists' Authorship Rights Act" differs from the California statute in several significant ways.[268] First, it defines "fine art" more broadly so that certain prints and photographs are included, and omitted is the California limitation of "recognized quality." Second, its focus is to prohibit the display in public of an altered, defaced, mutilated or modified form of a work of fine art whose display reasonably might damage the artist's reputation. It does not prevent the destruction of a work, as does the California statute. In addition, some argue that the language of the New York statute is too vague, and will provoke litigation. For example, museums and conservators have expressed concern fearing that their methods of exhibiting, preserving or restoring a work may be construed as unlawful alterations.[269]

---

264. Other states such as Massachusetts, Maine, Connecticut, Oregon and Washington are considering *droit moral* legislation. The often cited case to establish that there is no generally accepted *droit moral* right in the United States is *Crimi v. Rutgers Presbyterian Church*, 194 Misc. 570, 89 N.Y.S.2d 813 (1949). Mr. Crimi, as a commissioned artist, painted a mural in 1938 for a church in New York City. Years later, the mural was painted over when the church was redecorated. Mr. Crimi sued to have the painting restored or, in the alternative, for damages. The court could find no right that had been wronged and Mr. Crimi lost. See, also *Vargas v. Esquire, Inc.*, 164 F.2d 522 (7th Cir. 1947).

265. Cal. Civil Code § 987, as amended.

266. S. Weil, *Beauty and the Beasts* 228-9 (1983). See Weil for a history and analysis of the California Act in his chapter entitled "The Moral Right Comes to California." See also Hoffman, "The California Art Preservation Act," 5 *Art and the Law* 53 (No. 3 1980), for an analysis. For a discussion of all California statutes designed to benefit artists, see Karlen, "California Has Taken the Lead in Protecting Artists' Interests," *California Lawyer* 23 (March 1984). For a comparision of the California and New York legislation see Bostron, "The Moral Rights of Artists," *Museum News* 46 (April 1984).

267. Cal. Civil Code § 989 gives certain organizations standing to sue to prevent such activity.

268. Assembly Bill No. 5052-B (N.Y. General Business Law, article 12-J) signed Aug. 13, 1983, effective date, Jan. 1, 1984. As of December 31, 1983, it was republished as Article 14-A of New York's new Arts and Cultural Affairs Law.

269. See Robinson, "Art and the Law: 'Moral Rights' Comes to New York," *Art in America* 9 (October 1983).

The California and New York statutes are reproduced below. While each affects only activity within its respective state, both are of general interest as possible models for other jurisdictions interested in *droit moral*-type protection.

California Art Preservation Act

§ 987 of California Code

(a) The Legislature hereby finds and declares that the physical alteration or destruction of fine art, which is an expression of the artist's personality, is detrimental to the artist's reputation, and artists therefore have an interest in protecting their works of fine art against such alteration or destruction; and that there is also a public interest in preserving the integrity of cultural and artistic creations.

(b) As used in this section:

(1) "Artist" means the individual or individuals who create a work of fine art.

(2) "Fine art" means an original painting, sculpture, or drawing, or an original work of art in glass, of recognized quality, but shall not include work prepared under contract for commercial use by its purchaser.

(3) "Person" means an individual, partnership, corporation, association or other group, however organized.

(4) "Frame" means to prepare, or cause to be prepared, a work of fine art for display in a manner customarily considered to be appropriate for a work of fine art in the particular medium.

(5) "Restore" means to return, or cause to be returned, a deteriorated or damaged work of fine art as nearly as is feasible to its original state or condition, in accordance with prevailing standards.

(6) "Conserve" means to preserve, or cause to be preserved, a work of fine art by retarding or preventing deterioration or damage through appropriate treatment in accordance with prevailing standards in order to maintain the structural integrity to the fullest extent possible in an unchanging state.

(7) "Commercial use" means fine art created under a work-for-hire arrangement for use in advertising, magazines, newspapers, or other print and electronic media.

(c) (1) No person, except an artist who owns and possesses a work of fine art which the artist has created, shall intentionally commit, or authorize the intentional commission of, any physical defacement, mutilation, alteration, or destruction of a work of fine art.

(2) In addition to the prohibitions contained in paragraph (1), no person who frames, conserves, or restores a work of fine art shall commit, or authorize the commission of, any physical defacement, mutilation, alteration, or destruction of a work of fine art by any act constituting gross negligence. For purposes of this section, the term "gross negligence" shall mean the exercise of so slight a degree of care as to justify the belief that there was an indifference to the particular work of fine art.

(d) The artist shall retain at all times the right to claim authorship, or, for just and valid reason, to disclaim authorship of his or her work of fine art.

(e) To effectuate the rights created by this section, the artist may commence an action to recover or obtain any of the following:

(1) Injunctive relief.

(2) Actual damages.

(3) Punitive damages. In the event that punitive damages are awarded, the court shall, in its discretion, select an organization or organizations engaged in charitable or educational activities involving the fine arts in California to receive such damages.

(4) Reasonable attorneys' and expert witness' fees.

(5) Any other relief which the court deems proper.

(f) In determining whether a work of fine art is of recognized quality, the trier of fact shall rely on the opinions of artists, art dealers, collectors of fine art, curators of art museums, and other persons involved with creation or marketing of fine art.

(g) The rights and duties created under this section:

(1) Shall, with respect to the artist, or if any artist is deceased, his heir, legatee, or personal representative, exist until the 50th anniversary of the death of such artist.

(2) Shall exist in addition to any other rights and duties which may now or in the future be applicable.

(3) Except as provided in paragraph 1 of subdivision (h), may not be waived except by an instrument in writing expressly so providing which is signed by the artist.

(h) (1) If a work of fine art cannot be removed from a building without substantial physical defacement, mutilation, alteration, or destruction of such work, the rights and duties created under this section, unless expressly reserved by an instrument in writing signed by the owner of such building and properly recorded, shall be deemed waived. Such instrument, if properly recorded, shall be binding on subsequent owners of such building.

(2) If the owner of a building wishes to remove a work of fine art which is a part of such building but which can be removed from the building without substantial harm to such fine art, and in the course of or after removal, the owner intends to cause or allow the fine art to suffer physical defacement, mutilation, alteration, or destruction, the rights and duties created under this section shall apply unless the owner has diligently attempted without success to notify the artist, or, if the artist is deceased, his heir, legatee, or personal representative, in writing of his intended action affecting the work of the fine art, or unless he did provide notice and that person failed within 90 days either to remove the work or to pay for its removal. If such work is removed at the expense of the artist, his heir, legatee, or personal representative, title to such fine art shall pass to that person.

(3) Nothing in this subdivision shall affect the rights of authorship created in subdivision (d) of this section.

(i) No action may be maintained to enforce any liability under this section unless brought within three years of the act complained of or one year after discovery of such act, whichever is longer.

(j) This section shall become operative on January 1, 1980, and shall apply to claims based on proscribed acts occurring on or after that date to works of fine art whenever created.

(k) If any provision of this section or the application thereof to any person or circumstance is held invalid for any reason, such invalidity shall not affect any other provisions or applications of this section which can be effected without the invalid provision or application, and to this end the provisions of this section are severable.

New York Artists' Authorship Rights Act

Sec. 1. Legislative findings and declaration of purpose. The legislature finds that New York state is the home of many artists of international repute and that the physical state of a work of fine art is of enduring and crucial importance to the artist and the artist's reputation.

The legislature further finds that there have been cases where works of art have been altered, defaced, mutilated or modified thereby destroying the integrity of the artwork and sustaining a loss to the artist and the artist's reputation.

The legislature therefore finds that there are circumstances when an artist has the legal right to object to the alteration, defacement, mutilation or other modification of his or her work which may be prejudicial to his or her career and reputation and that further the artist should have the legal right to claim or disclaim authorship for a work of art.

§ 2. Short title. This act shall be known and may be cited as the "artists' authorship rights act."

§ 3. The general business law is amended by adding a new article twelve-J to read as follows:

ARTICLE 12-J
ARTISTS' AUTHORSHIP RIGHTS

Section	228-m.	Definitions.
	228-n.	Public display, publication and reproduction of works of fine art.
	228-o.	Artists' authorship rights.
	228-p.	Limitations of applicability.
	228-q.	Relief.

§ 228-m. Definitions. Whenever used in this article, except where the context clearly requires otherwise, the terms listed below shall have the following meanings:

1. "Artist" means the creator of a work of fine art;

2. "Conservation" means acts taken to correct deterioration and alteration and acts taken to prevent, stop or retard deterioration;

3. "Person" means an individual, partnership, corporation, association or other group, however organized;

4. "Reproduction" means a copy, in any medium, of a work of fine art, that is displayed or published under circumstances that, reasonably construed, evinces an intent that it be taken as a representation of a work of fine art as created by the artist;

5. "Work of fine art" means any original work of visual or graphic art of any medium which includes, but is not limited to, the following: painting; drawing; print; photographic print or sculpture of a limited edition of no more than three hundred copies; provided however, that

"work of fine art" shall not include sequential imagery such as that in motion pictures.

§ 228-n. Public display, publication and reproduction of works of fine art. Except as limited by section two hundred twenty-eight-p of this article, no person other than the artist or a person acting with the artist's consent shall knowingly display in a place accessible to the public or publish a work of fine art of that artist or a reproduction thereof in an altered, defaced, mutilated or modified form if the work is displayed, published or reproduced as being the work of the artist, or under circumstances under which it would reasonably be regarded as being the work of the artist, and damage to the artist's reputation is reasonably likely to result therefrom.

§ 228-o. Artists' authorship rights. 1. Except as limited by section two hundred twenty-eight-p of this article, the artist shall retain at all times the right to claim authorship, or, for just and valid reason, to disclaim authorship of his or her work of fine art. The right to claim authorship shall include the right of the artist to have his or her name appear on or in connection with the work of fine art as the artist. The right to disclaim authorship shall include the right of the artist to prevent his or her name from appearing on or in connection with the work of fine art as the artist. Just and valid reason for disclaiming authorship shall include that the work of fine art has been altered, defaced, mutilated or modified other than by the artist, without the artist's consent, and damage to the artist's reputation is reasonably likely to result or has resulted therefrom.

2. The rights created by this section shall exist in addition to any other rights and duties which may now or in the future be applicable.

§ 228-p. Limitations of applicability. 1. Alteration, defacement, mutilation or modification of a work of fine art resulting from the passage of time or the inherent nature of the materials will not by itself create a violation of section two hundred twenty-eight-n of this article or a right to disclaim authorship under subdivision one of section two hundred twenty-eight-o of this article; provided such alteration, defacement, mutilation or modification was not the result of gross negligence in maintaining or protecting the work of fine art.

2. In the case of a reproduction, a change that is an ordinary result of the medium of reproduction does not by itself create a violation of section two hundred twenty-eight-n of this article or a right to disclaim authorship under subdivision one of section two hundred twenty-eight-o of this article.

3. Conservation shall not constitute an alteration, defacement, mutilation or modification within the meaning of this article, unless the conservation work can be shown to be negligent.

4. This article shall not apply to work prepared under contract for advertising or trade use unless the contract so provides.

5. The provisions of this article shall apply only to works of fine art knowingly displayed in a place accessible to the public, published or reproduced in this state.

§ 228-q. Relief. 1. An artist aggrieved under section two hundred twenty-eight-n or section two hundred twenty-eight-o of this article shall have a cause of action for legal and injunctive relief.

2. No action may be maintained to enforce any liability under this article unless brought within three years of the act complained of or one year after the constructive discovery of such act, whichever is longer.

4. This act shall take effect on the first day of January succeeding the date on which it shall have become a law and shall apply to claims based on proscribed acts occurring on or after that date to works of fine art whenever created.

F. Acquisition Procedures

A museum should have established procedures for processing proposed acquisitions. This aids in assuring that important decisions are made in a timely manner and that necessary documentation is acquired promptly and placed on file. A museum's collection management policy can be an excellent vehicle for establishing such procedures, for delegating responsibilities for acquisition decisions and for promulgating general acquisition guidelines.[270]

The initial work in most acquisitions usually falls on the curator or staff member most knowledgeable in the area represented by the object in question. Depending on the type of material in question, museum procedures should set forth the kind of justification needed to support the acquisition and the level of internal review required before the object officially can be accepted or rejected. It is recognized that if the object is an insect specimen to be added to the extensive collection of a natural history museum, the justification required appropriately may be minimal with no need for review beyond curatorial level. However, when the object is a valuable piece of art or an item requiring extensive conservation work, level of justification and review would be expected to rise accordingly.

All important issues which must be addressed in any internal review process should be listed in the collection management policy. Some such issues are as follows: The relevance of the object to the collections; the ability and intention to use and care for the object effectively;[271] provenance concerns; and if restrictions are imposed, whether their acceptance is justifiable. If the acquisition is to be by purchase or exchange, instructions should be given as to when independent appraisals or outside consultations are to be sought. The decision-making process itself should be a matter of written record. Museum policy

---

270. See Chapter III, "Collection Management Policies."

271. Museums are becoming more aware of the cost of caring for collection objects with the realization that such costs can be a significant factor when making acquisition decisions. See Chapter VII, "Unclaimed Loans," footnote 21 for additional information. Also, the media used by the artist may raise questions about the advisability of acquisition. See, for example, Cannon-Brookes, "Impermanence: A Curator's Viewpoint," *The International Journal of Museum Management and Curatorship* 283 (No. 2 1983).

should establish who has the responsibility for maintaining such records and, with regard to objects actually acquired, who has the responsibility for seeing that all necessary documentation of title has been obtained and promptly recorded.

When objects are donated to a museum for the collections, the routine use of a formal Deed of Gift is a wise measure. Such a deed of gift should be drafted so that it is clear that the gift is without restrictions or if restrictions have been agreed to that these are stated expressly on the deed. Also, there should be language confirming the donor's belief that he owns the object and has the ability to pass title.[272] The deed form should require the signature of the donor, the date, and, if the gift is restricted, the form should be counter-signed by a museum official with authority to approve restricted gifts.

Lawyers sometimes tend to be overcautious when asked to prepare a deed of gift form. There is the desire to ward off a host of possible problems and this means the form can grow to be long and complicated. The average donor may feel intimidated when presented with such a document, or in good conscience may be reluctant to sign it for fear he cannot prove conclusively every representation. Common sense favors the use of a simple, straightforward form which is adequate for the museum's average transaction. Where circumstances indicate that title and provenance concerns need closer scrutiny, it is then the responsibility of museum staff to make suitable inquiries and, where necessary, to seek outside advice before there is any acceptance.

Two examples of relatively simple deed of gift forms appear at the end of this chapter. Before any form is adopted by a museum, however, it should be reviewed carefully in light of that museum's needs and procedures, and every word should be understood by museum staff involved in the acquisition process.[273]

It is important to note on museum records concerning donations the date on which each gift actually is placed in the custody of the museum, the date of the signing of the deed of gift (or other appropriate written evidence of donative intent) and the date of acceptance of the gift by the museum. Questions can arise between the donor and the Internal Revenue Service concerning the year in which a charitable gift was made, and copies of museum records may be requested for evidence. In the eyes of the Internal Revenue Service, a gift to a charity is not eligible for a tax deduction until the donor has relinquished all control over the object and has established that, in fact, title has passed. (Usually evidenced by a deed of gift or an exchange of letters.) Thus, evidence that the museum had a deed of gift in hand on December 31st does not secure a tax deduction for the donor for that year unless the museum also can verify

---

272. As mentioned in the section on "quality of title," such a statement by the donor does not cure bad title, but it may help rebut a challenge to the museum's title which occurs many years hence.

273. As a rule, it is sensible to have legal counsel review any form contemplated by the museum that concerns collection activity. Different approaches can be discussed and decisions made regarding what best meets the needs of that particular organization.

that it had dominion over and control of the gift before the end of the year.[274] (And, vice versa, if there is evidence that the gift was in hand on December 21st, the museum could be asked to document that there was in fact a deed of gift in that year.) It is sensible for a museum to keep these records meticulously.[275] Also, it is a wise precaution to go through existing records about October of each year looking for incomplete gift transactions. Donors then can be put on notice that if a tax deduction may be sought for that year, immediate action is necessary to complete Internal Revenue Service requirements.[276]

The insistence on delivery as a requisite for a tax deduction stems from earlier abuses when donors gave paper evidence of gifts to charitable organizations but delayed delivery indefinitely in order to have continued enjoyment of the objects in question. In effect, these "donors" had the benefit of a charitable deduction on their income tax with no concurrent benefit to the public. For this very reason museums should be careful not to lend objects back to their donors. Such activity not only jeopardizes the museum's reputation,[277] it also can place in question tax advantages sought or previously obtained by donors.

As explained in Section A on the meaning of the word "accession," and in Chapter XII, Section C, the Internal Revenue Code draws a distinction between gifts donated to a charity for the organization's "related use" and those donated for an unrelated use. The former affords a donor more favorable

---

274. The tax laws do not permit a charitable contribution deduction for a "future interest" in personal property of this type. Internal Revenue regulations state:

> The term "future interest" includes situations in which a donor purports to give tangible personal property to a charitable organization, but has an understanding, arrangement, agreement, etc., whether written or oral, with the charitable organization which has the effect of reserving to, or retaining in, such donor a right to the use, possession, or enjoyment of the property.

(Reg. § 1-170A-5(a)(4)). To be distinguished are fractional gifts (see Chapter XII, Section D, where the donor retains ownership rights proportional to the interest not yet donated to the charity).

275. The folly of back-dating museum records to assist in tax fraud is illustrated by the experience of several California museums in 1982. According to affidavits filed by the Internal Revenue Service in Los Angeles federal court, museum personnel in several prestigious local museums collaborated with an art dealer to produce false museum documents to support tax evasion schemes. The documents included back-dated deeds of gift. In addition to receiving extremely poor publicity, the museum officials named in the affidavits could face criminal charges for violating or conspiring to violate 26 U.S.C. § 7206(2) (providing or aiding in the providing of false statements, documents, etc.). Note also the *Brigham Young University* case mentioned in Chapter XVI, "Access to the Collections," footnote 30.

276. Exactly when possession of a gift passes can raise questions. Ordinarily, the mailing of a check or an endorsed stock certificate is deemed delivery if the check or certificate clears in due course. Stock certificates forwarded through the donor's broker or the issuing corporation are not deemed delivered until the stock is transferred on the books of the corporation (I.R.S. Regulations § 1-170A-1(b)). A pledge or promise to contribute is not delivery. Conditional gifts are not completed until conditions are met.

277. As a general rule, it is difficult for a museum to justify a loan of a collection object to any individual. See subdivision B(1), "To Whom Will Loans Be Made?," of Chapter VI for further discussion.

tax advantages. A museum's acquisition procedures, therefore, should recognize this distinction. Raising money is not considered a related use for a charity. Thus, if an object is being accepted by a museum so it can be sold, the proposed use should be a matter of record and it should be understood by the donor. The acknowledgment to the donor should be worded accordingly. Also, as previously explained, such an object is not "accessioned." The museum's goal should be to avoid even the appearance of collusion to circumvent tax requirements.[278]

---

278. Occasionally one hears reference to a "three-year rule" to the effect that if objects are held in the collections for three years then it is "safe" to dispose of them. The origin of the rule is uncertain. Perhaps it stems from the standard three-year time period (beyond the date of filing) within which the Internal Revenue Service can question the validity of a tax return. The use of the rule is not recommended. Under I.R.S. regulations § 1.170A–4(b)(3)(ii), a gift of tangible personal property to a charitable organization may be treated as put to a related use if (1) the taxpayer establishes that the property is not in fact put to an unrelated use by the donee; or (2) at the time the contribution is treated as being made, it is reasonable to anticipate that the property will not be put to an unrelated use by the donee. If a museum creates a situation where alternative (2) appears to be true and in fact establishes a pattern of holding such material for a set period of time and then disposing of it, the museum's true motivation is open to question. It is by far more prudent to observe the spirit as well as the letter of the law. Section 155 of the Tax Reform Act of 1984 contains a provision which could affect adversely a museum that is not careful in this regard. Under this section, if a museum disposes of certain donated property (usually of a value of $5,000 or more) within two years of receipt, the disposal must be reported to the I.R.S. and the donor.

XYZ MUSEUM DEED OF GIFT

Please complete this deed of gift and return this page to _____
_____. *Upon acceptance of your gift by the Trustees, a copy certifying the fact will be returned to you.*

I/We, _____ hereby give to the Trustees of the XYZ Museum absolute and unconditional ownership of the following, together with all copyright and associated rights which I/we have:

(ARTIST)   (WORK)   (MEDIUM)

I/We wish that the gift be identified to the public and in the records of the Museum as:

Gift of _____

To the best of my/our belief, the subject of this gift is free and clear of all encumbrances and restrictions and since _____ has not been imported or exported into or from any country contrary to its laws.

Date: _____   Signature of Donor: _____

Date: _____   Signature of Donor: _____

Address of Donor: _____

_____

Telephone No.: _____

(over)

Delivery: Works of Art offered to the Trustees should be physically present in the Museum for consideration at their next meeting. Please write or call _____ to obtain information on the dates of scheduled meetings of the Trustees and to make arrangements for transportation and insurance of your gift.

Provenance: For many reasons it is important that the Museum have as complete as possible a history of the subject of a gift. To that end, it will be helpful if you will forward any information or documentation which you may have with respect to your ownership, display and restoration, and all prior ownership, display and restoration, of the subject of your gift.

Valuation: The Museum may accept your valuation of your gift for insurance purposes but may not determine value for any purpose.

I certify that a deed of gift and the subject thereof were physically present in the XYZ Museum prior to the meeting of the Trustees of the Museum on _____ at which meeting the Trustees accepted the gift as described above.

_____

(Signed by the director of the museum)

DEED OF GIFT TO THE _____ MUSEUM

By these presents I(we) irrevocably and unconditionally give, transfer, and assign to the _____ Museum by way of gift, all right, title, and interests (including all copyright, trademark and related interests*), in, to and associated with the object(s) described below. I(we) affirm that I(we) own said object(s) and that to the best of my(our) knowledge I(we) have good and complete right, title, and interests (including all transferred copyright, trademark and related interests) to give.

1. Dated _____   _____
        (month)(day)(year)   *(signature of donor)*

2. Dated _____   _____
        (month)(day)(year)   *(signature of donor)*

The _____ Museum hereby acknowledges receipt of the above Deed of Gift.**

Dated _____   _____
       (month)(day)(year)   *(signature of curator)*

Attachments _____

---

*If less than all copyright, trademark and related interest are given, specify above.
**Note that on this form the museum is acknowledging receipt of the Deed of Gift, not the gift itself. A separate record is maintained for date of actual receipt of the gift.

CHAPTER V

The Disposal of Objects— Deaccessioning

A. The Practice of Deaccessioning
B. The Process
   1. Legality of Deaccessioning
   2. Procedure for Deaccessioning
      a. The Need to Establish the Museum's Clear and Unrestricted Title to the Object Under Discussion
      b. The Proper Authority to Approve a Decision to Deaccession
      c. Documentation Needed to Support Proposed Deaccessions
      d. The Appropriate Method of Disposal
      e. Notification to Donor of Deaccession
      f. Use of Proceeds Derived from Deaccessions
C. Requests for Return of Collection Objects

A. The Practice of Deaccessioning

The word "deaccession" does not appear in the dictionary. Apparently, linguists have not yet accepted the term, but this should come as no great surprise to the museum community. There are many who do not accept the practice. They view museums essentially as mausoleums dedicated to preserving, intact, the accumulations of successive generations. Collecting, however, is not a mechanical process. It is a combination of intelligent selection and thoughtful pruning. Periodic reevaluation is as important as acquisition, and deaccessioning, if properly used, can be a means toward true growth.[1]

    Deaccessioning, for the purposes of this text, is the process used to remove permanently an object from a museum's collection. The definition presupposes that the object in question once was "accessioned," that it was formally accepted and recorded as an object worthy of collection status. The practice of deaccessioning is not new, but, increasingly, more is heard about it. What makes the

---

1. "A . . . museum, if it is to serve the cultural and educational needs of the community, cannot remain static. It must keep abreast of the advances of the times, like every other institution whose purpose is to educate and enlighten the community." *Wilstach Estate*, 1 D&C 2d 197, 207 (Penn. 1954). But see Phillips, "The Ins and Outs of Deaccessioning," *History News* 7 (Nov. 1983), for one author's perception of how the public may view deaccessioning.

topic so newsworthy? In part, it may be the price of success. With increased public use of museums generally, there is a growing interest in every facet of museum operations and, quite understandably, people tend to take a more proprietary view of collection objects. Removal of an object from a collection can cause more apprehension than acquisition. Any decision to deaccession, therefore, is a potential subject of public concern.

Coupled with this increased public interest is a growing need on the part of many museums to consider deaccessioning. Several reasons can be given.

Museums are becoming more selective. They see a responsibility to prune collections in order to adhere to defined goals. Many museums grew unchecked in their early days. Areas of interest were broad, or perhaps, it would be more accurate to say that areas of interest were undefined, and almost anything offered was accepted. With the growing professionalism among museum personnel, it is now recognized that there must be some order and purpose in collecting. Frequently, this cannot be achieved without judicious weeding of existing holdings.

The costs of storage and conservation may no longer permit retention of excess objects. There are few museums that have excess storage space, and acquiring additional space is a major investment. Storage does not mean just space; the area should be secure, with proper atmospheric controls, and designed for efficient access to material. All of this costs money.[2] In addition, there is a greater awareness of conservation needs. There is an acknowledged obligation to use reasonable efforts to preserve and maintain stability of museum objects, and conservation work can be very costly.[3] These practical considerations may make it difficult for a museum to justify the retention of surplus objects.[4]

Growth may be possible only through exchange. As resources become limited, a common contemporary problem, priorities must be established. A museum may decide that it can best serve its purpose by focusing attention on its central collections, even if this means sacrificing auxiliary holdings. The deaccessioning and exchange of secondary holdings in order to acquire additions for core collections may present the only viable means for growth for a museum on a strict budget. Similarly, a decision to sacrifice lesser pieces in the core collections in order to substitute particularly choice objects could be justified by the facts of a particular situation.

Financial difficulties may force consolidation. Financial problems in a museum possibly could justify a decision to deaccession and sell collection objects in order to provide funds for capital improvement or even operating expense. For example, if capital improvements were necessary to safeguard or utilize the

---

2. See Chapter VI, "Loans, Incoming and Outgoing," footnote 21 for additional information on cost of caring for a collection object.

3. See Chapter XIV, "Care of Collections," section on conservation.

4. See *Johnson Trust*, 51 Pa. D&C 2d 147 (1970), wherein the court approved the deaccession of certain objects from the John G. Johnson Collection because they were not deemed of sufficient quality to warrant museum storage expense.

collection, and money was otherwise unavailable, a situation could arise where it would be deemed prudent to sacrifice selected collection objects in order to finance the improvements. Such decisions should be approached with utmost caution and with thorough exploration of all possible alternatives. Deaccessioning for routine operating expenses normally would be undertaken only as a last resort and only when it appears that the proceeds of the anticipated sales would enable the museum to regain financial stability.[5]

It should be noted also that deaccessioning legitimately can be viewed quite differently from discipline to discipline, and by virtue of the nature of the collection. For example, within an art museum, the art historian may argue for the retention of a fake while more curatorial-oriented colleagues press for its disposal. The ethnologist may find value in any object regardless of its condition for the bit of information it might add about a culture. In the local historical society, the third example of a weskit may be considered surplus; while to the botanist in the natural history museum next door, the one hundredth example of a grass may be viewed as hardly adequate. Because of the variables that arise, there can be considerable tension within the profession itself on the subject of deaccessioning if the impression is given that there are standard rules which must be applied to all collection objects or specimens. On the contrary, there are few constants. Deaccessioning essentially is an acknowledgment that museums cannot collect everything and, therefore, those charged with the administration of a museum must establish procedures for periodically reviewing and, if necessary, culling collections. Those procedures must be geared to the peculiarities of a collection, should permit the expression of a range of views and should clearly place responsibility for final decision making. The remarks contained in this chapter should be considered accordingly.

---

5. In 1982, Harvard's Fogg Museum announced plans to sell some pieces from the museum's collections in order to finance a new wing for its building. Proceeds from the proposed sale would be used to help fund a $3 million Art Museums Stabilization Fund to ensure the financial well-being of the university's museum complex. The works selected for sale were described as redundant or as "not playing a major role in the teaching mission of the museum." The plan generated much controversy and was reconsidered. In the late 1970s, the Peabody Institute in Baltimore experienced severe financial problems which prompted the sale of certain collection objects and even caused the trustees to offer the organization's art collections to the state as collateral in return for state assistance in rebuilding its endowment fund. In 1982, the Museum of Transportation in Boston found itself in severe financial difficulty with the prospect of bank foreclosure on its collections that had been used as collateral for loans. In 1982, the Corporation of Yale University established a policy on collections for its museums. The policy addresses the question of deaccessioning to support operating expenses. A deaccession for such purpose can be entertained only in extreme cases and subject to review by the corporation itself. A somewhat less stringent standard is set for deaccessioning for capital improvement. See *Yale Alumni Magazine* 4 (May 1982), for a report on the policy. In 1980, when the University of Glasgow (Scotland) announced plans to deaccession certain objects from its collections in order to meet financial pressures, there was a sharp public reaction. Subsequently, it withdrew its proposal to sell a group of paintings by James McNeill Whistler when the public responded to an appeal for funds. In 1982, when the university disclosed plans to sell certain nineteenth century books and photographs, a potential donor to the university mounted a campaign to stop further bequests to the institution arguing that such gifts would not be "safe." *The Chronicle of Higher Education* 13 (July 21, 1982).

B. The Process

1. Legality of Deaccessioning

The general authority of a museum to deaccession can be questioned even though there is no specific prohibition in the museum's charter limiting such activity. Without doubt, such a challenge reflects a natural cautiousness against disturbing the status quo. The case of *Wilstach Estate*[6] is an example. Mrs. Wilstach gave a collection of art to the City of Philadelphia, the collection

> to be preserved . . . and taken care of and kept in good order, as the nucleus or foundation of an Art Gallery for the use and enjoyment of the people. The collection to be kept together, and known and designated by the name of "the W. P. Wilstach Collection."[7]

Years later, the trustees of the collection sought court advice as to whether they had authority to dispose of certain works from the original collection as well as some after-acquired works. In deciding the question, the court quoted the *Restatement of the Law of Trusts*:[8]

> The trustee of a charitable trust can properly exercise such powers . . . as . . . are necessary or appropriate to carry out the purposes of the trust and are not forbidden by the terms of the trust.

In interpreting the "terms of the trust," in this case Mrs. Wilstach's will, the court concluded that her primary purpose was to furnish the people of Philadelphia with a public art gallery, and, reading her will as a whole, there was evidence that she contemplated changes in the collection. Deaccessioning was found to be a "necessary or appropriate" power for those charged with the operation of a public art gallery, and, hence, the court concluded that the trustees had authority to buy and sell paintings in their discretion.[9]

In *Rowan v. Pasadena Art Museum*,[10] the plaintiffs challenged the power of the trustees to change the focus of the museum collections by deaccessioning various pieces of contemporary art in order to acquire more traditional works.

---

6. 1 Pa. D&C 2d 197 (1954).

7. Ibid., at 201.

8. *Restatement (Second) Trusts* § 380.

9. *Frick Collection v. Goldstein*, 83 N.Y.S.2d 142 (1948), *aff'd* 86 N.Y.S.2d 464, questioned the authority of trustees to *add* to the museum's collection. The court was reluctant to read into the will any such restriction and confirmed the power of the trustees to accession material. See also *Parkinson v. Murdock*, 183 Kan. 706, 332 P.2d 273 (1958); *Taylor v. Baldwin*, 247 S.W.2d 741 (Missouri 1952); *Ranken-Jordan Home v. Drury College*, 449 S.W.2d 161 (Missouri 1976); *Gordon v. City of Baltimore*, 258 Md. 682, 267 A.2d 98 (1970). But see Gerstenblith, "The Fiduciary Duties of Museum Trustees," 8 *Art and the Law* 175 (No. 2 1983) for a different perspective. Gerstenblith argues that under the "public trust" concept, objects donated to museums cannot later be returned to private hands. It is suggested that this is a very strained extension of a "public trust" doctrine which is usually applied to unique natural resources. For example, courts frequently use such a "public trust" argument to invalidate any attempts to give exclusive control of navigable waters to a private party. To argue that any object donated to a museum is as essential to the public welfare as the ability to use navigable waters, does not comport with common sense.

10. No. C 322817 (Cal. Super. Ct., L.A. County, Sept. 22, 1981).

They argued that past practice had set permanently the direction of the museum. The court rejected this argument and found specifically that there was no impediment to the right of the board of trustees to change the direction of the museum by the exercise of its discretion.[11]

2. Procedure for Deaccessioning

A museum contemplating a deaccession should keep one thought in the forefront. A museum exists to serve the public, its beneficiaries, and to be truly effective, it must maintain the confidence of these beneficiaries. A decision to deaccession, therefore, should be weighed not just in light of what the museum perceives to be best for the people, but also in light of what the people may perceive to be their best interests. It is possible that in the eyes of experts a decision to sell a particular work may be well-justified, but if the public feels otherwise, or is unsure, caution should be exercised. This is not to say that every proposed deaccession should be submitted to public vote, a museum cannot delegate its responsibilities in this area, but it should be prepared to explain its plans and give due consideration to public reaction.[12] Because of this added dimension, a museum's deaccession process should be flexible; it should consider not just purely legal issues, but also what might be called the human factors.

In the spring of 1979, the Corcoran Gallery of Art deaccessioned and sold at auction some 100 European paintings from its collections. Apparently, much thought was given to all aspects of the proposed removal. The following statement by the Director of the Gallery[13] appeared in the front of the auction catalog, and it illustrates the museum's concern for its constituency:

Director's Statement

De-accessioning is a bold move which no museum would undertake lightly. After prolonged deliberation, the Corcoran Gallery of Art has decided to sell at public auction approximately 100 works from its European collection. Funds generated by this sale will be placed in a separate, restricted account designated solely for the purchase of American art of historical importance.

As Director of the Corcoran, I look upon this action as a means of keeping the museum's identity clear and focused, as a way of defining its mission and planning for its future, as well as a method of improving its collections. From its establishment in 1869, the Corcoran has enjoyed a preeminence in the field of American art. This sale will permit the Gallery— a private institute with very limited funds for acquisition—to fill some of the major lacunae in its outstanding American collection without diminishing the effectiveness of the institution.

---

11. The museum's charter did not limit the focus of the museum.

12. An example might be the Carnegie Institute's experience in 1979-80 regarding its proposal to deaccession its stamp and coin collections. Rather than engage in protracted legal proceedings to counter opposition to its court-approved deaccession plan, the Institute decided that the public would be better served by a compromise solution. See more detailed discussion in Chapter II, "Museums are Accountable to Whom?," on "Expanding Concept of Standing to Sue."

13. At this time, Dr. Peter C. Marzio was Director of the Corcoran Gallery of Art.

Conscious of its responsibility to donors and mindful of its obligation to the public, the Corcoran followed rigorous procedures in selecting the objects for this sale. From curatorial recommendation to final Board approval, each work was carefully scrutinized and its relevance to the Gallery's present and future programs weighed. It was decided that the works should be sold at auction to insure that they were offered to the largest possible audience. Trustees and staff of the Gallery, and members of their immediate families are restricted from bidding on these paintings.

Several of the works offered for sale were given to the Corcoran with the expressed purpose that they be sold and American works purchased with the resultant funds. In the case of the European paintings owned by William Wilson Corcoran, the donor himself, in what is an extraordinary example of farsighted museum philanthropy, stipulated in his deed of gift that their disposition was at the discretion of the Trustees. Donors of works sold will be acknowledged in future publications and on labels for art purchased through their generous gifts.

It is hoped that this sale will help make a great museum of American art even greater, and it is in this spirit and with this intention that we have taken this important step.

Certainly, the deaccession process should not be left to chance; written procedures are a prudent safeguard. Guidance to staff on at least the following issues should be offered in a museum's deaccession procedures.

a. The Need to Establish the Museum's Clear and Unrestricted Title to the Object Under Discussion

If title is uncertain, problems could be compounded by attempting to dispose of an object. For instance, if an object is sold and years later it is determined that the museum did not pass good title, the museum could find itself subject to a breach of warranty action with potentially dire consequences. Under section 2-714(2) of the Uniform Commercial Code, a disappointed purchaser who did not acquire good title and who is forced to return an object to its rightful owner can claim damages from his seller equal to the present value of the object.[14]

---

14. Under 2-714(2) "The measure of damages for breach of warranty is the difference at the time and place of acceptance between the value of the goods accepted and the value they would have had as warranted, unless special circumstances show proximate damages of a different amount." Under the reasoning of *Menzel v. List*, 267 N.Y.S.2d 804, 49 Misc. 2d 300 (1966) *aff'd* 28 A.D.2d 516, 279 N.Y.S.2d 608; third-party claim reversed on other grounds, 24 N.Y.2d 91, 298 N.Y.S.2d 979, 246 N.E.2d 742 (1969), the disappointed buyer is entitled to the value of the object as warranted as of the date the true owner recovered the object. It is possible that a museum could sell an object subject to unknown third party claims, thus disavowing a warranty of clear title, but the sales price would have to be reduced accordingly. Another alternative could be for the museum to limit the liability in the sale contract to an amount not exceeding the sale price. Note also *Jeanneret v. Vichey*, 541 F. Supp. 80, (S.D.N.Y. 1982), *rev'd* and remanded 693 F.2d 259 (2d Cir. 1982), in which the plaintiff, an art dealer, sued the defendant for breach of implied warranty. The defendant had sold the plaintiff a painting which, subsequently, the plaintiff learned had been exported from Italy without a permit. The plaintiff claimed the method of export created a cloud on the title and sued for the present day value of the painting, as warranted. The plaintiff prevailed in the trial court even though there was no clear determination of the precise nature of the "cloud," but on appeal the case was remanded for a new trial. In the opinion of the appeals court the plaintiff had to come forward with more proof to establish breach of warranty than that required by the trial court.

Thus, if an object had been sold by a museum for $5,000 and it had appreciated to $10,000 by the time the purchaser was aware that he did not have good title, the museum, as the seller, could be assessed damages of $10,000 in order to give the purchaser "the benefit of the bargain." What constitutes good title is a major topic in itself. In this regard, relevant sections of Chapter IV, which discuss the quality and completeness of title, should be reviewed. If it appears that title is uncertain or restricted, professional advice should be sought before any decisions are made regarding deaccessioning.

Without doubt, one of the most troublesome problems for many museums is the management of objects of uncertain ownership. A museum that has been in existence for any length of time invariably finds in its possession objects lacking any documentation and/or objects placed with it long ago "on deposit" or on loan but never claimed. As described in the chapters on "Objects Found in the Collections" and "Unclaimed Loans," often the law offers no clear solutions if a museum wants to dispose of such objects.

b. The Proper Authority to Approve a Decision to Deaccession
A safe rule is that the level of authority needed to remove an object from the collection should be equal to or higher than the authority needed to accession such an object. What that level should be in individual cases depends on various factors such as the monetary value of the object, its value as a research specimen, the extent of the proposed deaccession. For example, it may be quite proper in a museum to delegate to the director authority to approve the deaccessioning of objects of relatively modest value, reserving to the board of trustees the authority to pass on all other removals. However, in a large natural history museum even this division of authority may prove too cumbersome and unnecessarily restrictive. If there are frequent exchanges with other educational organizations of duplicate scientific specimens which have little if any market or scientific value, such deaccessions could appropriately be delegated at the curatorial level.[15] Similarly, where there are bottles and bottles of duplicate specimens of minimal value, the removal of several because they are flawed should be within the control of the department. Any system for deaccessioning, however, should have effective controls for monitoring adherence to museum policy and should require the maintenance of complete records. The museum goals are twofold: to have prudent deaccessioning procedures and to have the ability to demonstrate that, in fact, the procedures are followed.

If the object under consideration is of major significance or if a substantial portion of a museum's holdings are being considered for deaccessioning, some thought should be given to the advisability of discussing the matter with the state Attorney General's office. In New York, for instance, court approval is needed for a proposed sale of substantially all the assets of a not-for-profit corporation. This is to ensure that the terms of such a sale are fair and reasonable

---

15. An exchange essentially involves a deaccession and then an accession, and it should be treated as such with all relevant procedural safeguards.

and that the purpose of the organization will be promoted by the sale.[16] Notice of the sale must also be given to the Attorney General so that his views can be made known to the court. Somewhat similar precedents can be found in other states. In *Glenmede Trust Co. v. Dow Chemical Co.*,[17] a Pennsylvania case, the trustees of a charity, before consummating a sale of a substantial portion of trust assets, sought court approval. The Attorney General was held to be a proper defendant because under Pennsylvania law, it was deemed his duty to scrutinize the sale to determine if it was in the best interest of the beneficiaries.[18] Court review in such instances is limited to the issue of whether the museum's proposed action falls within the bounds of sound discretion.[19] But, even in cases where prior court approval is not mandatory, early consultation with the Attorney General can prove helpful when it is suspected that a proposed deaccession might provoke public debate. The views of the Attorney General, as representative of the people, afford an essential perspective which can be of great assistance to the museum in making its final decision.

c. Documentation Needed to Support Proposed Deaccessions
The range of issues which should be addressed in reviewing a proposed deaccession and the extent of documentation required necessarily are governed by the quality and/or quantity of the objects at issue. A museum's collection

---

16. Section 511 of the New York Not-For-Profit Corporation Law. See *Matter of Horticultural Society of New York* (N.Y. Sup. Ct., N.Y. County, as reported in *New York Law Journal* on April 1, 1980) wherein the Society sought to sell its McKenzie Collection of rare books. See also *In Re Conrad Poppenhusen Assoc. for an Order Approving the Sale of Assets*, Index No. 74-7/80 (N.Y. Sup. Ct., Queens County, Sept. 1980).

17. 384 F. Supp. 423 (E. D. Penn. 1974).

18. See *Zehner v. Alexander*, Vol. 89, Page 262 (Penn. 39th Jud. Dist., Franklin County Ct. of C. P., Orphans' Ct. Div., May 25, 1979). But see *Wilstach Estate*, 1 D&C 2d 197 (Penn. 1954) where the court noted that trustees of a museum did not need court approval for each sale of a collection object. As a practical matter, there may be no hard and fast rule as to when court review is required but, when in doubt, the Attorney General's office should be able to offer guidance.

19. *Conway v. Emery*, 139 Conn. 612, 96 A.2d 221 (1953) involved proposed action to close the Hill-Stead Museum in Connecticut. With regard to the trustees' decision, the court said "to the extent to which the trustees had discretion, the court will not attempt to control their exercise of it as long as they have not abused it. But the law will not tolerate its abuse, however great the creator of the trust intended the grant of discretion to be." (at 224). See also *Ranken-Jordan Home v. Drury College*, 449 S.W.2d 161 (Missouri 1970); *Attorney General v. President and Fellows of Harvard College*, 350 Mass. 125, 213 N.E.2d 840 (1966); and 3 *Scott on Trusts* § 187 (3rd ed.) which states: "In other words, although there is a field, often a wide field, within which the trustee may determine whether to act or not and when and how to act, yet beyond that field the court will control him. How wide the field is depends upon the terms of the trust, the nature of the power, and all the circumstances." *Zehner v. Alexander*, Vol. 89, Page 262 (Penn. 39th Jud. Dist., Franklin County Ct. of C.P., Orphans' Ct. Div., May 25, 1979), concerns an attempt by trustees of a college to close the school. A similar incident concerning the Mannes College of Music (New York) is reported in *The Chronicle of Higher Education* 9 (Nov. 5, 1979). In 1982, the Detroit Zoo was sued by a citizens' group protesting the planned euthanasia of several tigers. After protracted hearings, the court ruled that the deaccession decision had been made by the zoo after careful consideration and that the decision was not capricious, hence the court would not intervene. *Doppelberger v. City of Detroit*, No. 82-234592-CZ (Mich. Cir. Ct., Wayne County, December 10, 1982) *aff'd* Mich. Ct. of Appeals, November 14, 1984.

management policy should establish minimum criteria for reviewing proposed deaccessions of various classes of material. Acceptable reasons for removal should be listed and guidance should be given as to when outside opinions or appraisals should be sought.[20] The actions of those authorized to advise on or approve proposed deaccessions should be a matter of written record. In the case of *Lefkowitz v. Kan*,[21] at issue was the legality of a curator's roll in certain deaccessions conducted at a museum. The case was settled in January 1983 by a compromise agreement between the Attorney General of New York and the defendant curator, and the agreement contains this statement: "Good museum practice requires the complete and candid discussion of each step used in determining how an object from the collection was chosen for deaccession, and how the value of such an object was determined."

d. The Appropriate Method of Disposal

A decision concerning the method of disposal can be intrinsically tied to the decision whether to deaccession, but neither should be allowed to overshadow the merits of the other. For example, the fact that a museum desperately needs money should not dictate that collection objects must be sold, nor should a whimsical decision to sell a collection object gain an aura of legitimacy because sale proceeds will be used for a worthwhile cause. Persons charged with making deaccession decisions should weigh carefully and separately the merits of the removal itself and the merits of the mode of disposition.

Conway v. Emery[22] illustrates the pitfalls when this distinction is not made. In *Conway*, a testatrix left property to establish a museum for the citizens of the locality. Her will provided that if after a certain period of time the trustees of the museum "in their absolute discretion" determined there was not sufficient public interest in the museum to warrant its maintenance, the trustees could terminate the museum and transfer all its assets to a particular school. The museum was established and some years later it was called to the trustees' attention that the school was in grave financial difficulty. It was argued that if the museum stayed open, the school would have to close. The trustees voted to close the museum, and this decision was challenged by the Attorney General of the state. The court concluded that the trustees were in error. The essential question they had to decide in exercising their discretion was whether there was sufficient public interest in the museum to warrant its maintenance. In failing to focus on this issue, the trustees were not loyal to their trust. "In his dealings with his beneficiary [a trustee] must not be influenced by the interest of a third party."[23]

---

20. If an object of substantial value is to be sold or exchanged, frequently it is prudent for a museum to obtain one or two outside appraisals so there can be additional assurance that the price received or the exchange is fair.

21. Index No. 40082/78 (N.Y. Sup. Ct., N.Y. County, Jan. 3, 1978).

22. 139 Conn. 612, 96 A.2d 221 (1953).

23. Bogert, *The Law of Trusts and Trustees* § 543 (rev. 2d ed. 1977). See also *Henley v. Birmingham Trust National Bank*, 295 Ala. 38, 322 S.2d 688 (1975); *Attorney General v. President and Fellows of Harvard College*, 350 Mass. 125, 213 N.E.2d 840 (1966).

Assuming that an independent decision has been made that an object can be deaccessioned, care should be given to selecting an appropriate method of disposition. The museum's collection management policy should state what methods are acceptable and, perhaps, what circumstances may favor one method over the other. Here, again, the nature of the object in question greatly influences available options. In natural history museums, it is not uncommon for policies to favor or even require exchanges with other educational associations. This is based on a conviction that the museum's audience as well as the general public will benefit by keeping certain archaeological artifacts and scientific specimens in the public domain. As a rule, such methods of disposal are not stressed in art museums because, frequently, the marketplace offers the most realistic route for acquiring or disposing of art objects. There is no uniformly correct method of disposal. Based on its particular circumstances and the nature of its holdings, a museum, however, should be able to arrive at general guidelines with regard to methods of disposal for its various classes of objects.[24] In establishing these guidelines, consideration should be given first to the interests of the beneficiaries of the museum[25] and, thereafter, to the interest of the general public,[26] to the need to retain public confidence in the management of the museum,[27] and to any unusual considerations which may influence the selection

---

24. It is prudent, as a rule, to have a procedure for granting special exceptions to these general guidelines. If exceptions must be a matter of written record and require high-level approval, there is less chance for abuse.

25. As a general rule, a trustee has a duty to make trust property productive. *Scott on Trusts* §§ 181, 386 (3rd ed.).

26. It is not uncommon for a museum to be faced with a dilemma as to whether an object or collection should be sold at the best possible price in order to increase trust assets or whether a sacrifice should be made in order to retain the material in the public domain or within a certain locality. In a sense, it is a tug of war between favoring one's own beneficiaries or the general public. There is no easy answer, but it would seem that if the trustees of a museum appear to have weighed the merits of all arguments in good faith, their decision, if reasonable, should stand as within the limits of their discretionary powers. *Scott on Trusts* §§ 187, 382 (3rd ed.). See also *In Re Carnegie Institute*, No. 208 of 1979 (Penn. Ct. of C.P., Allegheny County, Orphans' Ct. Div., May 14, 1980).

27. Private sales, although not wrong per se, are more vulnerable to accusations of favoritism or inept bargaining by the museum. See, for instance, the complaint in *Lefkowitz v. Kan*, Index No. 40082/78 (N.Y. Sup. Ct., N.Y. County, Jan. 3, 1978). (Kan, a museum curator, deaccessioned and sold certain museum objects to a dealer. Kan also collected personally and did business with the same dealer. The Attorney General charged Kan with violating his fiduciary duties by not obtaining the best price for museum objects so that Kan could benefit in his personal transaction with the dealer. The case was settled in Jan. 1983.) See Brenson, "Auctions: The Museum Connection," *New York Times* C17 (Jan. 6, 1984), for a discussion of disposal routes used by New York City art museums. Private sales to employees and trustees rarely can be justified. American Association of Museums, *Museum Ethics: A Report to the American Association of Museums by its Committee on Ethics* at 29 (1978), states "No trustee, person close to him, or individual who might act for him may acquire objects from the collections of the museum, except when the object and its source have been advertised, its full history made available, and it is sold at public auction or otherwise clearly offered for sale in the public marketplace." Also on the issue of sales to trustees, see *Lefkowitz v. The Museum of the American Indian, Heye Foundation*, Index No. 41416/75 (N.Y. Sup. Ct., N.Y. County, June 27, 1975). If an object is to be sold frequently, public auction is the preferable method. On the issue of whether deaccessioned material should be sold in museum stores, the Code of Ethics of the Museum Store Association, Inc., contains the statement: "The sale of any deaccessioned material through the museum shop is unacceptable. Even though the item may have been properly

of a particular method of disposal.[28]

e. Notification to Donor of Deaccession

If an object is given to a museum without restriction, the donor retains no legal interest in it. The gift becomes the property of the museum to be administered for the benefit of the public.[29] If that object subsequently is deaccessioned, there is no legal requirement to seek the approval of the donor.[30] On their own accord, some museums have a "good will" policy of notifying donors of pending deaccession actions, and, frequently, objects obtained for the collections as a result of the deaccessions are noted on museum records as objects acquired through the original donor's generosity. Whether such a voluntary practice is feasible for a particular museum depends on the circumstances, and even with a general practice in force, individual cases often need to be weighed on their own merits. The desire of the museum to retain the good will of donors must be balanced with its obligation to carry out its responsibilities to its public in a reasonably efficient manner.[31]

If an object has been given with precatory (non-binding) language which bears on deaccessioning, the museum will want to proceed with thoughtful

---

deaccessioned, the public may perceive the transaction as the museum store participating in the liquidation of the museum's collection. Therefore, no deaccessioned items should be ever sold through the museum store." *Museum News* 51 (Jan. - Feb. 1982).

28. If deaccessioned objects have little, if any, monetary value, a museum well may be justified in donating them to worthy causes. Schools and universities often welcome gifts which can be used for teaching purposes, as theatrical props, etc. Such donations should not be in violation of the trust responsibility to preserve trust assets if, on balance, the museum gains by acquiring storage space and by being relieved of routine maintenance expenses. In this regard, see *Scott on Trusts* §§ 227.17, 389 (3rd ed.) which discusses the ability of trustees to invest or make gifts of trust assets based on moral or social considerations. A museum which is part of a governmental entity may be subject to limitations regarding methods of disposal. See, for instance, *Board of Supervisors of the City and County of San Francisco v. Dolan*, 45 C.A.3d 237, 119 Cal. Rptr. 347 (1975). If an object is being removed from the collection because it has been judged a fake, additional considerations arise concerning proper disposition. See "Report on Disposition of Fake Art," 26 *Record* 591 (Assoc. of the Bar of the City of N.Y. 1971); *New York v. Wright Hepburn Webster Gallery, Ltd.*, 64 Misc. 423, 314 N.Y.S.2d 661 (1970) *aff'd* 323 N.Y.S.2d 389 (1971); and the Code of Ethics for Art Historians and Guidelines for the Professional Practice of Art History (1973, 74, and 75). The latter suggests that owners of forgeries should be urged to donate them to museums for their study collections. If an animal is being removed from a zoo collection because of over population emotional issues can create major problems. See Luoma, "Prison or Ark," 84 *Audubon* 102 (No. 6, Nov. 1982), and the reference in footnote 17 to the law suit against the Detroit Zoo over planned euthanasia of several tigers. See also "Disposition of Wild Animals from Zoos and Aquariums: A Guideline of the American Association of Zoological Parks and Aquariums" (1978).

29. *Scott on Trusts* § 391 (3rd ed.), *Abrams v. Maryland Historical Society*, Equity No. A-58791/A513/ 1979 (Md. Cir. Ct., Baltimore City, June 20, 1979). Even if there are restrictions, the donor or his heirs may not have residuary interests. See, for example, *Amato v. The Metropolitan Museum of Art*, No. 15122/79 (N.Y. Sup. Ct., N.Y. County, Sept. 24, 1979); *Gifford v. First Nat'l Bank of Menominee*, 285 Mich. 58, 280 N.W. 108 (1938); *In Re Estate of Rood*, 41 Mich. App. 405, 200 N.W.2d 728 (1972).

30. Does an artist retain any rights in a work he sells? See Chapter IV, "The Acquisition of Objects—Accessioning," section on artist's rights. See later comments in this section on possible I.R.S. notification requirements.

31. For example, if heirs of a deceased donor cannot be located readily, or if the object to be deaccessioned was given generations ago, or if the object is of modest value, practical considerations may dictate against searching out donors and their heirs.

caution.[32] The decision to deaccession still rests with the museum, but such cases may present situations where consultation with the donor or his heirs strengthen confidence in the fairness of the museum's ultimate decision. An example in point is the deGroot incident[33] where the Metropolitan Museum of Art decided that it would not donate certain deaccessioned paintings to other museums, a course of action the testatrix favored but did not require. Instead, the trustees of the museum determined that the museum's interests would be better served by sale. The museum's decision was legal (it fell within the discretion of the museum trustees), but there was much adverse public criticism. Shortly after the deGroot sales, the museum voluntarily imposed these policy restrictions on its deaccession activity:

> (a) The Museum will, as in the past, consistently honor restrictions attaching to the gift or bequest of any work of art. In addition, requests which do not impose any legal obligation accompanying the bequest or gift of any work of art will be respected to the extent feasible, unless modified by the donor or, if the donor is not living, the donor's heirs or legal representatives, on notice to the Attorney General of the State of New York.

> (b) No work of art valued by the Museum at $10,000 or more will be disposed of within 25 years following its receipt if objected to, after appropriate notice, by the donor or the donor's heirs or legal representatives. This policy will apply to any work of art, including gifts or bequests which are not subject to any legal obligation or accompanied by any nonbinding request.[34]

The Committee on Ethics of the American Association of Museums in its 1978 report recommends a cautious approach:

> When precatory statements accompany the acquisition, they must be carefully considered, and consultation with the donor or his heirs should be attempted.[35]

The Board of Directors of the College Art Association promulgates the following advice:

> [W]here moral obligations are involved they must be evaluated within a moral context. Consultations with near relatives or locatable heirs is always a generous and wise procedure and should include a consideration of the use of the donor's name for the new acquisition.[36]

---

32. Precatory language places a moral rather than a legal obligation on the museum. For example, "It is my hope but not my command that . . . ." Court approval is not needed to deviate from precatory language.

33. See section on "Restricted Gifts" in Chapter IV. See also, "Report on Art Transactions 1971-1973," Metropolitan Museum of Art (June 20, 1973).

34. "Procedures for Deaccessioning and Disposal of Works of Art," Metropolitan Museum of Art (June 20, 1973).

35. American Association of Museums, *Museum Ethics: A Report to the American Association of Museums by its Committee on Ethics* 13 (1978).

36. College Art Association of America, Resolution Concerning the Sale and Exchange of Works of Art by Museums, Board of Directors (Nov. 3, 1973).

If an object is given with legally binding restrictions which affect the museum's ability to deaccession, the museum should not take any removal action without first consulting legal counsel. As a general rule, court approval is required to alter a legally binding restriction, and whether the donor is an appropriate party in such an action all depends on the particular circumstances.[37] In determining the consequences of a "gift over" in case a charity fails to carry out a restriction, the *Restatement (Second) of Property*, Donative Transfers, Section 1.6, makes these comments:

> A non-vested interest in an individual is subject to the rule against perpetuities even though it will vest, if it ever vests, by divesting a valid gift to a charity. The combination of interest in a charity followed by an interest in an individual does not justify excepting from the operation of the rule against perpetuities the non-vested interest in the individual.
>
> [Excluded] from the operation of the rule against perpetuities [is] a charitable interest that divests a charitable interest if the interest divested is valid so far as the rule against perpetuities is concerned.[38]

In effect, what these comments say is that if there is a gift over to a private party in case of a failure of a restricted gift to a charity, the gift over may be barred by the rule against perpetuities. If the gift over is to another charity, the rule against perpetuities does not apply. The rule against perpetuities states, in most general terms, that a gift must vest within twenty-one years after a life or lives in being at the time of the gift's creation. To the layman, all of this may be quite confusing, but for the lawyer such considerations may be crucial in determining the status of parties to question the administration of a restricted gift.

All of the above comments address the issue of whether the "approval" of the donor is needed in order to deaccession. With the passage of the Tax Reform Act of 1984,[39] there are now situations where the Internal Revenue Code requires that a museum "notify" the donor and the Internal Revenue Service if certain donated property is sold, exchanged or otherwise transferred within two years of the date of the gift. The information-reporting requirement applies if the amount of the charitable contribution for the property claimed by the donor under section 170 of the Internal Revenue Code exceeds $5,000 for any single item of such property or exceeds $5,000 in the aggregate for similar items of such property donated to one or more charitable donees. As explained in Section A of Chapter XII, such donations to a museum must, as of 1985, be accompanied by an appraisal summary from the donor which provides sufficient information so that the donee/museum knows whether an information notice to the donor and the Internal Revenue Service is required if the gift is transferred within two years of receipt. The information notice is

---

37. See Chapter IV, "Restricted Gifts," section E(1); also Chapter II, "Museums are Accountable to Whom?"

38. at 97. The text of this section discusses in detail the application of the Rule against Perpetuities, and notes state statutes that may address the public policies on which the rule is based.

39. See discussion in Chapter XIII, Section A.

precisely what its name implies, it gives the donor and the Internal Revenue Service information on the deaccession practices of the museum.[40] The requirement for an information notice, of itself, in no way alters the museum's ability to deaccession and pass title to the property in question.

f. Use of Proceeds Derived from Deaccessions

The common practice is to use proceeds from deaccessions for the acquisition of new collection material.[41] Such a practice usually serves the best interests of the public because it lessens the temptation to drain collections in order to meet support expenses. There are occasions, however, when a museum may be justified in diverting such proceeds to other uses.[42] Decisions of this nature must be made thoughtfully, with a careful assessment of all circumstances and in light of the museum's essential responsibilities. Ultimately, the burden rests with the museum's board of trustees to see that such proceeds are used properly. Mismanagement can expose the trustees and the director to personal liability.[43] The museum's collection management policy should address this particular issue so that, inadvertently, mistakes are not made.

C. Requests for Return of Collection Objects

Occasionally a museum is faced with a request to return a collection object. Such requests can take various forms and each has its particular problems. Experience demonstrates rather quickly that a museum must have basic guidelines to follow when handling requests for return of objects. Today, a museum may be asked for a very minor item, one deemed not worth much thought; tomorrow it may be a choice item. It is difficult to pick and choose battles and still retain credibility. If a museum's records on deaccessions are complete and open for inspection, a prudent policy, they should reflect consistency in handling all requests for returns.

In the first chapter of this book, the nature of a museum is discussed. It is pointed out that a museum holds its collections in trust for the public (the beneficiaries of the trust), and in managing these collections, the museum must consider first its responsibilities to the public. If a museum has acquired valid title to an object and has accessioned that object into its collections as a resource

---

40. In this regard, consider the discussion in Chapter IV, Section A on the meaning of the word "accession" and the concept of "related use" and also Chapter XII, Section C.

41. Association of Art Museum Directors, *Professional Practices in Art Museums: Report of the Ethics and Standards Committee* (1981) takes an unequivocal stand: "[F]unds obtained through disposal must be used to replenish the collection" (at 12). A. Ullberg and P. Ullberg, *Museum Trusteeship* (1981) suggests a more permissive approach: "Many museums specify as a matter of policy that proceeds from the sale of deaccessioned objects be used to replenish the collection" (at 19).

42. See "Legality of Deaccessioning" in earlier section, this chapter.

43. *People ex rel. Scott v. George F. Harding Museum*, 58 Ill. App. 3d 408, 374 N.E.2d 756 (1978) (trustees charged with using proceeds of deaccession to meet unnecessarily incurred operating expenses); *State of Washington v. Leppaluoto*, No. 11781 (Wash. Super. Ct., Klickitat County, April 5, 1977); and *Maryhill Museum of Fine Arts v. Campbell*, No. 78-2-01957-7 (Wash. Super. Ct., Yakima County, Oct. 23, 1979) (trustees and director charged with mismanagement of proceeds from deaccessions).

for the public, the object should not be removed without good cause. A trustee has less flexibility in handling trust property than he has in handling his own assets. If one owns property outright usually that property can be given away or even thrown away at will. A trustee, however, is under a duty to preserve and protect trust assets and to use such assets for the good of the trust beneficiaries. All of this is relevant when a museum is faced with a request for a return of an object. If there is no question of the validity of the museum's title to the object[44] the museum is not free to return the object without weighing carefully its obligations. Bursts of generosity or expedient solutions normally are avenues closed to a trustee. As stated in *Scott on Trusts*:[45]

> It is the duty of the trustee to use care and skill to preserve the trust property. . . . Where the loss to the trust is the result of his failure to use proper care or skill, where it is due to his negligence, he is liable to the beneficiaries for the loss.

Requests for return of collection objects can present complex legal and/or practical problems. This does not mean that in order to fulfill its responsibilities a museum must pursue to the bitter end every possible argument for retention. Trustees do have the power to compromise a claim where this seems prudent or to make a judgment that a claim should not be contested because of unusual circumstances.[46] The important points are that a museum when faced with a request should (1) ascertain the facts, (2) sift them carefully in light of trust responsibilities and (3) be prepared to defend action taken as prudent and done in good faith.

Consider, for example, the following hypothetical situations. Each presents a variety of issues that must be weighed before prudent decisions can be made.

Hypothetical Example 1. In 1970, Mr. X donated to the local historical society his grandfather's diary and scrapbooks. He signed a deed of gift stating he was giving all rights and interest to the society. The society placed the material in its archives, but never displayed it. In 1980, Mr. X asked that the diary and scrapbooks be returned. He explained that his family had become very interested in genealogy and this material had assumed a new importance for them. He indicated that he was mislead into making the gift because he thought it was of importance and would be placed on display. Mr. X's grandfather had been a local carpenter, he never achieved prominence in the community.

Consider:

(1) Was there a valid gift? Any question of fraud?

(2) Because of the nature of the material, should the family request be given special consideration?

---

44. If title is in doubt, this issue must be resolved first. If the requestor can establish that the object does in fact belong to him and that the museum has not acquired good title (or has no valid defense to an action for conversion), the museum is bound by law to return the object on demand. See Chapter X, "Objects Found in the Collections."

45. § 176 (3rd ed.).

46. See *Scott on Trusts* § 192 (3rd ed.).

(3) Would the public be served if a copy of the diary and scrapbook were made and the originals returned, or should the society consider only an offer to make a copy for Mr. X?

(4) What if the society no longer wants the diary and scrapbook? Should they be returned to Mr. X or should they be offered to other educational institutions so that they remain available to the public?

Hypothetical Example 2. In 1940, Mrs. B brings to the museum a doll, a family heirloom. She explains that it belongs to her seventeen-year-old daughter who is abroad at school, that the family is selling their large home and moving into an apartment, and that the daughter wants the doll placed in the museum. The museum gratefully accepts and writes the daughter, at her family's address, an acknowledgment for her generous gift. The doll is accessioned into the collections. On one or two occasions it is displayed briefly, but most of the time it is in storage. In 1979, the daughter requests the return of the doll. The museum refuses in the belief that there was a valid gift. The daughter then states that she never gave her mother permission to give the doll away, only permission to loan it.[47]

Consider:

(1) If the daughter was a minor when the gift was made was the gift void or voidable? (State law must be checked. In some jurisdictions, the gift would be void unless confirmed after majority. In others, a set period of time is given upon reaching majority when a gift can be declared void.)

(2) Even if the original gift were void, has the daughter delayed too long in bringing her claim? (See discussion on "Statutes of Limitations", "Laches" and "Adverse Possession" in Chapter VII, "Unclaimed Loans.")

Hypothetical Example 3. The state historical society has a collection of Indian artifacts that were obtained in the late 1800s. Several are objects associated with the religion of a particular tribe. Representatives of the tribe now ask for the return of these religious objects claiming (1) that the historical society could never have acquired good title because under tribal law such objects are always communally owned and (2) in retaining these objects, the historical society is infringing on the free exercise of religion by the tribe. In researching the objects, the historical society finds some evidence that the objects in question may be copies made specifically for a person who was not a member of the tribe.

Consider:

(1) Do the requestors have standing to make the claim? In other words, do they officially represent the tribe in question?

---

47. See *Magruder v. Smithsonian Institution*, Case No. 83-693-Civ.-Ca. (U.S.D.C. So. Fla., Sept. 15, 1983).

(2) In determining title to the objects, whose law is applied: the tribe's or the state's where the transfer took place?[48]

(3) Can (or should) the museum raise the defense that the tribe has waited too long to make the claim? In other words, the applicable statute of limitations has run.[49]

(4) In weighing the merits of the claim regarding the free exercise of religion, the American Indian Religious Freedom Act should be reviewed as well as relevant sections of the federal and state constitutions.[50]

(5) Is there any legal basis for the tribe to claim control over copies of their cultural objects?

Hypothetical Example 4. In 1900, Mr. C placed on loan with the museum four mineral specimens with the notation that he would call for them in a year or two. The specimens are still with the museum and museum records shed no additional light on whether there was further communication with the owner. The specimens have apparently borne an accession number for some time but when or why this was done is not documented. Heirs of Mr. C are now inquiring about the status of these specimens which have increased greatly in value over the years.

Consider:

(1) Have the heirs established their status to make the claim? Before any material is returned, a museum must assure itself that the return is made to the proper party. Otherwise, the museum remains liable to the true owner. Heirs should be required to prove that they are the sole and rightful claimants.

(2) What facts would be necessary to establish that the heirs have lost their right to claim the specimens?[51]

(3) Can any weight be given to the fact that items were accessioned? Is there other evidence that there was a subsequent donation?[52]

Hypothetical Example 5. The local historical society must move into new quarters and an inventory is being conducted of its holdings. Many objects are found to have no documentation. All that is known is that the items have been stored in the society's attic for years. Someone in the organization suggests a white elephant sale to dispose of unwanted items. Another suggests displaying the items and asking the townspeople to take back what might belong to them.

---

48. See discussion of *U.S. v. McClain* in Chapter IV, "The Acquisition of Objects—Acquisitioning," on issue of enforcing foreign laws and see section on the American Indian Religious Freedom Act in Chapter IV for an explanation of why an Indian tribe may be classified for some purposes as a foreign nation.

49. See Chapter VII, "Unclaimed Loans," for explanation of statutes of limitations.

50. See discussion of American Indian Religious Freedom Act in Chapter IV.

51. See Chapter VII, "Unclaimed Loans." From the fact that the owner said he would call for the objects "in a year or so," can there be inferred a reasonable term for the loan?

52. See Chapter VII, "Unclaimed Loans" and Chapter X, "Objects Found in the Collections."

Consider:

(1) It is important to verify the status of each article. Is an article placed on indefinite loan and never claimed more vulnerable to question than an article with no documentation?

(2) The value of articles can be an important consideration in determining prudent disposition.

(3) Is it safer to sell or give away objects which have clouded title?

(4) If objects are offered back to townspeople, how will claims be processed?[53]

---

53. See Chapter X, "Objects Found in the Collections," for issues raised in this hypothetical situation.

CHAPTER VI

Loans, Incoming and Outgoing

Loans, both incoming and outgoing, present distinct problems and invariably these problems are best managed by preplanning. It is prudent for a museum in its collections management policy to establish rules and procedures that are designed to encourage thoughtful attention to all aspects of loan procedure, whether objects are being borrowed or loaned. Issues which may be addressed in the policy are listed in Chapter III, "Collection Management Policies," in the section entitled "Guidelines for Preparing a Collection Management Policy." In this chapter, some of these issues will be explored in more detail.[1]

---

1. The subject of traveling exhibitions per se is not addressed. See, however, Gould, "Traveling Exhibitions: The Concerns of the Organizers, the Lenders, and the Exhibitors," ALI-ABA, *Course of Study Material on Legal Problems of Museum Administration* 181 (1975).

A. Incoming Loans

1. Liability Exposure

In everyday legal parlance, a loan creates a bailment. The term "bailment" is derived from the French word "bailier" meaning "to deliver":

> [It imports] a delivery of personal property by one person to another in trust for a specific purpose, with a contract, expressed or implied, that the trust shall be faithfully executed and the property returned or duly accounted for when the specific purpose is accomplished or kept until bailor claims it.[2]

When a loan is made to a museum, the lender is the bailor (the one giving), the museum, the bailee (the one receiving). The law recognizes innumerable forms of bailments; some are classified for the benefit of the bailor, some for the benefit of the bailee, and others of mutual benefit. The classifications are relevant when determining the rights and liabilities of the parties. For example, if the bailment is viewed primarily as a benefit to the bailor, the standard of care imposed on the bailee is more relaxed. He may be held liable only for gross negligence.[3] If, on the other hand, the arrangement also is for the benefit of the bailee, the law requires the bailee to exercise at least due care in managing the entrusted property.

While the law establishes general categories of bailments and sets forth duties imposed by each, these become of major importance only when there is no expressed contract governing the arrangements.[4] If there is an expressed contract, its terms prevail.[5] A museum is well-advised, therefore, never to accept a loan unless there is a written contract (that is, an incoming loan agreement) spelling out the rights and responsibilities of each party. Leaving the situation up to the common law could result in some unhappy surprises.

The museum's incoming loan agreement (the bailment contract) should recite the standard of care that will be accorded the object while on loan.[6] The most frequently used statement is that the museum will exercise the same care

---

2. *Commonwealth v. Polk*, 256 Ky. 100, 75 S.W.2d 761, 764 (1934).

3. Gross negligence is subject to different definitions. In the recently enacted California Art Preservation Act (see Chapter IV, Section E.3.), the term is defined to mean "the exercise of so slight a degree of care as to justify the belief that there was an indifference to the particular work of fine art."

4. See *Prince v. Alabama State Fair*, 17 So. 449 (Ala. 1895); *Colburn v. Washington State Art Assoc.*, 80 Wash. 662, 141 P. 1153 (1914).

5. Assuming the contract does not violate public policy. See also next footnote.

6. Whether a museum can release itself from any and all negligence as bailee is questionable. Sometimes, a release is held to excuse simple negligence but not gross negligence. There is also the issue of whether the bailor was sufficiently informed of the release. See *Picker v. Searcher's Detective Agency, Inc.*, 515 F.2d 1316 (D.C. Cir. 1975); *Smith v. Library Board of City of Minneapolis*, 59 N.W. 979 (Minn. 1894); *Kay County Free Fair Ass'n v. Martin*, 122 P. 2d 393 (Okla. 1942).

as it does in the safekeeping of its own objects of a similar type.[7] Some loan forms speak of "ordinary care and supervision" or "reasonable care."[8] Other museums seem to impose a slightly higher standard on themselves when they promise to take "every possible care of the object."

2. Insurance

Invariably, the incoming loan form addresses insurance for the objects. It is advantageous for the museum to have borrowed objects insured. If an object is lost or damaged while on loan, the museum, as bailee, has the burden of proving that it was not negligent.[9] In many instances, this is a difficult burden to sustain because the museum must come forward and prove due care. If there is uncertainty as to how an accident occurred, the party which must prove due care frequently suffers. Insurance offers a practical method for resolving lenders' claims and it protects the museum from possible catastrophic liability.

The incoming loan agreement usually offers the lender several options with regard to insurance. The insurance can be carried by the borrowing museum, the lender can carry his own insurance at the borrowing museum's expense or insurance can be waived. To enable the lender to make an informed decision, the loan agreement should describe briefly the insurance offered by the museum. Is it the "all risk" wall-to-wall policy subject to standard exclusions? (Be certain to list exclusions.) Also, it is sensible to have a provision in the loan agreement form stating that the amount payable by the insurance is the sole recovery available to the lender in case of loss or damage.

If the lender elects to maintain his own insurance at museum expense,[10] several points should be spelled out in the loan agreement. The museum should require that it be listed as an additional insured on the policy or that rights of subrogation be waived. This is to prevent a possible later rude awakening for the museum in the event of a loss. Suppose the lender provides his own insurance for a valuable piece lent to the museum. Through negligence on the part of a museum employee, the object is damaged and restoration costs are high. The lender's insurance company reimburses the lender for these expenses and, in so doing, the lender's rights arising out of the accident are subrogated

---

7. In *Gardini v. Museum of City of New York,* 173 Misc. 791, 19 N.Y.S.2d 96 (1940), the loan contract read "the museum is not responsible for the safekeeping of articles entrusted to it for exhibition beyond the exercise of such precautions as are now in force, or may hereafter be put in force, for the safekeeping and preservation of the property of the museum itself." The court held that this language entitled the lender to believe that his property would receive the care given by a reasonably prudent museum, and it did not absolve the museum from the responsibility of exercising reasonable care in safeguarding the property.

8. "The degree of care which a man may reasonably be required to take of anything (loaned) must . . . essentially depend upon the quality and value of the thing, and the temptation thereby afforded to theft. The bailee, therefore, ought to proportion his care to the injury or loss which is likely to be sustained by any improvidence on his part." Story, *Bailments* § 15. See, also, *Perera v. Panama Pacific International Exposition Co.,* 179 Cal. 63, 175 P. 454 (1918).

9. *Colburn v. Washington State Arts Association,* 80 Wash. 662, 141 P. 1153 (1914).

10. It is sensible to ask the lender on the loan form to estimate premium costs so that possible problems in this area can be resolved in advance of presentation of the bill.

(passed on to) the insurance company. The insurance company turns around and sues the museum for the restoration expenses caused by the museum's negligence. Certainly, the museum has not been protected by the lender's insurance. This can be avoided with some certainty by having the museum listed as an additional insured on the policy (the insurance company cannot seek reimbursement from the insured) or by having the lender waive the subrogation of his rights against the museum.[11]

Additional issues which should be clarified in the loan agreement when the lender insures are as follows. Some museums prefer to have in hand, before an object is shipped, a certificate of insurance verifying that the required insurance has been procured by the lender. Other museums look upon this requirement to monitor a commitment made by the lender as placing an undue burden on the receiving museums. They prefer to rely on a statement saying that failure of the lender to provide the agreed upon insurance constitutes a complete release of the receiving museum from any liability for damage to or loss of the property placed on loan. Even if a museum elects to request certificates of insurance, it may wish to include the added precaution that failure of a lender to secure insurance constitutes a complete release of the borrower of any liability. The loan agreement should also provide that the museum will not be responsible for any error or deficiency in information provided by the lender to his insurer or for any lapse by the lender in coverage.

Situations may possibly arise where, for practical reasons, a lender may wish to waive insurance coverage. Unless it is clear in the loan agreement that this waiver constitutes a release of the museum from any liability arising out of the loan, the museum can still be sued by the lender, exposing it to legal fees and possible damages. A release of liability, therefore, should go hand in glove with a waiver of insurance. It should also be remembered that even a waiver of liability might not protect a museum if loss is caused by the museum's gross negligence.[12] One additional caution is that if a lender elects to waive insurance coverage and sign a release because he is relying on protection from a blanket insurance policy he carries, the lender should inform his insurer in advance. Execution of the release by the lender without concurrence of his insurer could inhibit the lender's ability to pursue a later claim under his own policy. (In other words, the insurer might claim that the lender has signed away the insurer's right of subrogation without the insurer's permission.)

The valuation of lender's objects for insurance purposes can be troublesome. As a rule, the valuation should reflect fair market value, and this caution can

---

11. If the museum carries legal liability insurance, a common clause in most collection insurance policies, its own insurance company will defend if such a claim is brought against it. With legal liability insurance, it may not be so crucial to request a waiver of subrogation or to be named as an additional insured. See also *Housing Investment Corp. v. Carris*, 389 So. 2d 689 (Fla. 1980), and *Forten v. Nebel Heating Corp.*, 429 N.E.2d 363 (Mass. 1983). These cases discuss the proposition that when parties to a contract agree that one party will obtain insurance as part of the bargain, then the risk of loss from both of them is shifted to the insurance carrier. In other words, in such instances it may be implied that subrogation is not allowed.

12. *Smith v. Library Board of City of Minneapolis*, 59 N.W. 979 (Minn. 1894).

be printed on the loan form.[13] There are still some who, innocently or through design, grossly overvalue their objects. The issue is important whether the museum is insuring or whether the museum is paying the premiums for the lender's own insurance. In either event, there are obvious financial considerations and sometimes there are ethical considerations, which are subtle and more difficult to deal with. If there is a claim on an article that has been grossly overvalued, there are bound to be questions by the insurer. Has the museum by accepting the valuation tacitly endorsed it? Can the museum honestly say "It is not my problem" and yet retain the good will of the insurer and/or the lender? Even if no claim is ever presented on the overvalued object, has the museum nevertheless assisted in "hyping" the object? The owner can always demonstrate that the object was valued at that figure when loaned to the museum. It is generally conceded that there is some responsibility on the part of the museum to monitor gross overvaluation, as well as gross undervaluation. Frequently, this can be one of the more difficult tasks for museum staff, but it should not be skirted or left for someone to resolve frantically at the last minute. Curators or even the insurer may be able to suggest where valuations of comparable objects can be checked by the lender. If all else fails, the museum should reconsider at a very high level whether the loan should be pursued.

Sometimes lenders fail to give valuations. They do not want to be bothered or they do not know where to begin. To cover these situations, the loan agreement can provide that if a valuation is not given, the lender agrees to accept an insurance value set by the museum and that this value is not to be considered an appraisal. Museums are placed in an awkward position when they have the burden of setting an insurance figure on property owned by others, and it should be understood that under the circumstances all the museum will provide is a figure within reasonable limits.

In the case of long-term loans,[14] it should be clear who has the responsibility to update insurance valuations. Most loan forms have a statement notifying the lender that it is his responsibility to notify the museum if he wants adjustments on insurance values.

Some museums that have occasion to borrow fabricated works of art have seen fit in their loan agreements to limit insurance recovery in certain instances. A well-known museum administrator has some favorite examples that illustrate the problem. One concerns the sculptor who worked in fabricated steel, who lent his work, with an insurance value of $25,000, to a museum. The work was damaged while on loan and the museum quickly reported the accident to the sculptor and assured him that it would pay the $4,000 necessary to have the damaged portion replaced by the steel fabricator. (The plans were still with the fabricator.) The sculptor demanded $25,000. After much wrangling, there was a substantial settlement.

---

13. It is possible that the cost of restoring a damaged object may exceed its fair market value and the lender may request coverage of the greater figure because of the unique nature of the object. A museum is well-advised not to accept an arrangement where there is unlimited liability for restoration. Some compromise should be arrived at and a maximum figure set.

14. See section 6 of this chapter on "Duration of Loans."

The other example concerns a temporary exhibition of light works designed for a museum by an artist using neon tubes. After the artist prepared the specifications, the museum bought the parts and provided the labor to assemble the display. The total cost was $800. On the loan form, the exhibition was valued at $25,000 for insurance purposes. If some neon tubes are broken during the course of the loan, what is the recovery? This type of situation has prompted the inclusion in some loan agreements of a provision stating that in the case of works that have been industrially fabricated and can be replaced, the museum's liability, regardless of insurance valuation, is limited to the cost of such replacement.

3. Authority to Accept Loans
Having established that the acceptance of loans brings with it a considerable liability exposure for the museum, it is only prudent to establish clearly who in the museum has authority to approve an incoming loan.[15] In a large, complex museum with considerable loan activity, approval authority may have to be delegated and redelegated depending, for example, on the value and kind of objects involved. Such delegations frequently are accompanied with a caveat that unusual situations should be reserved for at least the director's attention. A clarification of approval authority and appropriate lines of delegation can be accomplished quite neatly by means of the collection management policy. Once adopted by a museum's governing board, a collection management policy that spells out incoming loan procedures and approval authorities should constitute valid delegation of power.

4. Loan Policy
It is a useful exercise to set out in writing the purposes for which loans can be accepted. This can prevent embarrassment. There are some who look upon museums as convenient warehouses, and with no clear policy direction, it can be difficult for the individual staff member to refuse with tact friends of the museum who want to store family treasures. For example, if a museum has an established policy that, unless written permission is obtained from the director (or board of trustees), loans will be accepted only for special exhibits or for approved research, a ready answer is available.

An exception procedure to the general rule is a sensible precaution. It is a fact of life that delicate situations can arise when potential donors are looking for receptive homes for their collections. Museums have been known to offer free storage and other considerations.[16] In New York, the Attorney General publicly questioned the legality of one museum's decision to offer long-term housing to a prospective donor's collection. At issue was whether funds dedicated to a public purpose were being ill-used in this instance. No legal action was taken, perhaps because these situations are rarely all black or all white. There is much that can be said on both sides and, invariably, some very hard

---

15. On the issue of whether a museum has an implied power to accept objects on loan, see *Smith v. Library Board of City of Minneapolis*, 59 N.W. 979 (Minn. 1894).

16. Museums are becoming increasingly aware of the fact that "storage" is costly. See Chapter VII, "Unclaimed Loans," footnote 21.

decisions have to be made by the museum. When venturing down this path, a museum is wise to bear in mind that what is deemed a reasonable or unreasonable exercise of discretionary power is colored by the perception of the beholder. At times, the public may have a justified interest in ongoing negotiations and an acknowledgment by the museum of this interest can help to dispel unwarranted hostility.

There are additional matters that are worth considering when setting incoming loan policy. The fact that an object has been exhibited in a museum invariably enhances its monetary worth. Lenders have been known to whisk their objects from the exhibit floor to the auction block touting recent exposure at a museum. Or the local museum of design might borrow for exhibit exemplary samples of contemporary crafts only to have the museum director later open the newspaper and read advertisements describing the crafts as "museum quality" or "selected by" the museum. Such potential problems should be brought to the attention of the staff. The first example is more difficult to control. The best protection is a perceptive staff that recognizes the pitfalls and selects lenders carefully. A simple precaution can control instances like the second example. If there is a possibility that the lender may use the loan for commercial advantage, he can be asked to sign a statement (or such a statement may be incorporated into the loan agreement) promising that no commercial exploitation will be made of the fact that the object was exhibited by the museum. If the lender objects to this provision, it may be prudent to look for another lender. A museum that gives even the appearance that favoritism or commercialism rather than scholarship dictates loan selections is courting trouble.

Closely allied is the subject of borrowing objects from board members or employees. Such loans are particularly vulnerable to accusations of self-dealing. A museum would do well to have very stringent rules regarding this practice.[17]

Provenance issues should be considered with regard to incoming loans. If, for example, an article is stolen property, imported illegally, or was taken in violation of certain endangered species laws, possibly the party having custody of the article can be embroiled in legal proceedings. A certain amount of caution is necessary. If staff members are well-instructed with regard to provenance criteria applicable to museum acquisitions, these same criteria can serve as guides in reviewing proposed incoming loans. Also, if a museum has committed itself publicly to an acquisition policy consonant with the goals of the UNESCO Convention on the Means of Prohibiting and Preventing the Illicit Import, Export, and Transfer of Ownership of Cultural Property,[18] the display of borrowed material acquired by its owners in contravention of those goals can be an embarrassment.

---

17. See Chapter I regarding the standard of care imposed on museum trustees. See also A. Ullberg and P. Ullberg, *Museum Trusteeship* Chapter V (AAM 1981). Any instructions in a museum's collection management policy on the subject of borrowing objects owed by trustees or employees should be coordinated with the museum's code of ethics on the subject of personal collecting.

18. See Chapter IV, "The Acquisition of Objects—Accessioning," section on "Objects Improperly Removed from their Countries of Origin."

A prudent provision in any incoming loan form is an affirmation by the signer of the form that he is either the owner of the object which is the subject of the loan or that he is a duly authorized agent of the owner with full authority to enter into the loan agreement. This affirmation isn't a cure-all, but it does demonstrate, if this point later becomes important, that the museum asked for and received assurance of authority to lend. Also, the very presence of the statement on the form might cause the uncertain lender to pause and resolve in advance any problems in this area.[19]

5. Handling and Use of Objects on Loan

It should not be assumed that lenders are familiar with what a museum may consider routine use of borrowed objects. To avoid misunderstanding, it is sensible to spell out these uses in the loan agreement. If the lender objects to specific provisions, these can be discussed prior to entering into a loan contract.

If a museum does not restrict the use of cameras by the general public in exhibition areas, this may be worth noting on the loan agreement. If the museum expects to be able to photograph or otherwise reproduce borrowed objects for catalog, educational or publicity purposes, this should be mentioned. Frequently, the subject of exhibit labels is important to the lender. The museum may wish to clarify its policy in this regard and reach written agreement regarding the wording of any credit line. If the museum reserves the right to fumigate objects and/or to examine them by photographic techniques, the loan form should so indicate. Most museums will not repair, restore, or in any way alter an object, without the lender's written permission. This is a sensible rule and one worth noting on the loan agreement. Even though a museum may reserve the right to cancel a loan at will, it might bear stating on the loan form that an object may be withdrawn from display at any time.[20] There have been occasional lenders who have considered it a breach of contract for a museum not to display continuously objects on loan.

Notice should be given to lenders of the museum's expectations concerning the condition and handling of borrowed objects. The average insurance policy covers a borrowed object "wall to wall." (From the time the object leaves the owner's wall, or custody, until it is returned.) The borrowing museum, therefore, has a definite interest in protecting its liability from the very inception of object movement. Where appropriate, several contract requirements can be imposed that lessen liability exposure. Some museums insert in their loan form a statement that the lender certifies that objects lent can withstand ordinary strains of packing, transportation and handling. Museums may also request that the lender send a written condition report prior to shipment of objects.

---

19. Consider, for example, this not uncommon occurrence. A museum eager to obtain the loan of a particular object for a special exhibition permits the loan form to be signed by someone with questionable authority or even permits two loan forms to be signed, each by a party claiming ownership. When the exhibition is over and it is time to return the object, the museum is faced with conflicting claims of ownership. The museum acts at its peril if it returns the object to the wrong party. The loan may end up costing the museum a sizable legal fee to unravel a situation it could have avoided.

20. See section 6 of this chapter on "Duration of Loans."

These two devices are designed to focus the lender's attention on his role in risk management. If for some reason the objects in question should not travel or should travel only with special handling, the owner has the opportunity to give notice. The borrowing museum may also wish to reserve some control over packing and transportation methods. It may reserve the right to prescribe such methods or to approve the owner's methods. Much depends upon the nature of the objects and the expertise of the lender.

A museum should have definite in-house procedures for monitoring the condition of loans. Immediately upon receipt, borrowed material should be inspected, photographed, if appropriate, and written notations made of findings. Damage or suspected damage should be investigated immediately and appropriate action taken to notify the owner and insurer. As a rule, this will not happen unless there is clear definition of responsibility. Who is responsible for receiving and opening packages? Who must inspect? Who within the museum must be notified if there is damage and who is responsible, for example, for compiling a record of findings and notifying the owner and insurer? Who handles any claim negotiations? So often a museum's claim payments increase in direct proportion to its degree of disorganization.

Similar instruction should be in force with regard to responsibility for monitoring loans and for prompt return of borrowed objects. The same attention should be given to inspection, packing and transportation when returning objects as is given upon receipt. This is the museum's last opportunity to verify in writing, and/or through photographs, the exact objects being returned and their condition.

The following example illustrates the value of extra care. Museum X had had on loan an exhibition of art work done on transparent acrylic material. Upon the owner's instructions, Museum X was to pack the exhibition and forward it to Museum Z for a subsequent showing. Museum X packed the art work carefully in specially constructed cartons listing, photographing and describing each piece inserted. Three cartons in all were forwarded to Museum Z, and, under separate cover, duplicate lists of shipped material were mailed to Museum Z. Several months later, a very excited owner called Museum X. He had just visited the opening of his show in Museum Z and two of his works were missing. Museum Z claimed it never saw them. The owner valued the works at $10,000. Upon investigation, Museum X was able to produce descriptions and photographs of the objects it claimed it forwarded. It could also produce duplicates of lists sent to Museum Z. Museum Z, in turn, could not explain why it had not noted the discrepancy between the shipping list and what it claimed it had received. In addition, Museum Z had to admit to destroying all the specially constructed transportation crates and the packing materials. Museum Z's insurer quietly paid the owner's claim when it was suggested that the two pieces of lost art probably had gone out with Museum Z's trash.

6. Duration of Loans

Lawyers who have museums as regular clients eventually meet their nemesis in the form of either the indefinite or permanent loan. Loans that are not monitored only invite trouble. Lenders move away or die, records become obsolete or disappear, and before long the museum finds itself saddled with objects over which it has little effective control. Can such objects be disposed of? If they need conservation or repair, has the museum the authority to initiate such work? Is it obliged to do so? Can heirs of lenders make contact generations later and claim these objects? As a rule, the law offers no quick solutions for the museum that is trying to clean house or assert title over objects left in its care for generations.[21] The only advice a lawyer may want to give with confidence is how to avoid these situations in the future.

With regard to prevention, it is most prudent for a museum to adopt a general policy that all incoming loans must be for a set period that cannot exceed a certain length of time. For example, a museum's rule might be that all loans must be for a set term but no term can exceed five years. This restraint forces regular evaluation of each loan situation.[22] If it is mutually desired, the loan can be renewed and insurance valuations updated. If the material is ready for return, the likelihood is good that the lender is available or easily traced. If the museum would welcome the material as part of its own collections, there is a convenient opportunity to discuss this possibility with the lender. On the whole, this procedure is plain good management for the modern museum.

With regard to the duration of incoming loans, a museum may wish to reserve to itself the ability to terminate a loan at any time before its expiration upon reasonable notice to the owner. Consider this instance. A museum is planning a major special exhibition that will consist mainly of objects borrowed from private individuals, and loan agreements are executed. Shortly before the exhibition date, the museum loses most of the funding for the show, and the exhibit is canceled or drastically curtailed. Some of the lenders are enraged. They have touted the fact that these objects will be on exhibit and they demand full execution of the loan agreement. Another unpleasant situation can arise when a museum has entered into a loan agreement only to find that there are serious problems concerning the provenance or ownership of the object it intends to borrow. If the museum goes through with the loan, it will be enmeshed in legal wrangling or professional criticism. Both situations can be solved easily if the loan agreement expressly warns that the museum may terminate the loan at will.

7. "Permanent" Loans

Loans by definition are temporary arrangements but, regardless of what Webster says, many museums are the possessors of permanent loans. And what is a permanent loan? If there are definitions, they are as varied as a roomful of museum professionals: "The opposite of short-term loan"; "Longer than an indefinite loan"; "A loan that ultimately will be given to the museum."[23] A

---

21. See Chapter VII, "Unclaimed Loans."

22. It is assumed that today museums have in place adequate registrational facilities and personnel for such a task, or are working toward that goal.

23. See Chapter XI, "Promised Gifts." It should be noted, however, that the term "permanent loan" as used in zoos is interpreted to mean a loan for the life of the specimen. In this sense, it is a loan for a definite period and not subject to many of the perils associated with permanent loan of inanimate objects.

lawyer turning to case law does not get much help, unless it is useful to know that in 1924 an English court stated:

> I do not think "permanent" [loan] means everlasting or perpetual and they are right in treating the word "permanent" in the sense that it is contra-distinguished from something that is temporary.[24]

Corpus Juris Secundum is closer to the mark. It notes:

> The significance of the term [permanent] depends on the subject matter in connection with which it is employed, and its meaning is to be construed according to its nature and in its relation to the subject matter of the instrument in which it is used.[25]

In reality, therefore, the term "permanent loan" in itself tells little and unless the parties spell out in detail precisely what is meant, uncertainty reigns. At best, some permanent loans are in written agreement form describing rights and obligations of the recipient museum. Most are bereft of such instructions and questions like the following constantly arise. Must the object be insured even if the museum does not insure its own collections? If the object is damaged, is the museum liable to the owner, and, if so, how are damages measured? Can the object be lent to other museums? What if the museum no longer can justify the expense of retaining the object? If the owner is available, answers can be sought, but the museum may find that it has limited bargaining power.

It is safe to venture that many permanent loan situations came about because the lender wanted to defer a hard decision and the recipient museum, eager for the object, thought mainly in terms of present needs. Situations of this kind rarely improve with age because there is even less incentive for the lender to make that "hard decision" once the museum has committed itself to care for the object. As time goes on, the attractiveness of the loan to the museum may begin to dull because of the expense of upkeep or because similar objects have since been acquired for the museum's own collections. If the lender is not readily accessible[26] much time and money can be spent trying to locate heirs or successors in interest in order to request renegotiation or termination. Even if the lender is known, the museum can only hope that he/it is sympathetic to changing the arrangements so that confrontation in court is unnecessary.

Consider this rather typical example. Organization X has acquired as a gift an extensive collection of books on the history of textiles. Under the terms of the gift, the organization can never dispose of the collection and must always keep it together in one room labeled as the collection of Donor Z. Before long, Organization X realizes that it has made a mistake, it has no urgent need for the collection and cannot justify the expense of upkeep. It turns to the local

---

24. *Yorkshire Railway Wagon Co. v. Inland Revenue Commissioners*, 94 Law Journal of King's Bench, New Series 134, 137 (1924).

25. 70 C.J.S. § 94, at 560. See also *Massachusetts Mutual Life Insurance Co. v. Montague*, 63 Ga. App. 137, 10 S.E.2d 279 (1940) and *Morgan Guaranty Trust Co. of New York v. The President and Fellows of Harvard College*, No. E 1855 (Mass. Probate Ct. of Worcester, Dec. 20, 1983).

26. It may be a question of locating heirs of a long-deceased lender or locating successors in interest to a defunct organization, etc.

museum and offers to place the material on "permanent loan."[27] The museum quickly accepts. As years go on, the museum takes a closer look at its coup. Many of the books need expensive conservation work. The collection is uneven in quality, and, if it were owned outright by the museum, it could be improved greatly by pruning and judicious exchange. In addition, the requirement that the collection be kept together in one room prevents its full utilization. The museum approaches Organization X which is very reluctant to discuss the matter. Any relief will require Organization X to initiate a *cy pres* or similar petition in court and the organization has no incentive to incur this expense.[28] In hindsight, the museum realizes it would have been much more prudent to take a firmer stand when the loan was initially offered. The museum could have agreed to support the organization's petition for court relief if the petition requested permission to make an unrestricted gift of the collection to the museum. Or, the museum could have accepted a loan of the collection for a limited period of time. At the termination date of the loan, the museum would have an unquestioned right to return the collection if a more suitable arrangement could not be negotiated. Faced with imminent return, Organization X might have had more incentive to resolve the matter.

It is difficult to imagine a situation where an indefinite loan is a more suitable arrangement than a series of term loans. Conceivably, however, a permanent loan between organizations or institutions might be justified in rare circumstances. For instance, one organization could have a very strong moral and/or cultural claim to material but cannot support with certainty a legal claim. The possessor organization might conclude with good reason that the public generally will benefit if the material is in the custody of the claiming organization, but there may be reluctance to pass title because of the possibility that someday the material could be transferred to a third party. A permanent loan, with the rights of each party carefully spelled out in an agreement, might be a legitimate solution.[29]

8. Change in Ownership

The incoming loan form should require the lender or his representative to give prompt notice to the museum if there is a change in ownership of the material on loan. Loan agreements impose obligations on a museum that require possible periodic consultation with the owner and, of course, the museum should be able to reach the owner at the termination of the loan or prior thereto if an early termination is sought. If the present owner cannot be ascertained conveniently and with certainty, the museum is at a grave disadvantage. It is sensible, therefore, to make it clear that as part of the loan agreement the owner or his

---

27. In loaning the material, organization X arguably is not "disposing" of it, it still retains title to the material. Thus, it is acting within the terms of the donor's restrictions.

28. See discussion in Chapter IV, "The Acquisition of Objects—Accessioning," on "Restricted Gifts."

29. Another, and perhaps better, solution might be for a museum to make a gift of the material to the claiming organization with the stipulation that before the material can be retransferred, it must first be offered back as a gift to the museum.

representative has a responsibility to keep in touch with the museum. This provision is especially helpful if the owner dies during the loan period. Notice to the museum by the estate at the owner's death permits consultation regarding oversight of the loan during probate proceedings and verification of who will succeed to the owner's rights. If mutually agreeable, a new loan agreement can be entered into with the party succeeding in interest, or the museum, with the assurance that it is dealing with the right party, can return the material. The notice provision also may help in those cases where the museum is unable to locate an owner and years later heirs appear to claim the property. If, in fact, no notice was given to the museum of the change in ownership, the failure to abide by the terms of the loan agreement would work to the heirs' detriment.

9. Return Provisions

Through experience, most museums have learned that all owners cannot be relied upon to retrieve their property. Too often museums have found themselves holding indefinitely property of owners who cannot be located, and the law affords them no clear guidance on how to resolve these matters.[30] Increasingly, museums are trying to prevent perpetuation of such situations by spelling out in their incoming loan agreements exactly what will happen if property is not claimed in a reasonable time. The technique is relatively new and there has been little practical experience in enforcing such provisions, but a museum would do well to consider the merits of the provision.

Such a clause now being used in some loan agreements provides as follows. If material cannot be returned at the termination of a loan, it will be maintained at the owner's expense and risk for a set number of years.[31] At the expiration of this final period, if the material is still unclaimed, the owner, in consideration of the museum's care, is deemed to have made an unconditional gift of the property to the museum. In drafting and implementing such a provision, several cautions should be observed. First, the loan agreement should be clear as to the date the loan terminates. This establishes the precise time when the owner should come forward. If this element is missing, the museum will have difficulty in establishing when the holding period begins. Without a time certain, the owner or his heirs can always argue that the loan was meant to last until he or they saw fit to demand the return of the property. Secondly, it should be clear which party has to initiate the return. Some loan forms provide alternative arrangements from which to select. The owner can request the museum to mail the object to his address or he can elect to retrieve the object himself. If options are offered, be sure a selection has been made. Finally, it would be a wise precaution for a museum to provide some form of written notice to the owner when the loan terminates stating that the material is being mailed or that it is time to retrieve it. If cautions such as these are observed and the museum maintains meticulous records documenting its efforts to return the property, the "gift provision" should withstand challenge.

---

30. See Chapter VII, "Unclaimed Loans."

31. Often this period is the local statute of limitations for bringing actions to recover wrongfully held property.

When borrowed objects are returned, the museum should have some form of a written receipt which is made a part of its loan record. In the case of objects retrieved in person by the owner/agent, proper identification should be requested, and the receipt immediately signed. Objects returned by mail should include a return receipt, or preferably, the receipt can be sent separately by certified mail. Experience has demonstrated that it is prudent to require the lender to return the receipt within a certain time period or else forfeit any claim for damage or loss. The purpose of the requirement is to encourage claim resolution while evidence is fresh, a fair procedure for all concerned.

10. Sample Incoming Loan Agreement

As with all sample forms, the model incoming loan agreement (on pages 170-173) should not be adopted by a museum without independent review by competent professionals. If the lender is another museum, quite possibly the lender may insist on using its outgoing loan forms. This is understandable because its objects are at issue. In such cases, each party should review carefully the other's form and differences should be resolved in advance. It is not unusual (assuming no major differences are apparent) for both forms to be signed with the expressed understanding that the terms of one (usually the lending museum's form) will prevail in case a conflict does develop.

Registrar's No. _____

NAME OF MUSEUM
ADDRESS OF MUSEUM
TELEPHONE NUMBER OF MUSEUM

AGREEMENT FOR INCOMING LOAN　　　　　Date: _____

From: _____　　Telephone: __( )_____
　　　　　　(name of lender)

　　　Address: _____

　　　　　　　_____

In accordance with the conditions printed on the reverse, the objects listed
below are borrowed for the following purpose(s):

_____

_____

for the period*_____ to _____
(*from estimated time objects leave lender's custody until their return and
receipt by lender; see "Shipping" below.)

Objects	Description (Please include size, materials, and report of condition; and attach a recent photo if possible.)	Insurance Value (Please itemize.)

(If additional space is necessary, attach extra sheet.)

Initiated by _____
　　　　　　　(museum curator)　　　*(museum department)*

SHIPPING: The following shipping arrangements will be followed unless
changed in writing by the museum after consultation with the Lender.

　　Objects will be shipped from: _____
　　　　　　　　　　　　　　　　　　(address)

　　to arrive no later than _____ via: _____

　　to be returned to above address (unless otherwise notified) via: _____

INSURANCE: (see conditions on reverse)
　　☐ to be carried by Museum
　　☐ to be carried by Lender: estimated premium charge $_____
　　☐ insurance waived

COSTS: The Museum will pay costs of packing, shipping, and insurance,

　　　　　unless otherwise noted here: _____

CREDIT LINE (for exhibition label and catalog): _____

SPECIAL CONDITIONS: _____

Museum Control No. _____

CONDITIONS GOVERNING LOANS

Care, Preservation & Exhibition

1. The Museum will give to objects borrowed the same care as it does comparable property of its own. Precautions will be taken to protect objects from fire, theft, mishandling, dirt and insects, and extremes of light, temperature and humidity while in the Museum's custody. It is understood by the Lender and the Museum that all tangible objects are subject to gradual inherent deterioration for which neither party is responsible.

2. Evidence of damage at the time of receipt or while in the Museum's custody will be reported immediately to the Lender. It is understood that objects, which in the opinion of the Museum may be damaged by infestation, may be fumigated at the discretion of the Museum.

3. The Lender will be requested to provide written authorization for any alteration, restoration or repair. The Museum, for its own purposes, may examine objects by all modern scientific methods.

4. The Museum retains the right to determine when, if, and for how long objects borrowed will be exhibited. The Museum retains the right to cancel the loan upon reasonable notice to the Lender.

Transportation and Packing

1. The Lender certifies that the objects lent are in such condition as to withstand ordinary strains of packing and transportation and handling. A written report of the condition of objects prior to shipment must be sent by the Lender to the Museum. Otherwise, it will be assumed that objects are received in the same condition as when leaving the Lender's possession. Condition records will be made at the Museum on arrival and departure.

2. Costs of transportation and packing will be borne by the Museum unless the loan is at the Lender's request. The method of shipment must be agreed upon by both parties.

3. Government regulations will be adhered to in international shipments. As a rule, the Lender is responsible for adhering to its country's import/export requirements and the borrower is responsible for adhering to its country's import/export requirements.

4. The Lender will assure that said objects are adequately and securely packed for the type of shipment agreed upon, including any special instructions for unpacking and repacking. Objects will be returned packed in the same or similar materials as received unless otherwise authorized by the Lender.

Insurance

1. Objects will be insured for the amount specified herein by the Museum under its "all-risk" wall-to-wall policy subject to the following standard exclusions: wear and tear, gradual deterioration, insects, vermin or inherent vice; repairing, restoration or retouching process; hostile or warlike action, insurrection, rebellion, etc.; nuclear reaction, nuclear radiation, or radioactive contamination. Insurance will be placed in the amount specified by the Lender herein which must reflect fair market value. If the Lender fails to indicate an amount, the Museum, with the implied concurrence of the

Lender, will set a value for purposes of insurance for the period of the loan. Said value is not to be considered an appraisal.

2. If the Lender elects to maintain his own insurance coverage, then prior to shipping the Museum must be supplied with a certificate of insurance naming the Museum as an additional insured or waiving rights of subrogation. If the Lender fails to provide said certificate, this failure shall constitute a waiver of insurance by the Lender (see No. 4 below). The Museum shall not be responsible for any error or deficiency in information furnished by the Lender to the insurer or for any lapses in such coverage.

3. In the case of long-term loans, it is the responsibility of the Lender to notify the Museum of current insurance valuations.

4. If insurance is waived by the Lender, this waiver shall constitute the agreement of the Lender to release and hold harmless the Museum from any liability for damages to or loss of the loan property.

5. The amount payable by insurance secured in accordance with this loan agreement is the sole recovery available to the Lender from the Museum in the event of loss or damage.

Reproduction and Credit

Unless otherwise notified in writing by the Lender, the Museum may photograph or reproduce the objects lent for educational, catalog and publicity purposes. It is understood that objects on exhibit may be photographed by the general public. Unless otherwise instructed in writing, the Museum will give credit to the Lender as specified on the face of this agreement in any publications. Whether individual labels are provided for objects on display is at the discretion of the Museum.

Change in Ownership and/or Address

It is the responsibility of the Lender or his agent to notify the Museum promptly in writing if there is any change in ownership of the objects (whether through *inter vivos* transfer or death) or if there is a change in the identity or address of the Lender. The Museum assumes no responsibility to search for a Lender (or owner) who cannot be reached at the address of record.

Return of Loans

1. Unless otherwise agreed in writing, a loan terminates on the date specified on the face of this agreement. If no date is specified, the loan shall be for a reasonable period of time, but in no event to exceed three years. Upon termination of a loan, the Lender is on notice that a return or renewal must be effected, or else a gift of the objects will be inferred.

2. Objects will be returned only to the Lender of record or to a location mutually agreed upon in writing by the Museum and the Lender of record. In case of uncertainty, the Museum reserves the right to require a Lender/claimant to establish title by proof satisfactory to the Museum.

3. When the loan is returned, the Museum will send the Lender a receipt form. If this form is not signed and returned within thirty days after mailing, the Museum will not be responsible for any damage or loss.

4. If the Museum's efforts to return objects within a reasonable period following the termination of the loan are unsuccessful, then the objects will

be maintained at the Lender's risk and expense for a maximum of _____ years. If after _____ years the objects have not been claimed, then and in consideration for maintenance and safeguarding, the Lender/Owner shall be deemed to have made the objects an unrestricted gift to the Museum.

Applicable Law

This agreement shall be construed in accordance with the law of

_____
(name of the applicable jurisdiction).

I have read and agree to the above conditions and certify that I have full authority to enter into this agreement.

Signed: _____ Date: _____
      (Lender)*

Title: _____

*If Lender is not the owner, complete the following two lines:

Name of owner: _____

Address of owner: _____

APPROVED FOR MUSEUM:

Signed: _____ Date: _____

Title: _____

(Please sign and return both copies.)

B. Outgoing Loans

1. To Whom Will Loans Be Made?

When a museum assumes the role of lender, several new considerations arise which have legal implications. A very basic decision that should be made early, is the museum's general policy regarding eligibility to borrow collection objects.

Most museums do not lend to individuals. There are sound reasons for this rule. Of paramount importance is the fact that museum collections are maintained for the benefit of the public; it is rare that one can justify their exclusive use by any individual.

And there are additional reasons:

- Adjustments made in the tax laws over a decade ago require donors to relinquish complete control over property donated to a museum if full charitable contribution tax deductions are to be taken. If museum policy permits donated property to be returned temporarily to the donor under a loan agreement, the validity of the donor's tax deduction could be called into question.

- Museum trustees and officers have a duty not to self-deal when managing museum assets and their acceptance of loans of collection objects for personal benefit could amount to a violation of this responsibility.[32] A museum policy that generally forbids loans to individuals serves as a useful reminder of this particular standard of conduct.

- When museum objects are on loan, they should be afforded the care and protection normally expected in a museum environment. As a rule, such requirements can be met more readily by institutional borrowers.[33]

Frequently, museums limit borrower eligibility even further by lending only to educational and/or nonprofit organizations. The purposes of the limitation are to focus loan activity on educational and research projects and to avoid entanglement in commercial ventures. The latter purpose warrants special attention by government-run or government-associated museums. Such museums could find their loan policies challenged on constitutional grounds if loan policies are drawn without reference to equal protection guarantees. Consider the following example.

The X Historical Society, run under the auspices of the county government, is asked to mount a small exhibit in the lobby of the local bank. The exhibition will be part of the bank's fiftieth birthday celebration and will depict life in the county fifty years ago. The historical society eagerly agrees to the loan because the exhibit will have prominent exposure and the bank promises to meet all temperature, humidity, and security requirements. The exhibit is a popular success. Some months later, the historical society is approached by the local department store which asks if it can borrow material for an exhibit on the local textile industry. The material will be incorporated in an "educational"

---

32. See Chapter I, "What is a Museum? What is Required of Its Board Members?"

33. When objects are lent for scholarly research even though the research is carried out primarily by an individual, the loan usually is made to the educational organization with which the individual is affiliated. That organization assumes the responsibility for the proper administration of the loan.

window display. Once again the Society agrees. When the local liquor store comes forward with a similar request, it is rejected because "it wouldn't be suitable." The owner of the liquor store protests and threatens legal action.

There is a good possibility that the liquor store will get its exhibit. Both federal and state constitutional safeguards generally guarantee equal access to government-offered benefits, and exceptions are narrowly construed. Once the X Historical Society, a part of the local government, extended a benefit to the bank and the department store, both commercial entities, it established a practice that the law may well require it to administer evenhandedly to all commercial entities in the area. The lesson, therefore, is simple, especially for government-run or government-associated museums:[34] Have a thoughtfully prepared loan eligibility policy and understand all its implications. Once certain actions have been taken, selection criteria may be severely limited.

2. What Will Be Loaned?

If proper handling is to be afforded all objects in a museum's care, some distinctions invariably must be made with regard to what can be placed on loan. A primary consideration is whether the museum has authority to loan a particular object. If the object is on loan to the museum rather than part of its own collections, no outgoing loan should be considered without evidence of written approval of the owner.[35] A normal use of an incoming loan does not include a reloaning of the object. If such is contemplated, permission of the owner should be expressly sought. Another consideration relating to authority to loan is whether the object is encumbered by restrictions that inhibit a loan. Accession records should be reviewed carefully to see if any such restrictions exist. When there is doubt regarding the existence or interpretation of restrictive language, professional advice should be sought.[36]

The value, rarity and/or condition of an object may dictate loan restrictions. No object should be exposed to loan conditions that may seriously threaten its safety, and there is an obligation on the museum to use due care in this regard.[37] What constitutes due care depends on the facts of each situation. Possibly, some objects should never be placed on loan because of fragility. If there is a serious question concerning the ability of an object to travel, it may be prudent to seek the opinion of a conservator.

---

34. What is a government-associated museum frequently amounts to a determination whether the museum is engaged in "government action." See discussion in Chapter IV, "The Acquisition of Objects—Accessioning" on the American Indian Religious Freedom Act.

35. There could be a possible copyright infringement problem if objects on loan, which are subject to copyright, are reloaned for display without the permission of the owner of copyright. See Chapter IV, discussion on "Should a Museum Strive to Acquire Copyright Interests?"

36. In a case discussed in the section in Chapter IV on "Restricted gifts," *In Re Trust of the Samuel Bancroft, Jr., Art Collection* Civil Action No. 6601 (Del. Ct. of Ch., New Castle County, Oct. 28, 1981), the Delaware Art Museum petitioned the court for instructions regarding the museum's ability to lend certain art objects. The objects had been given with the restriction that the museum "shall not . . . in any manner part with the possession of the objects." The court interpreted the restriction to permit loans.

37. As noted in Chapter I, a trustee has an affirmative obligation to preserve trust assets.

To assure that due regard is given to the question of what should be loaned, a museum is well-advised to have written guidelines for staff instruction. The guidelines also should be clear on the issue of who has the authority to approve loans.[38]

3. Loan Approval

As a rule, the basic authority to make loans resides in a museum's board of trustees.[39] The board may retain to itself the exercise of this authority or, barring specific legal restrictions to the contrary, may delegate and redelegate its exercise. Complete delegation, however, without guidance and oversight, is not in accord with normally accepted trust responsibility[40] and a museum's board will want to assure itself that policies and review procedures are in place which clarify who has the authority to make certain loans and what records must be maintained. If delegations are clear and adequate records must be kept, then effective oversight is possible.

When and how much authority to approve loans should be delegated is largely a matter of common sense. In a large, complex museum, there are very practical reasons why many routine outgoing loans can be left to the discretion of designated members of the professional staff. As a rule, such delegations are limited to loans not exceeding certain values or certain amounts, or are limited to objects in certain classes. The rule of thumb for the museum's board is whether the delegation is a reasonable one in light of the museum's overall size and activities.

4. Care of Objects

There is an obligation on the lending museum to take reasonable precautions to assure that museum objects placed on loan receive proper care. If the borrowing institution is not known to the museum, a facilities report may be in order or even an inspection visit by museum staff so that such matters as physical conditions and security standards can be judged. Also, it is sensible to have the loan agreement specify the care that should be afforded the borrowed objects so there are no misunderstandings. If a museum has a history of poor experience with a borrower, prudence would dictate that there be stringent review before any new loans are negotiated.

A loan agreement usually contains a standard clause requiring the borrower to give prompt, written notice to the museum of any damage or loss to loaned objects. Also, there is included a general caution that objects cannot be altered, cleaned or repaired without the written permission of the lending museum. If, in addition, a condition report is required of the borrower upon receipt of a

---

38. See *Johnson Trust*, 51 Pa. D&C 2d 147 (1970), where the court approved a specific outgoing loan policy for the John G. Johnson Collection held in custody by the Philadelphia Museum of Art.

39. In *Smith v. Library Board of City of Minneapolis*, 59 N.W. 979 (Minn. 1894), it was held that a museum has an implied power to accept objects on loan. Each museum, however, must examine its own situation to determine whether there are expressed restrictions that override any implied powers.

40. See Chapter I on the duties of trustees.

loan, not only is delivery confirmed, but any problems associated with transportation can be handled in a timely manner. Requiring a similar condition report before objects are packed and shipped for return helps to pinpoint responsibility if the objects are received back in damaged condition.

Packing and transportation methods should not be left to chance.[41] The borrowing institution should be on notice that certain requirements must be met when the objects are in transit. If special cases have been prepared in order to send the material, the borrower is usually instructed to retain the cases for use in return shipment. In any event, the lending museum should communicate clearly to the borrower any special care needed in unpacking the loan or in returning it. The loan agreement should also specify who is responsible for packing and transportation costs.

The cautions against indefinite and permanent loans mentioned in the prior section on "Incoming Loans" have application to the museum as a lender. It is difficult to imagine situations where it would be prudent for a lending museum to lend objects on an indefinite basis. Museums are obligated to use due care in overseeing collection assets, and if objects are loaned, the museum's responsibilities do not disappear. It is reasonable to interpret "due care" to mean that loan situations should be checked periodically to see that objects are safe, that they are being used for the agreed-upon purpose, and that insurance valuations are current. A practice of lending only for a stated term, subject to renewal, encourages adherence to the due care standard.

5. Insurance

Invariably, the lending museum insists on insurance coverage for all objects sent out on loan. Insurance offers the added measure of security that claims will be processed objectively and that resources will be available for payment of damages or replacement of the loaned object. As a rule, the borrower absorbs insurance costs by either providing insurance satisfactory to the lender or by reimbursing the lending museum for providing its own insurance.

If the borrower is to provide insurance, the lending museum will want evidence that adequate coverage has been obtained before objects are released. As a rule, a certificate of insurance or copy of the policy is requested prior to shipment. The borrower should also be warned that any cancellation or meaningful change in insurance coverage must be communicated to the lender immediately. A wise precaution is to add to the loan agreement a statement that failure of the borrower to have in effect the agreed-upon insurance will in no way release the borrower from liability for loss or damage. The purpose of such a statement is to rebut any inference that the lending museum may have waived its rights by any inaction on its part in monitoring the borrower's insurance. Even if there proves to be no insurance coverage, the lending museum still wants to preserve all legal rights it may have arising out of loss of or damage to its property.

---

41. As noted in Chapter XV, "Insurance," one insurance expert cites accidents during transportation as the leading cause of museum collection claims.

Occasionally, a borrower is not able to provide standard insurance coverage. It may, for example, be a governmental entity which self-insures.[42] In such instances, the lending museum will want to assure itself that there are reasonable expectations that the borrower will respond to any loss or damage claim. If the borrower has an established method for processing claims and can demonstrate a history of fair and timely attention to such matters, the lending museum may well decide that there is no undue risk in negotiating a loan. However, a clear statement in the loan agreement to the effect that the borrower agrees to indemnify the museum for any loss or damage occurring during the course of the loan is an added protection. It establishes that the borrower undertook the loan fully aware of potential liability.

Setting a value on objects for insurance can raise problems for the lending museum. For example, some natural history specimens may have no readily ascertainable market value, but their loss to the collections would be significant. Some objects may be irreplaceable or some, if damaged, may need restoration work that could be more costly than their market value. The insurance value of an object does not always equal fair market value, and in those cases where insurance estimates significantly exceed the traditional fair market value test, the lending museum should be prepared to defend its position. If the borrower does not question the valuation before entering into the loan, the insurer may well do so when a claim arises. When negotiating a loan, if there are serious differences of opinion between lender and borrower over insurance valuations, the advisability of going forward with the loan should be weighed. The costs of pursuing any claim that might arise and the potential for aggravating already strained relations may far exceed the perceived benefits from the loan.

6. Cancellation and Return

When an object is loaned for a definite term, there is a presumption that the borrower, as long as he does not breach the terms of the loan agreement, will have the right to use the object for the stated time. If the lending museum wishes to have the flexibility of canceling the loan before the termination date or of recalling the object for a period of time, then these conditions should be made an express part of the loan agreement. Without the benefit of such contract provisions, the lender who attempts to recall objects before the stated termination date may meet with a firm refusal or with a bill for damages accompanying the returned material.

If objects have been loaned on an indefinite basis, normally there is a presumption that either borrower or lender may request termination. However, the facts of each situation must be reviewed to see if there is evidence that both parties may have intended otherwise when the loan was negotiated. If a museum finds itself with objects out on indefinite or even permanent loan, it should consider the advantages of seeking to renegotiate each such loan for a stated term. As noted previously, indefinite or permanent loan situations tend

---

42. Sometimes there can be great confusion regarding the ability of a governmental entity to buy insurance. A possible solution might be for the lending museum to impose a modest "service fee" for such loans and then use this fee to cover the loaned material under its own insurance policy.

to produce problems that grow worse with time. A museum may find it prudent to take the initiative in clarifying such loans with the borrower before situations arise that make amicable resolution much more difficult.

Once a loan has terminated, the lending museum should retrieve its property promptly. There is a greater likelihood that unclaimed property may become lost or mislaid. Also, the borrowing organization could take the position that it owes a lesser standard of care to property left beyond the term of the loan agreement,[43] or, if the property is unclaimed for a long period of time, that there is an inferred gift, as described in subsection 9 of Part A of this chapter. Therefore, a museum is well-advised to have in place a system for monitoring loan terminations with clear guidance to staff regarding responsibility for seeing that loans are actually returned.

7. Sample Outgoing Loan Agreement

As with all sample forms, the model outgoing loan agreement (on pages 180-82) should not be adopted by a museum without independent review by competent professionals. If in a particular transaction the borrower wishes to utilize its incoming loan form as a supplement to the lender's outgoing form, both documents should be reviewed in advance for compatibility. Even where there appears to be no substantial conflict, the lender may still wish to specify that its form will be the controlling one.

---

43. Upon expiration of a loan agreement and failure of the owner to retrieve, the argument can be made that the bailee now holds the property strictly for the benefit of the owner, and, hence, is liable only for gross negligence. See general discussion on bailment in Chapter VI, "Loans, Incoming and Outgoing," section on "Incoming Loans."

Registrar's No. _____

NAME OF MUSEUM
ADDRESS
TELEPHONE NUMBER OF MUSEUM

AGREEMENT FOR OUTGOING LOAN   Date: _____

TO: _____
          (borrower's name)

     Address: _____   Telephone: (   ) _____

From: _____   Telephone: (   ) _____
       (curatorial unit)

In accordance with the conditions printed on the reverse, the objects listed
below are borrowed for the following purpose(s) only:

_____

For the period _____ to _____
         (approximate time objects leave Museum until their return
         receipt)

Locations of object(s) while on loan: _____

Initiated by: _____
        (curator's signature)

Accession or Index Number	Description of Objects (include size, materials, catalog numbers, etc.)	Insurance Value

(Attach continuation sheet if necessary.)

INSURANCE: (Please see conditions on reverse.)
    ☐ to be carried by Museum and premium billed to borrower
    ☐ to be carried by borrower
    ☐ insurance waived

SHIPPING AND PACKING:

     Object(s) will be packed by _____ charges to

     borrower: Yes _____ No _____

     Object(s) will be shipped to (address): _____

     from Museum ☐ or other: _____

Shipment to be via:

     OUTGOING: _____

     RETURN: _____

CREDIT LINE (for exhibition label and catalog) : _____

SPECIAL REQUIREMENTS for installation and handling:

_____

(attach continuation sheet if necessary)

The Borrower agrees to the following conditions of the loan:

Protection
Objects borrowed shall be given special care at all times to insure against loss, damage or deterioration. The borrower agrees to meet the special requirements for installation and handling as noted on the face of this agreement form. Furthermore, the Museum may require an inspection and approval of the actual installation by a member of its staff as a condition of the loan at the expense of the borrower. Upon receipt and prior to return of the objects, the borrower must make a written record of condition. The Museum is to be notified immediately, followed by a full written report, including photographs, if damage or loss is discovered. No object may be altered, cleaned or repaired without the written permission of the museum. Objects must be maintained in a building equipped to protect objects from fire, smoke or flood damage; under 24-hour physical and/or electronic security; and protected from extreme temperatures and humidity, excessive light, and from insects, vermin, dirt, or other environmental hazards. Objects must be handled only by experienced personnel and be secured from damage and theft by appropriate brackets, railings, display cases, or other responsible means.

Insurance
Objects shall be insured during the period of this loan for the value stated on the face of this agreement under an all-risk, wall-to-wall policy subject to the following standard exclusions: wear and tear, gradual deterioration, insects, vermin or inherent vice, repairing, restoration, or retouching process; hostile or warlike action, insurrection, rebellion, nuclear reaction, nuclear radiation, or radioactive contamination.

If the borrower is insuring the object, the Museum must be furnished with a certificate of insurance or a copy of the policy made out in favor of the Museum prior to shipment of the objects. The Museum Registrar must be notified in writing at least 20 days prior to any cancellation or meaningful change in the borrower's policy. Any lapses in coverage, any failure to secure insurance and/or any inaction by the Lender regarding notice will not release the borrower from liability for loss or damage.

Insurance value may be reviewed periodically and the Museum reserves the right to increase coverage if reasonably justified. In the event of loss or damage, the borrower's maximum liability will be limited to the insurance value then in effect.

If insurance is waived, the borrower agrees to indemnify the Museum for any and all loss or damage to the objects occurring during the course of the loan, except for loss or damage resulting from wear and tear, gradual deterioration, inherent vice, war and nuclear risk.

Packing and Transportation
Packing and transportation shall be by safe methods approved in advance by the Museum. Unpacking and repacking must be done by experienced personnel under competent supervision. Repacking must be done with the same or similar material and boxes, and by the same methods as the objects were received. Any additional instructions will be followed.

Reproduction and Credit
Each object shall be labeled and credited to the Museum. Unless otherwise stipulated in writing by the Museum, the visiting public may take impromptu photographs, but no other reproduction is permitted except photographic copies for catalog and publicity uses related to the stated purpose of the loan.

Costs
Unless otherwise noted, all costs of packing, transportation, customs, insurance and other loan-related costs shall be borne by the borrower.

Return/Extension/Cancellation
Objects lent must be returned to the Museum in satisfactory condition by the stated termination date. An extension of the loan period must be approved in writing by the Museum Director or his designate and covered by parallel extension of the insurance coverage. The Museum reserves the right to recall the object from loan on short notice, if necessary. Furthermore, the Museum reserves the right to cancel this loan for good cause at any time, and will make every effort to give reasonable notice thereof.

Interpretation
In the event of any conflict between this agreement and any forms of the borrower, the terms of this agreement shall be controlling. This agreement shall be construed in accordance with the law of _____.
                                                     (name of applicable jurisdiction)

I have read and agree to the above conditions and certify that I am authorized to agree thereto.

Signed: _____ Date: _____
                (borrower or authorized agent)

Title: _____

APPROVED FOR MUSEUM:

_____ Date: _____

Title: _____

(Please sign and return both copies.)

CHAPTER VII

Unclaimed Loans

A. The Problem
B. Statutes of Limitations
C. Laches
D. Adverse Possession
E. Discovery Rule
F. Legislative Solutions

A. The Problem

When museum professionals meet to discuss common problems, invariably someone asks what can be done about unclaimed loans. Many of these objects have been held for generations by museums in a state of limbo. Owners are unknown or cannot be located, and, lacking clear title, museums feel compelled to store and care for the objects. This places a considerable drain on a museum's resources, yet the alternatives are even less attractive. If the objects are disposed of, a museum may be vulnerable to claims by individuals who later appear and assert ownership. If extensive searches are mounted to locate owners, a museum faces substantial expenses with little assurance of remuneration or even success. It often comes as a shock to the earnest museum administrator that the law, and, frequently, even the public, offers him little solace.[1]

As explained in the preceding chapter, a loan gives rise to a relationship known in the law as a bailment. The bailor, the owner, places his property in the care of the bailee for a particular purpose. The bailee is responsible for holding the property for that purpose until the owner comes forward to claim it. What happens, however, when the owner fails to retrieve the property?

Assuming that there is a loan agreement stipulating that the loan is to terminate at a certain time, it can be argued that after the termination date the relationship of the parties is somewhat altered. While the loan agreement is in effect, the bailee is obliged to use and care for the property under the terms of the agreement, but after the expiration date, the "benefits" of the arrangement accrue only to the owner. This is so because upon failure of the bailor to retrieve, the bailee is left with the responsibility of care but with no express rights to use the property. A new form of bailment then exists, one essentially for the benefit of the bailor, and the bailee usually is held to a less strict standard

---

1. See discussion in Chapter VI, "Loans, Incoming and Outgoing," section on "Incoming Loans" for suggestions on ways to avoid future unclaimed loans.

of care. Also, if the bailee can demonstrate that expenses were incurred in caring for the property beyond the stipulated loan period, these usually can be recovered from the owner. This "involuntary bailment" situation is of little comfort to the bailee/museum, however, if the owner cannot be located or if, upon notice, he fails to retrieve the property. Are there steps a museum can take to resolve these situations? There are three doctrines in the law that possibly may afford relief if they can be set in motion. One is the relief afforded by "statutes of limitations," another is a defense called "laches" and the third is the doctrine of adverse possession.

B. Statutes of Limitations

Statutes of limitations[2] require that claims be brought within a certain stated period of time or else the right to claim is barred. The purpose of such statutes is to urge plaintiffs to action in a timely manner so that claims do not become stale.[3] In *Wood v. Carpenter*[4] the Supreme Court of the United States gave the following description:

> Statutes of limitation are vital to the welfare of society and are favored in the law. They are found and approved in all systems of enlightened jurisprudence. They promote response by giving security and stability to human affairs. An important public policy lies at their foundation. They stimulate to activity and punish negligence. While time is constantly destroying the evidence of rights, they supply its place by a presumption which renders proof unnecessary. Mere delay in extending to the limit prescribed, is itself a conclusive bar. The bane and antidote go together.[5]

The difficulty arises in trying to determine when a statute of limitations might begin to run in an "involuntary bailment" situation. The general rule is that the statute of limitations does not begin to run until the bailor has made a demand for the return of the property and has been refused, or until the bailee has acted in a manner inconsistent with the bailment.[6] When an owner is known, therefore, there are certain steps a museum can take that may trigger the running of a statute of limitations. A written warning, best delivered by certified mail, can be sent to the owner stating that the museum is as of such

---

2. See also discussion of statutes of limitations in Chapter IV, "The Acquisition of Objects—Accessioning," section on "Stolen Property."

3. "After all, statutes of limitation are statutes of repose and the principal consideration underlying their enactment is one of fairness to the defendant," *Lopez v. Swyer*, 62 N.J. 267, 300 A.2d 563, 567 (1973). See also Note, "Developments in the Law—Statutes of Limitations," 63 *Harv. L. Rev.* 1177 (1950) at 1185. But see *State of North Carolina v. West*, 293 N.C. 18, 235 S.E.2d 150 (1977), where the court held that in North Carolina a statute of limitations could not be applied against the state.

4. 101 U.S. 135, 25 L.Ed. 807 (1879).

5. Ibid., at 139.

6. *Irvine v. Gradoville*, 221 F.2d 544 (D.C. Cir. 1955); *Schupp v. Taendler*, 154 F.2d 849 (D.C. Cir. 1946).

and such date asserting title to the property in question unless the property is retrieved by that date:[7]

> Where the names and post office addresses of those affected by a proceeding are at hand, the reasons disappear for resort to means less likely than the mails to apprise them of its pendency.[8]

The purpose of the written communication is to establish evidence that the owner is on notice that the museum is "converting" (claiming as its own) the property in question. The owner should then be aware that he has a cause of action for conversion and if he fails to press this claim within the applicable statute of limitations, he may be forever barred from doing so.[9] All of this, of course, assumes that the owner is easily located and delivery of notice can be established.

If the owner of a terminated loan is unknown or cannot be located, the museum is faced with a dilemma. Extensive searches for an owner or his heirs are costly, and even if searches produce claimants, the museum acts at its peril if it returns objects to those having less than full ownership rights. How, practically, can effective notice be given to unknown owners? A notice in the newspaper? Perhaps, but there is an element of uncertainty. It all depends on whether this method is deemed sufficient by a court later called on to make the determination.[10] With regard to establishing proper notice for judicial

---

7. Even if the loan in question was for a term and the expiration date has long passed, it cannot be assumed that the courts will impose a duty on the lender to come forward, and it is safer to send such a notice. For example, in *Houser v. Ohio Historical Society*, 62 Ohio St. 2d 77, 403 N.E.2d 965 (1980), a loan made to a museum "for a term of one year or more" went unclaimed for over twenty years after the death of the owner. The court refused to apply the statute of limitations. In museum cases, the courts appear unwilling to concede that at some point lenders or their heirs should be on notice that loans cannot go on forever. Yet, in other situations, ignorance or lack of diligence has been held not to bar the statute of limitations from running: *Wood v. Carpenter*, 101 U.S. 135, 25 L.Ed. 807 (1879); *Fernandi v. Strully*, 35 N.J. 434, 173 A.2d 277 (1961); *Federal Insurance Co. v. Fries*, 78 Misc. 2d 805, 355 N.Y.S.2d 741, 747 (1974), "But ignorance does not stop the clock, unless the defendant engages in fraudulent or misleading conduct."

8. *Mullane v. Central Hanover Bank and Trust Co.*, 339 U.S. 306, 70 S. Ct. 652, 94 L. Ed. 865, 875 (1949). See also *Mennonite Board of Missions v. Adams*, 462 U.S. 791, 103 S. Ct. 2706, 77 L. Ed. 2d 180 (1983).

9. *Magruder v. Smithsonian Institution*, Case No. 83-693-Civ CA (U.S.D.C. So. Fla. Sept. 15, 1983). But see *DeBlanc v. State of Louisiana*, No. 79-13404 (La. Civ. D. Ct. for Parish of Orleans, Div. C, April 1980) and *Wogan v. State of Louisiana*, No. 81-2295 (La. Civ. D. Ct. for Parish of Orleans, Div. D, Jan. 1982) where under the peculiarities of Louisiana law a museum was not permitted to "convert" a loan.

10. In *In Re Estate of Therese Davis McCagg*, 450 A.2d 414 (D.C. 1982), the court suggests that if a museum is unable to locate heirs through reasonably diligent efforts "then constructive notice by publication might suffice." There is no elaboration on the nature of the publication. By statute in California, notice to unknown or unlocatable owners of unclaimed property left with museums is deemed sufficient if published at least once a week for three successive weeks in a newspaper of general circulation in both the county in which the museum is located and the county of the lender's address, if any. Other statutes on the same subject have slightly different procedures (see subsection F of this chapter). The Revised Uniform Disposition of Unclaimed Property Act (1981) does not cover property generally loaned to museums, but its notification provisions may be a useful point of reference if a museum is faced with determining what might constitute adequate notice in an unclaimed loan situation.

proceedings, the Supreme Court has said:

> This Court has not hesitated to approve of resort to publication as a
> customary substitute in another class of cases where it is not reasonably
> possible or practicable to give more adequate warning. Thus it has been
> recognized that in the case of persons missing or unknown employment of
> an indirect and even a probably futile means of notification is all that the
> situation permits and creates no constitutional bar to a final decree
> foreclosing their rights.[11]

It could be reasoned from this language that if a museum has no record
of names and addresses of the depositors of objects, or if named depositors
cannot be located with reasonable effort[12] then some form of general notice
may be sufficient to begin the running of applicable statutes of limitations. The
customary way of giving general notice is a notice in the local newspaper, but
any other method or combination of methods just as likely to produce the
desired end should be considered. Common sense, not mere custom, should
be the guide.[13] For example, if an object has been displayed publicly in a
museum for fifty years with a label identifying it as "on loan from John Smith,"
such a display could be construed an effective notice to John Smith's heirs that
a claim should be made immediately to the museum. Similarly, circumstances
may be such that a notice in the museum's newsletter and posters in the
museum itself may be deemed more likely to reach interested parties than a
notice in the city's newspaper.[14]

The situation regarding effective notice becomes even more tenuous when
the original loan was for an indefinite period. When do such arrangements
terminate? Normally, if there is no express evidence to the contrary, it is
assumed that either party to such a loan can terminate the arrangement upon

---

11. *Mullane v. Central Hanover Bank and Trust Co.*, 339 U.S. 306, 70 S. Ct. 652, 94 L. Ed. 865, 875
(1949). See also *Mennonite Board of Missions v. Adams*, 462 U.S. 791, 103 S. Ct. 2706, 77 L. Ed. 2d
180 (1983); *Cunnius v. Reading School District*, 198 U.S. 458, 25 S. Ct. 721, 49 L. Ed. 1125 (1905);
Blinn v. Nelson, 222 U.S. 1 (1911).

12. *Jacob v. Roberts*, 223 U.S. 261, 32 S. Ct. 303, 56 L. Ed. 429 (1911) discusses what constitutes
diligent search. Here various local residents were questioned and inquiries were made to local
officials in an effort to trace a former resident. This search was considered adequate. In *Schroeder
v. City of New York*, 371 U.S. 208, 83 S. Ct. 279, 9 L. Ed. 2d 255 (1962), another case involving "due
process," the court held that newspaper notice was not sufficient where with a good faith effort
the names and addresses of interested parties could have been obtained from city records. See
also *Walker v. City of Hutchinson*, 352 U.S. 112, 77 S. Ct. 200, 1 L. Ed. 2d 178 (1956). These cases
indicate that at a minimum, a museum should document that there was a systematic search of
public records, telephone directories, probate court records, etc., before a decision was made that
it was "not reasonably possible or practicable" to obtain actual addresses. For those faced with
the task of tracing long lost lenders, the U.S. Department of Health and Human Services publishes
a pamphlet entitled "Where to Write for Vital Records" (DHHS Publication No. (PHS) 82-1142).
The pamphlet gives the addresses of all state records offices, the scope of their records, fees for
duplication of records, etc.

13. See *Milliken v. Meyer*, 311 U.S. 457, 61 S. Ct. 339, 85 L. Ed. 278 (1940). *Grannis v. Ordean*, 234
U.S. 385, 31 S. Ct. 779, 52 L. Ed. 1363 (1913).

14. Of course, when claimants come forward, there is always the possibility that difficulties will
be encountered in determining who are the true parties at interest, and legal advice will be
necessary.

notice to the other. If the owner is known, therefore, a museum could give written notice that it is terminating an indefinite loan. Assuming that the notice is reasonable and the owner fails to collect the property, the museum can then attempt to force action by giving notice of intent to convert.[15] The more common situation, however, involves an unknown or unlocatable owner. This poses two problems for the museum: giving effective notice of termination and giving effective notice of intent to convert if the owner fails to retrieve. A museum could attempt to do both using a form of general notice it believes is defensible in light of all the circumstances.[16] Having given such notice, it could then prudently determine that the appropriate statute of limitations had begun to run, hoping that, if challenged, its actions will be upheld by the courts. At the present time, though arduous, this may be the safest course. Several other theories should be considered, however, which do not place all the burdens on the museum of establishing adequate notice in order to begin a statute of limitations. Rather, these theories infer an obligation on the depositor or his heirs to come forward.

There are cases that lend support to the argument that an owner should not be allowed to delay beyond a reasonable time in making his request for the return of property left on indefinite loan. In *Nyhus v. Travel Management Corporation*,[17] for example, the court reasoned as follows:

> Where a demand is necessary to perfect a cause of action, the statute of
> limitations does not commence to run until the demand is made. . . . [But] a
> party is not at liberty to stave off operation of the statute inordinately by
> failing to make demand; when statutorily unstipulated, the time for demand
> is ordinarily a reasonable time. That, however, is a matter of the parties'
> expectations, and a different result follows when an indefinite delay in
> making demand was within their contemplation.[18]

If the language of *Nyhus* is followed, a museum might find relief from a long overdue, indefinite loan by proving that the owner failed to make his demand for return within a reasonable time,[19] and this failure triggered the applicable

---

15. In *Bufano v. City and County of San Francisco*, 233 C.A.2d 61, 43 Cal. Rptr. 223 (1965), an artist sued the city for two of his sculptures which had been held by the city for seventeen years. The court held that a statute of limitations would not begin to run until the owner was on notice that the city claimed the sculptures as its own.

16. See this chapter, section F, "Legislative Solutions," for examples of statutory requirements concerning notice, and footnote 10. It is suggested that a notice contain at least the following information: A brief description of the reason for the notice and the property involved; approximate date of loan, if known; the name of any unlocatable owner; when a claimant must come forward and what happens if he/she does not; the name of a person at the museum to contact for more information; and the address for mailing claims.

17. 466 F.2d 440 (D.C. Cir. 1972). See also *Heide v. Glidden Buick Corp.*, 188 Misc. 198, 67 N.Y.S.2d 905 (1947); *Southward v. Foy*, 65 Nev. 694, 201 P.2d 302 (1948); *Slack v. Bryan*, 184 S.W.2d 873 (Ky. 1945); *Campbell v. Whorisky*, 170 Mass. 63, 48 N.E. 1070 (1898); *Wright v. Paine*, 62 Ala. 340 (1878).

18. *Nyhus*, at 452-3.

19. What is a reasonable time must be determined from the nature of the agreement and the probable intention of the parties. *Campbell v. Whoriskey*, 170 Mass. 63, 48 N.E. 1070 (1898). In *Desiderio v. D'Ambrosio*, 190 N. J. Super. 424, 463 A.2d 986 (1983), the court applied the statute of limitations period from the date the bailment began.

statute of limitations which has since run. However, a practical problem may be encountered in trying to convince a court that a "reasonable time" has elapsed for the owner to terminate the loan.[20] For many not familiar with the problems of running a museum, it seems perfectly reasonable to expect that a museum should be charged with holding indefinitely the property of some unknown party. It matters not whether the "indefinite" loan has gone on for ten years, forty years or one hundred years. The average museum administrator can only view such an attitude in complete disbelief, but it is an attitude that must be reckoned with.

If the facts reveal that the lender of an indefinite loan has long since died and that the estate or heirs failed to come forward to notify the museum, additional evidence may be available to support a loan termination date and a failure to make a demand in a reasonable time. Normally, when a person enters into an indefinite loan with a museum he is not contemplating an arrangement to survive his death, but rather a temporary disposition that will be subject to his later review. Indefinite loans are not viewed as testamentary instruments (instruments for determining the disposition of property after death), nor do they have the requisites established by law to be so classified. It is a fair inference, then, to hold that a lender when entering into an indefinite loan does not intend to have the loan last longer than his life. Rather, he expects that if he should die before recalling the loan the property will become part of his estate to be administered accordingly. In other words, from the nature of the agreement and the probable intent of the lender, the indefinite loan should be considered terminated at the death of the lender unless there is clear evidence that a contrary result was intended. There is an equally strong inference that a museum in entering into such a loan as bailee never intends that the loan should last beyond the life of the owner. To hold otherwise means that the museum willingly commits itself to a situation where it may face years of maintenance costs for objects over which it has no definitive control.[21] In

---

20. See *Houser v. Ohio Historical Society*, 62 Ohio St. 2d 77, 403 N.E.2d 965 (1980). In *Houser*, objects were placed on loan in 1931. In 1948, upon demand, one object was returned. In 1952, the lender died and in 1975 an administratrix was appointed for the lender's estate. The administratrix retrieved loan receipts from the lender's safe deposit box and requested the property from the historical society. The historical society claimed that the statute of limitations had run. The court quoted the rule which states that a demand must be made in a reasonable time but refused to invoke it for this "special circumstance." See also *In Re Estate of Therese Davis McCagg*, 450 A.2d 414 (D.C. 1982), where the court refused to find "an implied finite time for demand" in an indefinite loan which went unclaimed for almost fifty years after the death of the lender. It is difficult to reconcile these cases with *Desiderio v. D'Ambrosio*, 190 N. J. Super. 424, 463 A.2d 986 (1983), an unclaimed indefinite bailment situation that did not involve a museum. In *Desiderio*, the court held that a bailor was barred from reclaiming property left unclaimed for six-and-one-half years, even though the address of the bailor was known to the bailee.

21. One subject which deserves more attention by the museum profession is an analysis of the cost of maintaining a collection object. All too frequently, it is assumed that care or "storage" is a minor budgetary item which is of little significance in weighing the relative duties of lender and borrower. Some preliminary work in this area demonstrates that storage and/or exhibit of art objects and curation of scientific specimens involve substantial costs, and that loans or "deposits" to museums should be judged accordingly. With facts and figures on the cost of care available, a judge may pause before finding an indefinite loan of fifty years "reasonable." On the subject of

addition, common practice supports the view that museums actually treat indefinite loans as terminating at the death of lenders. In most of these situations, the estate or heirs come forward in a timely manner and, without hesitation, the museum returns the borrowed objects or, if mutually desired, a new loan agreement is entered into between the museum and the current owner. With the death of a lender, therefore, frequently there is persuasive evidence that an indefinite loan situation terminates. If the loan terminates, there should then be a responsibility on the part of the estate or heirs to come forward and demand the property. Undue delay may be grounds for arguing that the claim is now barred because the applicable statute of limitations began to run upon failure of the estate to make timely demand.[22]

C. Laches

The second legal doctrine that should be considered when trying to resolve unclaimed property situations is the defense of "laches." Laches is delay that makes it inequitable to give the relief sought or delay that warrants a presumption that the party requesting relief has waived his rights.[23] The defense usually is available if there is evidence that a party negligently delayed making a claim or enforcing a right, and this delay actually prejudiced the other party. In such cases, the law may imply a waiver of all claims on the part of the negligent party in order to avoid injustice to the prejudiced party:

> The doctrine of laches is based upon grounds of public policy which requires the discouragement of stale demands for the peace of society. Where there is difficulty in doing complete justice by reason of the death of

---

care of scientific specimens, see Marquardt, *et al.*, "Resolving the Crisis in Archaeological Collections Curation," 47 *American Antiquity* 409 (No. 2 1982); *The Curation and Management of Archaeological Collections: A Pilot Study*, Cultural Resources Management Series, U.S. Department of Interior, Washington, D.C. (1980). Nicholson, "The Obligation of Collecting," *Museum News* 29 (Oct. 1983). The North Idaho Regional Laboratory of Anthropology at the University of Idaho and the Institute of Archaeology and Anthropology at the University of South Carolina have developed fee schedules which reflect actual costs of curation and storage. At the 1983 ALI/ABA conference on "Legal Problems of Museum Administration" there was a presentation on the cost of maintaining a museum object as this relates to "indefinite loans." It was pointed out that a true analysis of cost should include such factors as: recording, periodic inventory, maintaining accessible records, environmental pest control, storage equipment, security, conservation, insurance and general overhead including management and building expense. Display can add considerably more to cost, especially if one realistically calculates total space used to create the ambience necessary for effective presentation. For more specific figures, see Washburn, "Collecting Information, Not Objects," *Museum News* 5 (Feb. 1984).

22. But see *In Re Estate of Therese Davis McCagg*, 450 A.2d 414 (D.C. 1982), where the court refused to find that the death of a lender triggered a duty to demand delivery. The root of the problem appears to be an unwillingness to impose any obligation on lenders or their heirs to inquire after property left with a museum. See also footnote 7 of this chapter. Note also that a state may have an escheat law, one which provides that unclaimed property left in a dead person's estate passes to the state. In such an instance, the state could attempt to assert a right to property held by a museum which has not been claimed by the heirs of a deceased lender.

23. *Thorpe v. Wm. Filene's Sons Co.*, 40 F.2d 269 (Mass. 1930); *Harrison v. Miller*, 124 W. Va. 550, 21 S.E.2d 674 (1942). The distinction is sometimes made that statutes of limitations apply to actions at law while laches is the analogous rule applied to equitable proceedings; see *Desiderio v. D'Ambrosio*, 190 N. J. Super. 424, 463 A.2d 986 (1983).

the principal witness or witnesses, or where the original transaction has become obscured by time because of gross negligence or deliberate delay, a court of equity will not aid the party whose application thus lacks good faith and reasonable diligence. Equity takes the view that such manifest neglect constitutes an implied waiver arising from a knowledge of the conditions and an acquiescence in them.[24]

What is an unreasonable time depends upon the facts,[25] but the defense of laches does require evidence of negligence on the part of the party asserting a right. In other words, in an unclaimed property situation, the bailee/museum would have to show that the claimant knew or should have known that he was sleeping on his rights.[26] Establishing the negligence aspect of laches carries with it the same or similar problems one encounters when trying to establish that a statute of limitations has begun to run.

If negligent delay can be established, the party asserting laches must also show that it has been prejudiced by the delay. A bailee/museum might be able to prove such prejudice if, for example, it can demonstrate that the undue delay has blurred evidence by which it could have shown that a deceased lender intended to make a gift of the property, or that timely notice would have put it in a better position to negotiate a gift or purchase of the property. If the museum has actually disposed of the property in good faith, it may well have a basis for proving prejudice when a long overdue claim is presented.

D. Adverse Possession

A third legal doctrine which may come into play in an unclaimed property situation is that of adverse possession.[27] Adverse possession is a method of acquiring title by possessing something for a statutory period of time under certain conditions.[28] The conditions are that the possession must be hostile (adverse to the owner), actual, visible, exclusive and continuous. The doctrine is associated, as a rule, with real property. For example, if one were to allow, without permission, a third party to build upon and occupy a piece of his property for years, the occupier may well develop a right to the real estate by adverse possession. The doctrine also has been applied to personal (moveable) property, but with less success. Whether or not possession of an object, as distinct from land, has been hostile, actual, visible, exclusive and continuous often defies conclusive proof, and, in addition, confusion can arise as to whether

---

24. *Kaufman v. Plitt*, 59 A.2d 634, 635 (Md. 1948). See also *Hoffa v. Hough*, 30 A.2d 761 (Md. 1943); *Brady v. Garrett*, 66 S.W.2d 502 (Tex. 1933).

25. *Kaufman v. Plitt*, 59 A.2d 634 (Md. 1948).

26. ''Laches cannot be imputed to a party who has been justifiably ignorant of the facts creating his right or cause of action, and has consequently failed to assert it.'' *Berman v. Leckner*, 66 A.2d 392, 395 (Md. 1949). In *Brady v. Garrett*, 66 S.W.2d 502 (Tex. 1933), the loan of an object for exhibit for fourteen years and the bailee's belief that a gift had been made by the owner's husband did not support a defense of laches and the owner was allowed to recover.

27. This doctrine is also discussed in the section on Stolen Property.

28. *Black's Law Dictionary* (4th ed. 1951).

the proper doctrine to apply is adverse possession or the running of a statute of limitations.[29] Consider, for example, the case of *Redmond v. New Jersey Historical Society*[30] and the previously discussed case of *O'Keeffe v. Snyder*.[31]

In *Redmond*, a Gilbert Stuart portrait was bequeathed by its owner to her son upon the condition that if the son were to die leaving no descendants, the portrait would go to the New Jersey Historical Society. The owner died in 1887 when her son was only fourteen years old. The portrait was delivered to the historical society. Fifty years later, the son died leaving children, and these children requested the return of the painting because, under the terms of their grandmother's will, title now vested in them. The historical society refused claiming it had acquired title to the portrait. The children sued. In deciding the case, the appeals court applied the doctrine of adverse possession and found that during the loan period[32] the historical society did nothing to establish that its possession of the painting was "adverse" or "hostile."

This application of the adverse possession concept to personal property gave the New Jersey Supreme Court trouble in *O'Keeffe v. Snyder*. *O'Keeffe* involved paintings allegedly stolen from the artist Georgia O'Keeffe and later found in the possession of an innocent purchaser. When O'Keeffe sued for the return of the paintings some thirty years later upon learning of their whereabouts, the question arose as to whether the doctrine of adverse possession should be applied. If adverse possession was the true test, the innocent purchaser could not prevail because the paintings had been displayed almost exclusively in private homes, and, hence, "hostile" and "visible" possession could not be proven. The court found that the doctrine of adverse possession did not provide a fair and reasonable means of resolving disputes involving personal property and overruled *Redmond* to the extent that it held the doctrine applied in New Jersey to personal property.

E. Discovery Rule

The court in *O'Keeffe* went on to adopt a new test for weighing conflicting claims to lost or stolen property. The test, called the discovery rule, could have

---

29. Two Louisiana cases demonstrate the difficulty a bailee may have in establishing a defense of adverse possession. *DeBlanc v. Louisiana State Museum*, No. 79-13404 (La. Civ. D. Ct. for Parish of Orleans, Div. C, April 1980) and *Wogan v. Louisiana State Museum*, No. 81-2295 (La. Civ. D. Ct. for Parish of Orleans, Div. D, Jan. 1982) involved claims against the Louisiana State Museum for loans allegedly converted by the museum. In both instances, the plaintiffs prevailed because under Louisiana law bailees "cannot prescribe whatever may be the time of possession." These cases also suggest that the public may not look too kindly on museums which silently change old loans to gifts in an effort to resolve title uncertainty through adverse possession.

30. 132 N.J. Eq. 464, 28 A.2d 189 (1942).

31. 170 N. J. Super. 75, 405 A.2d 840, 416 A.2d 862 (1980). See section on "Stolen Property" in Chapter IV.

32. The historical society knew or was presumed to have known that under the terms of the owner's will its claim to the painting could not be resolved until the son's death. Hence, it held the painting on loan as a bailee until this time. In effect, it held the painting on a loan for a definite term, the life of the son. In this regard, the *Redmond* case is quite different from the situation where there is an indefinite loan and the lender or heirs cannot be located.

important implications for the museum community if it is applied in similar cases in other jurisdictions:[33]

> The discovery rule provides that, in an appropriate case, a cause of action will not accrue until the injured party discovers, or by exercise of reasonable diligence and intelligence should have discovered, facts which form the basis of a cause of action. . . . The rule is essentially a principle of equity, the purpose of which is to mitigate unjust results that otherwise might flow from strict adherence to a rule of law.[34]

Applying this test to the *O'Keeffe* situation, the court reasoned as follows. Miss O'Keeffe's cause of action normally would have accrued in 1946 when she discovered that her paintings were stolen. In New Jersey, there is a six-year statute of limitations for bringing an action to recover stolen property and, thus, barring unusual circumstances, Miss O'Keeffe had to sue by 1952 or else she would loose her right to claim the property. In this instance, there were unusual circumstances because Miss O'Keeffe said she did not know where the paintings were until 1976, and hence could not make her demand until that time. Under the discovery rule, however, the running of the statute of limitations would not be postponed unless Miss O'Keeffe could establish that she exercised reasonable diligence in discovering the facts which formed the basis of her cause of action. In other words, the discovery rule placed a burden on Miss O'Keeffe to justify her lack of action for so many years.[35] Accordingly, the Supreme Court of New Jersey ordered the case to be returned to the trial court so that further evidence could be introduced by Miss O'Keeffe to establish reasonable diligence in pursuing her property.[36]

The discovery rule is an attempt to balance the repose that is essential to stability in human affairs (that is, the reason for statutes of limitations) with a desire to afford plaintiffs every opportunity to press claims in court. In the *O'Keeffe* case, the court considered it an unacceptable imbalance to permit owners of stolen property an indefinite period of time in which to claim their property, and by use of the discovery rule required such owners to justify long delays. In unclaimed museum loan situations, frequently it is an unacceptable imbalance to allow owners indefinite periods of time in which to claim their property, and here again, the discovery rule could be used to correct the imbalance. Its use, however, would be predicated on a court's willingness to place a time limit on the duration of an indefinite loan.[37] Consider, for instance,

---

33. In Maryland the discovery rule is applicable generally in all actions. *Poffenberger v. Risser*, 431 A.2d 677 (Md. 1981). See also Comment, "The Recovery of Stolen Art: Of Paintings, Statues and Statutes of Limitations," 27 *U.C.L.A. L. Rev.* 1122 (1980).

34. *O'Keeffe v. Snyder*, 416 A.2d 862 at 869 (N.J. 1980).

35. In *Poffenberger v. Risser* 431 A.2d 677 (Md. 1981), the court discusses the type of knowledge which is necessary under the discovery rule to start the running of the limitations period.

36. At this point, the parties entered into a private settlement and the case went no further in the courts.

37. An unwillingness by a court to place a time limit on the duration of an indefinite loan is, in effect, a disregard for the public policy behind statutes of limitations. If a court does not pinpoint some time at which a lender, or heirs, must come forward, then there is no point at which the statute of limitations can begin to run, and no possible period of repose. The case of *In Re Estate of Therese Davis McCagg* 450 A.2d 414 (D.C. 1982) illustrates this.

the following set of facts. In 1920, Mr. X loaned an antique clock to Museum Y. No time period was set on the loan, but the loan was acknowledged in writing by the museum and a loan receipt was given. Years passed and no further correspondence between the lender and the museum is shown in the museum's files, but museum records do indicate that in the 1940s some attempt was made by the museum to locate Mr. X or his family. During all this time, the clock remained on exhibit and was cared for by the museum. Museum records, which are open to the public, continued to record the clock as a 1920 loan from Mr. X. Some sixty years after the loan was made, heirs of Mr. X came forward and demanded the clock, which now had a substantial resale value. Does Museum Y have any basis for contesting the heirs' demand? If the adverse possession test is applied, the museum cannot prevail because it cannot demonstrate the necessary "hostile" possession. The museum never attempted to hide or change its records regarding the origin of the clock. But if the discovery rule is applied, possibly, in balancing the equities, the museum could prevail. The museum can argue that the 1920 indefinite loan must be examined in light of what the parties probably intended. It might be able to establish from the known facts that it is reasonable to infer that the indefinite loan terminated at the death of Mr. X,[38] or that under the reasoning of the *Nyhus* case, the court should infer a reasonable time within which a demand should have been made.[39] Upon termination of the loan, or upon expiration of a reasonable time for making a demand, there would then be an obligation on the part of Mr. X's estate or heirs to come forward and take action, and with this obligation the appropriate statute of limitations would begin to run.[40] Under the discovery rule, if the heirs hoped to postpone the running of the statute of limitations, the burden would be on them to show due diligence in pursuing their rights. A mere statement that they did not know of the clock until recently would not do. The discovery rule places a responsibility on owners to use reasonable care in looking after their property.[41] If Mr. X lost his loan receipt and never left evidence among his papers that the clock was on loan to the museum, he may well have violated the due care requirement and his heirs must suffer thereby. If evidence of the loan was left among his papers, his executor (and heirs) may well be unable to show due care in gathering all estate assets in a timely manner. If the existence of the clock had been known generally

---

38. See previous discussion on Statutes of Limitations.

39. See previous discussion on Statutes of Limitations and footnote 17.

40. In *Desiderio v. D'Ambrosio*, 190 N.J. Super. 424, 463 A.2d 986 (1983), the court applied the statute of limitations from the date the bailment began and thus did not consider the value of the discovery rule. The approach of first determining a reasonable time for the indefinite loan and then applying the statute of limitations appears to offer an equitable solution in a greater variety of cases.

41. In the case of *The Mary*, 13 U.S. (9 Cranch) 126 (1815), 3 L.Ed. 678, 684, Chief Justice Story commented "[I]t is part of common prudence for all those who have any interest in . . . [an object], to guard that interest by persons who are in a situation to protect it." Also, California recognizes an obligation on the part of lenders to keep in touch with museums. The California statute described in section F of this chapter states: "It is the responsibility of the owner of property on loan to a museum to notify the museum promptly in writing of any change of address or change in ownership of the property. Failure to notify the museum of these changes may result in the owner's loss of rights in the property."

to the family, some explanation would have to be given as to why there was no attempt to locate it. The fact that the clock was on public display at all times as a loan from Mr. X may cause some doubt as to whether any diligence was used by the family in searching for the property.

From a museum's standpoint, a court's willingness to find a reasonable time for the running of an indefinite loan and then permit the application of the discovery rule affords a fairer test and, arguably, one which is in accord with public policy. It discourages carelessness on the part of owners and, at the same time, it encourages museums to act in a forthright manner. Under the discovery rule approach, there is no pressure on museums to hide or change their records or to convert in order to ward off stale claims. The maintenance of accurate and open records actually works to a museum's advantage, because it creates a situation where forgetful owners cannot later claim that they used due diligence in looking for their property. On the other hand, evidence of deceit or lack of good faith on the part of a museum may well be used to justify a claimant's long delay in demanding property. The discovery rule also recognizes the reality that no museum alone can bear the burden and expense of keeping track of the current status of all its lenders, or their heirs, and that justice is better served when obligations are imposed on the lender as well as the borrower.

F. Legislative Solutions

Periodically, it is suggested that museums seek legislation to solve the problems associated with unclaimed property.[42] Drafting such statutes, however, can present formidable problems. In 1981, the State of Maine passed a relatively simple statute on this subject,[43] which, however, leaves unanswered many questions that time and experience may resolve. The statute reads as follows:

§ 601. Maine statute on unclaimed property in museums and historical societies.

1. Property to be considered abandoned. Any property held by a museum or historical society within the State which is held for 25 years or more, and to which no person has made claim shall be deemed to be abandoned and, notwithstanding Title 33, chapter 27, shall become the property of the museum or society, provided that the museum or society has complied with subsection 2.

2. Notice. The museum or society shall first cause to be published in at least one newspaper of general circulation in the county in which the

---

42. Many states have statutes regarding the disposition of abandoned property. Abandonment frequently is defined as the voluntary relinquishment of possession of a thing by the owner with the intention of terminating ownership but without the intention of vesting ownership in any other person. Leaving property unclaimed for a long period in a museum may not satisfy a court's interpretation of abandonment. Also, many statutes regulating abandoned property require that the property pass to the state.

43. 27 MSRA c19 § 601.

museum or society is located at least once a week for 2 consecutive weeks a notice and listing of the property. The notice shall contain:

A. The name and last known address, if any, of the last known owner of property;

B. A description of the property;

C. A statement that if proof of claim is not presented by the owner to the museum or society and if the owner's right to receive the property is not established to the museum's or society's satisfaction within 65 days from the date of the 2nd published notice, the property will be deemed abandoned and shall become the property of the museum or society.

3. Title to property. If no claim has been made to the property within 65 days from the date of the 2nd published notice, title to the property shall vest in the museum or society, free from all claims of the owner and of all persons claiming through or under him.

In 1983, Louisiana passed a similar statute (but applicable to property held merely ten years or more) which applies only to the Louisiana State Museum.[44] The State of Washington also has a statute which is directed to a single museum, the state museum at the University of Washington.[45] A much more comprehensive statute applicable to all museums within the state was enacted in California in 1983 (see pages 195-203). In 1984, the State of Tennessee joined the ranks of states with special legislation.[46] Tennessee's statute applies to all museums in the state.

Only time will tell how effective these legislative solutions prove to be within their respective states, and whether they have an effect beyond their jurisdictions. The statutes articulate a public policy that could cause courts generally to look more sympathetically at the plight of museums when long-silent lenders or their heirs appear to claim property.[47]

ANNOTATED VERSION
CHAPTER _____

An act to add Chapter 1.5 (commencing with Section 1899) to Title 4 of Part 4 of Division 3 of the Civil Code, relating to loans of property to museums.

The people of the State of California do enact as follows:

SECTION 1. Chapter 1.5 (commencing with Section 1899) is added to Title 4 of Part 4 of Division 3 of the Civil Code, to read:

---

44. See section c(1) of Act 687 of the 1983 regular session of the Louisiana State legislature. Note the two Louisiana State Museum cases described in footnote 29 which prompted this legislation.

45. RCW 27.40.034 (Washington State Statutes).

46. Senate Bill 2018 (Public Chapter No. 862) approved May 25, 1984.

47. In *Oliver v. Kaiser Community Health Foundation*, 5 Ohio St. 3d 111, 449 N.E.2d 438 (1983), the court adopted the discovery rule in a malpractice case citing the growing trend in this direction even though the state legislature had not acted upon a proposed discovery statute. See also *Berry v. Branner*, 245 Or. 307, 421 P.2d 996 (1966).

CHAPTER 1.5.

LOANS TO MUSEUMS FOR INDEFINITE OR LONG TERMS

Section 1899. *Findings.* The Legislature finds and declares as follows:

(a) Many museums have benefited greatly from having property loaned to them for study or display. Problems have arisen, however, in connection with loans for indefinite or long terms, when museums and lenders have failed to maintain contact. Many of these problems could be avoided by a clarification and regularization of the rights and obligations of the parties to loans for indefinite or long terms.

(b) An existing law, the Unclaimed Property Law (commencing with Section 1500 of the Code of Civil Procedure), is technically applicable to property on loan to a museum which has been left unclaimed by its owner for at least seven years.

(c) While the Unclaimed Property Law addresses problems similar to those which arise in the museum context when the parties to loans fail to maintain contact, there is need for an alternative method of dealing with unclaimed property in the hands of museums, one tailored to the unique circumstances of unclaimed loans to museums. These circumstances include the likelihood that the unclaimed property has significant scientific, historical, aesthetic, or cultural value but does not have great monetary value; that the public's interest in the intangible values of unclaimed property loaned to museums can best be realized if title is transferred to the museums holding the property; that often lenders intend eventually to donate property but place it on indefinite or long term loan initially for tax and other reasons; and that many museums have incurred unreimbursed expenses in caring for and storing unclaimed loaned property.

(d) There is an inherent tendency for the condition of tangible property to change over time. Loaned property often requires conservation work and conservation measures may be expensive or potentially detrimental to the property. Organic materials and specimens may serve as breeding grounds for insects, fungi, or diseases which threaten other more valuable property.

(e) Museums cannot reasonably be expected to make decisions regarding conservation or disposition of loaned property at their own risk and expense. Over time, however, lenders die or move, and museums and lenders lose contact. If a lender has failed to maintain contact with a museum, it is often impossible to locate the lender so that the lender can make decisions regarding conservation or disposition of loaned property.

(f) Since museums rarely relocate, it is easier for lenders, and those who claim through them, to notify museums of address or ownership changes so that museums can readily contact lenders when decisions must be made regarding conservation or disposition of loaned property.

(g) The best evidence of ownership of property on loan to a museum is generally the original loan receipt. The longer property remains on loan, the less likely it is that the original lender will claim it, and the more likely it is that any claim which is made will be made by someone who does not have the original loan receipt or other clear evidence of ownership. The state has a substantial interest in cutting off stale and uncertain claims to tangible personal property loaned to nonprofit and public museums.

(h) Most of the tangible personal property which escheats to the state under the Unclaimed Property Law is found in safe deposit boxes. Although 40–50 percent of the intangible property which escheats to the state is subsequently claimed, less than 1 percent of escheated tangible personal property is claimed. Of the few claims which are presented to the Controller for tangible personal property, most are presented within two years of the date the Controller gives notice of the escheat.

(i) The public interest is served by requiring lenders to notify museums of changes in address or ownership of loaned property, by establishing a uniform procedure for lenders to preserve their interests in property loaned to museums for indefinite or long terms, and by vesting title to unclaimed property on loan to museums in the museums which have custody of the property.

Section 1899.1. *Definitions.* For the purposes of this chapter:

(a) A "museum" is an institution located in California and operated by a nonprofit corporation or public agency, primarily educational, scientific, or aesthetic in purpose, which owns, borrows, or cares for, and studies, archives, or exhibits property.

(b) A "lender's address" is the most recent address as shown on the museum's records pertaining to the property on loan from the lender.

(c) The terms "loan," "loaned," and "on loan" include all deposits of property with a museum which are not accompanied by a transfer of title to the property.

(d) "Property" includes all tangible objects, animate and inanimate, under a museum's care which have intrinsic value to science, history, art, or culture, except that it does not include botanical or zoological specimens loaned to a museum for scientific research purposes.

Section 1899.2. *When Notice by Museum Deemed Given; Contents of Notices by Lenders and Museums; Location Defined.*

(a) When a museum is required to give a lender notice pursuant to the provisions of this chapter, the museum shall be deemed to have given a lender notice if the museum mails the notice to the lender at the lender's address and proof of receipt is received by the museum within 30 days from the date the notice was mailed. If the museum does not have an address for the lender, or if proof of receipt is not received by the museum, notice shall be deemed given if the museum publishes notice at least once a week for three successive weeks in a newspaper of general circulation in both the county in which the museum is located and the county of the lender's address, if any.

(b) In addition to any other information prescribed in this chapter, notices given pursuant to it shall contain the lender's name, the lender's address, if known, the date of the loan and, if the notice is being given by the museum, the name, address, and telephone number of the appropriate office or official to be contacted at the museum for information regarding the loan.

(c) For the purposes of this section, a museum is "located" in the county of a branch of the museum to which a loan is made. In all other instances, a museum is located in the county in which it has its principal place of business.

Section 1899.3. *Obligations of Museums.*

(a) If, on or after January 1, 1984, a museum accepts a loan of property for an indefinite term, or for a term in excess of seven years, the museum shall inform the lender in writing at the time of the loan of the provisions of this chapter. A copy of the form notice prescribed in Section 1899.5, or a citation to this chapter, is adequate for this purpose.

(b) Unless the loaned property is returned to the claimant, the museum shall retain for a period of not less than 25 years the original or an accurate copy of each notice filed by a claimant pursuant to Section 1899.4.

(c) The museum shall furnish anyone who files a notice of intent to preserve an interest in property on loan proof of receipt of the notice by mailing an original receipt or a copy of the receipt portion of the form notice prescribed in Section 1899.5 to the lender or other claimant at the address given on the notice within 30 days of receiving the notice.

(d) A museum shall give a lender prompt notice of any known injury to or loss of property on loan.

Section 1899.4. *Lenders' Notices.*

(a) It is the responsibility of the owner of property on loan to a museum to notify the museum promptly in writing of any change of address or change in ownership of the property. Failure to notify the museum of these changes may result in the owner's loss of rights in the property.

(b) The owner of property on loan to a museum may file with the museum a notice of intent to preserve an interest in the property as provided for in Section 1899.5. The filing of a notice of intent to preserve an interest in property on loan to a museum does not validate or make enforceable any claim which would be extinguished under the terms of a written loan agreement, or which would otherwise be invalid or unenforceable.

Section 1899.5. *Form Notice of Intent to Preserve an Interest in Property.*

(a) A notice of intent to preserve an interest in property on loan to a museum filed pursuant to this chapter shall be in writing, shall contain a description of the property adequate to enable the museum to identify the property, shall be accompanied by documentation sufficient to establish the claimant as owner of the property, and shall be signed under penalty of perjury by the claimant or by a person authorized to act on behalf of the claimant.

(b) The museum need not retain a notice which does not meet the requirements set forth in subdivision (a). If, however, the museum does not intend to retain a notice for this reason, the museum shall promptly notify the claimant at the address given on the notice that it believes the notice is ineffective to preserve an interest, and the reasons therefor. The fact that the museum retains a notice shall not be construed to mean that the museum accepts the sufficiency or accuracy of the notice or that the notice is effective to preserve an interest in property on loan to the museum.

(c) A notice of intent to preserve an interest in property on loan to a museum which is in substantially the following form, and contains the information and attachments described, satisfies the requirements of subdivision (a):

NOTICE OF INTENT TO PRESERVE AN INTEREST
IN PROPERTY ON LOAN TO A MUSEUM

TO THE LENDER: Section 1899.4 of the California Civil Code requires that you notify the museum promptly in writing of any change of address or ownership of the property. If the museum is unable to contact you regarding your loan, you may lose rights in the loaned property. If you choose to file this form with the museum to preserve your interest in the property, the museum is required to maintain it, or a copy of it, for 25 years. For full details, see Section 1899, et seq. of the California Civil Code.

TO THE MUSEUM: You are hereby notified that the undersigned claims an interest in the property described herein.

Claimant:

Name:_____

Address:_____

_____

_____

Telephone:_____

Social Security Number (optional):_____

Museum Name:_____

Date Property Loaned:_____

Interest in Property:

If you are not the original lender, describe the origin of your interest in the property and attach a copy of any document creating your interest:

_____

_____

_____

_____

Description of Property:

Unless an accurate, legible copy of the original loan receipt is attached, give a detailed description of the claimed property, including its nature and general characteristics and the museum registration number assigned to the property, if known, and attach any documentary evidence you have establishing the loan.

Registration #_____

Description:_____

_____

_____

_____

_____

(Attach additional sheets if necessary.)

I understand that I must promptly notify the museum in writing of any change of address or change in ownership of the loaned property.

I declare under penalty of perjury that to the best of my knowledge the information contained in this notice is true.

Signed:_____ Date:_____
                    (claimant)

OR

I declare under penalty of perjury that I am authorized to act on behalf of the claimant and am informed and believe that the information contained in this notice is true.

Signed:_____ Date:_____
            (claimant's representative)

RECEIPT FOR NOTICE OF INTENT
TO PRESERVE AN INTEREST IN PROPERTY

(For use by the museum.)

Notice received by:_____

Date of receipt:_____

Copy of receipt returned to claimant:

By_____

Date:_____

(d) Notices of intent to preserve an interest in property on loan to a museum filed pursuant to this chapter are exempt from the disclosure requirements of the California Public Records Act (commencing with Section 6250 of the Government Code).

Section 1899.6. *Conservation or Disposal of Loaned Property; Lien; Liability.*

(a) Unless there is a written loan agreement to the contrary, a museum may apply conservation measures to or dispose of property on loan to the museum without a lender's permission if:

(1) Immediate action is required to protect the property on loan or to protect other property in the custody of the museum, or because the property on loan has become a hazard to the health and safety of the public or of the museum's staff, and:

(A) The museum is unable to reach the lender at the lender's last address of record so that the museum and the lender can promptly agree upon a solution; or

(B) The lender will not agree to the protective measures the museum recommends, yet is unwilling or unable to terminate the loan and retrieve the property.

(2) In the case of a lender who cannot be contacted in person, the museum publishes a notice containing the information described in subdivision (a) of Section 1899.7 and there is no response for 120 days.

(b) If a museum applies conservation measures to or disposes of property pursuant to subdivision (a):

(1) The museum shall have a lien on the property and on the proceeds from any disposition thereof for the costs incurred by the museum; and

(2) The museum shall not be liable for injury to or loss of the property:

(A) If the museum had a reasonable belief at the time the action was taken that the action was necessary to protect the property on loan or other property in the custody of the museum, or that the property on loan constituted a hazard to the health and safety of the public or the museum's staff; and

(B) If the museum applied conservation measures, the museum exercised reasonable care in the choice and application of the conservation measures.

Section 1899.7. *Notice by Publication of Injury to or Loss of Property.*

(a) Except as provided in subdivision (b), if a museum is unable to give the lender the notice required by subdivision (d) of Section 1899.3 of injury to or loss of property on loan by mail, the museum shall be deemed to have given the lender notice of any injury or loss if in addition to the information required by subdivision (b) of Section 1899.2 the published notice includes a statement containing substantially the following information:

"The records of _____ indicate that you have property
                        (name of museum)
on loan to it. Your failure to notify it in writing of a change of address or ownership of property on loan or to contact it in writing regarding the loan may result in the loss of rights in the loaned property. See California Civil Code Sections 1899, et seq."

(b) If, within three years of giving notice of injury to or loss of loaned property by publishing the notice set forth in subdivision (a), the museum receives a notice from a claimant pursuant to Section 1899.4, the museum shall promptly advise the claimant in writing of the nature of the injury to or the fact of the loss of property on loan and the approximate date thereof. For the purposes of the limitation period in Section 1899.8, if the museum mails the information to the claimant within 30 days of the date the museum receives the notice from the claimant, the museum shall be deemed to have given the claimant notice of the injury to or loss of property on loan on the date notice by publication pursuant to subdivision (a) was completed.

Section 1899.8. *Limitation on Actions Because of Injury to or Loss of Property.* Effective January 1, 1985, no action shall be brought against a museum for damages because of injury to or loss of property loaned to the museum more than (1) three years from the date the museum gives the lender notice of the injury or loss, or (2) ten years from the date of the injury or loss, whichever occurs earlier.

Section 1899.9. *Termination of Loans; Expiration of Specified Term.*

(a) A museum may give the lender notice of the museum's intent to terminate a loan which was made for an indefinite term, or which was made on or after January 1, 1984 for a term in excess of seven years.

A notice of intent to terminate a loan given pursuant to this section shall include a statement containing substantially the following information:

"The records of _____ indicate that you have property
              (name of museum)
on loan to it. The institution wishes to terminate the loan. You must contact the institution, establish your ownership of the property, and make arrangements to collect the property. If you fail to do so promptly, you will be deemed to have donated the property to the institution. See California Civil Code Sections 1899, et seq."

(b) For the purposes of this chapter, a loan for a specified term becomes a loan for an indefinite term if the property remains in the custody of the museum when the specified term expires.

Section 1899.10. *Limitation on Actions for Recovery of Loaned Property.*

(a) The three-year limitation on actions to recover personal property prescribed in Code of Civil Procedure Section 338.3 shall run from the date the museum gives the lender notice of its intent to terminate the loan pursuant to Section 1899.9.

(b) Except as provided in subsection (e), effective January 1, 1985, no action shall be brought against a museum to recover property on loan when more than 25 years have passed from the date of the last written contact between the lender and the museum, as evidenced in the museum's records.

(c) A lender shall be deemed to have donated loaned property to a museum if the lender fails to file an action to recover the property on loan to the museum within the periods specified in subdivisions (a) and (b).

(d) One who purchases property from a museum acquires good title to the property if the museum represents that it has acquired title to the property pursuant to subdivision (c).

(e) Notwithstanding subdivisions (b) and (c), a lender who was not given notice that the museum intended to terminate a loan and who proves that the museum received a notice of intent to preserve an interest in loaned property within the 25 years immediately preceding the date on which the lender's right to recover the property otherwise expired under subdivision (b) may recover the property or, if the property has been disposed of, the reasonable value of the property at the time the property was disposed of with interest at the rate on judgments set by the Legislature pursuant to Section 1 of Article XV of the California Constitution.*

Section 1899.11. *Unclaimed Property Law.*

(a) The provisions of this chapter supersede the provisions of the Unclaimed Property Law (commencing with Section 1500 of the Code of Civil Procedure) except that at its option, a museum may report property which has been on loan unclaimed by its owner for more than seven years to the Controller pursuant to Section 1530 of the Code of Civil Procedure for disposition in accordance with the provisions of the Unclaimed Property Law.

(b) Not less than six months nor more than 12 months before reporting any loaned property to the Controller, a museum shall mail to the lender at the lender's address, if known, a notice of intent to report the property to the Controller. The notice shall include a statement containing substantially the following information:

"The records of ＿＿＿＿＿＿＿＿＿＿＿＿ indicate that you have property
(name of museum)
on loan to the institution. The institution wishes to terminate the loan. You must contact the institution, establish your ownership of the property, and make arrangements to collect the property before ＿＿＿＿＿＿＿＿ or the
(fill in date)
property will be disposed of in accordance with the provisions of the Unclaimed Property Law (commencing with Section 1500 of the California Code of Civil Procedure)."

SEC. 2. No appropriation is made and no reimbursement is required by this act pursuant to Section 6 of Article XIII B of the California Constitution or Section 2231 or 2234 of the Revenue and Taxation Code because the Legislature finds and declares that there are savings as well as costs in this act which, in the aggregate, do not result in additional net costs.

---

*This section amended by an Act approved July 17, 1984.

CHAPTER VIII

International Loans

A. Types of Loans
B. Immunity from Seizure
    1. Imported Objects
    2. Exported Objects
C. The United States Indemnity Program
D. *Force Majeure*
E. Checklists for Organizing and Implementing International Exhibitions

A. Types of Loans

International loans can take various forms, such as the importation of a single object from a foreign lender, the receipt of a prepackaged exhibition from a foreign museum, and a cooperative effort by a United States museum and a foreign museum to assemble from different sources an exhibition to tour both in the United States and abroad. International loans range from the relatively simple to the unbelievably complex. It is a fair statement to say that any museum contemplating initiating or receiving an international loan of any magnitude first should be sure that it has adequate staff expertise and ample time to devote to careful planning and resourceful execution.

It is beyond the scope of this text to detail the numerous legal problems that can arise when a museum is involved in an international loan. Rather, selected topics are discussed that generally affect international loan situations: providing for immunity from seizure of the imported or exported objects; the United States indemnity program; and the doctrine of *force majeure*. In addition, a series of checklists are provided that enumerate the various points that may have to be considered when planning, organizing and implementing international exhibitions.

B. Immunity from Seizure

1. Imported Objects
When a foreign lender transports valuable cultural objects into this country, certain legal risks are assumed which are quite distinct from those normally contemplated in a loan agreement. One is the possibility of seizure of the imported cultural objects by court order because of unrelated litigation initiated against the lender in this country. For example, if there are individuals or organizations in the United States which believe they have a claim against a

foreign lender, they cannot, as a rule, obtain jurisdiction over that lender in order to sue in the United States unless the lender is actually present in this country. If the lender is not actually present, an alternative is to attach property of the lender which may be in the United States, and use this property as a basis for litigating and/or satisfying the alleged claim. A foreign lender, therefore, might well be reluctant to allow cultural property to enter the United States for exhibition if there is a possibility that those objects might be used as a means to embroil him/it in legal controversy in this country.

In order to control this deterrent to international cultural exchange, Congress in 1965 passed "an immunity statute" which provides an immunity from seizure in certain instances.[1] The statute states that if an object of cultural significance is being imported into the United States for temporary exhibition, without profit, by a United States cultural organization, and the President of the United States, or his designee, determines that the object is of cultural significance and that the temporary exhibition is in the national interest, then that object may be declared immune from court seizure while it is within the confines of the United States.[2] By Executive Order[3] the President's responsibilities in this regard have been delegated to the United States Information Agency (U.S.I.A.)[4]

Any museum which is assuming responsibility for bringing in cultural artifacts from abroad should consider, in consultation with the lender, the advisability of seeking a declaration of immunity[5] The process should be initiated several months before the date of entry, usually by the sponsoring United States museum. The application is filed with the General Counsel of the U.S.I.A. and should contain the following:

(a) a schedule of all the items being imported for exhibition (including description and value);

(b) a copy of the agreement entered into between the foreign owner or custodian and the U.S. sponsoring cultural organization(s), and a copy of any agreements with U.S. participating museums;

(c) copies of any related commercial agreements between any or all of the U.S. institutions and the lender or other parties;

(d) a list of the places and dates of exhibition, especially the date the objects will arrive in the United States;

---

1. 22 U.S.C. § 2459 (Copy included in Appendix.)

2. The immunity statute has also been coordinated with Title III of Pub. L. 97-446, the "Convention on Cultural Property Implementation Act," (96 Stat. 2350 (1983), to be codified at 19 U.S.C. 2601, *et seq.* (See Chapter IV, "The Acquisition of Objects—Accessioning," Part D(6).) The terms of the Convention on Cultural Property Implementation Act do not apply to any archaeological or ethnological material or any article of cultural property which is imported into the United States for temporary exhibition or display if such material or article has been declared immune from seizure under the above-described immunity statute.

3. E.O. 12047 of March 27, 1978.

4. The name of the International Communications Agency was changed back to the United States Information Agency in 1982 (Pub. L. 97-241, § 303, 96 Stat. 291).

5. If the lender is a governmental entity of a foreign country, Chapter 97 of Title 28 of the U.S. Code should be consulted also. The chapter concerns the jurisdictional immunities of foreign states.

(e) a statement that the exhibition is being administered without profit (admission and similar fees that merely cover costs usually do not disqualify the exhibition for the immunity declaration, but a description of all charges or preferences in admission should be included in the application);

(f) a statement giving information as to why anyone might want to attach the property in the United States and an evaluation of the threat;

(g) a statement establishing the cultural significance of the objects; and

(h) evidence that the U.S. participants are cultural or educational organizations (a citation to the organization's I.R.C. § 501(c)(3) determination letter from the Internal Revenue Service usually satisfies this requirement).

Upon receipt of the application, the U.S.I.A. consults with the U.S. Department of State regarding the determination of national interest[6] and, as necessary, with experts to determine cultural significance. If all criteria are met to the satisfaction of the U.S.I.A., a notice to this effect is published in the Federal Register. Immunity from seizure is then in effect for the enumerated objects for the time period they are to be in the United States for purposes of the temporary exhibition.[7]

2. Exported Objects

An exported object, whether owned by the museum or by a lender contributing to the museum's exhibition, could be subject to seizure in a foreign country for the reasons just described. It is a sensible precaution to inquire of the borrower if the host country affords any form of protection from seizure. In this same regard, consider the situation raised in Canada by the *Heller* case (as described in footnote 73 of Chapter IV). In that case, an antiquity brought into Canada from the United States by a United States citizen was seized on suspicion of violating Canada's Cultural Property Export and Import Act. It is possible, therefore, that an antiquity which is not vulnerable to attack in the United States under our Convention on Cultural Property Implementation Act may become subject to seizure by the country of origin when brought into a foreign jurisdiction where the law implementing the UNESCO Convention permits the country of origin to sue. If the nature of the material to be exported in an international loan falls within the types addressed by the UNESCO Convention (described in Chapter IV) even though the material is legally possessed

---

6. In May 1980, a major exhibition from the Hermitage Museum of Leningrad was planned for viewing in the United States. An application for declaration of immunity was filed by the U.S. sponsoring museum, but the request was denied when the I.C.A. (now the U.S.I.A.) found the exhibition "not to be in the national interest." Just prior to the application, Russia had invaded Afghanistan severely straining Soviet-U.S. relations.

7. In 1979, when a number of U.S. citizens were held hostage in Iran, the President of the U.S. ordered the freezing of all Iranian assets in the United States. The question arose whether such an order took precedence over a declaration of immunity. In a chapter entitled "No Museum Is an Island," S. Weil in *Beauty and the Beasts* discusses these international incidents.

in the United States, its status in the importing country should be verified before the loan is made.

C. The United States Indemnity Program[8]

Insurance for a major international exhibition frequently accounts for a substantial portion of the exhibition budget.[9] In the last decade or two, as some international shows assumed grand proportions and insurance premiums rose accordingly, even well-endowed museums were not able to afford participation in certain international exhibitions without substantial outside funding or the assistance of special legislation.[10] General legislation was then sought for a government indemnity program on the basis that the country as a whole would benefit through increased international goodwill and understanding if cultural exchanges were fostered in this manner.[11] In 1975, Congress enacted the Arts and Artifacts Indemnity Act which established an indemnity program administered by the Federal Council on the Arts and Humanities.[12] Under the program, the U.S. government guarantees to pay loss or damage claims, subject to certain limitations, arising out of international exhibitions which have been previously certified for indemnity coverage.[13]

In order to qualify for coverage, eligible items must be on loan for display in the United States, or, if they are part of an exchange of exhibitions, eligible items may be covered while on display abroad, but both parties in the exchange cannot be covered. Eligible items are:

(1) works of art, including tapestries, paintings, sculpture, folk art, graphics and craft arts;

(2) manuscripts, rare documents, books, and other printed or published materials;

(3) other artifacts or objects; and

(4) photographs, motion pictures, or audio and video tape;

---

8. In 1981, Florida became the first state to pass an indemnity law to benefit state cultural organizations. The program insures works of art or exhibitions borrowed within the United States for display in Florida. Particulars on the indemnity program can be obtained from Florida's Cultural Affairs Division. In 1984, Iowa passed a similar statute. The Iowa Arts Council administers the statute.

9. Pfeffer, "Insuring Museum Exhibitions," 27 *Hastings L. Rev.* 1123 (May 1976).

10. In 1974, the U.S. government by special legislation (Pub. L. 93–287, 88 Stat. 141, and Pub. L. 93–476, 88 Stat. 1439) provided indemnification for a Chinese archaeological exhibition which traveled to the National Gallery of Art and for the U.S. portion of a major exchange of exhibitions between the Metropolitan Museum of New York and the Soviet Union.

11. Government indemnity programs have been in operation in other countries for some years. England is a notable example.

12. Pub. L. 94–158, 89 Stat. 826 (December 20, 1975) found in 20 U.S.C. §§ 971, *et seq.* (copy included in Appendix). For a general discussion of the indemnity program, see Alice Martin, "The Arts and Artifacts Indemnity Program," *Fed. B. News and J.* 45 (Jan. 1983). See also 45 C.F.R. pt. 1160.

13. See 20 U.S.C. § 273(c).

which are (A) of educational, cultural, historical, or scientific value, and (B) the exhibition of which is certified by the Director of the International Communications Agency[14] or his designee as being in the national interest.[15]

There is a monetary limit on the total amount that can be "insured" at one time[16] by the government indemnity program so it behooves an applicant to apply in a timely manner before all available coverage is apportioned. A museum planning quite far in advance can give written notice of its intent to apply at a future specified date and the Federal Council, in turn, after reviewing its known schedule, will give an opinion as to the likelihood that coverage will be available at that time. However, an opinion on the availability of coverage does not assure approval. When formally filed, each application for an indemnity must stand on its own merits.[17] Other indemnity limits are as follows:

- No indemnity agreement for a single exhibition can cover loss or damage in excess of $50,000,000.
- There is a deductible per exhibition and coverage comes into play after there is cumulative loss or damage exceeding the deductible regardless of the number of exhibiting museums. The deductible varies depending on the estimated value of the items covered by the indemnity agreement.[18]

Estimated Value of Items Covered	Aggregate Deductible
$2,000,000 or less	$15,000
more than $2,000,000 but less than $10,000,000	$25,000
$10,000,000 or more	$50,000

Frequently museums self-insure the deductible because insurance on a first dollar loss of this type invariably runs high. Private insurance to cover amounts in excess of the top limit of indemnity coverage, however, is usually available at reasonable rates.

It should be noted that valuations for purposes of indemnity coverage must be quoted in American dollars and any claim payments are in American dollars. These provisions sometimes cause foreign lenders some concern because of the fluctuations in currency rates. Also, once valuations are approved by the Federal Council for purposes of indemnity, these amounts, as a rule, cannot be changed.

---

14. The name of the International Communications Agency was changed back to the United States Information Agency in 1982 (Pub. L. 97–241, § 303, 96 Stat. 291).

15. 20 U.S.C. § 972(a).

16. The aggregate as of 1982 is set at $400,000,000 (20 U.S.C. § 974(b) as amended by the Arts and Humanities Act of 1980, Pub. L. 96–496, 94 Stat. 2583).

17. Applications are first reviewed by an Indemnity Advisory Panel (composed of museum directors and curators), with the panel making its recommendations to the Federal Council on the Arts and Humanities, the final approval authority. This process is conducted twice a year.

18. 20 U.S.C. § 974(b) as amended by the Arts and Humanities Act of 1980, Pub. L. 96–496, 94 Stat. 2583.

This means that care should be taken at the onset to encourage knowledgeable valuations. There is always the possibility, however, that gaps or limitations in indemnity coverage can be filled by private insurance.

Applications for indemnification require the following information:

 (1) name and address of applicant;
 (2) title and nature of proposed exhibition;
 (3) time period of indemnification;
 (4) place(s) and dates of exhibition;
 (5) total value and number of items to be indemnified and the amount of premium if privately insured;
 (6) total value of entire exhibition;
 (7) complete item-by-item description of objects to be indemnified, with U.S. dollar valuations;
 (8) itemized list of all objects in the exhibition *not* to be covered by indemnity;
 (9) a statement of the significance of the exhibition;
 (10) a description of packing, shipping and security arrangements;
 (11) a description of any insurance arrangements to supplement indemnity coverage;
 (12) a list of assured or anticipated financial support for the exhibition;
 (13) a description of all losses over $5,000 experienced by the applicant and each exhibiting institution during the three prior years;
 (14) a copy of an applying organization's Federal tax exemption letter or evidence that it is part of a state or local government; and
 (15) if applicable, a statement whether the applying organization is accredited by the American Association of Museums. (A lack of accreditation does not automatically make the organization ineligible for an indemnity.)

D. *Force Majeure*

When negotiating an international loan, there is an understandable tendency to be more concerned about events that cannot be controlled by the parties, such as natural disaster, war and political unrest. In a standard commercial contract governing the transport of commodities, such events may or may not be construed to relieve the parties of a duty to perform.[19] However, when the subject of the contract is unique, cultural property safety is a prime objective, and the normal preference is to excuse performance if events outside the control of the parties make performance hazardous. For this reason, the doctrine of *force majeure* (that is, superior or irresistible force) frequently is incorporated into an international loan agreement. By definition, *force majeure* is a term used in contracts "to protect the parties in the event that a part of the contract cannot be performed due to causes which are outside the control of the parties and

---

19. Berman, "Excuse for Nonperformance in the Light of Contract Practices in International Trade," 63 *Colum. L. Rev.* 1413 (1963). See also *Restatement (Second) of Contracts*, Chapter 14 and *Williston on Contracts* § 1936 (3rd ed.).

could not be avoided by exercise of due care."[20] By way of example, if a loan agreement states: "The provisions of this agreement are subject to the doctrine of *force majeure*," this is construed to mean that parties intend that unavoidable occurrences that make performance hazardous for the objects will excuse such performance.

Some contract provisions of this nature are quite simple, as the example given above. Others go into much detail. The following rather formidable paragraph was used in a contract for a major foreign exhibition shown in the United States:

> Anything herein contained to the contrary notwithstanding, neither party hereto shall be liable or be deemed to be in default to the other by reason of any act, delay or omission caused by epidemic, fire, action of the elements, strikes, lockouts, labor disputes, regulations, ordinances, or order of a court of competent jurisdiction, act of government, act of God, or of a public enemy, war, riot, civil commotion, earthquake, flood, accident, explosions, casualty, embargo, delay of a common carrier, inability to obtain labor, material facilities, transportation, power or any other cause beyond the reasonable control of the party hereto, or for any act, delay or omission not due to the negligence or default of that party hereto; provided, however, that the party whose performance shall have been so prevented shall give prompt written notice to the other of the nature thereof and the date when such condition commenced and give further notice to the other of when such conditions shall have ended. Upon receipt of such notice by either party, both parties shall confer with each other and with appropriate representatives of the . . . Government who shall determine whether the nature of the occurrence warrants cancellation of the Exhibition or its transfer to another location.

Another aspect of the *force majeure* problem is the allocation of costs if there is a premature termination of the contract. Consider, for instance, the situation where the exhibition is held successfully in Countries X and Y. Just prior to its delivery to Country Z for the last showing, the exhibition is terminated because of civil unrest. Must the museum of Country Z bear its full cosponsorship cost even though it never had the benefit of the exhibition? A clause in a loan agreement similar to the following establishes an equitable method for resolving such an issue:

> In the event of premature termination, the parties will agree on a just settlement of costs incurred prior to the date of termination. Such settlement will take into account any benefits already enjoyed by one or more of the participating museums.

E. Checklists for Organizing and Implementing International Exhibitions

International exhibitions in particular demand careful and thorough planning if legal problems are to be avoided. In addition to the normal exhibition problems, there are superimposed possible language difficulties, distance problems,

---

20. *Black's Law Dictionary* (5th ed. 1979).

variations in laws, customs and currencies, political tensions, and so on. The sensible approach is to start early, listing all anticipated steps and sketching out a program of action. Where possible, the schedule should allow leeway for the inevitable emergencies.

As planning guides there follow a series of checklists for organizing and implementing a sizable international exhibition. Checklist I (on pages 212-17) deals with the overall planning required of the organizers. Checklist II (on pages 218-21) concerns the loan agreement between the individual lender and the borrower/organizer. Checklist III (on pages 222-24) outlines points to be considered in drafting a contract between the lender/organizer and participating museum. The checklists were developed by Martha Morris Shannon, Registrar of the National Museum of American History, Smithsonian Institution.

I. CHECKLIST FOR ORGANIZING INTERNATIONAL EXHIBITIONS

I. INITIAL ORGANIZATION

   A. When should negotiations and planning begin?—as soon as possible
      . . . at least two years in advance is ideal.
   B. Who is involved?
      1. Assignment of project director or curator.
      2. Coordination of input from key museum staff: registrar, designer,
          public relations, education, development, administration.
      3. Is sufficient professional staff available? Will additional staff be
          needed?
      4. Additional support: legal counsel, insurance broker, guest cura-
          tor, and/or designer, participating museum, (co-organizers?).
   C. Development of projected budget. Be sure all costs are realistically
      high enough to cover contingencies.
   D. Approval of concept and budget by Director (and by Trustees, if
      required).
   E. Negotiations with corporate sponsor and/or application for Federal
      Grant (if applicable).
   F. Schedule/timetable. Delineation of staff responsibilities.

II. NEGOTIATIONS WITH FOREIGN LENDERS

   A. Will loans be negotiated with individual lenders or through one
      source, i.e., foreign government cultural office or co-organizing
      foreign museum?
   B. Organizer may be primary borrower and in turn lend exhibit to
      participant museums—when does each party take responsibility?
   C. How many countries are involved? Are U.S. lenders involved?
   D. If U.S. corporate sponsors are involved, do they have foreign branch
      offices that will be involved?
   E. Assistance from U.S. embassies/consulates in lender country? (Notify
      U.S. Department of State.)
   F. Final selection of objects/artwork—firm listings required by specific
      date; avoid last minute changes.
   G. Formalization of contract or loan agreement with co-organizing
      foreign museum/agency or individual lenders covering all relevant
      points; sharing of costs. Translations required? Review by legal,
      insurance and fiscal advisors.
   H. Prior to importation, complete application for *Immunity from Seizure*
      (see 22 U.S.C. 2459) . . . political considerations.

III. OBJECT CONSIDERATIONS: LEGAL & LOGISTICAL

   A. Documentation.
      1. ˙Loan Agreements
         a. All lenders must sign a loan agreement (which covers most of
            the points mentioned in section III).
         b. Is organizer or co-organizer a lender also?
         c. Lender's forms for your signature? Translation? Be sure condi-
            tions are acceptable.
         d. Loan fees charged?

2. Receipts
   a. Issued to lenders initially.
   b. Required as objects enter and leave custody of organizer and participant museums.
3. Condition reports
   a. Lender must document initial outgoing condition, and ideally, the organizer would be present to verify.
   b. Separate reports for each object are confirmed by organizer and participant museums as objects/works enter and leave custody (provide for translations).
   c. Require conservator or curatorial review.
   d. Photographs should be made and accompany written reports. (Who provides?)
   e. Borrowers should be prepared to photograph objects if change in condition occurs—who notifies lender if damage/loss occurs? Emergency restoration permission?
   f. Lender verifies final condition on receipt.
4. Photographs
   a. Design tools, condition records, publicity, catalog reproduction.
   b. Who provides?
   c. Does lender give permission?
5. Catalog listing—whose responsibility?

B. Logistics.
1. Packing
   a. Lender's option with organizer's approval . . . review techniques in advance or be on hand to supervise.
   b. Preservation and climate conditions.
   c. Marking containers for handling and identification.
   d. Crate lists and unpacking and repacking instructions.
2. Transit
   a. Via consolidated shipment arranged by commercial forwarder, or by organizers?
   b. Containerization?
   c. Via lender's chosen shipper?
   d. Via courier (should be experienced individual). What are reasonable costs?
   e. Via cargo or passenger flight?
   f. Security escorts?
   g. Split shipments as required by insurance/Indemnity?
   h. Are exhibit cases, equipment or graphics included?
3. Customs
   a. Can be complicated—usually preferable to hire a customs broker ("customs power of attorney").
   b. Has the lender met the export regulations of his country? What are U.S. import requirements?
   c. Require a through waybill to museum and an onsite inspection.
   d. Sometimes can arrange diplomatic clearance and avoid much paperwork (done by foreign embassy in the U.S.).

    4. Receiving loans
      a. Anticipate object flow within museum.
      b. Holding area—acclimatization—storage capacity? Convenience to exhibit area, other services?
      c. Security (alarms, guards, who has access?).
      d. Unpacking, customs inspection, condition reports; use identifying tags (indicating exhibit catalog number).
      e. Storage of packing material.

C. Preservation.
    1. What are objects' conservation needs?
      a. Lender's requirements?
      b. Restoration prior to travel (whose cost?).
      c. Permission to reframe, remat, clean, etc.?
      d. Environmental conditions (temp./rh%) monitoring?
      e. Fumigation?
      f. Lighting: levels, types, filtered?
      g. Access to services of professional conservator?
    2. Handling restrictions
      a. Who is authorized to handle?
      b. Require special equipment/manpower?
    3. Installation
      a. Requirements for special methods or materials?
      b. Dust filters for cases?
      c. Provide designers with physical descriptions and photographs as early as possible.
    4. Security
      a. Physical guarding—current capability vs. additional needs?
      b. Electronic—wiring objects/cases; TV monitors.
      c. Perimeter alarms for exhibition galleries?
      d. Regular inventory.
      e. Confidentiality of information.

D. Insurance/Indemnity.
    1. Contracted for in agreements with lenders.
    2. Point of liability at leaving lender's custody or elsewhere?
    3. Who insures? Lender's choice.
      a. Lender's policy—factors to consider:
        1. ask for translation.
        2. type of coverage; transit limits?
        3. exclusions?
        4. require certificate waiving subrogation (also for participant museums, but not carrier).
        5. how would claims be handled?
        6. premium cost.
      b. Your own policy. Advantage in familiarity with coverage and personnel would lead to ease in claim settlement.
      c. Split coverage. More than one company covering loan creates potential problems—who is ultimately responsible when claim occurs?
      d. Federal Indemnity (Federal Council on the Arts/NEA). See PL-94-158; Application, key provisions.

    1. regulations require considerable documentation of exhibition details—well in advance of importation.

    2. deadlines for coverage require application April 1 for exhibits beginning July 1 and October 1 for exhibits beginning February 1.

    3. criteria for acceptance.

    4. may require organizer travel to foreign lender's premises to oversee packing (expense factor).

    5. valuations are fixed at time of application in U.S. currency—problem with devaluation of dollar against certain foreign currencies.

    6. how are deductibles covered? (additional expense).

    7. coverage in excess of limit per show? (additional expense).

    8. with competition from other museums, can you be guaranteed indemnification? (total $ limit restrictions).

    9. should you accept partial indemnity?

    10. foreign lenders agree to U.S. government indemnity? (must be in loan agreement).

    11. how will claims be settled?

    12. changes in plans after indemnity granted may require resubmission of application.

E. General consideration for insurance or indemnity:

    1. valuation—must be fair market value; currency fluctuations need to be considered in coverage.

    2. deductibles—how to cover.

    3. excess coverage needed?

    4. claims—what is procedure for reporting, adjusting, arbitrating disputes?—settle per values agreed upon; depreciation is allowed in partial losses.

    5. subrogation—whose right to waive?

    6. insurance or indemnity—must be the sole monetary recovery available to the lender in the event of loss or damage.

    7. consider exclusions—limited to standard . . . add war risk.

    8. what is the most cost effective decision? compare all costs of commercial vs. indemnity (how much premium will be saved with indemnity vs. costs to obtain indemnity?).

    9. maintain close contact with insurance broker or agent throughout.

IV. CIRCULATION OF EXHIBITION

A. Negotiation with participant museums via contract.

B. Use of facilities reports in gathering information on participant's physical capability, professional staffing, and potential hazard to objects.

C. Can entire show travel? Will other objects be added?

D. Scheduling showing to include preparation and travel time.

E. Preparation of traveling exhibition instructions for object handling, packing & unpacking, crate lists, press kits, catalogs, condition report book.

F. Who will insure? Waiver of subrogation.

G. Who will pack? Inhouse or outside firm? What carrier(s) will be used?—shipment consolidation and insurance requirements (security escorts, split shipments). Lender's courier required?

H. Who will oversee installations, etc.? Organizer send project director or curator to each site.

I. Cost allocations—problem of *force majeure*.

J. Sharing of revenue from catalog or other product sales?

V. DISPERSAL

A. Will show be extended? Have all lenders and participants agreed to extension in writing? Insurance extended? (Difficult to extend Indemnity).

B. Disperse from last exhibitor or return to organizer? Organizer's responsibility to lenders is paramount.

C. Outgoing condition check, photos, packaging.

D. Scheduling returns with lenders, coordinating with couriers.

E. How to be returned? To one foreign point for distribution or direct to lenders?

F. Who covers costs? Where do liabilities begin or end?

G. Are customs formalities in line? Return to country of origin to avoid problem of reentry.

H. Obtaining final receipts from lenders (time limit—insurance requirement).

VI. OTHER CONCERNS

A. Inhouse or outside designers?

B. Public relations.
   1. Opening, other events, receptions.
   2. Press, TV, radio coverage (local or national).

C. Credit to lenders (per loan agreement).

D. Acknowledgment of sponsors (federal and/or corporate).

E. Who is allowed to photograph? Can the public? (per loan agreement).

F. Educational.
   1. Lectures or symposia?
   2. Audio tours?
   3. Films?
   4. Visitor interpretation/evaluation?

G. Catalog.
   1. Multilanguage publications? Import problems?
   2. Who produces essay, edits, designs, publishes? Who approves? Who sets production deadlines? Number ordered? Selling price?
   3. Distribution of complimentary copies.

H. Posters, postcards, reproductions of artifacts.
   1. Quality control.
   2. Who manufactures? Amount of order? Who sells? Cost to exhibitors? Sales revenue to whom?

I. Securing reproduction rights (in loan agreement). SPADEM.

J. Graphics and banners? Printing forms, invitations, etc.

K. Are admission fees charged? Disposition of revenue?

L. Accommodation of increased number of visitors?

M. Competition from other exhibitions.

VII. MAJOR BUDGETARY CONSIDERATIONS
    A. Drain on daily operations/resources? Overhead?
    B. Curatorial travel.
    C. Escort travel.
    D. Shipments, including customs broker.
    E. Packing.
    F. Insurance premiums.
    G. Catalog, brochures, posters & reproductions.
    H. Loan fees.
    I. Restoration/preparation costs.
    J. Design & installation—major reconstruction of exhibit area?
    K. Publicity photography, advertising, opening reception.
    L. Security: guards and hardware.
    M. Phone bills.
    N. How are costs shared with participants?
    O. How are costs shared with co-organizers?
    P. Is revenue to be shared?
    Q. Billing, bookkeeping, and financial reports.

II. CHECKLIST FOR LOAN AGREEMENT (international exhibitions) BETWEEN ORGANIZER/MUSEUM AND INDIVIDUAL LENDER

A. Factual Information
  1. Parties to the Agreement: individual Lender & Borrower (organizer) for each: name, address, phone, telex or cable numbers
  2. Purpose of the loan: name of exhibition
  3. Dates of the exhibit; dates of loan period (wall-to-wall) (If circulating, name participant museums, their addresses and dates of showing)
  4. Object(s) Description:
      type of object
      title (if applicable)
      artist or maker
      date of execution
      medium or materials
      size: height, width, depth
      weight
      number of parts or pieces
      museum or collection number(s)
      inscriptions or identifying marks and locations
      provenance, bibliographic references, etc.
      insurance value
  5. Design and installation considerations: permission to reframe, remat, clean or alter works for display? (must be reversible process) special requirements for installation?
  6. Reproduction and Credit
      request for photographs (black and white, color, etc.)
      request for permission to photograph for:
        —publicity
        —condition reports
        —catalog illustration
      request permission to reproduce for:
        —publicity
        —catalogs
        —slides
        —postcards
      Copyright restrictions?
      Indicate credit line for publication and label
  7. Insurance
      by lender? If so, need certificate waiving subrogation against borrowers. Premium costs? by borrower(s)? Insurance value must be fair market. Will you accept US Federal Indemnity?
  8. Packing and Transportation
      a. preferred method of packing?
          pack by lender or outside firm? (include packing instructions)
          permission to repack by borrower for consolidated tour?
          Address object to be returned to, if different from above.
      b. preferred method of transportation
          preferred carrier? (if lender has no preference all arrangements will be made by borrower or agent)
          date due at borrowing museum?

9. Handling & Preservation
   —any handling restrictions?
   —any special requirements for lighting, temperature, humidity?
   Do we have permission to perform emergency conservation measures if necessary?
   Will there be any special preparation or restoration costs?
   Please prepare a written condition report at time of packing the objects for loan and forward to the borrower.

B. Loan Conditions

Loans are made subject to the following conditions; participant museums (as named above) have contracted with borrower (name) and will also comply with these conditions:

1. Care and Preservation
   a. Borrower promises to devote to all objects lent the same care as afforded similar objects in its own collection. Objects will be displayed out of reach under 24 hour security with guards during public hours. Efforts will be made to maintain conditions necessary to the conservation of objects such as lighting, climate control, and dust filtering.
   b. Lender certifies objects are in such condition as to withstand normal stress of packing, and unpacking, handling, and transits. Any potential problem will be discussed with the Borrower and/or knowledgeable conservator prior to loan. The Borrower will not be liable for normal wear and tear or for damage or loss due to conditions inherent or previously existing in the objects.
   c. Condition reports will be made by the Lender prior to shipment and by Borrower and participating museums at packing, unpacking and regular intervals while on display. Photographs will be made to document condition and travel with the exhibition.
   d. Evidence of damage or loss to an object will be promptly communicated to the Lender. No cleaning, repair or restoration will be undertaken by the Borrower without written authorization, except in an obvious emergency situation to curtail further deterioration.

2. Insurance
   a. If the Borrower is insuring, objects will be insured at the Lender's herein stated value against all risks from wall-to-wall subject to standard exclusions (listed). Insurance will be placed with the Borrower's insurance company (named) or under a U.S. Government Indemnity (if applicable) for the entire period of the loan, as stated herein. The amount payable by this insurance or indemnity is the sole recovery available to the lender in event of loss or damage. Valuations should reflect fair market value. If U.S. indemnity is secured, objects will be insured in U.S. dollars at their value as of the application date. Currency fluctuations affecting value of claims at a later date are not recognized under indemnity.
   b. The above insurance/indemnity will reimburse loss or damage occurring during the loan period. Restoration costs and depre-

ciation in value will be covered, but are subject to mutual agreement. Total losses are reimbursed at the value as agreed herein, and are subject to salvage.

c. If the Lender prefers to maintain his/her own insurance, then the Borrower and participating museums must be named as additional insureds on the policy. Otherwise, they are to be released from all liability and held harmless for any loss or damage to the loaned objects.

3. Shipping and Packing

a. Unless other arrangements are herein stated, foreign loans will be consolidated for packing and/or shipping to and from the United States at mutually agreeable location and time. Shipments will be by (chosen method) and will be accompanied by the Borrower's authorized agent(s). Packing must be of highest professional quality and done under the supervision of the Lender and/or Borrower. Packing should be of a quality to withstand shocks of handling and changes in climate. Unpacking and repacking instructions should be included. Borrower will provide security protection during packing, transit and storage periods.

b. Lenders and Borrower will adhere to their respective government customs regulations in exporting and importing loans and will protect objects from possible damage during inspections.

c. Lenders who accompany their own loans will provide qualified couriers. Arrangements will be subject to advance agreement with the Borrower.

4. Reproduction, Photography and Credit

a. Unless expressly denied herein, the Lender gives permission to the Borrower and participants to photograph, film, and reproduce objects for publicity, condition record, catalog illustration or other educational uses. Credit will be given as stated herein for publication and labels. Copies of the catalog will be furnished to each lender. (English or foreign language edition)

b. Photography will be done under supervision of curators and excessive lighting will be prohibited.

c. It is understood that the general public may photograph objects for personal use.

d. Lender must inform Borrower of any existing copyright.

5. Possession and Return

a. Objects will remain in the Borrower's possession for the period indicated herein and be displayed at the Borrower's discretion.

b. In case of change in legal ownership, Borrower must be given satisfactory proof before objects will be released.

c. Objects will be returned to the Lender or his authorized agent at the address given herein. If efforts to return the objects within a reasonable time are unsuccessful, the Borrower may place the objects in storage at the Lender's risk and expense. Failure of the Lender to sign and return the official return receipt within 30 days of final shipment will absolve the Borrower of any further liability for the loaned objects.

6. Costs

All reasonable costs of effecting the loan, e.g. insurance, transit, packing, will be covered by the Borrower. Lender must inform Borrower of all known costs incidental to the loan herein.

C. Certification and Signature (example below)

I have read and agree to the above conditions and certify I am authorized to agree thereto.

Signed:_____ Date_____
          Lender (owner or authorized agent)

_____ Date_____
Borrower

III. CHECKLIST FOR INTERNATIONAL EXHIBITION CONTRACT BETWEEN ORGANIZER/MUSEUM AND BORROWER/MUSEUM (may be co-organizer or participant)

1. Name and address of Borrower and Lender as parties to the Contract. Lender is organizer, Borrower is co-organizer, or participant.
2. Purpose—exhibition title and description.
3. Time frame and location—exact location of exhibition showings and approximate dates for the loan including sufficient time to cover shipment, receipt, unpacking, installation, public exhibit, dismantling, repacking, and return shipment.
4. Objects or artworks included in the exhibit should be referenced by an attachment (catalog listing) or a statement in the contract that the listing will be provided by Lender on a specific date.
5. Name(s) of curatorial individual(s) (or duly appointed successors) responsible for the exhibition, acting on behalf of the borrowing and lending institutions.
6. Division of responsibility between organizers and participant museums regarding:
   a. Loan selection and negotiation with other lenders.
   b. Design and printing of any special loan agreement forms, receipts, condition report forms or stationery.
   c. Period of responsibility/liability for objects.
   d. Signing individual Lender's agreements, which should not differ materially from the standard terms agreed upon for borrowing (if Organizers are Lenders, agreement to the same standard terms).
   e. Acceptance and payment of loan fees.
   f. Responsibility for collection, packing, shipping, courier arrangements, security, etc.
   g. Applications for immunity from seizure; Federal indemnity.
7. Description of packing methods and materials
   a. In accordance with the most advanced techniques in order to assure rapid safe and secure transport.
   b. Provision for borrower to review packing technique, especially where insurance liability in effect.
   c. Crate lists, packing and unpacking instructions.
8. Condition reports
   a. Organizing curators (with conservator) to prepare master report and photographs. Condition checked at time of preparation and packing for transport to borrowing organization.
   b. Responsible individual to check condition of objects at packing and repacking points along the tour.
   c. Requirement for receipts.
   d. Notice that damage or loss will be recorded and reported promptly to Organizer and Lenders.
9. Transportation arrangements
   a. Selection of carrier for each leg of journey.
   b. Transit via mutually agreeable carrier and scheduled time.
   c. Security arrangements for transit.

  d. How shipment(s) will be moved from museum to port for overseas flight/(ocean voyage).

  e. Indicate necessity to split shipment on more than one conveyance to meet insurance or indemnity requirements.

  f. Provision for curatorial escort of main shipments.

  g. Provision for reasonable travel expenses for lender escort (as required by loan agreements).

10. Customs responsibility for lending organization or individual Lenders

  a. Clearance of customs in foreign countries (export licenses?)

  b. Arrangement for US customs clearance and outside inspection on Borrower premises.

  c. Assignment of customs broker.

11. Insurance/Indemnity

  a. Statement regarding who will arrange for insurance under indemnity or through commercial carrier.

  b. Approximate total value and specific period of coverage.

  c. Indication if there will be a split coverage situation.

  d. Notice that insurance/Indemnity is sole recovery available in the event of loss or damage.

  e. Requirement that lending organization(s) should cooperate fully in providing necessary information for completing Indemnity application.

  f. Note that Indemnity requires coverage in US dollars at a set value with no provision for fluctuation in market valuation or currency devaluation.

  g. Provision for covering insurance of the deductibles and any excess.

  h. Description of commercial coverage to be sought in lieu of Indemnity.

  i. Provision for sending insurance certificate to Lenders.

  j. Indication that Lenders preferring their own insurance will have borrowers as additional insured or waive subrogation against borrowing institution(s) as referenced in the loan agreements.

  k. Indication of how Lender insurance premium will be paid.

12. Preservation/installation

  a. Borrowers promise to use best efforts to protect exhibition from damage and loss while in custody.

  b. No conservation treatment will be undertaken without approval of lenders.

  c. Request special instruction for handling care and installation be provided in loan agreements.

  d. Installation of the exhibit; design concept and selected site will be organizer's and participants' full responsibility and privilege.

  e. Participant exhibitors may omit objects from showings for good cause with prior knowledge of lender.

  f. Allowance for couriers or Lender representatives to be present at unpacking and installation.

g. Provision for security alarms and guards for exhibit areas.
13. Catalog
    a. Designation of curatorial staff or outside contractor responsible for editing, designing, writing and/or translating catalog.
    b. Indication of where catalog will be produced.
    c. Number of catalogs in order and suggested price.
    d. Foreign language editions and provisions for translation.
    e. Banner, poster, cards, and artifact reproductions.
    f. Reproduction permission: provision for resolving copyright problems and paying royalties or reproduction fees.
14. Publicity
    a. Control of the labelling, press release, promotion, public service TV film, photographs, etc.
    b. Credit lines for sponsors (corporate and/or federal).
    c. Allowance for view of press releases in advance by organizer and borrower.
    d. Opening invitation and reception.
15. Provision for who, how, and when photography to be allowed.
16. Statement on admission fees.
17. Indication of any extra material to travel with the exhibit such as exhibit cases, graphics, panels, other hardware and responsibility for returning.
18. Dispersal—primary borrower (organizer) will be responsible?
19. Sharing of costs and revenues.
20. Timetable for completion of various portions of project.
21. Agreement to cooperate and resolve mutual problems—modifications of agreement can be made in writing.
22. Provision for sharing costs should exhibit be subject to early cancellation.
23. Both parties sign.

CHAPTER IX

Objects Left in the Temporary Custody of the Museum

A. Objects in Temporary Custody as Distinguished From Loans
B. Temporary Custody Procedures
C. Return Provisions
D. Sample Temporary Custody Receipt Form

A. Objects in Temporary Custody as Distinguished From Loans

There are valid distinctions to be made between objects loaned to a museum for exhibition and/or research and objects deposited with a museum for identification, authentication, examination for purchase, and the like. The first mentioned invariably are sought out by the museum and subsequent loans benefit both museum and lender. The second classification covers objects left with the museum on the initiative of the owner in order to accomplish an objective of particular interest to the owner. Both situations result in bailments, but the form of the bailment can vary. As explained in the section on loans, when a bailment is for the mutual benefit of the parties, the bailee (museum) is held to a higher standard of care than when the bailment is for the benefit of the owner. A museum, therefore, can justify having a different agreement regarding liability with those who leave objects for their own benefit. Frequently, such an agreement is called "a temporary custody receipt" to be distinguished from the traditional loan.[1]

The temporary custody receipt may recite the fact that the bailment is for the benefit of the owner and the museum is responsible only for gross negligence, or it could notify the owner that while reasonable care will be used, safety is not guaranteed and no insurance will be carried. Either statement, or variations thereof, should put the owner on notice that the museum, with cause, is limiting its liability with regard to the deposited material. It should be recognized, however, that such statements probably will not absolve a

---

1. Questions can arise in some instances as to whether a temporary custody receipt or an incoming loan agreement is in order. For example, if someone offers to donate an object to the museum and the museum wishes to have the object in hand for a period of time in order to make a decision on whether to accept, a short-term, incoming loan agreement may be more appropriate. The justification would be that the museum is requesting a period of custody for its own purposes and hence it is fairer to provide the owner insurance coverage. Common sense should be the guide.

museum from liability if there is clear-cut evidence of obvious negligence, but they should afford some protection against weak claims or situations where misfortune rather than negligence is the cause.[2] A museum prudently may decide that it will not insure individually objects left for the benefit of owners because of the more limited risk exposure. However, such a decision should be made only after it is clear whether other insurance carried by the museum may come into play in cases of obvious negligence and/or whether the museum, within limits, can self-insure.

Another distinction which can be made between true loans and objects left for the benefit of owners is that frequently the second category of objects should be processed expeditiously in order to limit expense and liability exposure. Experience demonstrates that there is a greater chance that unsolicited objects can be lost or forgotten if they are not given immediate attention. Time spent later on searching for such objects and their owners, or trying to recall promises made, is costly. It is a wise precaution, therefore, for a museum to devise and follow a system designed to monitor the flow of such material.

B. Temporary Custody Procedures

Every collection-type object which comes into a museum should be a matter of record. Accessioning procedures provide a system of immediate notation of objects known to be destined for the collections, and a similar recording system invariably is in place for incoming loans. The use of a temporary custody receipt provides the catch-all for recording those objects which, when received, fall into neither the "to be accessioned" or true incoming loan category. To be effective, the temporary custody receipt system needs central coordination with established procedures for issuing receipts and for the filing and timely follow-up of all such receipts.

A museum can find itself overwhelmed with material deposited for identification and other assorted purposes unless guidelines are established in the museum's collection management policy regarding what and when objects can be taken into custody for the benefit of owners. For example, a museum may find that its liability exposure is greatly reduced if instead of accepting objects on deposit for identification, it sets aside certain times when objects can be brought in for immediate viewing by museum staff. These articles never leave the custody of their owners and only oral opinions are given.[3] This, then, may become the general rule with exceptions made only for unusual situations. If, on the other hand, a museum generally permits objects to be placed in custody, there should be a system in the collection management policy for alleviating backlogs. If too many objects are accumulating, perhaps a mechanism for instituting a moratorium on the acceptance of additional objects until the backlog

---

2. See Chapter VI, Part A, "Incoming Loans" regarding ability to limit liability, and footnote 3 for definitions of "gross negligence."

3. See Chapter XIII, "Appraisals and Authentications," for other problems pertaining to an authentication service.

is reduced to a manageable level may be in order. The museum should not encourage problems by taking in objects when it is evident that prompt attention cannot be given them. The museum's collection management policy also should make it clear who has the authority to approve the issuance of temporary custody receipts.

How an object is received should be a matter of record. For example, if an unsolicited object is mailed to a museum, its method of delivery may be an important piece of information in weighing museum liability if the owner later claims negligence.[4] If the temporary custody receipt form has a space for describing mode of delivery, this information is captured. Ideally, unsolicited objects mailed to a museum should be returned immediately with or without requested information, or a temporary deposit receipt mailed for signature. By definition, the ideal is not reality.

Another important consideration is the establishment of a maximum duration period for the temporary custody receipt. Every such receipt when issued should have a clearly specified termination date so that owner and museum staff are aware that a return date must be met. This encourages prompt processing by the museum and it establishes a time for the bailment to end, which can be important if the owner fails to retrieve the property. While staff may be given some discretion in setting the term of a custody receipt, a museum-wide maximum term should be established which cannot be exceeded without special permission. Ninety days is a maximum period used by some museums, but each museum can tailor the period to suit its own capabilities and needs.

The temporary custody receipt form may wish to address certain other topics which can prove troublesome if not explained in advance. Some museums have found to their dismay that owners who have temporarily deposited objects have then misused museum custody for personal gain. For instance, a temporary custody receipt usually requires the owner to describe briefly the object and its value. Owners have been known later to tout their attribution and/or valuation as "museum endorsed," merely because the information was accepted by the museum without comment. Another example is the owner who drops off his object at the museum for possible sale. If there is no sale, the object is then offered elsewhere with the added provenance that it was once on loan to X museum. Cautions against such misuse can be included in the list of conditions that frequently appear on the back of the temporary custody receipt form.

If the museum wishes to have the right to photograph such objects or to examine them by generally accepted methods, this should be noted on the form. The form can also explain how this information will be used. As with incoming loans, a museum avoids restoring, treating or otherwise altering objects left in its temporary custody unless the written permission of owners

---

4. It may legitimately be argued that when a museum receives unsolicited objects in the mail for identification, or similar reasons, a constructive bailment is created. In a constructive bailment, the law implies a bailment even though there is no mutual consent between the parties, but the unconsenting bailee usually is held to a low standard of care. If the museum consents to the bailment by issuing a temporary custody receipt, usually a slightly higher standard of care is expected.

has been obtained. It may be prudent to note this particular policy on the receipt form.

If the temporary custody receipt is used occasionally for objects which are being offered to the museum for donation or sale, the museum may wish to have the owner warrant at this stage his ability to pass good title. By including such a provision in the custody receipt, the offeror is put on early notice that proof of title is important and possible difficulties in this area can then be resolved before internal museum review procedures are set in motion.

C. Return Provisions

Two major purposes in establishing a temporary custody receipt procedure are to assure prompt return of objects to their owners, and, if return cannot be made, to prevent museum storage areas from becoming cluttered with unclaimed objects. As with incoming loans, these purposes cannot be accomplished effectively unless certain precautions are taken when the objects are received. The temporary custody receipt form should require the owner to specify exactly what method should be used to return the object when the period of custody ends. It should also describe the steps the museum will take if the object cannot be returned after reasonable efforts are made. Finally, the form can provide that an unrestricted gift of the object to the museum will be inferred if the object is not claimed after a specified holding period. The section entitled "Return Provisions" in "Incoming Loans" in Chapter VI and "Unclaimed Loans" (Chapter VII), should be reviewed for an understanding of why these provisions may prove important to the museum. The section on "Change in Ownership" in Chapter VI also is relevant when a museum is designing its temporary custody receipt form.

D. Sample Temporary Custody Receipt Form

The example of a temporary custody receipt (on pages 229-30), as with any form, should not be adopted without question by a museum. Before any form is used, every provision should be understood by staff and judged appropriate. If there is uncertainty, professional assistance should be sought.

Registrar's No. _____

NAME OF MUSEUM
ADDRESS

TEMPORARY CUSTODY RECEIPT

The object(s) listed below are received subject to the CONDITIONS printed on the reverse.

Received from: _____
            (name and address of depositor)

_____

_____ Phone: __( )_____

For the following purpose:

_____

_____

Removal date is: _____
(Unless otherwise mutually agreed on, the object(s) shall remain in custody for a limited period of time, not to exceed _____ days. See CONDITIONS on reverse.)

Return of Object(s)
  ☐ will be picked up by depositor

  ☐ Museum will send by _____ to this address: _____

_____

Packing and shipping to be paid by ☐ Depositor   ☐ Museum.

Description of Object(s): (include condition)	Depositor's Valuation

Curatorial Unit: _____

Date received: _____   Signed: _____

(over)

Museum Control No. _____

COPY DESIGNATION

CONDITIONS

(1) The objects are accepted by the Museum for the benefit of the deposi-tor and the Museum assumes no responsibility except the avoidance of gross negligence. The depositor hereby agrees to release and hold harmless the Museum, its employees, officers, and agents from any liability in connection with the objects while on deposit or in transit except for clear gross negligence.

(2) Insurance of the objects is the responsibility of the depositor.

(3) Attributions, dates, and other information shown on the face are not to be considered appraisals or official opinions by the Museum. The fact that objects have been in the Museum's custody shall not be misused to indicate Museum endorsement.

(4) Objects may be photographed and examined by modern scientific methods by the Museum for its own purposes, but will not be restored, treated or otherwise altered without written permission of the depositor.

(5) In forwarding imported objects for deposit, the depositor is required to comply with all government regulations.

(6) If there is a change in the identity and/or address of the depositor or the owner, the Museum must be notified promptly in writing. Objects must be claimed on or before the removal date noted on the face of the Receipt. If one other than the original depositor claims objects, the Museum reserves the right to request proof of legal authority to receive the material before objects will be released.

(7) If objects are to be returned to the depositor by mail or other carrier, the depositor will be sent an Outgoing Receipt at time of shipment. Failure to sign and return said Receipt within 30 days of shipment of said objects shall release the Museum from any further liability for the deposited property.

(8) If the depositor of record fails to collect the objects or if delivery cannot be effected after the removal date, the Museum will mail the depositor at its address of record a warning to remove. The Museum assumes no responsi-bility to search for a depositor (or listed owner) not located at the address of record. If after _____ years from the removal date noted on the face of this Receipt objects have not been claimed, then, and in consideration for their maintenance and safekeeping during such period, the objects shall be considered unrestricted gifts to the Museum.

(9) In the event the objects are being offered for sale or donation to the Museum, the depositor, in the absence of written notice to the Museum to the contrary, warrants that he/she upon request is prepared to pass full and clear title to the objects, including any copyright interests.

(10) This agreement shall be construed in accordance with the law of

_____.
(name of the applicable jurisdiction)

- -

I have read and agree to the above CONDITIONS, and I certify that I have full authority to agree thereto.

Date:_____ Signed:_____
                                 Depositor*

*If Depositor is not the owner, complete the following:

Name of owner:_____

Address of owner:_____

_____

_____

CHAPTER X

Objects Found in the Collections

A. The Problem
B. When Claims Are Made
C. When the Museum Wishes to Dispose of Objects Found in the Collections

A. The Problem

The phrase "objects found in the collections" frequently is used in the museum profession to describe items that lack any significant documentation as to how they were added to the collections. In other words, the museum knows that these objects have been in its possession for some time yet, if called upon, it cannot prove ownership with certainty because there are no definitive records. For the purposes of this discussion, the phrase does not include unclaimed loans, a subject discussed in a prior chapter. As a general rule, objects found in the collections are distinguishable from unclaimed loans because their continued undisturbed possession by the museum usually supports a presumption of a valid initial transfer of ownership. This presumption must be rebutted by a claimant. In the case of unclaimed loans, however, it is clear that there was no initial transfer of ownership to the museum and if the museum hopes to retain the material, it must come forward with a successful argument as to why the lender has lost the right to claim the property. In this latter case, as the law now stands the museum has the burden of proof, and this can make a crucial difference.

The fact that undocumented objects are fairly common in museum collections should come as no great surprise to one familiar with the history of museums. Many museums were begun by public-spirited individuals operating with limited funds and/or without the help of well-trained support staff. (The museum registrar of today is a fairly recent addition to the professional ranks of the museum community.) If there were funds and staff available for record-keeping, these systems often were quite personalized and hence lacked continuity. Also, the orderly preservation of records and the periodic checking of records against museum inventory are costly tasks which, realistically, do not gain priority if funds are short. It can be easily understood, therefore, why museums, particularly those which were founded generations ago or which had very informal beginnings, now have undocumented objects in their collections. The problem is a cause of general concern, but it becomes more acute when a museum wishes to dispose of such objects or when someone comes forward to claim one of the objects. What is the position of the museum?

B. When Claims Are Made

First, consider the undocumented object that is being claimed. Normally, as previously explained, the burden of proving ownership rests on the claimant. In other words, to prevail the claimant must show that he and he alone now holds title to the object in question. Until this is done, the museum need not budge. In order to weigh the merits of the claim certain information is usually required by the museum from the claimant:

(1) A clear explanation of why the claimant believes he holds title, with copies of supporting evidence.

(2) A statement from the claimant that he is either the sole party at interest or that he is authorized to represent all parties at interest, with supporting proof.

Sometimes the second request can be a stumbling block for the claimant. If, for example, his claim is based on the allegation that the object in question was lent to the museum years ago by an ancestor, he must show, by family records, relevant testamentary instruments, etc., that he is the sole heir of that ancestor. If he is not the sole heir, he must produce satisfactory proof that all other heirs have given him permission to represent them in the matter.

When the precise nature of the claim is known and the claimant appears to have the right to make the demand, the museum will want to review its records with great care to see whether it can find evidence that supports or contradicts the claim, and whether it has evidence which will support a valid defense. Defenses which most often come to mind are: the running of a statute of limitations, laches and adverse possession. Each of these has been discussed in some detail in Chapter VII, "Unclaimed Loans." Essentially, the kind of evidence the museum looks for to support a defense in claims of this nature are:

(1) Evidence that the claimant knew, or should have known, that the museum thought it owned the object and that the claimant delayed in bringing his action to the detriment of the museum.

(2) Evidence that the claimant "slept on his rights," that is he failed to use due diligence in seeking out his property.

(3) Evidence that the museum has publicly displayed the object as its own or otherwise publicized it as such.

After relevant information has been gathered, the evaluation of a claim frequently should be done with professional advice. The museum also will want to review its general trust responsibilities regarding protection of trust assets, as described in the section entitled "Requests for Return of Collection Objects" in Chapter V.

If there is legitimate doubt as to the validity of a claim or if the claim appears to be valid but there are several claimants and some are reluctant to see the object removed from public use, one alternative worth suggesting is as follows. If the claimant or claimants are willing to give to the museum in writing every right, title and interest he/they may have in the object, possibly there may be legitimate tax advantages. In either case, there is a relinquishment of a chance to win a judgment in court and, in effect, this chance to win is being donated to the museum. The value that legitimately can be placed on such a gift is a matter for resolution between the donor and the Internal Revenue Service. If such a quitclaim-type deed of gift is executed, the museum's title to the object should then be secure.

C. When the Museum Wishes to Dispose of Objects Found in the Collections

The disposal of objects of unconfirmed ownership presents risks. These risks should be understood so that informed decisions can be made when there is pressure to prune such objects from the collections. As explained,[1] as a general rule, if a museum cannot refute successfully a third party's assertion and proof of ownership to an object, that object must be returned upon demand. If the object is no longer in the possession of the museum because the object has been given away or sold, and the claimant pursues his interest against the present holder, the museum can expect repercussions.

If the museum sold the object to the present holder without reservations about title and the holder subsequently must return the object to the true owner, the museum may be forced to pay the holder the value of the object as of the date of its return. This is so because under the Uniform Commercial Code[2] there is a general implied warranty that a seller conveys good title, and the Code also provides that if a purchaser does not acquire good title, he can elect to claim damages against his seller equal to the present value of the object.[3]

A museum could attempt to protect itself from suit by a disappointed purchaser by selling an object and expressly not warranting title. Naturally, it then can expect that the purchase price will reflect this limitation. Another alternative is to state in the sale agreement that any recovery by the purchaser is limited to the sale price. Here again this provision may affect what the purchaser is willing to pay.

If the museum gives away an object of unconfirmed ownership, the Uniform Commercial Code should not be applicable, and if the present holder ultimately is forced to return the object, the holder may have no recourse against the donor/museum.[4] In order to sue the museum successfully, the holder, as a rule, would have to demonstrate that it was damaged because of the donation.

---

1. See discussion in Chapter IV, "The Acquisition of Objects—Accessioning," section on "Circumstances Which Can Affect the Quality of Title" and Chapter VII, "Unclaimed Loans."

2. Section 2-231. See discussion on Uniform Commercial Code in Chapter IV, "Acquisition of Objects—Accessioning."

3. Section 2-714(2) of the Uniform Commercial Code. Consider, also, that in such a sale there need not be an intervening third party. If the purchaser subsequently learns title is faulty, he may elect to return the object to the seller and seek present-day value.

4. An exchange of objects normally would constitute a sale, not a gift.

However, if the true owner cannot retrieve the object from the present holder or if the object has been damaged, the museum may well find itself subject to suit.

When considering the disposal of objects of unconfirmed ownership, the museum rarely can deal in generalities. The facts of each particular case must be researched and weighed so that informed judgments can be made as to the strength of the museum's position if there is a challenge, and the potential risks. Additional factors that might be considered in such an analysis are as follows:

- What is the value of the object in question? This bears on the extent of the potential liability. Value also may indicate whether a third party will ever seriously search out the item.[5]
- Is the object quite distinctive so that it is readily identifiable? The more common the object, the more difficult it might be to establish ownership.
- Has the object ever been displayed publicly as property of the museum? In other words, if the museum has consistently and publicly held the object out as its own, there is greater chance that the museum may have a valid defense if a third party later comes forward to claim it.[6]
- What is the proposed method of disposal, sale or donation, and how urgent is the need? For instance, it should be easier to justify the donation to a charitable organization of several large, relatively worthless objects because space is needed desperately than it is to justify the sale of small, costly objects in order to feed the museum's general acquisition fund.

All in all, there are no quick, easy answers to the problems raised by "objects found in the collections." However, if a museum can afford the time and money required to research records carefully and to obtain necessary professional advice, some ameliorating steps may present themselves as worthy of consideration.

---

5. However, certain objects have been known to increase in value dramatically because of changes in public taste.

6. See prior discussions in Chapter VII, "Unclaimed Loans," on the defenses of statutes of limitations, laches and adverse possession.

CHAPTER XI

Promised Gifts

A. Obstacles to Enforcement
B. Arguments for Enforcement
C. Pledge Forms

A. Obstacles to Enforcement

If an object (or money) has been promised to a museum and the gift is not completed, does the museum have any recourse? There usually are difficulties in enforcing such promises because of a lack of what is called "consideration." If all the elements of a valid gift cannot be established, then to be enforceable, a promise must be shown to have the requisites for a valid contract. Contracts require a demonstration of "consideration" on the part of both parties:

> To make a valid gift *inter vivos* [during life], there must be a clear intention to transfer title to the property, and also a delivery by the donor and an acceptance by the donee. It is essential to the validity of such a gift that the transfer of both possession and title shall be absolute and shall go into immediate effect. In other words, the donor must intend not only to deliver possession, but also to relinquish the right of dominion. If a gift has reference to future time when it is to operate as a transfer, it is only a promise without consideration, and cannot be enforced either at law or in equity.[1]

Consideration is "an act or forebearance or the promise thereof done or given by one party in return for the act or promise of another."[2] Both parties to a contract must proffer consideration. In the typical promised gift situation, the prospective donor has already made a promise to act (the donor's consideration), the problem, usually, is to find consideration on the part of the donee, the recipient museum.

Another frequent obstacle to enforcement of a promised gift is the statute of frauds. Most states have a statute requiring that certain kinds of understandings must be in writing and signed before a cause of action can be brought on them. These statutes are patterned on the old English statute of frauds and hence the common use of that name when referring to laws of this type. If the

---

1. *Berman v. Leckner*, 66 A.2d 392, 393 (Md. 1949). See, also *Whalen v. Milholland*, 89 Md. 199, 43 A. 45 (1899). But see Temple, "Gifts Effected by Written Instrument: *Faith Lutheran Retirement Home v. Veis*," 35 Montana L. R. 132 (Winter 1974).

2. *Webster's Dictionary*.

promise to donate to a museum has not been reduced to writing and signed, it is quite possible that it might run afoul of the local statute of frauds, and, thus, not be enforceable in court.[3]

B. Arguments for Enforcement

The enumerated obstacles are not insurmountable, and there is a tendency on the part of many courts to favor the enforcement of charitable subscriptions as a matter of public policy.[4] Each case, however, must stand on its own merits, and the peculiarities of applicable state law must be researched. Two avenues frequently taken by the courts to uphold promised gifts, are: (1) reliance as demonstrated by the subsequent conduct of the promisee is deemed consideration and (2) the doctrine of promissory estoppel.

A classic situation of the first type was presented to a New York court in 1978.[5] A donor had promised a large sum of money to a museum for the construction of an addition to the museum building. It was understood that the pledge would be paid over a period of five years. There was no written pledge agreement. Several substantial payments were made to the museum through the donor's bank, acting as agent. The donor died before all payments were due and when the museum requested the balance of the pledged sum, the matter was taken to court by the donor's estate. The museum prevailed. In this particular case, the evidence demonstrated that upon receiving the pledge, the museum initiated building construction. The court found that this liability incurred in reliance on the pledge constituted adequate consideration.[6] With regard to the statute of frauds, the court held that it could look to other writings submitted in evidence to satisfy the purpose of that statute. There was evidence that the donor had signed papers that referred to the pledge and this was held sufficient to satisfy the New York requirement that such a pledge had to be in writing and signed by the party from whom performance was sought.[7] Of interest to all charities are the comments of the court concerning the manner in which the particular pledge was made:

> The loss of litigation by donors' estates should be of no solace to charitable donees for such litigation, caused by inexcusable casualness, may cause less charitable gift-giving by others. These proceedings would not have been necessary if the Museum had followed reasonably prudent business methods and had the decedent sign a simple pledge form.[8]

---

3. See *Restatement (Second) of Contracts*, Chapter 4, for a listing of state statutes which qualify as Statutes of Frauds.

4. See, for example, *Woodmere Academy v. Steinberg*, 41 N.Y.2d 746, 363 N.E.2d 1169 (1977).

5. *In Re Charles S. Payson*, File No. 177095 (N.Y. Sur. Ct., Nassau County, July 11, 1978).

6. See also *I&I Holding Corp. v. Gainsburg*, 276 N.Y. 427, 12 N.E.2d 533 (1938); *In Re Field's Will*, 181 N.Y.S.2d 922 (1959); *In Re Field's Estate*, 172 N.Y.S.2d 740 (1958); *In Re Kirby's Will*, 240 N.Y.S.2d 214 (1963); *Liberty Maimonides Hospital v. Feldberg*, 4 Misc. 2d 291, 158 N.Y.S.2d 913 (1957).

7. See also *In Re Field's Will*, 181 N.Y.S.2d 922 (1959) on the statute of frauds issue.

8. *In Re Charles S. Payson*, File No. 177095 (N.Y. Sur. Ct., Nassau County, July 11, 1978) at 11.

What constitutes sufficient reliance on the part of a donee to enforce a gift is a question of fact:

> First, it can be said with assurance that the action or forebearance must amount to a substantial change in position. . . . A generous promise of a gift of $100 will not be made enforceable by the fact that the promisee walks a few blocks to the bank in the reasonable belief that the promise will there be performed. . . . What is substantial[?] Beyond doubt, it is relative to the other circumstances and especially to the content of the promise and the cost to the promisor of his promised performance.
>
> Secondly, it can be said with equal assurance that the action or forebearance must either have been actually foreseen by the promisor, or must be of such a kind as a reasonable person in his position would have foreseen when making the promise.
>
> Thirdly, an actual promise must have been made, and this promise must itself have induced the action or forebearance in reliance on it.[9]

With regard to charitable subscriptions in particular, the *Restatement of Contracts* makes this comment:

> American courts have traditionally favored charitable subscription . . . and have found consideration in many cases where the element of exchange was doubtful or nonexistent. Where recovery is rested on reliance in such cases, a probability of reliance is enough, and no effort is made to sort out mixed motives or to consider whether partial enforcement would be appropriate.[10]

As mentioned, the other reason given by some courts for enforcing charitable contributions is the doctrine of promissory estoppel. In such instances, there usually is evidence that the promisee took action as a result of a promise, the action was known or should have been expected by the promisor, the promisor failed to take reasonable steps to warn the promisee there would be no performance, and under existing circumstances, it would be an injustice to the promisee if the promise was not enforced. When these facts are present, a court may hold that as a matter of fairness, the promisor is estopped from raising such defenses as the statute of frauds or lack of consideration.[11] It is argued by some experts that the use of the doctrine of promissory estoppel in such cases amounts to the application of the previously described "reliance" approach. In other words, upon analysis, there is only one theory, that of

---

9. Corbin, *Contracts* § 200. See, also, *Restatement (Second) of Contracts*, § 90. In *Mount Sinai Hospital of Greater Miami v. Jordan*, 290 So. 2d 484 (Fla. 1974), the court refused to enforce a pledge of funds made for no specific purpose and where there was no actual evidence of detrimental action on the part of the charity. See also *Jordan v. Mount Sinai Hospital of Greater Miami*, 276 So. 2d 102 (Fla. 1973).

10. § 90 (2d ed.). See also *Salsbury v. Northwestern Bell Telephone Co.*, 221 N.W.2d 609 (Iowa 1974). But note this caution stressed in the *Mount Sinai Hospital* cases, *supra.* at 487 and 108:

> Courts should act with restraint in respect to the public policy arguments endeavoring to sustain a mere charitable subscription. To ascribe consideration where there is none, or to adopt any other theory which affords charities a different legal rationale than other entities, is to approve fiction.

11. See Seavey, "Reliance Upon Gratuitous Promises or Other Conduct," 64 *Harv. L. Rev.* 913 (1951); *Allegheny College v. National Chautauqua County Bank of Jamestown*, 246 N.Y. 369, 159 N.E. 173 (1927); *In Re Field's Estate*, 172 N.Y.S.2d 740 (1958); and *Restatement (Second) of Contracts* § 90.

reliance.[12] A defense phrased as promissory estoppel may be particularly compelling, however, if the conduct of the promisor appears to be less than honorable. Consider, for example, the following situation. A frequent donor to the XYZ Museum of Technology lends the museum a very rare, recently acquired printing press, saying that as soon as it is financially advantageous for him to do so, he will make a gift of the press. Museum staff spend much time, money and effort restoring, researching and publicizing the piece.[13] This is done with the knowledge of the lender who never indicates that he may have changed his mind about the promised gift. As a result of the museum's efforts, the value of the press has increased greatly. The lender then announces that he wants the press returned so that it can be sold. Because of the element of unjust enrichment to the promisor if a return is made, the defense of promissory estoppel may be quite effective. Also, this defense may avoid entirely the issue of the statute of frauds.[14]

Another situation which is not uncommon for a museum also may call into play the doctrine of promissory estoppel. A choice item is offered to the Hillandale Historical Society by Mrs. A, an elderly lady of limited means. Mrs. A offers to sell it to the museum for a modest sum explaining that she cannot afford to give it outright. Acquisition funds for the historical society are very low, and the director approaches Mr. Z who has expressed an interest in helping the Society. Mr. Z says he will be delighted to buy the piece from Mrs. A at the quoted price, place it on loan to the Society, and then, when tax consequences are favorable, donate it to the Society. Mr. Z, in fact, buys the object, lends it, but later demands its return, informing the Society that no gift will be forthcoming. Possibly, the Society can successfully refuse to return the piece arguing that Mr. Z is estopped from enforcing a demand for its return.[15]

A case involving the papers of the poet W. H. Auden illustrates other facts which may have to be resolved when the issue is whether an enforceable gift has been made.[16] Auden bequeathed his entire estate to his friend, Chester Kallman. While Auden's estate was still in the process of being settled, Kallman arranged to have Auden's manuscripts and papers delivered from London to the New York Public Library. Several months after the delivery, Kallman died. When Kallman's estate requested the return of the manuscripts and papers, the New York Public Library refused contending that a gift of the material had been made by Kallman to the library. As previously noted, the requirements for a completed *inter vivos* gift are: intent of the donor to make such a gift;

---

12. See Corbin, *Contracts* § 204, and *Restatement (Second) of Contracts* § 90. See also *Greiner v. Greiner*, 293 P. 759 (Kan. 1930).

13. The wisdom of such action might be questioned, but there can be circumstances where such reliance by a museum is understandable.

14. See *Illinois Railway Museum v. Hansen*, No. 80 Ch. 229 (Ill. 19th Judicial Cir., McHenry County, Woodstock, Oct. 1980).

15. If the facts are such that it can be established that Mrs. A sold to Mr. Z at the reduced rate expressly so that the museum would ultimately benefit, possibly the museum also could sue as the third party beneficiary to enforce the contract between Mrs. A and Mr. Z.

16. *Estate of Kallman*, 425 N.Y.S.2d 398, 103 Misc. 2d 339 (1980).

delivery of the property involved; and acceptance by the donee.[17] The burden of establishing each of these elements rests on the donee.[18] In the Auden case, it was conceded that the poet's papers had been delivered to the library, but Kallman's estate claimed that the papers had been transferred only for safe-keeping and not with the intent to make an immediate gift. The library, not without difficulty, was able to convince the court otherwise. The "ambiguous" delivery can be a problem for museums because frequently objects are placed on loan and then later donated. The mere fact that an object is delivered to a museum does not then necessarily infer that there is a contemporaneous intent to transfer title. It is important to record promptly the status of each object delivered to a museum with appropriate documentation forwarded to the trans-feror. If objects are delivered on loan status with the understanding that the owner intends to make a gift at a later date,[19] this should be clarified in writing. If the promise is meant to be enforceable, this should be stated also, possibly with mention of how the museum is relying on the promise.[20] In any event, it is preferable to write the loan agreement for a relatively short period of time so that the situation can be monitored.

C. Pledge Forms

It is recognized that frequently when dealing with prospective donors there is a reluctance on the part of the museum staff to require the execution of printed forms or to request that a particular understanding be committed to writing. There is the fear that such procedures will appear overly aggressive to donors and may sour what up until then have been good relations based on mutual trust. This reaction is understandable, but if given the opportunity for further reflection, donors usually appreciate the wisdom of providing for all contin-gencies. And, as exemplified by the previously described *Payson* case, a judge may loose patience with a museum which invites a lawsuit by failing to commit such a promise to writing.

Properly executed, written memoranda can save time, tempers and needless expenditures for legal fees. A museum is well-advised to prepare with profes-sional assistance, and use, whether the gift is money or objects, appropriate pledge forms that spell out the intentions of all parties. The use of such a form will not necessarily guarantee enforcement of a pledge, and, in fact, this may not be the parties' intention, but it should avoid later legal confrontations.[21]

The examples of pledge forms (on pages 240-41), as with all such examples, should not be adopted for use by a museum without careful professional review.

---

17. Ibid., at 940.

18. *In Re Moffett's Estate*, 266 N.Y.S.2d 989, 49 Misc. 2d 225 (1966).

19. Tax consideration frequently influences the timing of a gift.

20. For example, the museum may be giving up other gift opportunities in reliance on the promise or it may be making certain commitments in expectation of the gift.

21. Fractional gifts, as described in Chapter XII, "Tax Considerations Relevant to Gifts," raise pledge-type problems. What happens if the donor dies or changes his mind before all portions of the gift pass? Such eventualities should be addressed in the initial agreement between the donor and the museum.

EXAMPLE OF A PLEDGE INTENDED TO BE BINDING

Pledge to the _____ Museum

By this writing, I hereby confirm my agreement to give to the Museum at or before _____ the following:

I have represented to the Museum that I consider this a binding commit-ment. I understand that the Museum is relying on this commitment of mine, more specifically that the Museum's acquisition program is being adjusted in reliance on this pledge, and that my pledge may be used by the Museum to encourage others to make similar commitments.

Should this gift not be completed during my lifetime, it is understood that this agreement shall be binding on my executors or administrators, heirs and assigns, and that any failure to include such a specific bequest in my will shall not release my executors or administrators from the obligation of completing the gift to the Museum.

Accepted on_____   Pledgor:_____

the Museum   Date:_____

By_____

                                   *WITNESSES FOR PLEDGOR:

                                   _____

                                   _____

---

*It could be argued that a promise which, in fact, is enforceable at the death of the pledgor must satisfy the local Statute of Wills, which sets forth a certain format for testamentary instruments. Legal counsel advising a museum of the sufficiency of a pledge form may wish to review the applicable law on this point.

EXAMPLE OF PLEDGE INTENDED TO BE NONBINDING

I hereby pledge to give to the _____ Museum at or

before _____ the following:

It is mutually understood that this pledge is not binding, that it may be revoked at any time by the pledgor, and that it is not enforceable on and after the death of the pledgor.

Accepted on_____   Pledgor:_____

the Museum   Date:_____

By_____

CHAPTER XII

Tax Considerations Relevant to Gifts[1]

A. The Tax Status of the Donee/Museum

B. Income Tax Consequences of Charitable Gifts to "Publicly Supported" Museums

C. Concept of "Unrelated Use"

D. Spreading Out Charitable Deductions

E. The Bargain Sale

F. The Museum's Position Regarding Donor Deductions

A. The Tax Status of the Donee/Museum

No member of a museum's staff should attempt to play the role of a tax advisor to donors or prospective donors. Nevertheless, a general understanding of the tax consequences of charitable gifts is necessary if the museum expects to act intelligently and with integrity when matters of this nature are at issue. Instances can arise when it is quite appropriate for the museum to suggest to a potential donor a possibly advantageous method of giving (with the understanding that the donor will pursue this with his own advisors), just as there may be occasions when a museum should give a firm "No, thank you" to certain offers. Without some knowledge of the intricacies of the tax consequences of various gifts, a museum is hardly able to comport itself with any assurance. What follows, however, is only a basic outline of the most common gift situations and relevant federal tax law.[2]

In this discussion, it is assumed that the museum has requested and received a determination letter from the Internal Revenue Service (I.R.S.) recognizing the museum as an exempt organization under 501(c)(3) of the Internal Revenue

---

1. See also Chapter IV, "The Acquisition of Objects—Accessioning," section F on "Acquisition Procedures" regarding record-keeping for tax purposes, when a gift is complete for tax purposes, etc., and Chapter II, "Museums Are Accountable to Whom?," section E on "Oversight by Taxing Authorities."

2. For more comprehensive discussions of tax considerations see Comment, "Tax Incentives for Support of the Arts: In Defense of the Charitable Deduction," 85 *Dick. L. Rev.* 663 (1981); S. Goldberg, *Taxation of Charitable Giving* (1973); I.R.S. Publication No. 526, "Charitable Contributions"; A. Anderson and Co., *Tax Economics of Charitable Giving* (1982).

Code.[3] Section 501(c)(3) provides an exemption from federal income taxes for organizations that are formed and operated exclusively for charitable (including educational) purposes.[4] If such organizations also can demonstrate that they receive a substantial part of their support from governmental units or from the general public, they qualify as "publicly supported" charities.[5] Under § 170(c) of the Code, donors to such publicly supported charities receive the maximum possible deductions for their charitable contributions.

B. Income Tax Consequences of Charitable Gifts to "Publicly Supported" Museums

Cash. A gift of cash is deductible, at its dollar amount, up to 50 percent of the individual donor's "contribution base" (essentially, adjusted gross income).

Securities and Real Property. A gift of real estate or of intangible personal property (such as securities), if it has been held for six months[6] or more, would qualify as a contribution of "capital gain property" and would be deductible at its "fair market value,"[7] up to 30 percent of the individual donor's "contribution base."[8]

Tangible Personal Property. The typical museum donation, however, is of tangible personal property—items donated to the collections. For these, the tax laws impose additional considerations in determining the deduction. The allowable deduction may be cost (or other basis), cost (or other basis) plus 60 percent of any appreciation in value, or the fair market value of the property. A determination of which deduction is appropriate depends on whether the tangible personal property must be classified as ordinary income property or capital gain property, and, if the later, whether it is put to a "related use" by the donee.

Ordinary Income Property. If the donor created the property (as an artist his

---

3. I.R.S. Publication No. 557, "How to Apply for Recognition of Exemption for an Organization" should be consulted for instructions regarding application for exempt status.

4. Under I.R.S. regulations, an organization will be regarded as "operated exclusively" for an exempt purpose if it engages "primarily" in activities which accomplish such purpose (Treasury Regulations 26 C.F.R. § 1-501(c)(3)–1(c)(1)).

5. If a 501(c)(3) organization such as a museum cannot demonstrate "publicly supported" status (by one of several tests), it is treated as a private foundation. A private foundation is subject to special record-keeping and reporting requirements, is restricted in its dealings with certain organizations and individuals, and offers less favorable tax consequences to its donors.

6. Prior to the Tax Reform Act of 1984 (Section 1001), such property had to be held one year or more.

7. Fair market value is defined by the Internal Revenue Service as the price at which property would change hands between a willing buyer and a willing seller, neither being under any compulsion to buy or sell, and both having reasonable knowledge of the relevant facts. See I.R.S. Publication No. 526, "Charitable Contributions." See also I.R.S. Revenue Rulings 79-419, 1979-2 C.B. 107; and 80-69, 1980-1 C.B. 55.

8. A taxpayer-donor might elect to claim as a deduction the "fair market value" reduced by 40 percent of the realizable long-term capital gain. He then could take the resulting deduction up to 50 percent of his "contribution base." This election is usually of interest, however, only where the donated property has appreciated very little over the donor's basis (usually cost) but nonetheless amounts to over 30 percent of his contribution base.

painting or a writer her papers), its sale would result in ordinary income to the creator. Therefore, if donated by the creator, it is a gift of "ordinary income property" for which the allowable deduction is the donor-creator's "basis" in the property (for the artist, generally the cost of the canvas and paint).[9] Donations of certain property by others, notably dealers and other business people who regularly trade in the type of property which is donated, would also be considered donations of ordinary income property and would be equally limited in the allowable deduction to mere basis.[10]

In addition, short-term capital gain property (capital gain property held less than six months[11] before its donation or sale) is treated as ordinary income property for tax purposes. Thus, a donor of this property also would be limited to his basis in the property in claiming a charitable contribution deduction.[12]

Capital Gain Property. If the sale of the tangible personal property (at a profit) by an individual would have resulted in a long-term capital gain, its donation to a "publicly supported" museum usually entitles the donor to a charitable contribution deduction of the fair market value of the object contributed,[13] up to 30 percent of the donor's contribution base. There is, however, one important condition on this deduction: the donation of tangible (capital gain) property to a publicly supported museum will result in an allowable fair market value deduction only if the contributed property will be used by the museum for a purpose which is "related to" the museum's educational purposes.[14]

An explanation of related use and the tax consequence of a gift that is "unrelated" follows as Part C.

C. Concept of "Unrelated Use"

As defined by the I.R.S., the term "unrelated use" is a "use which is unrelated to the purpose or function constituting the basis of the charitable organization's

---

9. Note, "Tax Treatment of Artists' Charitable Contributions." 87 *Yale L.J.* 1244 (1979). There have been several bills introduced into Congress to give relief to artists, etc., who wish to donate their own works to charity but as of 1984, none has been enacted.

10. Though it is but small consolation, donations of "ordinary income property" are not held to the capital gain property deduction limit (30 percent of contribution base) discussed hereafter. Thus, though one can claim only basis, one can deduct for "ordinary income property" contributions up to 50 percent of one's "contribution base." Note all that this discussion concerns is federal income tax laws; state laws may vary.

11. Prior to the Tax Reform Act of 1984, the holding period was one year or more.

12. Since for a purchased item, the donor's basis is generally the purchase price, it is only when the item's fair market value is significantly higher than the purchase price (though it was purchased only a few months earlier) that a donor need be concerned about this point. If a prospective donor is aware of or anticipates a significant increase in the value of a recently acquired object, he may prefer to place it on loan with the museum and defer any gift until six months have passed from the date of acquisition.

13. See footnote 6, *supra*, for definition of fair market value.

14. This "related use" restriction applies to gifts for which an income tax charitable contribution deduction is taken. There is no similar restriction on estate tax charitable contribution deductions (except for § 2055(e)(4) of the Internal Revenue Code which applies to bequests of property with copyright ramifications). Also, an estate has an unlimited charitable deduction—there are no restrictions to 30 percent or 50 percent of the estate income.

exemption under section 501."[15] Clearly, therefore, an object donated for a museum's collections is for a related use and the donor is entitled to a fair-market-value charitable contribution deduction. However, when a group or collection of objects is offered to a museum and only a portion is suitable for its collections, a question of unrelated use may arise. Assuming that the museum can justify accepting the entire offering, does the fact that some of it will not be placed in the museum's collections jeopardize the "related use" of the entire gift? I.R.S. regulations contain the following statement:

> If a set or collection of items of tangible personal property is contributed to a charitable organization or governmental unit, the use of the set or collection is not an unrelated use if the donee sells or otherwise disposes of only an insubstantial portion of the set or collection.[16]

Whether "insubstantial portion" refers to quantity, quality or dollar value is not clear, however, and caution should be exercised.

In addition to the issue of the amount of the donation that will be put to a particular use, questions also arise concerning the relatedness of the use itself. I.R.S. regulations give the following examples of "unrelated use":

> [I]f a painting contributed to an educational institution is used by that organization for educational purposes by students, the use is not an unrelated use, but if the painting is sold and the proceeds used by the organization for educational purposes, the use of the property is an unrelated use. If furnishings contributed to a charitable organization are used by it in its offices and buildings in the course of carrying out its functions, the use of the property is not an unrelated use.[17]

If the tangible personal property is given expressly for an "unrelated use" by the museum, the donor's allowable deduction is limited to fair market value less 40 percent of the long-term gain that would have been recognized had the property been sold.[18] If the museum is soliciting contributions for an unrelated use (as, for example, its annual fundraising auction), care should be taken to document such planned use in a written communication to such donors so as not to mislead potential donors as to the tax consequences of such gifts.[19]

D. Spreading Out Charitable Deductions

Because there is a limit to the amount of charitable deductions a donor can claim in a year,[20] it is useful to know that there is a five-year carryover period.

---

15. Regulations 26 C.F.R. § 1.170.A-4(b)(3). See also Code § 170(e)(1)(B).

16. Ibid.

17. Ibid.

18. Stated another way, the donor's allowable deduction is cost (or other basis) plus 60 percent of gain.

19. See also comments in Section B(2)(e) of Chapter V, "The Disposal of Objects—Deaccessioning," which explain I.R.S. notification requirements if certain gifts are transferred by a museum within two years of receipt.

20. That is, the standard 50 percent of adjusted gross income for the year or the special 30 percent of adjusted gross income applicable to donations of certain capital gain property (see discussion under Part B, *supra*).

In other words, if a donor makes such charitable gifts in one year that the allowable deductions exceed 50 percent (or 30 percent, as applicable) of his adjusted gross income for that year, he may deduct the excess in each of the five succeeding years until it is used up.[21] Thus, a donor, in effect, has six years in which to absorb the tax benefit of a substantial gift to charity.

It is possible that the six-year period will not be enough to take the full tax advantage of a major gift, or it may be that the donor may anticipate a substantial raise in the value of his gift in the years to come. In such cases, a fractional gift might be considered.[22] In a fractional gift situation, the donor gives the museum ownership in a portion of the property at issue, with (one hopes) the understanding that the remaining portion(s) will be given at a later date. Suppose, for instance, that Mrs. X has a very valuable collection of dolls, and she wishes to give the collection to the local historical society. In her tax bracket, however, six years will be insufficient time for her to use up the allowable charitable deduction. Mrs. X could give the historical society immediately an undivided one-half interest in the collection with the understanding that six years later she will convey the remaining one-half interest. The entire collection could be turned over to the historical society with Mrs. X's one-half undivided interest held as a loan. Properly done, this arrangement would give Mrs. X twelve years to absorb the tax benefits of her gift.

Fractional gifts should be prepared with expert assistance so that Internal Revenue Service criteria are met and eventualities are provided for in writing. What if the donor dies before the gift is completed? Is there a provision in the will bequeathing the remaining portion(s) to the charity? What if the object(s) are damaged or destroyed before the completion of the gift? Who bears the loss? Who insures? Is the donor's promise to convey the remainder interest considered binding? If so, will this affect anticipated tax consequences? Before a fractional gift situation is entered into, there should be a carefully drafted, written agreement between donor and museum which sets forth the full understanding of the parties.

E. The Bargain Sale

A bargain sale (or donative sale) arrangement may be proposed by the owner of an object which is desired by a museum. Here the owner offers to sell the object to the museum for less than its fair market value, because, in this way, the owner receives some remuneration plus a charitable contribution for the

---

21. However, each year's maximum must be utilized before there can be a carryover to the following year.

22. Tax considerations need not be the sole reason for using the fractional gift. Consider this example. Mr. Y has a collection of gems that he would like to give to the local natural history museum. However, he is in the process of writing a treatise on gems and for several years he will need periodic access to the collection. Through a fractional gift arrangement, the collection could be placed in the museum with Mr. Y having the right to withdraw all or a portion for stated periods of time (reflecting the portion of ownership still retained) pending completion of the gift.

portion "given" to the museum.[23] Such an arrangement is legitimate if, in fact, it is a true "bargain sale." While the burden of proving fair market value to the Internal Revenue Service rests on the donor, this is one instance in which it may be proper for the museum to comment on the value of a donated object— by acknowledging in writing the fact that it perceives it is purchasing the object at less than fair market value. Such an acknowledgment, which should not attempt to state or confirm a fair market value dollar figure, merely rebuts the normal presumption that the sale is an arms-length transaction.

In handling a bargain sale, the following points may prove helpful: (1) the museum should have written evidence that the owner has a donative intent in setting the sale price (that is, evidence the donor is intentionally setting a low price); (2) there should be an informed judgment made by the museum that the purchase price is significantly less than apparent fair market value; (3) the museum should not approve or appear to approve any dollar figure as constituting fair market value; and (4) clearly the museum should not put itself in a position where it endorses or appears to endorse an inflated value in order to give the owner undeserved tax advantages. The prudent museum proceeds very cautiously if there appears to be inflated value, and at a certain point, a rather frank discussion with the owner may be in order before negotiations continue.

If the museum enters into the bargain sale, a deed of gift need not be used because title has passed by virtue of the contract of sale. It is appropriate, however, to note on the contract of sale and on accession records that the transaction is a bargain sale or donative sale. After payment has been made and the object received, usually a letter is sent to the seller acknowledging the museum's perception that the transaction was a bargain sale and expressing gratitude for the resulting "gift" to the museum.

F. The Museum's Position Regarding Donor Deductions

Considerable discussion is generated when the topic is the proper role of the museum with regard to tax consequences of donors' gifts. Some favor a complete "hands off, it's not our problem" approach, while others argue that museums should take an active role in probing apparent abuses. If there is a "right" answer for a museum it probably lies somewhere in between. Good intentions must be reconciled with what is possible and even with a prudent general policy in place, staff must stay informed and be vigilant for the unusual circumstances which require special treatment. Consider the following examples.

Hypothetical Example 1. A respected friend of the museum donates a painting represented as a Corot and appraised at $25,000. The painting is accepted but not put on display. Some years later, several researchers establish that the painting is not authentic. Upon investigation, it is learned that the director of

---

23. In a bargain sale, the donor's basis must be allocated between the sale and contribution elements of the transaction. See I.R.S. Regulations 26 C.F.R. § 1.1011-2 for an explanation of existing law. See also A. Anderson and Co., *Tax Economics of Charitable Giving*, Chapter V (1982) and I.R.S. Publication No. 526, "Charitable Contributions."

the museum had serious doubts about the authenticity of the work when the gift was made, but felt that the museum should not intervene in a matter essentially between the donor and the Internal Revenue Service. The painting was stored out of public view for over three years, the statutory period during which the Internal Revenue Service could have questioned the deduction taken (that is, the claimed value of the charitable donation).

Hypothetical Example 2. A museum has on loan an unusual ethnographic object which it would like to have for its collections. The owner explains that he cannot afford to give the work, but asks the museum to help him search for a prospective donor who will buy the object and then, after an appropriate period, give the piece to the museum. A prospective donor is located and the museum becomes privy to the fact that the donor will pay a reasonable sum for the object but plans to overvalue it grossly for gift purposes. Appraisals that support the exaggerated valuation are shown to the museum. Nothing is said and the museum waits patiently for the deed of gift, anticipating its arrival as soon as sufficient time has passed so that the donation will qualify as long-term capital gain property.

Hypothetical Example 3. Curator X finds himself flooded with offers of donations of a particular type of specimen which he knows is being promoted and sold as a tax shelter. The museum's collections are already well-represented in this area, but nothing is refused. It is apparent that the donors have acquired the specimens merely to donate them later for tax benefits far in excess of their investments. Valuations substantially over the purchase price are being claimed. Curator X plans in due time to sell or exchange most of this material, but the realities are never openly discussed by the donors or the museum.

In each of the above examples, it is quite possible that a museum might come forward with a legitimate explanation for its conduct, based on particular circumstances, but such explanations tend to wear thin when a pattern develops. To the careful observer, museum personnel who "look the other way" appear (at a minimum) unethical; a consistent pattern of such behavior in recurring situations might amount to participation as a silent co-conspirator in a tax evasion scheme. In any event, even the mere appearance of participation in systematic abuse can tarnish the museum's reputation in the eyes of the general public.[24]

There are indications that certain practices now considered by some to raise serious ethical questions may, in fact, involve legal questions as well. For example, in the case of *United States v. Wolfson*,[25] the defendant was in charge of a charitable donation program at certain Florida schools. He solicited donations of property and gave appraisals. The defendant was indicted for aiding

---

24. See, for example, the *Washington Post*, page 1 for March 27, 28, and 29, 1983 for articles describing certain accession and deaccession activity in the gems and minerals department of the Smithsonian Institution's Museum of Natural History. If there is reasonable evidence of consistent donor abuse of tax statutes regarding donations to a museum, the I.R.S. could invoke 26 U.S.C. § 7609(f) and (h) in order to obtain access to the museum's records. See *United States v. Brigham Young University*, 679 F.2d 1345 (10th Cir. 1982).

25. 78-1 U.S.T.C. ¶ 9456, 573 F.2d 216 (5th Cir. 1978). See, also, *Blake v. Commissioner*, T. C. Memo 1981-979.

in the preparation of fraudulent tax returns because the Internal Revenue Service alleged that he had a pattern of giving overstated appraisals. He was found guilty and appealed. One of the issues on appeal was whether the defendant could be found guilty under 26 U.S.C. § 7206(2) for the preparation of fraudulent tax returns:[26]

> [The defendant] contends that his conduct could not fall under the statute, because he did not prepare returns *per se*. At best, he provided only an appraisal that the taxpayer or his accountant used to prepare a return.
>
> We hold, however, that it is possible for . . . [the defendant] to be prosecuted under this statute. . . . [The defendant] does not have to sign or prepare the return to be amenable to prosecution. If it is proved . . . that he knowingly gave a false appraisal with the expectation it would be used by the donor in taking a charitable deduction on a tax return, it would constitute a crime.[27]

It should be noted that as of 1982 a new section was added to the Internal Revenue Code, 26 U.S.C. § 6701. This section makes it a *civil* offense to engage in the preparation of fraudulent tax returns. (As a rule, it is easier to prove a civil violation than a criminal violation.) Pertinent portions of 6701 describing the prohibited conduct read as follows:

> (a)—Any person—
>
> (1) who aids or assists in, procures, or advises with respect to, the preparation or presentation of any portion of a return, affidavit, claim, or other document in connection with any matter arising under the internal revenue laws,
>
> (2) who knows that such portion will be used in connection with any material matter arising under the internal revenue laws, and
>
> (3) who knows that such portion (if so used) will result in an understatement of the liability for tax of another person,
>
> shall pay a penalty with respect to each such document in the amount determined under subsection (b).
>
> . . . .
>
> (c). . .
>
> (1) In general.—For purposes of subsection (a), the term "procures" includes—
>
> (A) ordering (or otherwise causing) a subordinate to do an act, and

---

26. 26 U.S.C. § 7206(2) reads:

> Any person who willfully aids or assists in, or procures, counsels, or advises the preparation or presentation under, or in connection with any matter arising under, the internal revenue laws, of a return, affidavit, claim, or other document, which is fraudulent or is false as to any material matter, whether or not such falsity or fraud is with the knowledge or consent of the person authorized or required to present such return, affidavit, claim or document . . . shall be guilty of a felony and upon conviction thereof, shall be fined not more than $100,000 . . . ($500,000 in the case of a corporation), or imprisoned no more than 3 years, or both together with the costs of prosecution.

(The monetary penalty was increased in 1982.)

27. 78-1 U.S.T.C. § 9456, 573 F.2d 216, 225 (5th Cir. 1978) (the case was returned to the trial level on other grounds).

(B) knowing of, and not attempting to prevent, participation by a subordinate in an act.

(2) Subordinate.—for purposes of paragraph (1), the term "subordinate" means any other person (whether or not a director, officer, employee, or agent of the taxpayer involved) over whose activities the person has direction, supervision, or control.

In 1982, another incident made the news which sounded a strong cautionary note even closer to home.[28] On the West Coast, the Internal Revenue Service had occasion to investigate the activities of an art dealer who allegedly was arranging improper tax shelters for clients involving donations to local museums. In affidavits filed in federal court, the Internal Revenue Service described the following sequence of events.[29] Internal Revenue Agents, posing as prospective clients, approached the art dealer and inquired about tax shelters. The dealer explained that for a fee he could arrange a donation of art to certain museums and obtain back-dated gift receipts and inflated appraisals. With such documentation, a client in the higher brackets could take an immediate, healthy tax deduction. The agents, using their assumed identities, then approached the two named museums directly and asked if it were possible to have a deed of gift predated and if the museums would appraise gifts. In both instances, they were told it was against museum policy to predate and to appraise. The agents then returned to the dealer with money for an art purchase. Within a short time, they were provided with signed evidence from the two museums that donations had been received in the prior year. Names of museum officials were given in the affidavits and 26 U.S.C. § 7206(2) was cited as the relevant statute.[30]

---

28. "Museum Officials Falsified Records on Gifts, I.R.S. Says," *Los Angeles Times*, June 2, 1982, page 1.

29. See Affidavit for Search Warrant concerning investigation of M_____ R_____ filed by Special Agent Harper in Federal Court, District of Los Angeles; May 1982.

30. Note also statutes such as 26 U.S.C. § 6700 that imposes penalties on individuals who promote abusive tax shelters. See *United States v. Buttorff*, 563 F. Supp. 450 (N.D. Tex. 1983).

Chapter XIII

Appraisals and Authentications

A. Appraisals
    1. The Museum's Position
    2. When Appraisals Are Required
    3. I.R.S. Appraisal Procedures
    4. I.R.S. Review of Valuations
    5. Recommending Appraisers
B. Authentications
    1. Misrepresentation
    2. Disparagement
    3. Defamation

A. Appraisals

1. The Museum's Position

Should a museum provide monetary appraisals for donors or prospective donors? The question prompts much discussion. On the one extreme are those who view such museum activity as an essential service in the competition for important donations. On the other extreme, it is looked upon as a practice bordering on illegality.[1] There are all shades of opinion in between.[2]

One basic fact that frequently is overlooked by donors and museum staff alike is that in any gift situation, the museum is an interested party. The museum is the donee or prospective donee. Invariably an appraisal is being sought for tax purposes and the Internal Revenue Service wants impartial appraisals. One from a donee is immediately suspect. When this is explained to donors, many gratefully look elsewhere for their appraisals. This self-interest problem of the museum/donee is now recognized in the Tax Reform Act of 1984.[3] Under that legislation as of 1985, a museum/donee is disqualified from

---

1. While this practice was quite common years ago, it has been more closely scrutinized with the increasing importance to donors of the tax consequences of gifts.

2. See "On Being a Print Collection: Eight Views," 11 *The Print Collector's Newsletter* 73 (July-Aug. 1980). Speiller, "The Favored Tax Treatment of Purchases of Art," 80 *Colum. L. Rev.* 214 (1980); Anthoine, "Deductions for Charitable Contributions of Appreciated Property - The Art World," 35 *Tax L. Rev.* 239 (1979-80). In "A Code of Ethics for Curators," *Museum News* 36 (Feb. 1983), there is this statement:

    Curators may prepare appraisals only for internal use at their institutions (e.g., insurance, valuations for loans) and, with the approval of the curator's museum, for other nonprofit institutions.

3. See discussion of Tax Reform Act of 1984 which follows.

appraising for federal income tax purposes property over a certain value which is contributed to it.

Some museums have a practice of paying for third-party appraisals of donated objects. It is argued that this is a courtesy deserved by a donor and that the procedure affords the donor a more creditable opinion. There is much to be said for this position, but also there are possible drawbacks. If all donors are provided appraisals, it can prove to be costly and beyond a museum's budget. If appraisals are provided only to certain donors, the selection criteria can be difficult to draft. If a particular appraiser routinely is used, his impartiality may be open to question or his competitors may complain.[4] One additional consideration should not be forgotten. For some donors an appraisal is a matter of vital interest. The closer the museum is to the appraisal process, the more likelihood there is that the museum could be drawn into controversy if appraisal results are disappointing.[5]

Many museums establish a general policy that monetary appraisals will not be provided. This, perhaps, is the easiest solution for the museum, but it, too, is not without drawbacks. Some prospective donors may be offended and go elsewhere, and true hardship cases can arise. At times, there are situations where museum staff may feel uncomfortable about an apparent intention on the part of a donor to inflate grossly the value of his gift for tax purposes.[6] In such cases, a complete hands-off policy by the museum regarding appraisals could be viewed as contributing to the suspected manipulation. In the public interest, the museum may wish to take a more active role. Sometimes just informing a prospective donor that a known appraisal might not withstand an Internal Revenue Service audit has a salutary effect, and there is always the alternative that the gift be declined. A polite refusal can convey a message as effectively as a dogmatic judgment.[7]

---

4. For instance, under Section 155 of the Tax Reform Act of 1984, Pub. L. 98-369, 98 Stat. 494, 691, if a museum/donee is disqualified from acting as an appraiser with regard to a particular donation, an "employee" of that museum is also disqualified. If there is a longstanding relationship between the museum/donee and a particular outside appraiser that would cause a reasonable person to question the independence of the appraiser, the appraiser could be considered an "employee" and hence disqualified. I.R.S. regulations addressing this issue are to be promulgated by 1985.

5. New provisions in the Internal Revenue Code (26 U.S.C. § 6659) impose additional penalties on taxpayers who substantially overvalue property reported as charitable contributions. The additional tax is imposed only when the value overstatement exceeds 150 percent of the amount determined to be the correct value and when the resulting tax underpayment exceeds $1,000. While these penalties should encourage more caution on the part of donors, they also raise the stakes when serious disputes develop between donors and the I.R.S. In addition, such penalties cannot be waived by the I.R.S. if, among other things, the donor cannot demonstrate that the claimed value was based on an appraisal by a "qualified" appraiser. Thus, a too close relationship between the donor and museum on the appraisal issue could possibly affect the waiver process also. (See section 155 of the Tax Reform Act of 1984, Pub. L. 98-369, 98 Stat. 494, 691.)

6. The popularity of some "tax shelter donations" (possibly abusive) has aggravated this problem.

7. See Chapter VII, "Tax Considerations Relevant to Gifts," for a discussion of the problems that can arise. Note also that under Section 155 of the Tax Reform Act of 1984, the museum/donee must receive copies of and "acknowledge" certain appraisal summaries donors are required to file with the I.R.S. The legislative history of this provision contains the following statement: "The donee's acknowledgment signature on the summary appraisal solely represents acknowledgment

It is difficult to defend the position that there is only one acceptable way for all museums to handle the appraisal question. There is room for variation, but these comments are worth mentioning:

(1) It is prudent to establish in advance a general rule for the guidance of staff that is in accord with current Internal Revenue Service regulations regarding appraisals. A strictly ad hoc approach makes the museum more vulnerable and can result in unfairness to donors, embarrassment to staff and possible liability for the museum.

(2) The general rule should be such that it affords the museum a reasonably practical way to avoid abuses, and museum staff should understand the underlying reasons for the rule so that in appropriate situations additional guidance will be sought.

(3) There should be an avenue of appeal to designated museum officials for exceptions to the general rule. Before an exception is granted, its precedential effect should be weighed carefully.

Even if a museum's policy does not permit the giving of monetary appraisals, knowledgeable staff members still can offer certain practical advice to members of the public. Internal Revenue Service Publication No. 56l, entitled "Determining the Value of Donated Property," explains when appraisals are necessary to support a claimed charitable contribution tax deduction, lists what should be included in an appraisal, and describes how the Internal Revenue Service reviews appraisals.[8] Information also is given on methods of valuing various types of property. Staff members familiar with the publication, can, in appropriate cases, call it to the attention of donors or prospective donors. A current copy of Publication No. 561, which can be obtained from any Internal Revenue Service office, is a handy reference to have on file.[9]

2. When Appraisals Are Required

Appraisals are not necessary to support every claimed charitable contribution deduction:

- If the property donated is worth $200 or less, little if any documentation is needed.
- If the property exceeds $200 in value, but does not exceed $5,000 in value (and similar items given to all charitable donees in the year do not have

---

of receipt of the items described in the summary appraisal and in no way is to be construed as indicating the donee's agreement with or acceptance of the amount claimed for the donated property on the appraisal summary." (Conference Report on H.R. 4170, June 23, 1984, at 998.) The observations made in the text, however, about the appropriateness of action by the museum in certain instances may well be considered when a "summary appraisal" is received before a gift is consummated.

8. With the passage of the Tax Reform Act of 1984, the Internal Revenue Service by 1985 must promulgate extensive new regulations implementing mandatory appraisal requirements for certain charitable contributions valued at $5,000 or more. It is assumed that I.R.S. Publication No. 561 will be revised to incorporate these new regulations.

9. See also Rev. Proc. 66-49 (Part 1, § 170; 26 C.F.R. 1.170-1), which gives detailed guidelines for making appraisals of donated property for Federal income tax purposes. I.R.S. Publication No. 526 treats the general subject of "Charitable Contributions" and is a useful companion to Publication No. 561.

an aggregate value in excess of $5,000), Internal Revenue Service regulations require that certain information be filed with the tax return, such as the fair market value of the contributed property and the method used to determine value. This information can be in the form of a professional appraisal signed by the appraiser, but it is not always the only alternative.[10] There may be instances where fair market value can be established with some certainty by supplying evidence to the Internal Revenue Service of contemporary sales at public auction of similar property. If the museum is aware of published records of such sales, there is no reason why these cannot be called to the attention of a donor who requests assistance. As a rule, it is wise to supply such references with the caution that additional research by the taxpayer may be in order to confirm the relevance of the published sales to the gift at issue and/or to verify that the published sales reflect market conditions similar to those that would govern the valuation at issue.

- Under the Tax Reform Act of 1984, if the amount claimed as a charitable deduction by a taxpayer for a year exceeds $5,000 for any single item or exceeds $5,000 for the aggregate of items of a similar nature given by the taxpayer to all charities, then the taxpayer must fulfill certain statutorily prescribed appraisal requirements. If these statutory requirements are not followed, the charitable deduction will be disallowed. The requirements are explained more fully hereafter, and they apply to charitable contributions made after December 31, 1984. Current Internal Revenue Service regulations should be consulted especially with regard to effective dates.

3. I.R.S. Appraisal Procedures

It is necessary to distinguish between appraisal procedures in effect before January 1, 1985, and those in effect on and after that date. Prior to the Tax Reform Act of 1984,[11] there was no specific statutory requirement that donors obtain appraisals to verify the fair market value of donated property. Internal Revenue Service regulations, however, did set forth guidelines on the preparation of appraisals because invariably donors of substantial items chose to verify value by means of professional appraisals. With the passage of the Tax Reform Act of 1984, prescribed appraisal procedures are mandatory with regard to certain donations in order to obtain tax benefits, and by January 1, 1985, the Internal Revenue Service must promulgate regulations to implement these statutory requirements. It is necessary, therefore, to describe first the guidelines in place as of 1984 (subdivision (a)) and then to explain what new procedures are required as of 1985 (subdivision (b)):

(a) As of 1984, under Internal Revenue Service guidelines, a complete professional appraisal contained at least the following information:

---

10. I.R.S. Regulation 26 C.F.R. § 1.170A-1(a)(2)(ii).

11. The Tax Reform Act of 1984 is Division A of the Deficit Reduction Act of 1984, Pub. L. 98-369, 98 Stat. 494 (approved July 18, 1984).

(1) A summary of the appraiser's qualifications to appraise property of the type and quality at issue;

(2) The reason for having the appraisal done (such as for income, estate or gift tax purposes);

(3) A full description of the item to be valued, including, where applicable, the name of the creator, approximate date of creation, medium and subject matter;

(4) A statement of the value placed on the object and the appraisers definition of value;[12]

(5) The basis on which the appraisal was made, including restrictions, understandings, or agreements or obligations limiting the gift or disposition of the property;

(6) The effective date of the valuation (such as, the date the gift was accepted by the museum); and

(7) The date of the appraisal.[13]

To support his conclusion, the appraiser included relevant background information, such as:

(1) A history of how the object was acquired and its cost (or other basis);

(2) A history of the ownership of the item and public exhibitions;

(3) A good-size photograph of the item;

(4) Recent comparable sales and/or, if the artist is still living, the artist's asking price for similar works; and

(5) The state of the market at the time of valuation, especially with regard to objects like the one at issue.

(b) As of January 1, 1985, these procedures must be followed with regard to contributions of certain property to museums for which a charitable deduction is sought. In order to trigger the requirements the contribution must be valued in excess of $5,000, or contributions by the taxpayer of similar objects in the taxable year to all charities must total a value in excess of $5,000.

(1) The taxpayer must obtain a "qualified appraisal" of the property contributed;

(2) An appraisal summary must be attached to the return on which such deduction is first claimed;

(3) The appraisal summary must be in such form as the Internal Revenue Service prescribes and it must be signed by the appraiser and carry the tax identification number of the appraiser;

(4) The appraisal summary must be acknowledged by the donee/museum in such manner as the Internal Revenue Service prescribes;[14] and

---

12. The issue usually is the fair market value of the property. "The 'fair market value' is the price at which the property would change hands between a willing buyer and a willing seller, where neither is under any compulsion to buy or sell and both are cognizant of the relevant facts," *Posner v. Commissioner*, 35 T.C.M. 943 (1976). See also I.R.S. Publication No. 526, "Charitable Contributions" and I.R.S. Revenue Rulings 80-69, 1979-2 C.B. 107, and 79-419, 1980-1 C.B. 55.

13. See I.R.S. Publication No. 561 for more details. For a less technical discussion, see Stapleton and Sparkman, "How Do You Know What You've Got?" *Connoisseur* 92 (Nov. 1982).

14. See footnote 7.

(5) The appraiser must be a "qualified appraiser."

A "qualified appraisal" is defined to mean:

[A]n appraisal prepared by a qualified appraiser which includes—

(A) a description of the property appraised
(B) the fair market value of such property on the date of contribution and the specific basis for the valuation
(C) a statement that such appraisal was prepared for income tax purposes
(D) the qualifications of the qualified appraiser
(E) the signature and TIN (tax identification number) of such appraiser, and
(F) such additional information as the . . . [Internal Revenue Service] prescribes . . . [by] regulations.[15]

The term "qualified appraiser" is defined to mean:

[A]n appraiser qualified to make appraisals of the type of property donated, who is not—

 (i) the taxpayer
 (ii) a party to the transaction in which the taxpayer acquired the property
(iii) the donee
(iv) any person employed by any of the foregoing persons or related to any of the foregoing persons . . . or
 (v) to the extent provided in . . . [Internal Revenue Service] regulations, any person whose relationship to the taxpayer would cause a reasonable person to question the independence of such appraiser.

The Act further states:

For . . . [these purposes] an appraisal shall not be treated as a qualified appraisal if all or part of the fee paid for such appraisal is based on a percentage of the appraised value of the property. The preceding sentence shall not apply to fees based on a sliding scale that are paid to a generally recognized association regulating appraisers.[16]

4. I.R.S. Review of Valuations

For some years now to assist in reviewing valuation placed on art work,[17] the Internal Revenue Service has maintained an Art Advisory Panel and an Art Print Panel.[18] The requirements set forth in the Tax Reform Act of 1984 should not affect the functions of these panels. Each panel is composed of experts, and they recommend acceptance or adjustment of values claimed for major art works. A work with a claimed market value of $20,000 or more usually is referred to one of the panels. A work of lesser value may be referred if circum-

---

15. Section 155 of the Tax Reform Act of 1984, Pub. L. 98-369, 98 Stat. 494, 691. Undoubtedly when promulgating regulations describing more fully what constitutes a "qualified appraisal" for these purposes, the Internal Revenue Service will incorporate much of what is contained in its existing guidelines on appraisals.

16. Section 155 of the Tax Reform Act of 1984, Pub. L. 98-369 contains most of the above-described provisions.

17. The I.R.S. defines a work of art as a painting, drawing, print, sculpture or antique furnishing.

18. See I.R.S. News Release of February 1, 1948, which announced the establishment of the Art Advisory Panel. See also Mullaney, "I.R.S. Art Advisory Panel: A Regulatory Paper Tiger?" 7 *The New Art Examiner* 3 (May 1980).

stances warrant special review. The Internal Revenue Service, in addition, has staff appraisers or it may seek advice from outside experts.[19]

5. Recommending Appraisers

Many times museums may be asked to recommend appraisers.[20] Rather than recommend just one, it is wiser to suggest several sources, allowing the individual to make the final selection.[21] If only one is suggested and the appraiser proves to be a disappointment, the irate donor may focus his anger on the museum.[22] Also, it is a more cautious procedure not to have a prepared list of appraisers for distribution to requestors. The fact that there is a prescribed list may be construed as a museum endorsement, despite a disclaimer. In addition, the existence of such a list may cause appraisers not on the list to demand inclusion. This can raise awkward situations if the appraiser is not known to the museum or is not held in high regard.

B. Authentications

Invariably, the initial issue raised is whether it is an appropriate museum activity to provide *gratis* to the public opinions on the authenticity of objects or works of art.[23] As is so often the case, this essentially is a policy question rather than a legal one, and it must be weighed in light of a museum's particular circum-

---

19. Some cases dealing with contested valuations of charitable contributions are: *Cukos v. Commissioner*, 27 T.C.M. 89 (1968); *Posner v. Commissioner*, 35 T.C.M. 943 (1976); *Farber v. Commissioner*, 33 T.C.M. 673 (1974) (authenticity as well as fair market value at issue). See also I.R.S. Rev. Rul. 80-69, 1980-1 C.B. 55, which concerns the fair market value of gem specimens donated to museums or universities.

20. The appraisal fee paid by the donor is not treated as part of the charitable contribution, but the donor may deduct it as a "miscellaneous expense" incurred in preparing the tax return when itemizing deductions on the standard 1040 tax form.

21. For example, the Art Dealers Association of America, Inc., has a set of forms available upon request to those interested in obtaining appraisals. The set includes a form "Letter Agreement" between the donor and the Association, a list of "Conditions of Appraisal" and a list of background information on the work to be appraised that must be supplied to the Association. For more information contact: Art Dealers Association of America, Inc., 575 Madison Avenue, N.Y., N.Y. 10022. There are several large appraisers' associations in the United States that may be of assistance. For instance: The Appraisers Association of America, 60 East 42nd Street, N.Y., N.Y. 10165; American Society of Appraisers, Dulles International Airport, P.O. Box 17265, Washington, D.C. 20041; International Society of Appraisers, P.O. Box 726, Hoffman Estates, Ill. 60195. For an interesting two-part article on appraising see Rosenbaum, "Appraising the Appraisers," *Artnews* 92 (Nov. 1983) and 99 (Dec. 1983).

22. Note the previous comments regarding possible disqualification of an appraiser because of close ties with a donee. Also, under Section 156 of the Tax Reform Act of 1984, Pub. L. 98-369, 98 Stat. 494, 695, appraisers who have violated certain I.R.S. statutes may be barred from participating in documentation of federal tax returns.

23. This discussion does not cover the question of museum personnel who appraise or authenticate for a fee in addition to their museum employment. Such "outside employment" raises additional ethical and legal issues and is beyond the scope of this text. For information on this question see: American Association of Museums, *Museum Ethics: A Report to the American Association of Museums by its Committee on Ethics* (1978), "A Code of Ethics for Art Historians and Guidelines for the Professional Practice of Art History" (College Art Association 1973, 1974), "A Code of Ethics for Art Museum Directors," published as an appendix to Association of Art Museum Directors, *Professional Practices in Art Museums* (1981), and "A Code of Ethics for Curators" published in *Museum News* 36 (Feb. 1983).

stances. Some museums view it as a public service and/or find that such activity ultimately benefits their ability to advance scholarship because through the authentication process a wide variety of interesting objects and information is brought to the attention of curatorial staff.[24] For others, any such benefits are outweighed by undue burdens on staff time and/or by real or apparent misuse of the service by individuals or businesses. To assure that a prudent policy is set, there must be a careful balancing of pros and cons in light of the museum's obligations to acquire and manage its collections in the best interests of the public and to maintain the confidence of the public. *Museum Ethics*[25] states:

> Performing appraisals or authentications can be useful to a museum and the public it serves; however, there should be institutional policy covering the circumstances where appraisals are desirable or permissible as an official museum-related function.

If a decision is made that authentications will be given as a matter of policy, a few precautions should protect the museum and its staff from undue liability. The museum wants to avoid possible claims based on any theory of misrepresentation, disparagement or defamation.

1. Misrepresentation

In general, a misrepresentation is "any manifestation by words or conduct by one person to another that under the circumstances, amounts to an assertion not in accordance with the facts."[26] Usually to create liability, a misrepresentation must be intentional,[27] but there are instances when negligent misstatements can invite lawsuits. Such instances usually occur when there is direct, foreseeable harm to an individual because of a misstatement[28] and the injured party is considered justified in relying on the information given.[29] If this test

---

24. The College Art Association (C.A.A.), a group composed mainly of art historians, takes the position that authenticating works of art is a responsibility for a scholar (See C.A.A.'s "Code of Ethics for Art Historians and Guidelines for the Professional Practice of Art History" (1973, 1974).) It should be noted that as a rule art historians are permitted more freedom by their university/college to engage in outside consulting work than that accorded museum staff. For an article dealing with museum practices, see Stapleton and Sparkman, "How Do You Know What You've Got?" *Connoisseur* 92 (Nov. 1982).

25. American Association of Museums, *Museum Ethics: A Report to the American Association of Museums by its Committee on Ethics* 13 (1978).

26. *Black's Law Dictionary* (4th ed. 1951).

27. For this reason, misrepresentation frequently is associated with the tort of deceit.

28. Courts are often reluctant to find a duty of care if the resulting liability might be "an indeterminate amount for an indeterminate time to an indeterminate class." *Ultramares Corp. v. Touche, Niven and Co.*, 255 N.Y. 170, 179; 174 N.E. 441, 444 (1931). See also Prosser, "Misrepresentation and Third Persons," 19 *Vand. L. Rev.* 231 (1966). "[T]he mere reasonable anticipation that the statement will be communicated to others whose identity is unknown to the defendant, or even knowledge that the recipient intends to make some commercial use of it in dealing with unspecified third parties, is not sufficient to create a duty of care toward them." Prosser, *Law of Torts* 708 (4th ed. 1971). But see *Citizens State Bank v. Timm, Schmidt, and Co.*, 335 N.W.2d 361 (Wisc. 1983); *Rosenblum, Inc. v. Adler*, 461 A.2d 138 (N.J. 1983); *Page v. Frazier*, 383 Mass. 55, 445 N.E.2d 148 (1983).

29. The issue of reliance sometimes takes the form of finding a duty between the plaintiff and defendant which duty requires the defendant to exercise reasonable care.

is applied to museum situations involving authentications, several other considerations frequently bear on the "reasonable reliance" issue: the authentications are given *gratis* and usually can be construed as opinions.

It is commonly held that to find liability for a negligent misrepresentation, the giver of the information must have a direct or indirect pecuniary interest.[30] A direct pecuniary interest would be an authentication done for a fee, not the type of situation under discussion in this chapter. An example of an indirect interest is illustrated by the following. A physician on the way to his office meets a neighbor who is not a patient and in the course of a conversation offers some curbstone medical advice. Upon reaching his office, the physician receives a call from another neighbor who is a patient and he offers free medical advice. In the first instance, a truly *gratis* situation, all that is required is an honest answer; in the latter, where there is indirect pecuniary benefit, there usually is found to be a duty of care and hence potential liability for negligence. But even the ramifications of a truly *gratis* situation can change if there is a perceived public duty to supply the information in question. In such cases, which frequently involve health and safety matters, there is a tendency to impose a duty of care toward those members of the public designed to be served even though there was no direct or indirect pecuniary relationship with the plaintiff.[31] The facts in each such case led the court to find that the defendant by his conduct had assumed a duty of care toward the plaintiff.[32] While such exceptions to the *gratis* rule generally should not apply to museum authentication situations, it should be borne in mind that there is a strong temptation to find liability even when services are offered free if there is evidence of blatant carelessness and disregard for consequences.

Authentications frequently amount to expressions of opinion and, like the *gratis* situation, this also can effect the reasonableness of a plaintiff's reliance on the representation. But whether a statement is a fact or an opinion can generate much discussion. From one viewpoint, any opinion is a factual statement of an individual's conclusions, that is, it is a statement of what is in one's mind. If there is evidence that an opinion is not given in good faith, for some this amounts to a misstatement of fact.[33] If an opinion is given in the form of a statement of fact by someone who purports to be an expert, does this justify reliance by the nonexpert? Possibly it could on the theory that in expressing the opinion the expert infers the existence of facts known to him to be true which justify his opinion. This situation could be further colored if the expert

---

30. *Restatement (Second) of Torts* § 552 (1981). But intentional misrepresentation is actionable even when made gratuitously. Also, if one makes statements knowing that he does not know what he says is true, this can be intentional misrepresentation. See Prosser, "Misrepresentation and Third Persons," 19 *Vand. L. Rev.* 231, 234 (1966).

31. *Restatement (Second) of Torts*, Comment on Subsection 3 of § 552.

32. Prosser, "Misrepresentations and Third Persons," 19 *Vand. L. Rev.* 231, 236-7 (1966). See, for instance *DeLong v. County of Erie*, 455 N.Y.S.2d 887 (1982).

33. "Fraud includes the pretense of knowledge when knowledge there is none." *Ultramares Corp. v. Touche, Niven and Co.* 255 N.Y. 170, 174 N.E. 441, 444 (1931).

knows that the recipient intends to rely on the opinion.[34] There are many extenuating circumstances that can shape a judgment concerning the reasonableness for relying on an opinion. As one expert notes:

> It is stated very often as a fundamental rule in connection with all of the various remedies for misrepresentation, that they will not lie for misstatements of opinion, as distinguished from those of fact. The usual explanation is that an opinion is merely an assertion of one man's belief as to a fact, of which another should not be heard to complain, since opinions are a matter of which many men will be of many minds, and which is often governed by whim and caprice. Judgment and opinion, in such case, implies no knowledge. . . .

But this explanation is scarcely adequate.[35] This same reluctance to accept a simple method of classification is reflected in the case law. In *Reeves v. Corning*,[36] for example, the court stated:

> There is no certain rule of law by the application of which it can be determined when false representations constitute matters of opinion, or matters of fact. Each case must, in large measure, be adjudged upon its own circumstances. In reaching its conclusion, the court will take into consideration the intelligence and situation of the parties, the general information and experience of the people as to the nature and use of the property, the habits and methods of those dealing in or with it, and then determine, upon all the circumstances of the case, whether the representations ought to have been understood as affirmations of fact, or as matters of opinion or judgment.[37]

Consider the following situation which illustrates some of the points mentioned: Museum M routinely allows staff members to give opinions regarding authenticity as part of their employment. No cautions are prescribed. Curator X receives a letter from Miss Y with a photograph of an early American portrait. Miss Y explains that the picture has been in her family for years and it always has been attributed to the well-known artist Z. Circumstances now force her to sell many of her possessions, and she needs an expert's opinion of the portrait. Curator X writes back, "Clearly, this is not the work of artist Z. It has little monetary value." Shortly thereafter, Miss Y sells the work for a pittance. Within months, it is resold for $20,000 as a portrait by Z.

---

34. See Prosser, *Law of Torts* 707 (4th ed. 1971). Frequently courts are more inclined to impose liability when such reliance is evident. See also discussion of "pure" and "mixed" opinion in section on defamation, this chapter.

35. Prosser, *Law of Torts* 720-21 (4th ed. 1971).

36. 51 F. 774, 780 (Ind. 1892). See also Keeton, "Fraud: Misrepresentation of Opinion," 21 *Minn. L. Rev.* 643 (May 1937).

37. An analogy can be drawn to breach of warranty cases involving misattributed art. For example, in two classic English cases, *Jendwine v. Slade*, 170 Eng. Rep. 459 Nisi Prius 1797, and *Power v. Barham*, 111 Eng. Sep. 865 K.B. 1836, different results were reached on the issue of seller's liability. In *Jendwine* the seller's attribution was held to be only "opinion" because the artist in question lived centuries before. In *Power* the seller's attribution was found to be a fact or "warranty" probably because the artist in question was more recent. The *Power* court refused to follow *Jendwine* saying each case must be decided on its own circumstances.

A similar situation is presented to Curator A of the Q Historical Society. Curator A's reply reads as follows: "After studying the photograph you sent me, I do not believe that the portrait is by Artist Z. However, this opinion is based on the limited information provided me, and it should not be relied on as definitive."

Curator A took simple precautions which make it highly unlikely that Miss Y would even threaten to sue. Curator X's conduct, on the other hand, is such that the museum could well be drawn into a lawsuit with the volatile issue of "reasonable reliance" as pivotal.

In summary, a museum's exposure to a suit based on misrepresentation should be slight if a little caution is exercised.[38]

2. Disparagement

When derogatory information about an object or a work of art is conveyed to someone other than the owner, there is a possibility of incurring additional legal liabilities. One is an action for disparagement, or, as it is sometimes called, "injurious falsehood."[39] The gist of the alleged wrong is interference with the prospect of sales or some other advantageous use of the property. For example, if in giving an authentication the museum staff person, without the permission of the owner of the article, makes statements to third parties discrediting the quality of the article, the elements for an action for disparagement could exist.[40] In order to prevail in an action for disparagement, the plaintiff has the burden of proving at least the following:

(a) his interest in the object in question;

(b) the nature of the derogatory statements made;

(c) the falsity of the derogatory statements;

(d) the publication of these statements to a third party (or parties) without plaintiff's consent; and,

(e) as a result of the publication, a definite pecuniary loss was incurred.

There is confusion as to whether another element, that of malice, must also be proved. Some experts and cases support the view that the intent of the defendant is not relevant in establishing disparagement as long as the above five elements are present. In other words, if there is a false statement which causes pecuniary loss, there is liability regardless of intent.[41] This view is countered

---

38. See also the discussion on disclaimer forms in the following section on "Disparagement."

39. Defamation also involves communication. See next section.

40. *Restatement (Second) of Torts* § 626 (1965). If the owner of the object requests the authentication, it is inferred that he consents to the information being given to him. Thus, there can be no claim for disparagement when information has been conveyed only to a requesting owner. If the owner requests that the information be conveyed to someone else, this disclosure also would be protected from suit provided the publication did not exceed the scope of the consent. See *Restatement (Second) of Torts* § 646A (1965). In *Fisher v. Washington Post Co.*, 212 A.2d 335, 337 (D.C. App. 1965), an art gallery owner requested a newspaper art critic to review his new exhibition. When the review proved to be most unflattering, the gallery owner sued the newspaper. The court stated, "He should not be heard to complain if the criticism *so invited* is not gentle." (emphasis added).

41. See, however, *Gertz v. Robert Welch, Inc.*, 418 U.S. 323, 94 S. Ct. 2997 (1974) which limited strict liability in defamation cases.

by other experts and cases arguing that proof of injurious intent or malice is required. Also, it has been suggested that the best rule takes the middle ground and holds the defendant liable for disparagement "only when a reasonable man would have foreseen that his statement would disparage and would have ascertained that the statement was false."[42] The issue is still debated[43] and this is understandable. Disparagement cases because of their very nature usually involve a balancing of interests. The individual making the statement invariably claims a sufficiently important reason for the publication (usually referred to as a privilege, see later discussion), and this must be weighed against the interests of the complaining party. In difficult cases, the malice issue can be used by the court as the pivotal point in achieving what is perceived to be the desirable result.

In light of the given criteria, the risk of suit for disparagement is not great for the curator who exercises a little prudence when giving authentications. It is the plaintiff's responsibility to prove the falsity of the statements made, and even if this burden is sustained, the plaintiff also may have to prove some element of ill-will or serious negligence on the part of the curator. In addition, the plaintiff must show that the publication of the statement was a substantial factor in causing him a pecuniary loss.[44] Accordingly, if a curator does not attempt to stray outside his area of expertise, if he uses some care in making his judgments and to whom he expresses them, and if he avoids dogmatic language liability exposure should be very slight.

As added precautions, some museums use a disclaimer form before an authentication is done and/or agree to give only oral opinions. If a disclaimer form is used, frequently it contains one or more of the following points, and it is signed by the owner of the object prior to the authentication:
   (a) a formal request for the opinion by the owner;
   (b) an acknowledgment that the opinion is being given *gratis*;
   (c) a statement that the opinion will not be used in connection with any commercial transaction; or,
   (d) in consideration for receiving the opinion, a promise not to sue the museum for any reason growing out of the authentication and to hold the museum harmless for any damages or expenses it may incur because of any suit brought by anyone else growing out of the authentication.

Two of the often-cited cases involving disparagement of art highlight other facets which frequently color a result. In *Hahn v. Duveen*[45] the flamboyant art dealer, Sir Joseph Duveen, after seeing only a photograph of a picture claimed to be "La Belle Ferroniere" by da Vinci, declared to a newspaper reporter that the picture was a copy. The owner, who was engaged in negotiating the sale of the picture to an art museum, sued Duveen for disparagement. When a long

---

42. Stebbins, "Possible Tort Liability for Opinions Given by Art Experts" in F. Feldman and S. Weil, *Artworks: Law, Policy, Practice* 988 (1974).

43. See *Restatement (Second) of Torts* § 623A (1965) and Prosser, *Law of Torts* 919-922 (4th ed. 1971).

44. *Restatement (Second) of Torts* § 632 (1965).

45. 133 Misc. 871, 234 N.Y.S. 185 (1929).

trial proved inconclusive, Duveen settled the claim for a sizable sum of money. In *Gott v. Pulsifer*[46] there had been much publicity over a statue called "Cardiff Giant" or "Onondaga Statue" which was purported to be a major archaeological find. The defendant newspaper wrote an article stating that the statue was a fake and that it had been purchased by the owner for eight dollars. The owner, who had been in the process of selling the statue for $30,000, sued the newspaper. The newspaper prevailed on the trial level, but on appeal the case was returned for a new trial on the issue of malice. Both cases raised questions of "privilege."

The law recognizes that certain derogatory statements should be privileged[47] (that is, permitted without liability), because the public good to be gained by permitting free expression outweighs the harm that may be done to the individual. A few privileges are classified as absolute because they protect the individual even from inquiry into the truth of his statement or his motivation. Absolute privilege usually is conferred by virtue of one's office or position which, for the public good, requires freedom from threat of suit.[48] Examples would be judges or legislators who usually enjoy absolute immunity for statements made in the course of their official proceedings. Other privileges commonly are referred to as conditional or qualified privileges:

> These are based upon a public policy that recognizes that it is desirable that true information be given whenever it is reasonably necessary for the protection of the actor's own interests, the interests of a third person, or certain interests of the public. In order that this information may be freely given, it is necessary to protect from liability those who, for the purpose of furthering the interests in question, give information which, without their knowledge or reckless disregard as to its falsity, is in fact untrue.[49]

As explained, this second type of privilege is qualified or conditional because it can be lost if it is shown that the defendant knew his statement was false or exhibited gross disregard as to whether it was true or false, if there is sufficient evidence to impute improper motive, or if the extent of publication is deemed excessive.[50] Thus, even though a curator may believe that his motive for communicating his opinion[51] is purely to advance scholarship, some degree of caution is necessary. The appearance that he is "grandstanding," seeking

---

46. 122 Mass. 235 (1877).

47. The term "privileged" is also used with regard to statements consented to by the individual (see footnote 32).

48. If a museum is part of a governmental unit, inquiry should be made to see if employees, as public officials, have any form of absolute immunity from suits based on another theory—that the governmental unit has not waived its immunity regarding certain types of actions. Such immunity is not a "privilege," but it is another form of effective defense.

49. *Restatement (Second) of Torts* § 584, Introductory Note and at 258-261 (1965). See also Prosser, *Law of Torts* 924-926 (4th ed. 1971).

50. As previously discussed, scholars still debate whether malice is a necessary element for a disparagement action. In part, the controversy is due to the interaction of elements of privilege in many disparagement actions. If malice is in fact a necessary element, there should be far fewer cases requiring the defense of a conditional privilege.

51. See later discussion in this chapter on "fair comment" in section on "Defamation" and prior discussion of opinion v. fact in section on "Misrepresentation."

headlines or cocksure, only invites a challenge as to whether any privilege that may exist has been misused. The test frequently employed is whether the privilege has been exercised for the purpose for which it was given, and with reasonable care to ensure that no more harm should be done than is necessary to accomplish the permitted end.

Occasions that may be covered by a conditional privilege include:

- The protection of a lawful interest of the person making the statement, other than an interest in competition for prospective pecuniary benefits.
- The desire of the person making the statement to protect a lawful interest of a third person or to enable that third person to protect the interest. The publication, however, must be within current standards of permissible conduct and hence it is usually important whether the information was volunteered or was given in response to a request.
- The information affects a sufficiently important public interest and certain communications are required to protect the public interest.[52]

The existence of conditional priviledge could be an important consideration if a museum is confronted with a situation where it appears that a previous authentication given by one of its staff may be inaccurate. Withdrawal of an authentication frequently requires communication beyond the individual who requested or received the initial opinion, and hence, there may be fear that remedial action by the museum will provoke a disparagement suit. This fear should be allayed by review of the conditional privilege defense and with thoughtful planning of remedial action so that communication is limited to those most likely affected by the initial opinion.

3. Defamation

Defamation is an invasion of a person's interest in his reputation and to be actionable, it requires a communication to another or others which has a derogatory effect on that reputation:

> A communication is defamatory if it tends so to harm the reputation of another as to lower him in the estimation of the community or to deter third persons from associating or dealing with him.[53]

Defamation can be in the forms of libel (the written word) or slander (the spoken word).[54] Historically, the law has been harsher on libel than on slander with libel actionable without proof of damage, but slander requiring such proof. This distinction gradually is fading with many courts permitting an action for slander without proof of damage if the slander involves a major social disgrace (such as commission of a crime) or describes conduct or a condition which

---

52. These privileges also apply in actions of defamation. In the following section on defamation note, however, the discussion of the *Gertz* case. The case concerns defamation, but its First Amendment argument could be applied to other wrongs involving expressions of opinion. See *Restatement (Second) of Torts* § 634 (1965), and Prosser, *Law of Torts* 792 and § 118 (4th ed. 1971).

53. *Restatement (Second) of Torts* § 559 (1965), *Kraushaar v. LaVin*, 42 N.Y.S. 2d 857 (1943) (questioning professional competence). In some states, publicity that puts someone in a false light in the public eye may also give rise to an action for invasion of privacy.

54. Libel can include pictures, signs, statues, motion pictures, or even conduct that tends to defame. See, for example, *Yorty v. Chandler*, 13 Cal. App. 3d 419, 91 Cal. Rptr. 709 (1971); *Silberman v. Georges*, 456 N.Y.S. 2d 395 (1982).

adversely affects the fitness of an individual to conduct his business or profession.[55]

In the authentication process, the threat of a suit for defamation could arise if, for example, the statements made about the object in question are construed to reflect poorly on the reputation of the owner of the object, an interested dealer or a fellow critic.[56] However, in a defamation case, it is usually necessary to distinguish between fact and opinion, a most difficult task. This is due in good part to a 1974 U. S. Supreme Court decision, *Gertz v. Welch*[57] In *Gertz*, the court said:

> Under the First Amendment, there is no such thing as a false idea. However pernicious an opinion may seem, we depend for its correction not on the conscience of judges and juries, but on the competition of other ideas. But there is no constitutional value in false statements of fact.[58]

This case, which gave constitutional protection to expressions of opinion, caused the *Restatement of Torts* to revise substantially its view regarding liability for defamatory communications which take the form of opinion.

The *Restatement* distinguishes between two types of opinion.[59] The "pure type" occurs when an individual states the facts on which he bases his opinion of another and then expresses a comment as to that person's conduct, qualifications or character. The statement of facts and the statement of opinion based on the facts are separate matters. A "pure type" of opinion also occurs when an individual does not himself state the alleged facts on which he bases his opinion, but all parties to the communication know the facts or assume their existence. The second type of opinion, the "mixed type" occurs when an opinion, in form or context, appears to be based on facts regarding an individual or his conduct that have not been stated by the individual making the communication nor are such facts assumed to exist by the parties to the communication. In other words, the expression of the opinion infers the existence of undisclosed facts that justify the opinion.

Traditionally, expressions of opinion of the "pure type" could be actionable as defamatory, and even though the privilege of fair comment[60] was available as a defense, the defendant had no quick way to end legal proceedings.[61] In

---

55. See *Restatement (Second) of Torts* §§ 569-574 (1965), and Prosser, *Law of Torts* 751-760 (4th ed. 1971).

56. The fact that the publication of the libelous matter purports to be based on rumor usually is no defense. *Cobbs v. Chicago Defender*, 308 Ill. App. 55, 31 N.E.2d 323 (1941).

57. 418 U.S. 323, 94 S. Ct. 2997 (1974). See also *Old Dominion Branch No. 496 v. Austin*, 418 U.S. 264, 94 S. Ct. 2770, 41 L. Ed. 2d 745 (1974); Note, "Fact and Opinion After *Gertz v. Robert Welch Inc*: The Evolution of a Privilege," 34 *Rutgers L. Rev.* 81 (No. 1 Fall 1981).

58. *Gertz v. Robert Welch, Inc.*, 418 U.S. 323, 339-40, 94 S. Ct. 2997 (1974).

59. *Restatement (Second) of Torts* § 566 (1965).

60. Expressions of opinion on matters of public concern were viewed as "in the public interest" and hence privileged (protected in whole or in part from liability) because in fostering their expression, the benefit to the public outweighed possible damage to the individual.

61. For example, Prosser states "There has been . . . more willingness [in the case of defamation] than in the case of misrepresentation to find that an opinion carries with it assertions of fact and even when the facts are fully known to the hearer, an unprivileged comment or opinion is now generally regarded as sufficiently defamatory in itself." Prosser, *Law of Torts* § 111 at 742 (4th ed., 1971).

light of the *Gertz* decision, there is now far less chance that certain expressions
of opinion will ever be legally challenged. Because of *Gertz*, the *Restatement of
Torts* presently takes the position that the two described types of opinion have
constitutional significance which cannot be ignored.[62] Accordingly, the *Restatement* now holds:

> A simple (pure) expression of opinion based on disclosed or assumed
> nondefamatory facts is not itself sufficient for an action of defamation, no
> matter how unjustified and unreasonable the opinion may be or how
> derogatory it is. But an expression of opinion that is not based on disclosed
> or assumed facts and therefore implies that there are undisclosed facts on
> which the opinion is based, is treated differently. The difference lies in the
> effect upon the recipient of the communication. In the first case, the
> communication itself indicates to him that there is no defamatory factual
> statement. In the second, it does not, and if the recipient draws the
> reasonable conclusion that the derogatory opinion expressed in the comment
> must have been based on undisclosed defamatory facts, the defendant is
> subject to liability.[63]

Under the *Gertz* analysis, an authentication[64] that contains no expressed or
inferred defamatory facts is not actionable. If, however, defamatory statements
of fact were made or inferred, litigation could proceed and other factors would
have to be considered in determining whether there is liability:

- There is no liability for defamation if the communication is true.
- If the plaintiff is a public official or public figure,[65] usually he can prevail

---

62. Even though *Gertz* involved public communications on matters of public concern, in the view
of the *Restatement*, "the logic of the constitutional principle would appear to apply to all expressions
of opinion of the . . . pure type." *Restatement (Second) of Torts* at 173.

63. *Restatement (Second) of Torts* at 173, and see, for example, *Burns v. McGraw-Hill*, 659 P. 2d 1351
(Colo. 1983). Once again, this analysis depends on the ability to distinguish fact from opinion, a
matter easier said than done. In *Information Control Corp. v. Genesis One Computer Corp.*, 611 F. 2d
781, 784 (9th Cir. 1980) under California law, recovery for defamation could be had only for false
statements of fact, not for statements of opinion. In distinguishing between fact and opinion, the
court stated:

> In sum, the test to be applied . . . requires that the court examine the statement in its
> totality in the context in which it was uttered or published. The court must consider
> all the words used, not merely a particular phrase or sentence. In addition, the court
> must give weight to cautionary terms used by the person publishing the statement.
> Finally, the court must consider all of the circumstances surrounding the statement,
> including the medium by which the statement is disseminated and the audience to
> which it is published.

A 1983 decision, *Ollman v. Evans*, 713 F.2d 838, which is still being litigated, may provide
further light on the issue of what is opinion and what is fact.

64. Authentications frequently involve matters of general public interest and this could encourage
the adoption of the *Gertz* approach in deciding liability.

65. In the *Gertz* case (418 U.S. 323 at 345), the Supreme Court gave this definition of "public
figures":

> For the most part those who attain this status have assumed roles of especial promi-
> nence in the affairs of society. Some occupy positions of such persuasive power and
> influence that they are deemed public figures for all purposes. More commonly, those
> classed as public figures have thrust themselves to the forefront of particular public
> controversies in order to influence the resolution of the issues involved. In either
> event, they invite attention and comment.

in a defamation action only if he can prove with clear and convincing evidence that the defendant had knowledge of the falsity of his statement or acted in reckless disregard of truth or falsity.[66]

- If the plaintiff is a private person,[67] as a rule, he can prevail in a defamation action if it can be proven that the defendant knew that his statement was false and defamatory, acted in reckless disregard of such matters, or acted negligently in failing to ascertain the truth of his statement.

If, in fact, suit is brought, the defendant also may have available the defense of consent and the privileges described in the previous section on disparagement.

It should be noted, that much of the case law on defamation involves the media as a defendant, and, hence, there are strong public policies for affording these defendants greater "free speech" leeway. If, however, a case involves a defendant who cannot raise such public policy issues (a defendant, for example, who is pursuing strictly commercial interests), a court is more inclined to demand more of the defendant.[68] A second caution is that whenever defamation questions arise applicable state law should be consulted. In the previously mentioned *Gertz* case, the United States Supreme Court held that the states could define for themselves the appropriate standard of liability for a publisher of defamatory falsehoods injurious to a private individual. Hence, the law and its interpretation can vary from state to state.[69]

The case of *Porcella v. Time Inc.*[70] was decided before *Gertz v. Welch*, but its reasoning, using the "fair comment" doctrine, closely parallels the *Gertz* approach.[71] Mr. Porcella put himself forth as an art expert and he frequently

---

In *Bufalino v. Associated Press*, 692 F.2d 266 (2d Cir. 1982) the court held that the "public official doctrine" would not apply if the plaintiff was not identified in the publication as a "public official" and the plaintiff's name is not otherwise immediately recognized in the community as a public official. As to whether an art critic is a public figure, see *Mount v. The Viking Press, Inc.*, No. 7036/74 (N.Y. Sup. Ct. Dec. 16, 1974); *Mount v. The Boston Athenaeum*, No. 74-4837-T (D. Mass. July 25, 1975) *aff'd* 530 F. 2d 961 (1st Cir. 1976), *cert. denied* 431 U.S. 916 (1977); and the later described case of *Porcella v. Time, Inc.*, 300 F.2d 162 (7th Cir. 1962).

66. See *New York Times Co. v. Sullivan*, 376 U.S. 254, 84 S. Ct. 710 (1964) and its progeny. This rule does not apply if the defamatory statements concern a purely private matter not bearing on conduct, fitness or role in a public capacity. If the matter is "purely private," the plaintiff is treated as a private person. Public officials and public figures are exposed to freer criticism because, it is reasoned, they usually enjoy greater access to channels of effective communication and hence have more realistic opportunities to counteract false statements. In addition, their public stature justifies a free flow of ideas. The *New York Times* test was applied to communications involving "matters of public or general concern" in *Rosenbloom v. Metromedia, Inc.*, 403 U.S. 29, 91 S. Ct. 1811 (1971) (but modified by the *Gertz* case), and to product disparagement in *Bose Corp. v. Consumers Union*, _____U.S. _____, 104 S. Ct. 1949, 80 L. Ed. 2d 502, 52 U.S.L.W. 4513 (1984).

67. See *Hutchinson v. Proxmire*, 443 U.S. 111, 99 S. Ct. 2675, 61 L. Ed. 2d 411 (1979) for discussion of public v. private figure.

68. See, for instance, *Greenmoss Builders, Inc. v. Dun and Bradstreet, Inc.*, 461 A.2d 414 (Vt. 1983).

69. The Libel Defense Resource Center, 32nd Floor, 708 Third Avenue, N.Y., N.Y. 10017, publishes a current survey of libel law in the 50 states.

70. 300 F.2d 162 (7th Cir. 1962).

71. Some would argue that if there can be no recovery for "pure opinion" in light of *Gertz*, then the privilege of "fair comment" no longer has independent significance. See *Restatement (Second) of Torts*, Appendix § 566 (1981).

did appraisals and authentications for museums, collectors and others. The defendant, in one of its magazine articles, described some of Porcella's activities and Porcella alleged that the article libeled him because it charged or implied that he was incompetent as an art expert and untrustworthy. The defendant's answer was that the article fell within the limits of fair comment. The trial court dismissed the suit on motion of the defendant and Porcella appealed.

In affirming the lower court opinion, the appeals court stated:

> Certainly plaintiff would be entitled, as any other person would be, to redress against any false statements of fact maliciously published in regard to him. However, [o]ur analysis of the alleged libelous article convinces us that, insofar as the complaint charged it to be false, it is an expression of the publisher's comments and opinions upon the activities of plaintiff as an art expert with a description of the entire setting in which he was active. It might well be characterized as a satirical recital by an author who made no effort to conceal his belief that there were some authenticators of paintings less reliable than others. The article, insofar as it offended plaintiff, merely expressed the author's opinion, rather than made a false statement of any fact. Plaintiff was engaged in a field which he admits (and even boasts) was in the public domain and, as such, he was subject to comment by the public press as to his activities in that field.[72]

A more recent defamation case is *Mount v. Sadik*.[73] Mount, an art critic, authenticated a portrait of George Washington as a Gilbert Stuart. The organization owning the portrait sent a photograph of the picture to the defendant Sadik, a museum director, asking for his opinion. Sadik wrote in reply: "There is no possibility whatever in my opinion that your portrait of George Washington could be by Gilbert Stuart." Later, Sadik studied the painting itself and confirmed his belief. The dispute between Mount and Sadik was widely covered by the press and two such articles formed the basis of the defamation suit. Sadik moved to have the case against him dismissed. In granting the motion the court said:

> The statements in the articles attributed to Sadik are expressions of his belief, concededly differing from that of Mount, that the painting was not by Stuart. The words of Sadik as quoted or paraphrased even if construed to be a rejection of plaintiff's views, are not defamatory. They merely indicate to the reader that Sadik and Mount have differing opinions of the painting's origin. They do not attack Mount personally, but merely call into question one opinion he has expressed. The law of defamation has never gone so far as to provide that, once an expert has expressed an opinion, all other experts must keep silent on the matter, lest they expose themselves to legal action.[74]

---

72. *Porcella v. Time Inc.*, 300 F.2d 162, 166-7 (7th Cir. 1962). See also *Brewer v. Hearst Publishing Co.*, 185 F.2d 846 (7th Cir. 1951).

73. No. 78 Civ. 2279 (S.D.N.Y. Oct. 26, 1978). See also *Mount v. Sadik*, No. 78 Civ. 2279 (S.D.N.Y. April 7, 1980) which discusses the liability of the magazine that published a story on the controversy.

74. *Mount v. Sadik*, No. 78 Civ. 2279, slip op. at 6 (S.D.N.Y. Oct. 26, 1978). Articles of general interest on the subject of authentications are: Stebbins, "Possible Tort Liability for Opinions Given by Art Experts" a somewhat dated treatise appearing in F. Feldman and S. Weil, *Art Works: Law, Policy, Practice* (1974) and Gross, "Libel Law—Past and Present," *Case and Comment* 25 (May–June 1983).

CHAPTER XIV

Care of Collections

A. The Duty
B. Inventory Procedures and the Reporting of Missing Objects
C. Other Security Precautions
D. Conservation

A. The Duty

A museum has a responsibility to provide reasonable care for the objects entrusted to it. With regard to objects owned by the museum, this responsibility springs from the museum's charitable trust status, as explained in Chapter 1. Trustees have a responsibility to use the care and skill of persons of ordinary prudence in preserving trust property, and they are under a similar duty to use care in preventing theft of trust property and damage to it by the unlawful acts of third parties.[1] With regard to objects on loan to a museum, the responsibility to provide care is governed by the bailment relationship created by the loan agreement.[2] With regard to objects other than loans placed in the custody of the museum, the degree of responsibility assumed by the museum should be set forth in the temporary custody receipt, described in Chapter IX. As a practical matter, this means that a museum's governing body should be able to assure itself that policies and procedures are in effect that afford museum objects prudent care and protection in light of existing circumstances.[3] Here,

---

1. *Scott on Trusts* § 176 (3rd ed.).

2. See Chapter VI, "Loans, Incoming and Outgoing" section on "Liability Exposure." See also *Johnson Trust*, 51 Pa. D&C 2d 147 (1970) wherein the court discussed appropriate protection measures for the John G. Johnson Collection held in custody by the Philadelphia Museum of Art.

3. *Harris v. Attorney General*, 31 Conn. Sup. 93, 324 A.2d 279 (1974) discusses the responsibility of museum trustees to provide insurance and adequate security against theft and fire. In weighing the conduct of the trustees, the court considered the particular circumstances of the museum. In *Parkinson v. Murdock*, 183 Kan. 706, 332 P.2d 273 (1958), a question at issue was whether trustees of an art collection have implied authority to employ a conservator to evaluate the care and condition of objects in the collection. The court stated at 277:

> As a necessary incident to the carrying out of the expressed intention to provide an art collection that would last throughout the years, the trustees also have the duty to see that the objects of art purchased are properly housed and cared for so as not to deteriorate after a relatively short period of time. to achieve this end, the trustees have the power . . . to use all reasonable and necessary means to ascertain the condition of the objects of art.

See also *State of Washington v. Lappaluoto*, No. 11781 (Wash. Super. Ct., Klickitat County, April 5, 1977). In this case, which was eventually settled without going to judgment, it was alleged by the Attorney General that the defendant trustees failed to require proper maintenance of the museum's collection and this failure constituted a breach of their fiduciary duties. In a case still in litigation,

again, the museum's collection management policy can be the vehicle for implementing prudent measures. The policy can articulate the desired objectives, assign responsibility to staff for making certain decisions, establish procedures for bringing problems to the attention of appropriate staff, and require periodic reports to the museum's governing board on the status of care and security of the collections. Pertinent topics that may be addressed in the collection management policy include:

- inventory procedures and the reporting of missing objects;
- security controls;
- fire and natural disaster hazard protection;
- conservation; and
- insurance (discussed in Chapter XV).

B. Inventory Procedures and the Reporting of Missing Objects

The task of doing a complete inventory of a museum's collections frequently is looked upon as an unrealistic goal. It requires a major diversion of staff time, careful planning, and a willingness to forego projects which promise more immediate gratification. As a museum grows, however, effective management usually demands that a continuing inventory system be in place if intelligent decisions are to be made regarding collection use, growth, storage and security. And, it is never too late to begin such an inventory project, as is evidenced by the experience of the Smithsonian Institution's National Museum of American History. That museum initiated a complete inventory when its collections were estimated to include more than 14 million stamps, 800,000 numismatic specimens, a half-million photographs, and over one million additional objects ranging from political memorabilia to locomotives.[4]

In addition to the readily apparent benefits to research, documentation and storage; an ongoing inventory system can be an essential security device. The knowledge that spot inventory checks can and will be done routinely is an effective deterrent to misappropriation of collection objects, and if there is, in fact, a theft the museum is in a better position to detect the loss and take necessary action. If a museum is unable to demonstrate with certainty that a collection object is missing and, as a result, reasonable efforts are not made to retrieve the property, the museum could be vulnerable to charges of mismanagement.

Consider the following situation. It comes to the attention of Museum X that two of its paintings are in the possession of Mr. Y. A demand is made upon Mr. Y to return the works, but he refuses stating that he purchased the paintings in good faith from a dealer many years ago. The museum turns to its lawyer for advice. Upon investigation, it develops that the museum cannot

---

People of the State of Illinois v. Silverstein, No. 76, Ch. 6446 (Ill. Cir. Ct., Cook County, Oct. 1976), the Attorney General is suing museum trustees for, among other things, permitting a large portion of the museum's collection to remain in storage under poor conditions that are accelerating deterioration.

4. Evelyn, "Taking Stock in the Nation's Attic," *Museum News* 39 (July–Aug. 1981). The article discusses practical problems encountered in initiating an effective inventory.

establish when the paintings might have been taken because it has no ongoing inventory system. In addition, staff members admit that they had looked in the past for the paintings but decided not to say anything when they could not be found. It was assumed that some day the paintings would turn up and the museum did not want the embarrassment of reporting a loss. Upon learning all the circumstances, the museum's lawyer is less than enthusiastic about bringing suit. He cites the case of *O'Keeffe v. Snyder*.[5] In *O'Keeffe*, the plaintiff sought the return of paintings which she claimed had been stolen from her many years previously. The defendant, the present holder, alleged that he had purchased the paintings in good faith from another party. The court held that the plaintiff would be barred from pursuing her claim after the passage of so much time unless she could establish that she had exercised reasonable diligence in discovering the facts which formed the basis of her cause of action. Under this test, the burden was on the plaintiff to prove that she had been diligent and prompt in trying to establish when her paintings had been stolen and that she had taken reasonable measures at that time to alert law enforcement officials and the art world that the works had been unlawfully removed from her possession. In the given hypothetical case, if Museum X were to sue to retrieve the paintings, and the court adopted the *O'Keeffe* case reasoning,[6] the museum would not be in a strong position to prove due diligence in keeping track of its property and in taking constructive action to seek its return. Taking such a situation one step further, if the museum were barred from recovering because of negligence, can the museum's board members be charged with the loss on the grounds of mismanagement?[7] There is no one answer; the facts of each situation will determine if there is negligence and if it amounts to misfeasance on the part of board members. However, the lesson is that a museum is well-advised to have some reasonable system for keeping track of its collection objects, and if a loss is suspected it should be museum policy to pursue the matter with diligence.[8]

---

5. 170 N. J. Super. 75, 405 A.2d 840, 416 A.2d 862 (1980). This case is discussed in more detail in the section on Stolen Property.

6. But under cases such as *State of North Carolina v. West*, 293 N.C. 18, 235 S.E.2d 150 (1977) and *Menzel v. List*, 267 N.Y.S.2d 804, 49 Misc. 2d 300 (1966) *aff'd* 28 A.D.2d 516, 279 N.Y.S.2d 608; third-party claim *rev'd* on other grounds, 24 N.Y.S.2d 91, 298 N.Y.S.2d 979, 246 N.E.2d 742 (1969) the museum might not have to explain its lack of action.

7. See, for instance, *Lynch v. Redfield Foundation*, 9 Cal. App. 3d 293, 88 Cal. Rptr. 86 (1970) where trustees of a charitable corporation were held personally liable for sums lost to the corporation because of their negligence. See also *Stuart v. Continental Ill. Nat'l Bank and Trust Co. of Chicago*, 68 Ill. 2d 502, 369 N.E.2d 1262 (1977) *cert. denied* 444 U.S. 844.

8. Diligent pursuit could involve some or all of the following: reporting to local police; reporting to Federal Bureau of Investigation (F.B.I.) and Interpol if property exceeds a certain value and interstate and/or international traffic is suspected; seeking publication in circulars similar to *Art Theft Archive Newsletter* (published by International Foundation for Art Research, Inc., N.Y., N.Y. 10021). See also Mason, "Art Theft Investigations," *F.B.I. Law Enforcement Bulletin* (Jan. 1979), for a description of the "International Guide to Missing Treasures." *BAMBAM* (Brookline Alert Missing Books and Manuscripts, N.Y., N.Y. 10021) operates a rare book and manuscript database to assist in the identification and recovery of stolen material of this type. A museum's ability to recover under an insurance policy when inventory records are incomplete is discussed in *Insurance Co. of North America v. Univ. of Alaska*, 669 P.2d 954 (Ala. 1983).

C. Other Security Precautions

Security is one of the topics weighed in the accreditation of a museum by the American Association of Museums. The following questions are used as guides in the accreditation process and they reflect a common understanding of what constitutes museum security:

(1) Is the museum and its collections protected against burglary?

(2) Against theft and pilferage?

(3) Against vandalism?

(4) Are guards on regular schedules?

(5) Are all parts of the collections kept locked or under scrutiny during open hours?

(6) Are mechanical or electronic systems in operation?

(7) Are there written procedures to be followed in case of fire?[9] In case of holdup? In case of vandalism? In case of rowdyism?

(8) Are these procedures known to all employees?

(9) Do all employees know procedures in case of illness or personal injury to staff or visitor?

(10) Are records adequate to furnish usable descriptions of missing specimens to police?

(11) Is the building adequately insured?[10]

In seeking to provide reasonable security for its collections, there are precautions which can be taken beyond the ones enumerated above. Many of these additional precautions involve the establishment of internal rules which require staff to be conscious of security and accountability. For example, museum procedures can require that a written notation be made on appropriate records whenever a collection object is moved, even if the move is only an internal one. With such a requirement in effect, there is an immediate warning to staff of possible misappropriation when a collection object is missing without a written explanation. A package pass system and/or a requirement that all packages must leave through a designated check-out area is another precaution worth considering. Policies regarding access to collections, whether by staff or outsiders, also can be reviewed to be sure that procedures are in place that afford reasonable protection yet do not unduly inhibit collection use.

In *Museum Ethics*,[11] this statement is made:

> An ethical duty of museums is to transfer to our successors, when possible in enhanced form, the material record of human culture and the natural world. They must be in control of their collections and know the location . . . of the objects that they hold.[12]

---

9. See Chapter XVII, "Visitor and Employee Safety as It Relates to Collections," for discussion of fire safety.

10. See Chapter XV, "Insurance," for discussion of insurance of collection objects.

11. American Association of Museums, *Museum Ethics: A Report to the American Association of Museums by its Committee on Ethics* (1978). The report was first published in the March–April 1978 issue of *Museum News*.

12. Ibid., at 11 of American Association of Museums, *Museum Ethics*.

Whether a museum's security procedures fall so short of accepted ethical standards as to constitute a violation of legal responsibilities, all depends upon the
facts of a particular situation. But it stands to reason that if little thought has
been given to security, a museum is placing itself in a vulnerable position.[13]

D. Conservation[14]

The 1981 version of Professional Practices in Art Museums contains this reference to conservation:

> Once an object enters the museum, its preservation is the responsibility of
> the Director in consultation with the Curator concerned and Conservators.
> To assure the Board's (Board of Directors) full awareness of preservation as a
> primary museum function, it may be that the Director should report
> periodically on the state of the collection.[15]

This advice is in accord with trust law[16] and it is valid for all types of museums.[17]
In addition, the quotation offers suggested procedures for carrying out conservation responsibilities. It places a duty for making decisions in particular cases
on one individual and it specifies the other parties normally contributing to the
evaluation process. The suggestion that periodic reports be given to the governing board is a sensible one. Conservation work can be costly and the condition
of a museum's collection may well be an important consideration when budget

---

13. Joseph Chapman discusses the physical security of museum collections in C. Keck, *et al.*, *A Primer on Museum Security* (1966). See also Dierker and Burke, "Legal Questions in Providing Security for Museum Objects," *ALI/ABA Course of Study Materials on Legal Problems of Museum Administration* 163 (1980) for an annotated outline on legal issues associated with security measures; Shaines and Dierker, "Problems Relating to Theft by Museum Staff—The Legal Risks of Catching the Employee Thief," *ALI/ABA Course of Study Materials on Legal Problems of Museum Administration* 121 (1982); L. Fennelly, *Museum, Archive and Library Security* (1983); T. Weber, *Alarm Systems and Theft Prevention* (1979); R. Tillotson, *Museum Security* (1977); and D. Menkes, ed., *Museum Security Survey* (1981) (both publications available through the American Association of Museums); J. Hunter, *Security for Museums and Historic Houses: An Annotated Bibliography*, Technical Leaflet 114 (AASLH 1979); Schna-bolk, "Museum Security: A Well-Kept Secret," *Museum News* 5 (Aug. 1983); P. Waters, *Procedures for Salvage of Water-Damaged Library Materials* (Library of Congress 1975); J. Martin, ed., *The Corning Flood: Museum Under Water* (Corning Museum of Glass 1977); Musgrove, "A New Look at Fire Protection," *Museum News* 11 (Aug. 1984).

14. See also the discussion of pest control in Chapter XVII, "Visitor and Employee Safety as It Relates to Collections."

15. See Association of Art Museum Directors, *Professional Practices in Art Museums, Report to the Ethics and Standards Committee*, paragraph 30 (1981). "Enters the museum" is presumed to mean "accessioning." Conservation work on objects on loan to the museum or otherwise in its custody should not be undertaken without a written agreement with the owner regarding the nature of the work to be done, the responsibilities assumed and insurance provisions. If museum staff in their individual capacities are permitted to use museum facilities to do conservation work, aside from the ethical questions that must be addressed, there can be potential negligence liability for the museum. Unless the relationship between staff member and museum is clearly spelled out, insurance aspects are considered, and appropriate "hold harmless" clauses executed, the museum could be drawn into a conflict between the owner and the conservator.

16. See section A, this chapter.

17. Conservation needs can be varied. Consider the case of a new aquarium in Baltimore, Maryland, which met with overwhelming popularity. After six months of operation, it became apparent that the long visiting hours and crowd stress were fatiguing the fish. Prudently, steps were taken to limit evening hours and to reduce the number of visitors permitted inside the building at one time.

priorities are being established. If conservation problems reach a certain magnitude, the situation certainly needs the attention of a museum's board. Board members could be questioned for permitting less pressing expenditures or for incurring additional museum responsibilities when the collections are in dire need of care.[18] *Museum Ethics* sets forth this guidance:

> The physical care of the collection and its accessibility must be in keeping with professionally accepted standards. Failing this, museum governance and management are ethically obliged either to effect correction of the deficiency or to dispose of the collection, preferably to another institution.[19]

It is worth noting that the American Association of Museums' accrediting standards address the conservation and preservation of a museum's collection. From a very practical standpoint, if a museum hopes to obtain or retain accreditation, it should keep abreast of AAM standards in this area. Also, these standards may offer some guidance on what is "professionally acceptable" in certain situations.[20]

---

18. Caroline Keck, a noted conservator, is less than sanguine when discussing management's willingness to give conservation its due:

> Conservators place an irritating emphasis on the impermanence of artifacts. It can spoil the very nature of collecting to encourage the contemplation that upkeep costs, suggestions of inherent vice or other built-in deteriorations be added to a purchase price. Art conservation, however gratifying in theory, in practical application is often a downstairs waste of time and money which upstairs is disinclined to justify. Let it have lip service with an occasional gratuity, but keep it out of the museum council chamber.

Keck, "Conservation's Cloudy Future," *Museum News* 35 (May–June 1980). See also, "On Being a Print Curator: Eight Views," 11 *The Print Collector's Newsletter* 73 (July–Aug. 1980). Two articles which discuss current problems concerning adequate care of archaeological collections are: Marquardt, *et al.*, "Resolving the Crisis in Archaeological Collections Curation," 47 *American Antiquity* (No. 2 1982) and "The Curation and Management of Archaeological Collections: A Pilot Study," Cultural Resources Management Series, U.S. Department of Interior, Washington, D.C. (1980). See also Washburn, "Collecting Information, Not Objects," *Museum News* 5 (Feb. 1984).

19. American Association of Museums, *Museum Ethics* 11.

20. Some sources of information on conservation matters are: (1) the National Institution for the Conservation of Cultural Property (formerly the National Conservation Advisory Council). The newly formed Institute is a nonprofit, educational organization established (a) to provide for voluntary cooperation and planning among institutions, programs and individuals in the United States concerned with conserving cultural property, (b) to provide information, education and scientific support programs for conservation professionals, and (c) to increase public awareness and support of conservation efforts. The address of the Institute is c/o A&I 2225, Smithsonian Institution, Washington, D.C. 20560; (2) American Institute for Conservation of Historic and Artistic Works, 1511 K Street, N.W., Suite 725, Washington, D.C. 20005; (3) American Association for State and Local History, 1400 Eighth Avenue, South, Nashville, Tennessee 32703; and (4) National Trust for Historic Preservation, Education Services Division, 740-48 Jackson Place, N.W., Washington, D.C. 20006. Another information source is a publication entitled: "Pest Control in Museums: A Status Report" (1980). Inquiries concerning this publication may be addressed to the Association of Systematics Collections, Museum of Natural History, University of Kansas, Lawrence, Kansas 66045. C. Keck, *et al.*, *A Primer on Museum Security* (1966) has chapters on environmental problems affecting museum collections, the effect of light on museum objects and miscellaneous other problems that are of interest to the conservator. Additional publications of possible interest are: R. S. Reese, comp., *Care and Conservation of Collections*, Vol. 2 of *A Bibliography on Historical Organization Practices*, published by the American Association for State and Local History (1977); G.

Thomson, *The Museum Environment* (1978); N. Brommelle and P. Smith, eds., *Conservation and Restoration of Pictorial Art* (1976); B. Feilden, *Conservation of Historic Buildings* (1982); "Where to Look: A Guide to Preservation Information" (compiled by the Advisory Council on Historic Preservation) U.S. Government Printing Office, Washington, D.C. 20402; E. Johnson and J. Horgan, *Museum Collection Storage* (1979); S. Williams, *et al.*, *A Guide to the Management of Recent Mammals Collections*, Carnegie Museum of Natural History, Special Publication No. 4 (1977); *Reusing Old Buildings; Preservation Law and the Development Process* (study materials from a 1982 conference sponsored by the Conservation Foundation, the National Trust for Historic Preservation, and the American Bar Association), published by the Conservation Foundation, 1717 Massachusettes Avenue, N.W., Washington, D.C. 20036. In "Conservation Treatment Facilities in the United States," a pamphlet published in 1980 by the National Conservation Advisory Council (now the National Institute for the Conservation of Cultural Property, see above), various conservation arrangements are discussed, and the Code of Ethics and Standards of Practice of the American Institute for Conservation of Historic and Artistic Works are reproduced.

CHAPTER XV

Insurance

A. Scope of Discussion
B. Obligation to Insure
C. The Role of Insurance
D. Selecting a Policy

A. Scope of Discussion

This chapter is a general discussion on insuring objects owned or under the control of a museum. It does not cover what might be called "people insurance," such as trustees and officers liability insurance, personal injury insurance, and bond coverage on employees. The latter types of protection certainly are of interest to a museum and should be weighed in reviewing the organization's overall insurance programs, but they are outside the scope of this text which focuses on collection objects.[1] Nor does this chapter attempt to give a comprehensive treatment of the subject of collections insurance. Excellent publications are available that afford detailed information.[2] Rather, the purpose of this discussion is to comment, from a lawyer's point of view, on the museum's obligation, if any, to insure and to suggest an approach to insurance that is consonant with a museum's overall responsibilities. Specific insurance questions arising in such matters as the management of loans and the care of objects placed in the custody of the museum are discussed in the chapters that address these specific arrangements.

B. Obligation to Insure

Collection-type objects that may be the subject of insurance fall into various categories:

    (1) collection objects owned by the museum (whether on premises or off);

---

1. Articles that address "people insurance" issues are: Babcock, "Insure Against Employee Theft," *History News* 19 (Sept. 1981); Bishop, "Sitting Ducks and Decoy Ducks: New Trends in the Indemnification of Corporate Directors and Officers," 77 *Yale L. J.* 1078 (1968); Knepper, "Corporate Indemnification and Liability Insurance for Corporation Officers and Directors," 25 *Sw. L. J.* 240 (1971); Myers, "Liability of Trustees and Officers," *Business Officer* 18 (April 1978); Porth, "Personal Liability of Trustees of Educational Institutions," 1 *J. of College and Univ. L.* 84 (Fall 1973); Sugerman and Feinberg, "Protecting Directors of Nonprofit Organizations from Liability," *Foundation News* 25 (Sept./Oct. 1979).

2. See, for example: P. Nauert and C. Black, *Fine Arts Insurance: A Handbook for Art Museums* (1979); D. Dudley, *et al.*, *Museum Registration Methods* (1979); Pfeffer, "Insuring Museum Exhibitions," 27 *Hastings L. J.* 1123 (1976); Pfeffer and Herrick (eds.), *Risk Management Manual for Museums* (1974, 1975); C. Keck, *et al.*, *A Primer on Museum Security* (1966).

(2) objects borrowed by the museum for exhibition, study, and the like;[3] and

(3) objects placed in the custody of the museum for other than loan purposes (for example, for identification or possible purchase).

Whether there is an obligation to insure for each category and, if there is no such obligation, whether it is prudent to insure depends on the circumstances. If the objects are owned by the museum, normally an obligation to insure is not inferred as a requirement of due care.[4] It is reasoned that frequently museum collections are irreplaceable and, therefore, prudent management may dictate that available funds be spent for security and care of the objects rather than for insurance which can only compensate for loss. This argument is more persuasive when the objects are on-premises and under the museum's immediate control. When the museum's objects are off-premises, however, insurance may be a prudent safeguard. Off-premises there is greater likelihood of loss or damage which cannot be controlled by museum staff and, frequently, the cost of insuring can be imposed on the recipient of the objects.

General guidance concerning the insuring of a museum's own collections properly should come from the museum's board of trustees. The board is charged with providing due care for the collections and it must determine how best to carry out this obligation within the museum's resources. Barring specific restrictions to the contrary and based on a museum's particular circumstances, a board, acting prudently, could determine that it was more practical not to insure the collections, or that the collection should be insured but only for a portion of its value, or that the collection should be insured for full value, or that the collections should be insured only when off-premises. What is important is that periodically the board review the situation and make an informed decision regarding the insurance program.

If the objects in question are items on loan to the museum, different considerations arise with regard to insurance. The loan agreement may require insurance by the museum; so, clearly, there is then an obligation to provide coverage. If the loan agreement is silent on the issue or if the lender merely has waived insurance, this does not preclude the lender from suing to recover for loss or damage caused by the museum's negligence.[5] The museum may well determine that it is prudent to insure to protect itself from possible claims (or such claims that exceed an amount which the museum can self-insure). If a lender has waived insurance and has agreed in writing to hold the museum

---

3. In 1981, Florida passed an Arts Indemnification Act designed to insure works of art or exhibitions borrowed from within the U.S. for display in Florida. Florida is the first state to adopt such a program. In 1984, Iowa passed a similar statute. When assessing insurance needs, a check of state statutes may be in order.

4 See *Harris v. Attorney General*, 31 Conn. Supp. 93, 324 A.2d 279 (1974); *In Re Petition of Trustees of the Hyde Collection Trust*, No. 17023 (N.Y. Sup. Ct., Warren County, decision—March 25, 1974; judgment—June 18, 1974), See also *Restatement (Second) of Trusts* § 176 (1959) and *Scott on Trusts* § 176 (3rd ed.).

5. As noted in Chapter VI, "Loans, Incoming and Outgoing," the museum, as a bailee, has an obligation to exercise reasonable care in the handling of the loaned property. If the property is damaged or lost while in the museum's custody, usually the museum must assume liability.

harmless from loss or damage arising out of the loan, then there may be little need to insure.[6]

If the objects in question are in the custody of the museum primarily for the benefit of their owners (for example, for identification), the law usually imposes a less demanding standard of care. As explained in Chapter IX, "Objects Left in the Temporary Custody of Museums," it is sensible to have a special museum form documenting the receipt of such objects and explaining the degree of care that will be afforded them. Such clear notice to owners strengthens the museum's position if there is an accident. Barring a specific agreement with the owner to the contrary, it is difficult to infer an obligation on the part of the museum to insure such objects. Whether it is prudent to carry insurance on this category of objects or to self-insure is a decision for each museum. Much will depend on the volume of the objects involved, their relative value, the efficiency of the museum in processing such objects, and the ability of the museum to absorb some liability. If there is a desire to insure, the museum should be able to negotiate a very reasonable rate for the coverage, assuming that it has a thoughtfully prepared temporary custody receipt form and a system for its implementation.

C. The Role of Insurance

Insurance should not be used as a cure-all for poor management. The "Don't worry, we're insured" approach may be the simplest, but it hardly comports with responsibilities to care for and preserve cultural objects. If viewed from the proper perspective, insurance, as a rule, should be the last resort for the museum manager. Prevention rather than reimbursement should be the primary goal.

The term "risk management" is in vogue, and fundamentally it is the application of analysis and common sense to perceived risks. Museum officials responsible for advising on insurance needs should be familiar with the risk management technique, because it puts insurance in its proper place. Risk management deals with the identification, analysis and the evaluation of risk, and the selection of the most advantageous methods for handling it. It is an aggressive approach that seeks first to avoid, control, reduce or accept an identified risk before insuring against it. For example, if a museum has many valuable small objects in its collections and the question is whether they should be insured on-premises, the risk manager looks at such things as storage security, exhibit procedures, display cases, detection equipment, crowd control, inventory and record procedures, all with an eye to avoiding or reducing possible loss or damage. Such a review might demonstrate that museum time and funds are better spent on improving preventive procedures and equipment rather than on insurance coverage. Similarly, if the museum is experiencing a high rate of loss for incoming loans, the risk manager does not automatically budget more for insurance. First there is an investigation of why losses are increasing. Are too fragile objects being accepted? Are unpacking and packing

---

6. Even with a waiver of liability, a museum could be held liable for gross negligence.

procedures at fault? Are condition reports being done routinely so there is certainty as to when loss or damage occurs? An elevated loss rate is accepted only when the risk manager is satisfied that reasonable care has been taken down the line to avoid or control the situation. The general risk management approach is inherent in any prudent review of a museum's collection procedures, with the insurance program viewed as the last bastion in the defense.

D. Selecting a Policy

An insurance policy amounts to a contractual arrangement between the museum and the insurance company with regard to specified risks. Having identified the types of risks it wishes to cover, a museum should be able to bargain intelligently regarding the terms of its insurance contracts. Effective bargaining requires some comprehension of the factors that will be weighed by the insurance company[7] in deciding whether it will accept a risk (and at what price), otherwise the museum cannot hope to put its best foot forward. Effective bargaining also requires the museum to accept only a policy which meets its precise needs and which does not strain staff capabilities.

According to Patricia Nauert and Caroline Black, authors of *Fine Arts Insurance, A Handbook for Art Museums*,[8] the committee of the Inland Marine Underwriters Association specializing in fine arts insurance[9] considers the following to be the most common problems encountered when evaluating a museum risk:

(1) *Record-keeping*. The museum's records do not reflect accurately what is in storage, what is on display or what is on loan. As a result, insurance is either insufficient or excessive.

(2) *Security*. There may be little protection against theft.

(3) *Valuation*. There can be a range of problems associated with setting values and keeping them current.[10]

Other experts such as Irving Pfeffer[11] list the following as significant risk factors for museums:

(1) *Hazards*. Fire and the related perils of smoke and water damage.

(2) *Storage*. Careless placement of artifacts in storage containers as well as poor storage areas.

(3) *Transportation*. Packing and shipping methods frequently are negligent.[12]

---

7. It is the insurance underwriter who actually evaluates the risk and decides whether the company should accept certain coverage and at what rates. Naturally, a museum wants its circumstances to be presented to the underwriter in a favorable light.

8. Published in 1979 by AAMD and distributed by the American Association of Museums.

9. Fine arts insurance is a form of inland marine insurance.

10. P. Nauert and C. Black, *Fine Arts Insurance: A Handbook for Art Museums* 27 (1979).

11. Pfeffer, "Insuring Museum Exhibitions," 27 *Hastings L. J.* 1123 (1976).

12. One well-known insurance broker, Huntington Block, cites as the number one cause of museum collection claims "accidents while objects are being handled or transported." See Chapter 9 of D. Dudley, *et al.*, *Museum Registration Methods* (1979).

A museum preparing to bargain for insurance coverage is well-advised to review its situation with regard to the above, compile needed statistics, and, if necessary, initiate corrective measures that improve its attractiveness as a risk. Once again, the museum's collection management policy can come into play as a means of implementing good internal procedures and of demonstrating to a prospective insurer that management in the museum is not left to chance. Armed with relevant facts and figures on its operation, the museum is in a better position to bargain realistically (that is, sell its risk, not buy insurance) for the insurance it actually needs.

Any insurance policy that is under discussion should be reviewed carefully to be sure that it offers adequate protection and that it does not impose unrealistic demands upon the museum.[13] A wise precaution is to involve museum staff who will bear the burden of implementing policy requirements in the review. These points warrant special scrutiny:

(1) Does the coverage clearly define the property the museum wishes to cover? For example, if a museum maintains several types of collections (permanent, study, education), is it clear which are covered? Is it clear which incoming and outgoing loan situations are covered and when coverage goes into effect? Are partial gift situations, jointly held property, remainder interest in property, and so on, covered? Are frames, display cases, and other auxiliary materials covered?

(2) Are the territorial limits of coverage adequate, and what is the most economical method for obtaining coverage for occasional shipments beyond normal traffic areas?

(3) Are the perils insured against and the exclusions realistic? Most policies are "all risks" with named exclusions. This is a more advantageous approach for museums because it is easier to evaluate specified exclusions than it is to list all possible perils. There is some leeway in negotiating certain exclusions, with corresponding rate adjustments, but the exclusions that usually survive in an "all risk" policy are:

- wear and tear, gradual deterioration, insect, vermin, inherent defects (sometimes referred to as inherent vice) or damages caused by repairing, restoration or retouching;
- war, insurrection, rebellion, revolution or civil war;
- nuclear damage; and
- shipments by mail, unless registered, first-class or insured parcel post (and with possible limitations on dollar value).[14]

---

13. For example, if the policy calls for the museum to "warrant" or "guarantee" that something will be done, it is worth requesting that this be changed to read that the museum "to the best of its ability" will, etc. Time limits should be checked for reasonableness and, rather than have to do something "immediately," the museum might request a change to "as soon as practicable." With regard to "proof of loss" provisions, see *Insurance Co. of North America v. Univ. of Alaska*, 669 P.2d 954 (Ala. 1983).

14. D. Dudley, *et al.*, *Museum Registration Methods* 144 (1979).

(4) Are the procedures for establishing valuations realistic? For example, if valuation is based on the fair market value at the time of loss, there is no critical pressure to constantly readjust book valuations. But what if a claim is for a borrowed object with an insurance value preset by the owner under the terms of the loan agreement? It may be necessary to distinguish between procedures used in valuing objects loaned to the museum and those used in valuing the museum's own objects. In any event, the museum should understand clearly the policy terms in this area and make sure that its internal methods for setting values mesh.

(5) A "pairs and sets" clause can be important. Such a clause provides that if any of the pieces which make up a pair or set is lost, the insured has the option to claim a total loss for the pair or set. However, it should be borne in mind that if total loss is paid, the remainder of the pair or set (as with an object declared a total loss) becomes the property of the insurance company.

(6) Consider, also, a "buy back" provision. This gives the insured the right to buy back from the insurance company a lost or stolen item that is recovered after the claim has been paid.

(7) Is it prudent to include deductibles or franchises in order to reduce premiums? With a deductible, no claim is made if the loss is less than the stated deductible. With a franchise, the insurance pays the entire amount if the loss equals or exceeds the amount of the franchise. In deciding whether such clauses are prudent, the museum must consider its ability to respond with museum funds to cover losses or repairs falling below these limitations.

A museum purchasing insurance coverage for collection objects can be faced with a variety of proposals. Selection can be difficult because there is no standard collections insurance policy presently in use. Efforts have been made to draft model forms[15] but only recently has one such proposal begun to attract considerable attention. That proposal, the work of Phillip Babcock and Marr Haack (on pages 282-87)[16] can serve as a useful checklist when evaluating insurance proposals, and, in addition, the model purposely was written in "plain English" so that it can be understood even by the novice. In time, if a standard policy is adopted by the museum community, most questions between borrower and lender concerning the adequacy of insurance coverage should disappear.

---

15. See form prepared by John Lawton in C. Keck, *et al.*, *A Primer on Museum Security* 26-30 (1966). See also Vance, "A Proposed Standard Insurance Policy," *Museum News* 21 (Sept. 1969), and Babcock and Haack, "Plain English Collections Insurance," *Museum News* 22 (July–Aug. 1981).

16. This model policy has been endorsed by the American Association of State and Local History. It is reproduced in this text with the approval of the authors.

Sample Model Policy

Coverage Features*

The Museum Collections form contains three insuring agreements, relating to permanent collections, loan collections, and legal liability for loan collections in the insured's care. The permanent collection can be insured for different amounts while on premises, in transit, and at other locations. The loan collections agreement provides "wall-to-wall" coverage on borrowed collections the insured has agreed to insure, regardless of the duration of the loan. This agreement also applies to property owned by the insured that has been loaned to others. As with the permanent collection agreement, separate amounts can be arranged for loan collections on premises, in transit, and at other locations. The legal liability agreement applies to the insured's liability (and related defense costs) for loss to collectibles in the insured's care when the insured has been instructed *not* to insure the property.

Coverage under all agreements is on an *all risks* basis, with the usual exclusions of wear and tear, gradual deterioration, insect or animal damage, inherent vice, nuclear risks, and war. In addition, loss by extremes of temperature or humidity (mold or mildew, for example) are excluded if the property is not protected by environmental controls, unless loss results from another covered peril. Especially pertinent to museum exposures, loss resulting from repairing, restoration, or retouching processes is also excluded. There are also exclusions of loss due to inventory shortage, loss to property shipped under an "on deck" bill of lading, and loss to property sent by mail (other than first-class or registered mail—see sample form).

Finally, there is an exclusion of loss caused by dishonest acts of officers or employees—an often underestimated loss exposure faced by museums. However, the form does cover such losses to the extent they exceed the museum's Fidelity bond limit or the Fidelity coverage deductible shown in the declarations. In other words, the policy can be written to provide excess Fidelity coverage.

Valuation of lost or damaged property is stated to be fair market value at the time of loss not to exceed the applicable limit of liability. There are a number of special provisions that apply to valuation in some instances, however. Loaned property, for example, is valued at the amount agreed upon by the lender and borrower. If there is no agreement, the amount of loss is valued at fair market value at the time of loss. Another special provision states that if the lost or damaged property is contemporary art that was designed by an artist and then constructed by the artist or a technician, the insurer may pay only for the cost of repair or replacement if the work can be repaired or replaced to the artist's specifications. Another clause permits the museum to buy back property for whose loss the insurer has already paid the museum. The terms of this provision are clearly stated in the sample form under "Buy-back option." The form also contains a "Pairs and Sets" clause.

Of special interest is a condition stipulating that insured property will be packed and unpacked only by trained packers. There is also a clause entitled

---

*This introductory summary was first published in F.C.&S. Bulletins, August 1981.

Conflicting terms stating that the terms and conditions of the Museum Collections form prevail whenever they are in conflict with any other terms or conditions of the museum's policy. This refers to the fact that the Museum Collections form is not a free-standing document and is intended to be attached to the museum's regular Property insurance policy or, perhaps, the insurer's skeleton form for Inland Marine coverages.

Endorsements

The drafters have prepared two endorsements for use with the policy. One provides for reporting of values on either a monthly or an annual basis, and the other provides international coverage for property in transit or at another location. Without the latter endorsement, the regular policy territory is the continental United States, Alaska, Hawaii, and Canada, including losses occurring in transit between these places.

Museum Collections Coverage

This agreement is designed to protect museum collections against all risks of direct physical loss or damage with some limitations.

Coverage Summary	Limits of	coverage
Permanent Collection — locations		
1.	$	
2.	$	
• All other locations	$	
• In transit	$	
Loan Collection — locations.		
1.	$	
2.	$	
• All other locations	$	
• In transit	$	
Legal Liability.	$	
International Coverage. This coverage applies only if a limit is shown and the International Coverage Endorsement is attached.	$	
All Loss From any One Event. This is the most we'll pay for all loss from any one event no matter how many protected persons, property owners or financial interests are involved. This applies to all losses, expenses and salvage charges combined. Any amount we pay for a loss won't reduce this limit for loss from other events.	$	

Deductibles.

$	Permanent collection
$	Loan collection
$	Fidelity Coverage

Reporting. If the museum Collection Reporting Endorsement is attached, we'll figure your premium on the basis of written reports you make to us. You'll report on a monthly or annual basis and pay the rate as indicated below.

☐ Monthly — Rate   per $100

☐ Annual — Rate   per $100

If we issue this agreement after the date your policy takes effect, we must complete these spaces and our representative must sign below.

Policy issued to

Authorized representative

Agreement takes effect

Policy number

What This Agreement Covers

This agreement protects museum collections indicated in your Coverage Summary against all risks of direct physical loss or damage. By museum collections we mean property of rarity or of artistic, scientific or historical significance. This includes property such as paintings, statuary, ancient artifacts and other property normally exhibited in museums. Frames, glasses, shadow boxes and other protective enclosures used to display the property are also covered.

Of course, there are some limitations to your coverage which will be explained later in this agreement.

Permanent collection. Your permanent collection consists of property you own and is covered on your premises. It's also covered while in transit to and from another location and while it's temporarily kept at that location for repair, restoration or storage.

We'll cover your permanent collection up to the separate limits shown in your Coverage Summary for premises, other locations and in transit.

Loan collection. Your loan collection consists of property of others loaned to you which you've been instructed to insure (verbably or in writing) and property owned by you which you've loaned to others. Your loan collection includes property on extended loan of six months or more as well as temporary loans. We'll cover this property on a "wall to wall" basis, whether on exhibition or not. "Wall to wall" means that we cover from the time Insured property is removed for shipping from the place it's normally kept, until it's returned there. Coverage also applies during transit and all phases of shipping and exhibition. If, before the return shipment, the owner specified that the property be returned elsewhere, we'll cover the property until it's returned to that place;

We'll cover your loan collection up to the separate limits shown in your Coverage Summary for premises, other locations and in transit.

Legal liability. If a limit is shown in the Coverage Summary for legal liability, we'll defend any suit brought against you for loss or damage to other people's collectibles in your care. This coverage applies when the owners of the property have instructed you not to insure it. Of course, if you have a signed release of liability from the owner, this coverage doesn't apply.

The limit shown in the Coverage Summary is the most we'll pay for defense costs and any judgment in any one loss.

Who's protected under this agreement. While this agreement is in effect, we'll cover your interest and the interest of the owners of covered property. We'll also cover the interest of temporary borrowers you've given custody of the property. But we won't cover the interest of transportation carriers, packers, or shippers. Nor will we cover the interest of others having temporary custody of property for storage or for any repairing, retouching or restoring process.

Where We Cover

We'll cover losses that occur in the continental United States, Alaska, Hawaii and in Canada. We'll also cover losses that occur in transit between these places.

If the International Coverage Endorsement is attached we will also cover losses according to that endorsement.

Exclusions—Losses We Won't Cover

Wear—deterioration—pests. We won't cover loss or damage resulting from any of the following causes:
• Wear and tear;
• Gradual deterioration; or
• Insect or animal pests like termites, moths or mice.

Inherent nature. We won't cover loss or damage resulting from the inherent nature of the property. By inherent nature we mean a quality in the property that causes it to deteriorate or to destroy itself.

Extremes of temperature or humidity. We won't cover loss or damage that results because covered property is kept at a location that isn't protected from extremes of humidity or temperature, unless the loss or damage results directly from another covered peril. For example, if your museum doesn't have the environmental controls to prevent excessive humidity, we won't cover mold or mildew damage to a painting unless that damage was directly caused by flooding or a leaking water pipe.

Repair. We won't cover loss or damage resulting from any repairing, restoration or retouching process if the loss results from this work. But if the work results in a loss that would otherwise be covered, we'll pay for the loss that results directly from the covered peril.

Mail. We won't cover loss or damage to property sent by mail unles it's sent by registered or by first class mail. But property sent by first class mail isn't covered if its value is more than $1,000.

Inventory shortage. We won't cover loss resulting from inventory shortage. Inventory shortage means a loss reflected in your records, but it can't be determined where, when or how the loss occurred.

Fidelity. We won't cover loss caused by any fraudulent, dishonest, or criminal act or series of related acts committed by your officers or employees even if there are others involved. However, we'll cover this loss once it exceeds your fidelity bond limit or the fidelity coverage deductible shown in the Coverage Summary, whichever is greater.

"On deck" shipments. We won't cover loss or damage to property shipped under an "on deck" Bill of Lading.

Nuclear activity. We won't cover any loss caused by nuclear reaction, nuclear radiation, or radioactive contamination. And we don't intend these causes of loss to be considered fire, smoke, explosion, or any other insured peril. But we will cover direct loss by fire resulting from nuclear reaction, nuclear radiation or radioactive contamination if the loss

would otherwise be covered under this agreement.

War and government seizure. We won't cover any loss, damage or injury caused by: war (declared or undeclared), invasion, insurrection, rebellion, revolution, civil war, seizure of power, or anything done to hinder or defend against these actions. We won't cover seizure or destruction of your property under quarantine or Customs regulations, or confiscation by any government or public authority. Nor will we cover illegal transportation or trade.

Setting A Value On Property
If there's a covered loss, we'll consider the value of covered property to be the fair market value of your interest in the property, at the time of loss. But in no case will we pay more than the applicable limits shown in the Coverage Summary.

The following special rules apply.

Loaned property. Property loaned to you which you've been instructed to insure or for which you may be liable will be valued at the amount agreed upon by you and the owner. If you and the owner didn't agree upon a value in advance, you and we will agree upon a value based on the fair market value at the time of loss.

Pairs and sets. There may be a total loss of one or more articles which are part of a pair or set. If you choose, we'll pay you the fair market value of the pair or set up to the limits of your coverage. If you choose this option, you'll give us whatever remains of the pair or set.

Contemporary art. Some contemporary art is designed by artists and then constructed by them or by technicians. If such a work is damaged and can be repaired or replaced to the artist's specifications, we'll pay only the cost of repair or replacement.

Buy-back option. If we recover property for which we have already paid you, you have the right to buy the property back from us. If the property is not damaged, you'll pay the same amount we paid you, plus an amount for loss adjustment, recovery expenses and interest.

Page 3 of 4

The interest will be computed at 1% above the prime rate during the period between the date we paid you and the date you chose to re-purchase

If we paid you for a total loss on damaged property, you have the right to buy back the damaged property. You'll pay the fair market value of the damaged property at the time of re-purchase.

We'll make every effort to notify you of your right to buy back damaged or recovered property. You'll have 60 days from the time you receive our notice to re-purchase the property.

Who We'll Pay

We'll adjust any loss with you or with the owners of the covered property. Our payments for losses will be made to you or any other person or organization you name.

Your Deductible

Your Coverage Summary may show deductibles for your permanent and your loan collections or for fidelity loss. If so, you'll be responsible up to that amount for each loss. We'll pay the rest of your covered loss up to the applicable limit of your coverage.

Other Insurance

Other insurance may be available to cover a loss. If so, we'll pay the amount of your loss that's left after the other insurance has been used up. But we won't pay more than the applicable limit of coverage under this agreement.

This section doesn't apply to insurance that the owners of property loaned to you may have. And the existence of the owners' insurance won't affect our responsibility to pay for a covered loss.

Of course, we won't pay a loss if you or the owner have already collected the loss from others.

Excess insurance. You agree not to purchase excess insurance without our permission. Excess insurance is insurance that applies after the limits of coverage under this agreement are used up.

Other Rules For This Agreement

Packing. You agree that the insured property will be packed and unpacked by trained packers.

Preserving your rights. You must do all you can to preserve any rights you have to recover your loss from others. If you do anything to impair these rights, we won't pay for your loss. You can, however, accept ordinary bills of lading from a shipper, even if they limit the carrier's liability for losses.

We won't attempt to recover any loss from museums or any other place borrowing covered property for exhibition. However, we must give our permission before you give a written release from responsibility of loss to any person or organization other than a museum.

Conflicting terms. The terms and conditions of this agreement apply whenever they are in conflict with any other terms or conditions in your policy, such as the General Rules or Conditions.

Expenses for reducing loss. When a covered loss occurs, you must do everything possible to protect the property from further damage. Keep a record of your expenses. We'll pay our share of reasonable and necessary expenses incurred to reduce the loss or protect covered property from further damage. We'll figure our share and your share of these expenses in the same proportion as each of us will benefit from them.

Insurance for your benefit. This insurance is for your benefit. No third party having temporary possession of the property, such as a transportation company, can benefit directly or indirectly from it.

Certificate of insurance. We may issue certicates of insurance to you. You'll have the authority to give these certificates to others.

Museum Collections Reporting Endorsement

This endorsement changes your Museum
Collections Coverage

How Your Coverage Is Changed

Your Coverage Summary indicates that your premium is based on either annual or monthly written reports you make to us. We'll figure your premium by applying the rate shown for monthly or annual reporting to the values you report. You agree to keep accurate records of the location of covered property for the purpose of these reports.

Monthly reporting. Based on your records, you agree to make monthly reports to us in writing. Each month you'll report the total values of your loan collection (loans of less than 6 months durations) that were covered the previous month. Your reports are due within ten days after the last day of each month.

If the International Endorsement is attached, these conditions also apply to it. You'll also report the total values of your loan collection, that were covered while in international transit and at international locations during the previous month.

Annual reporting. Based on your records, you agree to make an annual report to us in writing. Each year you'll report the total values of your loan collection that were covered during each month. Your annual report is due within thirty days after the anniversary date of your policy or whenever your policy ends.

Other Terms

All other terms of your policy remain the same.

International Coverage Endorsement

This endorsement changes your Museum
Collections Coverage

If a limit is shown for International Coverage in your Coverage Summary, we'll cover losses that occur at locations outside the continental United States, Alaska, Hawaii and Canada, except as noted below.

We'll also cover losses that occur while in transit to and from these locations.

Reporting Terms. The terms of the Museum Collection Reporting Endorsement also apply to International Coverage. You'll report on a monthly basis and pay the rate as indicated.

    International Transit rate per shipment:

Airborne Shipments	per $100
Waterborne Shipments	per $100

    International Locations

Rate per month	per $100

Where We Won't Cover. We won't cover losses that occur in transit to and from or at locations in:

Ocean Marine Terms. International Coverage as provided in this endorsement is also subject to the following American Institute Clauses:

   • Delay   • Marine Extension Clauses

All other terms and conditions of the Policy not in conflict with the foregoing remain unchanged, it being particularly understood and agreed that the F.C. & S. clause remains in full force and effect, and that nothing in the foregoing shall be construed as extending this insurance to cover any risks of war or consequences of hostilities.

Chapter XVI

Access to the Collections

A. Visiting Hours
B. Availability of Collection Objects
C. Access to Collection Records
D. Handicap Access
    1. Legal Requirements
    2. The Rehabilitation Act of 1973
    3. Effect on Historic Preservation Projects

    Legal issues regarding access to museum collections can take various forms. The sufficiency of a museum's visiting hours may be questioned, disputes can arise concerning access to the objects themselves or to records concerning the objects, or handicapped individuals may protest the inability to take part in a museum program or activity.

A. Visiting Hours

The issue of adequacy of visiting hours usually does not rise to the level of a legal question unless visitors are so restricted that the status of the museum as a public-oriented or "charitable" organization is placed in doubt. The challenge might come in the form of a denial of tax exempt status or as a charge of mismanagement against trustees for failure to carry out the purposes of the museum.[1] The classic illustration is the litigation involving the Barnes Foundation of Pennsylvania.

    The Barnes Foundation, a Pennsylvania nonprofit corporation, was established in 1922 under terms set down by Albert C. Barnes. The Foundation administered an art gallery and arboretum as an "educational experiment" to benefit primarily students of art. By instruction of the donor:

> [T]he gallery and the arboretum shall be open five days in each week, except
> during the months of July and August of each year, and solely and
> exclusively for educational purposes, to students and instructors of
> institutions which conduct courses in art and art appreciation, which are
> approved by the trustees of Donor. On Saturday of each week, except
> during the months of July and August of every year, the gallery and the
> arboretum shall be open to the public between the hours of ten o'clock in

---

1. Access by the public also may bear on eligibility for federal grants. See, for instance, the regulations implementing the Institute of Museum Services, 45 C.F.R. pt. 1180.

the morning and four o'clock in the afternoon, under such rules and regulations as the Board of Trustees of Donor may make. It will be incumbent upon the Board of Trustees to make such rules and regulations as will ensure that the plain people, that is men and women who gain their livelihood by daily toil in shops, factories, schools, stores and similar places, shall have free access to the art gallery, and the arboretum upon those days when the gallery and arboretum are to be open to the public, as hereintofore provided. On Sunday of each week during the entire year, the gallery and the arboretum shall be closed to students and public alike.

The art gallery and arboretum were denied exemption from state and local taxes on the grounds that they were not "purely public" as required by state law. It was argued that the admission policy, as interpreted by the trustees, was so restrictive that both entities could not meet the "purely public" test. The trustees of the Foundation contested this interpretation[2] and won. The court stated:

> It must be borne in mind that the gallery is used not as an art gallery as that term is ordinarily understood, but that it is an integral part of a new educational experiment, and the unrestrictive admission of the public would be as detrimental to the work of the Barnes Foundation as it would be to the work carried on in the laboratories and clinics of the University of Pennsylvania. . . . Reasonable regulations for admission of the public do not destroy the charitable nature of a gift where it is otherwise found to be so.[3]

The Foundation continued to pursue a very restrictive admissions policy and a later attempt by a private citizen to question it was unsuccessful.[4] Then, in 1958, the Attorney General of the state initiated legal action claiming that as representative of the people of the state he had the obligation to ascertain why the Foundation as a public charity had closed the doors of the art gallery to the public. The court affirmed the power of the Attorney General to bring such a suit, found a general intent on the part of the donor to give the public at least limited access to the gallery, and ordered the Foundation to justify its admission policy.[5] The court stated:

> Naturally, the general public cannot use the gallery at will. The general public cannot even use a public library at will. Orderliness requires that there be hours of opening and closing of libraries, that hours or days be set aside for rest of personnel, for taking inventory, for cleaning and repairing the property and facilities. But no library would be considered public if the public could be admitted only upon the caprice, whim and arbitrary will of its administrators.[6]

At this point, the Foundation and the Attorney General entered into an agree-

---

2. *Barnes Foundation v. Keely*, 314 Pa. 112, 171 A. 267 (1934).

3. Ibid., at 268.

4. *Wiegand v. Barnes Foundation*, 374 Pa. 149, 97 A.2d 81 (1953).

5. *Commonwealth v. Barnes Foundation*, 398 Pa. 458, 159 A.2d 500 (1960).

6. Ibid., at 506.

ment, later approved by the court, which permitted limited but regular public access to the gallery.

A more recent case questioning the hours of a museum is *People of the State of Illinois v. Silverstein*,[7] also known as the *Harding Museum* case. The Harding Museum, a not-for-profit organization incorporated under the laws of Illinois, was, for a number of years, an active museum in the city of Chicago. The Attorney General of Illinios in 1976 began legal proceedings against the museum's trustees charging, among other things, that since the museum relocated within the city in the mid-1960s its collections have been mainly in storage with only a small portion of them open to the public on a limited basis. This, he claims, amounts to mismanagement on the part of the museum trustees because such a lack of access is in derogation of the intended purpose of the museum. It is not disputed by the trustees that the general public has not been welcomed since the relocation and that parts of the collection are shown only by appointment. The matter still is in litigation.

Another indication of what the courts and the public today might consider reasonable access is found in the case of *In Re Stuart's Estate*.[8] Here a donor had left a collection of books, manuscripts and paintings to a library with the condition, among others, that the collection be exhibited to the public at all reasonable times, but "never on the Lord's Day." Years later, the library sought court approval to waive the Sunday restriction claiming it was not practical and was ill-suited to public need.[9] It was pointed out that most people had the time to visit the collection on Sundays. The court agreed to the waiver stating that the dominant purpose of the donor was to make it possible for the public to see his collection and, in this day and age, access on Sunday served this purpose.

It is worth noting that in the definition of "museum" as used in the Museum Services Act,[10] objects must be exhibited to the public "on a regular basis." The regulations interpreting this phrase read as follows:

(1) An institution which exhibits objects to the general public for at least 120 days a year shall be deemed to meet this requirement.

(2) An institution which exhibits objects by appointment may meet this requirement if it can establish in light of the facts under all the relevant circumstances that this method of exhibition does not unreasonably restrict the accessibility of the institution's exhibits to the general public.[11]

The Association of Art Museum Directors in its *Professional Practices in Art Museums*,[12] defines the art museum as an institution which exhibits works of

---

7. No. 76 CH 6446 (Ill. Cir. Ct. of Cook County, Oct. 1976) and 408 N.E.2d 243 (Ill. 1980). See also *People ex rel. Scott v. George F. Harding Museum*, 58 Ill. App. 3rd 408, 374 N.E.2d 756 (1978), and *People ex rel. Scott v. Silverstein*, 412 N.E.2d 692 (Ill. 1980) and 418 N.E.2d 1087 (Ill. 1981).

8. 183 N.Y. Misc. 20, 46 N.Y.S.2d 911 (1944).

9. See Section E of Chapter IV on Restricted Gifts.

10. 20 U.S.C. §§ 961–968.

11. See 48 Fed. Reg. 27729 (June 17, 1983). It should be noted that this definition is used for the purposes of grant eligibility, not tax status, trustee liability, etc.

12. Association of Art Museum Directors, *Professional Practices in Art Museums: Report of the Ethics and Standard Committee* (1981).

art to the public "on some regular schedule." Practice as well as case law supports the view that museums should have regular hours for attendance and, in setting these hours, the convenience of the public should be taken into consideration.[13]

B. Availability of Collection Objects

What responsibility does the museum have to provide access to objects which are not on public display or to respond to requests for the loan of objects? The problem may be that the museum simply does not have the staff to provide controlled access or to service all loan requests, or it may be that the objects in question are so fragile that the museum believes limited access is a necessity. Basically, it is a matter of trying to balance perceived needs in conservation, exhibition and research,[14] and in all such instances so much depends on the eye of the beholder. There are some who insist that if a museum is publicly supported, the emphasis should be on exhibition and access. Others stress the responsibility to conserve for future generations. Who must make the decisions?

Museum Ethics[15] has this to say on the availability of collections:

> Although the public must have reasonable access to the collections on a nondiscriminatory basis, museums assume as a primary responsibility the safeguarding of their materials and therefore may regulate access to them. . . .
>
> . . .
>
> The judgment and recommendation of professional staff members regarding the use of the collections must be given utmost consideration. In formulating his recommendation the staff member must let his judgment be guided by two primary objectives: the continued physical integrity and safety of the objects or collection, and high scholarly or educational purposes.
>
> The governing board holds the ultimate fiduciary responsibility for the museum and for the protection and nurturing of its . . . collections and related documentation. . . .[16]

On the same subject, the Association of Art Museum Directors offers this guidance:

> The collection is the primary responsibility of the museum. The preservation and conservation, growth and presentation of the collection are the cardinal responsibilities of the Board and the Director to whom it delegates these activities. In all matters relating to the collection, the Director

---

13. In *In Re Estate of Hermann*, 454 Pa. 292, 312 A.2d 16 (1973), the court discusses the question whether a museum ceases to exist if, in fact, the public never visits it.

14. Added to this list might be "acquisition." There are some who believe that the ability to make the object accessible to the public should be a major consideration in any acquisition decision. Stressing the public nature of the museum, they find it difficult to approve the use of museum resources for objects that must be kept under wraps.

15. American Association of Museums, *Museum Ethics: A Report to the American Association of Museums by its Committee on Ethics* (1978).

16. Ibid., 14, 27-28.

must, therefore, keep the Board advised since the Board remains ultimately responsible for the collection.

. . .

The collection exists for the benefit of present and future generations; it should be as easily accessible as is consistent with the safety of the individual objects.[17]

Professional practice recognizes that ultimately a collection access policy must receive its direction from the museum's board of trustees. And the law, while conceding that such a board has discretion in setting policy, insists that informed judgments be made.[18] Thus, while staff recommendations regarding an access policy certainly are in order, the board in approving any such recommendation will want to assure itself that the proposal reflects its informed judgment concerning the goals of the museum and that resources are in fact available to carry out the proposed policy. If a museum is ever challenged on its access policy, evidence that the policy was adopted by its board after prudent review should lend considerable weight to its defense.[19]

As a practical matter, the museum's access policy can be a part of its total collection management policy. The board, having established access guidelines, can delegate their implementation in the collection management policy. Many unfortunate incidents concerning access to the collections occur because procedures implementing basic policy have not been thought out and/or disseminated. Even though a museum may have very good reasons for denying access, it may find itself with a major public relations problem if those reasons are given only after bureaucratic shuffling and staff indecisiveness.[20]

C. Access to Collection Records

In weighing an object access policy, thought must be given also to a corollary policy on access to collection records. A museum professional would be the first to agree that an object without its documentation has limited value and that same professional, as a rule, would protest vehemently if documentation was censored before it was made available to him. A museum must reconcile this attitude with some very practical problems encountered with regard to record access.

For purposes of this discussion, collection records are deemed to include

---

17. Association of Art Museum Directors, *Professional Practices in Art Museums: Report of the Ethics and Standards Committee* 10, 11 (1981).

18. See Chapter I, "What is a Museum? What is Required of its Board Members?" Note *Conway v. Emeny*, 139 Conn. 612, 96 A.2d 221 (1953) and *Scott on Trusts* § 187 (3rd ed.) on the question of trustee discretion.

19. *Olds v. Rollins College*, 173 F.2d 639 (N.C. 1949).

20. Articles that address practical problems involved in collection access are: Richoux, *et al.*, "A Policy for Collections Access," *Museum News* 43 (July-Aug. 1981); Force, "Museum Collections: Access, Use and Control," 18 *Curator* 249 (1975); "On Being a Print Collector: Eight Views," 11 *The Print Collector's Newsletter* 73 (July-Aug. 1980).

two general categories of material.[21] The first includes records which are commonly associated with registration functions. These primarily document the legal status of an object within the museum, possibly the object's value, and that object's movement and care while under the control of the museum. The second category includes records associated with curatorial functions. These provide a broad body of information about an object which establishes the object's proper place and importance within its cultural or scientific sphere. With regard to the first category, more common access problems concern possible privacy considerations of donors or lenders, commercially motivated requests (such as the dealer who wants to check appraisal data) and the very legitimate fear that important documents will be lost or damaged if registration folders are handled by outsiders. With regard to requests for records in the second category, there may be reluctance to provide access for fear research notes will be pirated or curatorial observations or correspondence will be misused.[22]

Before attempting to establish a record access policy, it should be determined whether there are any laws or regulations affecting the release of collections records. The federal government[23] and most states have freedom of information-type statutes that require the release of certain public records,[24] as well as open meeting or "sunshine" laws that require that certain governmental bodies conduct their proceedings in public.[25] Municipalities may have similar requirements. If a museum is part of a governmental unit or closely associated with one, laws of this nature could affect access to collections records.[26] For

---

21. Archival collections can raise even more complex questions. Archives as such are not covered in this discussion.

22. An associated problem is the case of the curator who wants exclusive access to certain records (and possibly collection objects), because he is engaged in active research. Such situations are especially prone to criticism and a strictly enforced internal method for reviewing all such arrangements affords protection to all concerned.

23. The federal Freedom of Information Act (5 U.S.C. § 552) applies only to the Executive Branch of government. Records produced under a federal grant normally would not be subject to the federal Freedom of Information Act unless such records were on file in a federal Executive Branch agency. Possibly, the terms of a particular federal grant could impose conditions concerning the accessibility of records produced by the grantee.

24. "Public records" frequently are defined to include all writings made, maintained or kept by the state or any agency, institution, or political subdivision thereof for use in the exercise of functions required or authorized by law or administrative rule or involving the receipt or expenditure of public funds. The term "writings" may be defined to include a broad range of documentary material regardless of physical form. As of 1982, Mississippi became the last state to enact some type of public records law which permits access to records of state agencies, although some question whether Illinois has an effective statute on this subject.

25. 73 *Mich. L. Rev.* (No. 5 April 1975) is devoted to an extensive analysis of state "open record" laws and gives citations to all such laws in existence as of 1975. See also Simon, "The Application of State Sunshine Laws to Institutions of Higher Education," 4 *J. of College and Univ. L.* 83 (Winter 1976-77).

26. See *Wake County Hospital System, Inc. v. News & Observer Publishing Co.*, 284 S.E.2d 542 (N.C. Ct. App. 1982). Even if a museum is not covered by a freedom of information statute, if the museum shares collection records with an organization that is subject to such an act, those records may fall within the purview of the act as records "maintained" by a covered entity. Consider the implication of this if, for instance, many museums decide to computerize and share collection data.

example, an applicable freedom of information-type statute may leave a museum with little discretion regarding access to collection records. If there is also an applicable sunshine law, the public probably will have access to the museum board's decisions concerning the collections. On the other side of the coin, the federal government and some states have privacy statutes that restrict the release of most information which could be classified as personal to an individual.[27] If museum's collection records are covered by both a privacy statute and an open-record statute, thorny problems can arise.[28]

Experience demonstrates that it is preferable to favor openness with regard to collection records. When viewed objectively, most of what is in these records should be available to the public. Normally, how a museum acquires and disposes of objects is a proper public concern, and provenance records are gathered primarily to further scholarship and public appreciation of collection objects. A policy of secrecy only breeds distrust and may produce an atmosphere where the public is intolerant of even legitimate reasons for withholding information. A more prudent approach is to treat information in collection records as open to the public unless there is a clearly defensible reason, consonant with applicable statutes, for denying a specific request.[29] With such a

---

27. The Libel Defense Resource Center (LDRC) publishes a current and comprehensive fifty-state survey of privacy law. Information on the publication can be obtained from LDRC, 32nd Floor, 708 Third Avenue, N.Y., N.Y. 10017.

28. In 1980, the National Conference of Commissioners on Uniform State Laws endorsed a model Uniform Information Practices Code. The purpose of the code is to provide a consistent approach to freedom of information and privacy issues at the state level. This can be accomplished only if all or most states adopt the proposed model code.

29. Information generally is withheld if its disclosure would constitute an unwarranted invasion of personal privacy; encourage theft or expose an individual to physical harm; release business secrets or propriety information; inhibit ongoing negotiations or litigation, etc. However, statutes vary and a museum should study carefully any applicable to it. Of general interest to museums are two recently enacted exceptions to the federal Freedom of Information statute. Section 501 of the National Historic Preservation Act Amendments of 1980 (now 16 U.S.C. § 470w-3) reads as follows:

> The head of any Federal agency, after consultation with the Secretary shall withhold from disclosure to the public information relating to the location or character of historic resources whenever the head of the agency or the Secretary determines that the disclosure of such information may create a substantial risk of harm, theft, or destruction of such resources or to the area or place where such resources are located.

Section 9 of "The Archaeological Resources Protection Act of 1979," Pub. L. 96-95 (now 16 U.S.C. §§ 470aa—47011) states:

> (a) Information concerning the nature and location of any archaeological resource for which the excavation or removal requires a permit or other permission under the Act or under any other provision of Federal law may not be made available to the public under subchapter II of chapter 5 of title 5 of the United States Code or under any other provision of law unless the Federal land manager concerned determines that such disclosure would—(1) further the purposes of this Act or the Act of June 27, 1960 (16 U.S.C. §§ 469–469c), and (2) not create a risk of harm to such resources or to the site at which such resources are located. (b) Notwithstanding the provisions of subsection (a), upon the written request of the Governor of any State, which request shall state—(1) the specific site or area for which information is sought, (2) the purpose for which such information is sought, (3) a commitment by the Governor to adequately protect the resource from commercial exploitation, the Federal land manager concerned shall provide to the Governor information concerning the nature and location of archaeological resources within the State of the requesting Governor.

policy of openness in force, however, it is almost a necessity to delegate to one or two well-informed staff members the responsibility for deciding the hard cases.[30] Consistency and fairness are essential. Also, a policy of openness does not mean that access must be granted on demand. It assumes that a request will be made with some precision and that the person having custody of the records will have sufficient time to review the request so it can be determined whether all of the material can be released.

Any policy on access to collection records must consider also record security and the ability of the museum financially to accommodate requests. Record duplication and monitoring record use by outsiders are costly and time consuming. Inordinate demands in these areas invariably must be borne by other museum programs. In recent years, many museums have experienced dramatic growth in requests from the public for collection record information.[31] A good portion of these requests come from persons engaged in commercial ventures and/or from individuals who need constant staff assistance. Obviously, decisions have to be made as to what the museum can and should do to promote equitable use of its resources and, once again, the burden of setting policy rests with the museum's board.

D. Handicap Access

1. Legal Requirements
There have been federal,[32] state and municipal laws[33] in effect for many years which regulate building accessibility for the handicapped. However, it was not until the mid-1970s, with the passage of the Rehabilitation Act of 1973, that public attention was focused on access problems experienced by the handicapped. The 1973 act is directed at program access, as distinct from building access, and it provides the handicapped with effective enforcement procedures for a broad range of barrier problems. Prodded by the threat of legal sanctions, government agencies initiated more aggressive enforcement of all federal accessibility statutes and this, in turn, encouraged similar action by state and local governments. Museums were bound to feel the repercussions.

Today, most museums are much more aware of the problems that can be experienced by visitors and staff who have disabilities. In order to assure that

---

30. An example of a hard case is the experience of Brigham Young University. In 1982, after a legal battle to protect the privacy of its donors, the university was ordered to turn over to the Internal Revenue Service the names and addresses of all donors to the university. The appeals court held that the I.R.S. had established "a reasonable basis" for believing that many donors had overvalued their gifts to the university. Thus, under 26 U.S.C. § 7607(f) (2), the university properly was ordered to release a list of all donors. *United States v. Brigham Young University*, 679 F.2d 1345 (10th Cir. 1982).

31. See, for example, Black, "New Strains on Our Resources," *Museum News* 18 (Jan.–Feb. 1978).

32. For instance, the Federal Architectural Barriers Act of 1968, as amended (Pub. L. 90-480, 42 U.S.C. § 4151, *et seq.*) requires that buildings constructed, altered or leased with federal money be accessible to the handicapped.

33. All states have some type of accessibility laws which govern new construction done with state funds. Some of these statutes extend to alterations and renovations, and some may even cover privately owned buildings that are open to the public. Municipalities can have similar regulations.

it is meeting its legal obligations in this regard, a museum should be familiar with all federal, state and local laws which may affect any construction, renovation or leasing it might do or which may affect its programs and practices.[34] It is infinitely easier to do it right the first time. Energy and money spent on confrontations and/or required changes can balloon actual costs and inevitably feelings are bruised in the process.

2. The Rehabilitation Act of 1973

As explained in Section F of Chapter II, "As Recipients of Federal Financial Assistance," a museum that receives federal support, directly or indirectly, probably falls within the purview of § 504 of the Rehabilitation Act of 1973.[35] Section 504 prohibits discrimination on the basis of handicap in any programs or activities receiving federal support. Because the term "handicap" is defined broadly and each form of handicap can present unique accommodation challenges, this statute has had far-reaching effects for museums.

The term "handicapped person" is defined in agency regulations implementing § 504 as follows:

> [A]ny person who has a physical or mental impairment that substantially limits one or more major life activities, has a record of such an impairment, or is regarded as having such an impairment.

The phrase "physical or mental impairment" covers the broadest range of physical and mental disorders, including drug addiction and alcoholism.[36] But, it should be noted that § 504 applies to "qualified" handicapped persons. With respect to employment, a qualified handicapped person is one who, with reasonable accommodation, can perform the essential functions of the job in question. With respect to services, a qualified handicapped person is one who

---

34. See 36 *History News* (No. 7 July 1981), which devotes several articles to handicap access in museums and historical societies; Molloy, "504 Regulations: Learning to Live by the Rules," *Museum News* 28 (Sept.–Oct. 1978); A. Kenney, *Access to the Past: Museum Programs and Handicapped Visitors* (1980); H. Snider, *Museums and Handicapped Students* (Smithsonian Institution 1977); C. Steiner, *Museums and the Disabled* (Metropolitan Museum of Art 1979).

35. See Chapter II, "Museums Are Accountable to Whom?," for a definition of coverage and a discussion of legal remedies available to persons who believe they have been discriminated against by the organization receiving the federal support.

36. The definition of "physical or mental impairment" used in agency regulations implementing § 504 is as follows:

> "Physical or mental impairment" means:
> (i) Any physiological disorder or condition, cosmetic disfigurement, or anatomical loss affecting one or more of the following body systems: neurological; musculoskeletal; special sense organs; respiratory, including speech organs; cardiovascular; reproductive; digestive, genitourinary; hemic and lymphatic; skin; and endocrine; or (ii) Any mental or psychological disorder, such as mental retardation, organic brain syndrome, emotional and mental illness, and specific learning disabilities.
> The term "physical or mental impairment" includes, but is not limited to, such diseases and conditions as orthopedic, visual, speech, and hearing impairments, cerebral palsy, epilepsy, muscular dystrophy, multiple sclerosis, cancer, heart disease, diabetes, mental retardation, emotional illness, and drug addiction and alcoholism.

For other definitions see the current regulations of various federal agencies implementing § 504. In *Vickers v. Veterans Administration*, 549 F. Supp. 85 (D.C. 1982), hypersensitivity to tobacco smoke was held to be a handicap within § 504.

meets the essential eligibility requirements for the receipt of such services. Applying these definitions to actual situations has been no easy task[37] and if a museum is faced with a situation that requires a definitive answer, expert opinion should be sought regarding the current state of the law.

Several important elements of § 504 should be borne in mind. First, the statute does not require that every program and activity be accessible, but that the handicapped have access to *the* program or activity. Translated into practical situations, this means that if two performances of a show are given, at least one must be accessible, and if identical classes are run, at least one must be accessible. Second, the statute does not require that all buildings and facilities of the recipient be accessible,[38] only that the programs and activities be accessible. For example, a museum which does not have an accessible building of its own possibly could comply with the statute by holding its federally supported program (or at least one presentation of it) at an outside accessible location. Third, accessibility means not just access for the mobility impaired, but also access for the deaf, the blind, the mentally retarded, and so on. This may require of a museum such action as the redesign of exhibit labels, the providing of Braille catalogs or recordings for the blind, the installing of amplification devices or arranging for interpreters for the hearing impaired, and the altering or expanding of programs to accommodate the mentally retarded, to mention a few. Fortunately, technical services in this area are growing and frequently state arts agencies can offer consulting services or general advice. The National Endowment for the Arts has funded several projects to help the arts achieve accessibility, and information on these can be obtained by writing directly to the Endowment.[39] The U.S. Architectural and Transportation Barriers Compliance Board[40] and the U.S. General Services Administration[41] can supply infor-

---

37. In *Southeastern Community College v. Davis*, 442 U.S. 397, 99 S.Ct. 2361 (1979), the U.S. Supreme Court discussed what is meant by an "otherwise qualified handicapped individual." Ms. Davis had been refused admission to the nursing program of the community college because of a severe hearing impairment. Evidence established that she would need extensive assistance if she enrolled in the program, and she would not be able to perform some routine nursing tasks. The court held there was no violation of § 504 because Ms. Davis was not an "otherwise qualified handicapped individual." "Section 504 imposes no requirement upon an educational institution to lower or to effect substantial modification of standards to accommodate a handicapped person" (at 413). The Court acknowledged, however, that the line between illegal discrimination against a handicapped person and a lawful refusal to extend affirmative action may, at times, be very thin. In *Barnes v. Converse College*, 436 F. Supp. 635 (S.C. 1977), a college, regardless of the financial burden placed upon it, was ordered to provide interpreter services for a deaf student. See also *Dopico v. Goldschmidt*, 687 F.2d 644 (2d Cir. 1982); *Doe v. New York University*, 666 F.2d 761 (2d Cir. 1981); *Strathie v. Dept. of Transportation*, 716 F.2d 227 (3rd Cir. 1983); and *Nelson v. Thornburgh*, 567 F. Supp. 369 (Pa. 1983) on interpretation of "otherwise qualified."

38. While § 504 may not require complete building and facility access, other federal, state or local laws could impose such a requirement. The source of construction, renovation and program funds often can trigger several statutes, each with their own requirements.

39. Arts and Special Constituencies Office, National Endowment for the Arts, Washington, D.C. 20506.

40. Architectural and Transportation Barriers Compliance Board, Washington, D.C. 20201.

41. Write: Assistant Commissioner for Design and Construction, Public Buildings Service, General Services Administration, Washington, D.C. 20405.

mation on current accessibility standards for use in the design, construction or alteration of facilities, and regional libraries for the blind and physically handicapped can assist in transcribing printed material into Braille.[42]

3. Effect on Historic Preservation Projects

Questions can arise concerning the interaction of accessibility statutes and laws designed to protect buildings of historical, architectural and cultural significance. For example, if a museum is housed in an historic structure and a federal grant or loan is obtained for renovation work, there must be compliance with both federal handicap access and federal historic preservation laws.[43] Major problems can arise if the building's original design severely inhibits handicap access. The Advisory Council on Historic Preservation has issued guidelines concerning the approach that should be taken in such instances. Current information on these guidelines can be obtained by writing the Council.[44] If state or local laws are at issue, and they appear irreconcilable, the local historic preservation commission usually can offer assistance.[45]

---

42. Write: Library of Congress, 1291 Taylor Street, N.W., Washington, D.C. 20542.

43. The National Historic Preservation Act of 1966 (Pub. L. 89-665, 16 U.S.C. § 470); Executive Order 11593, "Protection and Enhancement of the Cultural Environment" (1971), and regulations for the "Protection of Historic and Cultural Properties," 36 C.F.R. pt. 800. Also see Chapter IV, "The Acquisition of Objects—Accessioning," Section D.8.b. on the National Historic Preservation Act itself.

44. Division of Federal Program Review, Advisory Council on Historic Preservation, Suite 530, 1522 K Street, N.W., Washington, D.C. 20005.

45. A very useful booklet on reconciling handicap access and preservation goals is "Access to Historic Buildings for the Disabled: Suggestions for Planning and Implementation," Heritage Conservation and Recreation Service Publication No. 46 (1980), U.S. Department of the Interior. Copies are for sale by the Superintendent of Documents, U.S. Government Printing Office, Washington, D.C. 20402.

CHAPTER XVII

Visitor and Employee Safety As It Relates to Collections

A. Responsibility Owed the Public
B. Responsibility Owed Employees
C. Safety and Health Guides; Other Assistance
    1. Fire and Related Hazards
    2. Employee Safety
    3. Fumigation Hazards

A. Responsibility Owed the Public

A museum invites the public to enter its premises and view its displays. The law infers, therefore, that the museum will act in a reasonably prudent manner to assure that the visiting public is safe from hazards. This duty applies not only to the condition of the museum's stairs and walkways, the traditional slip and fall areas, and the coat-check booths, which spawn umbrella claims, but also to the exhibits themselves. Consider the following situations.

Hypothetical Example 1. The Mellow Museum of Modern Art has a light show exhibit which is described by the critics as "Stunning! An Emotional Tour de Force!" The euphoria generated by the show's reception is somewhat dampened when the museum is sued by Ms. Delicate for injuries sustained in a fall when she became "disoriented" by the exhibit. Shortly thereafter, a similar suit is filed by Mr. Elderly who claims he became nauseous when viewing the exhibit and "blacked out" upon leaving the museum. Obviously Mellow Museum has a problem and expert advice is needed.[1]

Hypothetical Example 2. The Hoosier Historical Society plans to refurbish the grand salon of its Governor Grover House. Much care is being taken to find authentic fabrics, carpets and decorative items. Someone asks whether fire safety must be considered when selections are made and installed even if this jeopardizes the "integrity" of the finished exhibit.

Hypothetical Example 3. The Seaside Science Museum is exhibiting space capsules and related equipment. Children are particularly attracted to the display

---

1. In 1982, the Whitney Museum in New York City was faced with lawsuits of this nature arising from a light show featured on its premises.

and as a precautionary measure, several signs are posted that say: "Do not climb on exhibits." During the course of a busy morning, an eight-year-old youngster, while touring the museum with his school class, manages to injure himself seriously when attempting to climb into one of the artifacts. How will the museum fare when the inevitable claim is brought?

In the eyes of the law, art, historical integrity and "meaningful educational experiences" usually must bow to safety and health considerations. Local fire and safety codes, local building codes, and the law's traditional test in negligence cases, "the reasonably prudent man rule,"[2] invariably apply to museums and historic structures.[3] A museum is well-advised, therefore, to make safety a prime consideration when choosing the objects it collects, the objects it displays, and its methods of exhibit. There are a few practices that can be instituted which draw safety into these routine museum activities in a timely manner.

A museum's collection management policy can require a safety evaluation among its accessioning criteria as well as its incoming loan criteria. Objects posing safety problems usually demand special handling, special display and/ or special insurance, none of which, upon reflection, a museum may want to assume. Calling attention to the safety factor before a decision is made to accession or borrow allows for a more objective analysis of the merits of the acquisition. The spinning mobile, the angular piece of fabricated art or the highly flammable but authentic carpeting may lose some of its attractiveness when considered in a crowded museum setting. What is the potential for injury? Are there simple yet effective measures that can be taken to protect the public? A sign saying "Don't climb" isn't effective for the young child who cannot read[4] and a movable stanchion may be a totally inadequate guard if surrounding exhibits draw a visitor's attention elsewhere. Is the object one that can be viewed satisfactorily from a distance or from behind protective barriers, or will such methods of display only frustrate the visiting public? Each proposed acquisition of a potentially hazardous item raises its own safety consideration that deserves early and thoughtful evaluation.

---

2. In most negligence cases, the standard of care imposed is that of a reasonably prudent man. In other words, the individual charging negligence must demonstrate that the act or condition complained of was not something that a reasonably prudent man would do or permit.

3. If a museum is part of or associated with a governmental unit, local statutes and case law should be checked to see if the museum benefits from the doctrine of sovereign immunity. Under the traditional doctrine of sovereign immunity, a government cannot be sued (i.e., the king is above the law), but today, in most jurisdictions within the United States, this doctrine has been modified or waived by statute. These waiver statutes take a variety of forms, but usually they permit designated types of claims to be brought against the governmental unit as long as certain procedural requirements are followed. Also to be considered is the doctrine of charitable immunity. Traditionally, charitable organizations were not subject to suit on the theory that their charitable endeavors would suffer if private individuals were permitted to obtain large judgments. In most jurisdictions, this doctrine has been abolished or seriously modified. A museum may find it advisable to have a professional opinion on record regarding the applicability of both doctrines (sovereign immunity and charitable immunity) to its activities.

4. As a rule, more caution is expected of the museum when children are known to frequent an area or when the object or location at issue is one which normally would attract children.

Frequently the mode of exhibit can ameliorate a safety hazard inherent in a collection object, but just as frequently the manner of exhibit, not the object, can create the hazard. This is especially true if the exhibit is an elaborate one utilizing background construction, special lighting and audio visual equipment, and the like. The curator and the designer in their efforts to achieve an authentic and effective display may lose sight of safety factors. The change of lighting in the exhibit area may be too drastic or there may be tripping hazards caused by inadequate demarcation of levels. Both conditions are particularly hazardous in an area that may be crowded and where visitors are encouraged to look at displayed objects and not at the walkway. Proper ventilation is another important consideration as well as adequate traffic patterns and unobstructed, visible exit routes. It is a wise precaution for a museum to have a firm policy that no exhibit proceeds beyond the preliminary design stage without review for safety considerations.[5] As a rule, aesthetics, authenticity and the law co-exist quite comfortably and economically if time is allowed for consultation and adjustment.

The above-described procedures for early consideration of safety issues will not work unless someone within the museum has been assigned responsibility to keep abreast of applicable rules and regulations so that information is available in an efficient manner. Equally important is a commitment on the part of the museum to budget for safety needs. Too often safety is very low on the list of priorities when museum funds are being allocated.

B. Responsibility Owed Employees

The Occupational Safety and Health Act of 1970[6] affects the working conditions of just about everyone employed in a museum located in the United States. The Act extends to all employers "engaged in a business affecting commerce"[7] and their employees, and it requires that each employer "shall furnish to each of his employees employment and a place of employment which is free from recognized hazards that are causing or are likely to cause death or serious physical harm to his employees."[8] This general duty has been translated by the U.S. Department of Labor, through its Occupational Safety and Health Administration (OSHA), into numerous, quite specific OSHA standards which regulate work environment and work practices. OSHA standards are divided into four major categories: General Industry, Maritime, Construction, and Agriculture. General Industry and Construction are the categories of particular

---

5. At the same time, a review for any applicable handicap access requirements can be conducted (see Chapter XVI).

6. 29 U.S.C. §§ 651, *et seq.*

7. "Commerce" is defined to mean "trade, traffic, commerce, transportation, or communication among the several states or between a state and any place outside thereof, or within the District of Columbia, or a possession of the United States . . ., or between points in the same state but through a point outside thereof." 29 U.S.C. § 652(3).

8. 29 U.S.C. § 654(a).

interest to museums. All OSHA standards are found in Title 29 of the Code of Federal Regulations (parts 1910, *et seq.*)

OSHA requirements can bear directly on a museum's collection management activities. Museum specimens and their preservatives may present health hazards which are addressed by specific OSHA standards. On-site conservation work should be examined for adherence to OSHA standards. The display and demonstration of certain historic machinery and craft techniques have been known to run afoul of OSHA standards because required protective shields or safety equipment were not used. For employee protection, OSHA standards must be applied also in the fabrication, layout and location of exhibits. If OSHA standards have been met in these general areas, as a rule, visitor safety requirements will have been satisfied as well.[9]

Implementation of the Occupational Safety and Health Act is the responsibility of the U.S. Department of Labor, but by statutory design, most local compliance is administered through the states under federally approved state programs. A museum should be familiar with the enforcement arrangements in the locality. Quick and complete information on local jurisdictions can be obtained from the nearest regional or area office of the U.S. Department of Labor, Occupational Safety and Health Administration.[10] Employees have the right to file health and safety grievances with their employer or directly with the enforcement authority without fear of retribution.[11] Failure to comply with the Act's requirements can expose an employer to civil and criminal penalties.

Another federal safety statute which bears on collection activity and employee health is the Federal Insecticide, Fungicide, and Rodenticide Act (FIFRA), as amended.[12] All museum collections, whether they be paintings, textiles, and manuscripts, archaeological specimens, botanical specimens, or historic structures are susceptible to damage or destruction by a variety of pests. In attempting to conserve their objects, museums use a variety of chemicals and techniques for pest control, and a good portion of such activity now is subject to government regulations. FIFRA, for example requires that all pesticides must be properly labeled, and that consumer use must be in accordance with label instructions. The Act further provides that some pesticides (those labeled for "restricted

---

9. In the application of all rules, common sense is an important ingredient. When touring a museum sculpture display, an OSHA official, who, fortunately, is an art lover, pointed out that several figures with extended arms posed possible striking hazards. Under OSHA regulations, such hazards are to be marked with bright yellow paint. To the museum's great relief, no recommendation was made that the limbs of the figures be painted.

10. Offices are located in Boston, Mass.; New York, N.Y.; Philadelphia, Pa.; Atlanta, Ga.; Chicago, Ill.; Dallas, Tex.; Kansas City, Mo.; Denver, Col.; San Francisco, Cal.; and Seattle, Wash.

11. 29 U.S.C. § 660(c)(1) states:

> No person shall discharge or in any manner discriminate against any employee because such employee has filed a complaint or instituted or caused to be instituted any proceeding under or related to . . . [the Occupational Safety and Health Act] or has testified or is about to testify in any such proceeding or because of the exercise by such employee on behalf of himself or others of any right afforded by this . . . [Act].

Violation of this provision can subject an employer to suit.

12. 7 U.S.C. § 135, *et seq.*, 40 C.F.R. pt. 162, *et seq.*

use") can be applied only by a certified pesticide applicator or by someone under the direct supervision of a certified pesticide applicator. What all of this means for museums is:

(1) there can be no mixing of one's own pesticides;

(2) labels on registered pesticides must be read to see if the use intended is one enumerated on the label;

(3) label instructions regarding procedures must be followed carefully; and

(4) if pesticides labeled for "restricted use" are to be applied by museum staff, sufficient persons must be certified as applicators to comply with FIFRA requirements.[13]

In many states, FIFRA requirements are enforced by state agencies under programs approved by the U.S. Environmental Protection Agency (EPA). If a state does not have an approved program in place, enforcement is handled directly by EPA. Here, again, a museum should be familiar with local requirements and local enforcement authorities.

C. Safety and Health Guides; Other Assistance

In pursuing its safety programs for both visitors and employees, a museum will find the following publications particularly helpful:

1. Fire and Related Hazards

The Life Safety Code (NFPA 101), the work product of the National Fire Protection Association, Inc., is a generally accepted standard code for establishing minimum requirements for a reasonable degree of safety to life from fire in buildings and structures. Each museum must conform to its local fire safety regulations, and these can vary from municipality to municipality. However, most local standards do not vary significantly from NFPA 101 and with a copy of that publication in hand a museum has a comprehensive source of reference. There are several other NFPA publications that treat both general and specific museum fire problems:

NFPA 910—Protection of Libraries and Library Collections (1980)

NFPA 911—Protection of Museums and Museum Collections (1980)

NFPA 40—Cellulose Nitrate Motion Picture Films (1974)[14]

Pamphlets 910 on Libraries and 911 on Museum Collections contain handy fire safety self-inspection forms designed to disclose conditions that need correction.[15]

---

13. If a museum has a fumigation chamber, it is most likely that applicable regulations will require that the chamber be operated by or under the direct supervision of a certified individual.

14. All publications are available from the National Fire Protection Association, Inc., Batterymarch Park, Quincy, Massachusetts 02269.

15. See also R. Tillotson, *Museum Security* (1977); J. Hunter, *Security for Museums and Historic Houses: An Annotated Bibliography*, AASLH Technical Leaflet 114 (1979); J. Martin and C. Edwards, eds., *The Corning Flood: Museum Under Water* (1977); J. Morris, *Managing the Library Fire Risk* (2d ed. 1979); Musgrove, "A New Look at Fire Protection," *Museum News* 11 (August 1984). See also Chapter XIV, Section C.

Frequently, a museum's insurance company may have fire and safety consultants who are available to offer advice and the local fire department or regulatory agency may provide similar assistance. In addition there are professional fire and safety consultants who can be retained to evaluate existing or proposed conditions.

2. Employee Safety

Occupational Safety and Health Standards cover hundreds of pages in the U.S. Code of Federal Regulations. There are certain standards, however, which are of recurring interest to a museum. They include but are not limited to the following which all appear in Part 1910 of Title 29 of the Code of Federal Regulations:[16]

Subpart D—Walking-working Surfaces
Subpart E—Means of Egress
Subpart G—Occupational Health and Environmental Control with special
                emphasis on 1910.95 (Occupational Noise Exposure)
Subpart H—Hazardous Materials
Subpart I—Personal Protective Equipment
Subpart J—General Environmental Controls
Subpart K—Medical and First Aid
Subpart L—Fire Protection
Section 1910.176—Handling materials—general
Section 1910.212—General requirements for all machines
Section 1910.213—Woodworking machinery requirements
Section 1910.215—Abrasive wheel machinery
Subpart P—Hand and Portable Powered Tools and Other Hand-held Equip-
                ment
Subpart Q—Welding, Cutting and Brazing
Subpart S—Electrical
Subpart Z—Toxic and Hazardous Substances

3. Fumigation Hazards

In 1981, a very useful document was published which addressed specific problems encountered by museums in pest control. "Pest Control in Museums: A Status Report"[17] contains proceedings and recommendations from a 1980 interdisciplinary conference called to define the problems associated with the use of pesticides in museums. In addition to the conference proceedings, there are included:

(1) results of a survey conducted by the New York State Museum in order to document how natural history museums store their collections, what pests cause damage, and what methods are being used to protect specimens;

---

16. See also Malaro, "Better Safe than Sorry," *Museum News* 16 (Sept. 1974); *All About OSHA*, U.S. Dept. of Labor Publication No. OSHA 2056.

17. Compiled and edited by S. Edwards and B. Bell, Association of Systematics Collections, University of Kansas, Lawrence, Kansas 66045.

(2) a summary of federal statutes and regulations governing the use of pesticides, as well as an annotation of federal pesticide regulations;

(3) technical reports on various pesticides used in museums;

(4) an illustrated guide to common insect pests;

(5) a bibliography of literature pertaining to pest control; and

(6) a listing of state and federal agency contacts with expertise in pest control matters.[18]

---

18. Other publications of interest are National Fire Protection Association Standard on Fumigation (NFPA 57-1973), National Fire Protection Association, Batterymarch Park, Quincy, Massachusetts 02269; "Fumigants: Procedures, Precautions and Institutional Responsibility for Their Safe Use," 4 *Association of Systematic Collections Newsletter* 5 (No. 1 1976); J. Frank, "Fumigants and Poisons: A Guide to Herbarium Practice," *Handbook for Museum Curators* (1965); R. Lewis, *Manual for Museums* (1976); S. Williams, *et al.*, *Fumigation: A Guide to the Management of Recent Mammal Collections*, Carnegie Museum of Natural History, Special Publication No. 4 (1977). The Center for Occupational Hazards, N.Y., N.Y. 10038, is a nonprofit organization that serves as a clearing-house for research and information on health hazards in the arts. The Director of the Center's Hazards Information Center, Monona Rossol, is the author of "Keeping Your Health: Health Hazards for Artists" which appears in L. Caplin (ed.) *The Business of Art* (1982).

Appendixes

A. Public Law 95-158, Arts and Artifacts Indemnity Act

Public Law 94-158
94th Congress, S. 1800
December 20, 1975

𝔄𝔫 𝔄𝔠𝔱

To provide indemnities for exhibitions of artistic and humanistic endeavors, and
for other purposes.

*Be it enacted by the Senate and House of Representatives of the
United States of America in Congress assembled,*

Arts and Arti-
facts Indemnity
Act.

SHORT TITLE

SECTION 1. This Act may be cited as the "Arts and Artifacts
Indemnity Act".

20 USC 971
note.

FEDERAL COUNCIL

SEC. 2. (a) The Federal Council on the Arts and Humanities (hereinafter in this Act referred to as the "Council"), established under
section 9 of the National Foundation on the Arts and the Humanities
Act of 1965, is authorized to make agreements to indemnify against
loss or damage such items as may be eligible for such indemnity
agreements under section 3—

    (1) in accordance with the provisions of this Act; and
    (2) on such terms and conditions as the Council shall prescribe,
by regulation, in order to achieve the purposes of this Act and,
consistent with such purposes, to protect the financial interest of
the United States.

(b) For purposes of this Act, the Council shall be an "agency"
within the meaning of the appropriate definitions of such term in
title 5, United States Code.

20 USC 971.

20 USC 958.

ELIGIBLE ITEMS

SEC. 3. (a) The Council may make an indemnity agreement under
this Act with respect to—

    (1) works of art, including tapestries, paintings, sculpture,
folk art, graphics, and craft arts;
    (2) manuscripts, rare documents, books, and other printed or
published materials;
    (3) other artifacts or objects; and
    (4) photographs, motion pictures, or audio and video tape;
which are (A) of educational, cultural, historical, or scientific value,
and (B) the exhibition of which is certified by the Secretary of State
or his designee as being in the national interest.

(b)(1) An indemnity agreement made under this Act shall cover
eligible items while on exhibition in the United States, or elsewhere
when part of an exchange of exhibitions, but in no case shall both parts
of such an exchange be so covered.

(2) For purposes of this subsection, the term "on exhibition"
includes that period of time beginning on the date the eligible items
leave the premises of the lender or place designated by the lender and
ending on the date such items are returned to the premises of the
lender or place designated by the lender.

20 USC 972.

"On exhibition."

20 USC 973.

SEC. 4. (a) Any person, nonprofit agency, institution, or government desiring to make an indemnity agreement for eligible items under this Act shall make application therefor in accordance with such procedures, in such form, and in such manner as the Council shall, by regulation, prescribe.

(b) An application under subsection (a) shall—

(1) describe each item to be covered by the agreement (including an estimated value of such item);

(2) show evidence that the items are eligible under section 3(a); and

(3) set forth policies, procedures, techniques, and methods with respect to preparation for, and conduct of, exhibition of the items, and any transportation related to such items.

(c) Upon receipt of an application under this section, the Council shall, if such application conforms with the requirements of this Act, approve the application and make an indemnity agreement with the applicant. Upon such approval, the agreement shall constitute a contract between the Council and the applicant pledging the full faith and credit of the United States to pay any amount for which the Council becomes liable under such agreement. The Council, for such purpose, is hereby authorized to pledge the full faith and credit of the United States.

INDEMNITY AGREEMENT

20 USC 974.

SEC. 5. (a) Upon receipt of an application meeting the requirements of subsections (a) and (b) of section 4, the Council shall review the estimated value of the items for which coverage by an indemnity agreement is sought. If the Council agrees with such estimated value, for the purposes of this Act, the Council shall, after approval of the application as provided in subsection (c) of section 4, make an indemnity agreement.

(b) The aggregate of loss or damage covered by indemnity agreements made under this Act shall not exceed $250,000,000 at any one time.

(c) No indemnity agreement for a single exhibition shall cover loss or damage in excess of $50,000,000.

(d) Coverage under this Act shall only extend to loss or damage in excess of the first $15,000 of loss or damage resulting from a single exhibition.

REGULATIONS

20 USC 975.

SEC. 6. (a) The Council shall prescribe regulations providing for prompt adjustment of valid claims for losses which are covered by an agreement made pursuant to section 5, including provision for arbitration of issues relating to the dollar value of damages involving less than total loss or destruction of such covered objects.

(b) In the case of a claim of loss with respect to an item which is covered by an agreement made pursuant to section 5, the Council shall certify the validity of the claim and the amount of the loss to the Speaker of the House of Representatives and the President pro tempore of the Senate.

AUTHORIZATION OF APPROPRIATIONS

Sec. 7. There are hereby authorized to be appropriated such sums as may be necessary (1) to enable the Council to carry out its functions under this Act, and (2) to pay claims certified pursuant to section 6(b).

20 USC 976.

REPORT

Sec. 8. The Council shall report annually to the Congress (1) all claims actually paid pursuant to this Act during the preceding fiscal year, (2) pending claims against the Council under this Act as of the close of that fiscal year, and (3) the aggregate face value of contracts entered into by the Council which are outstanding at the close of that fiscal year.

20 USC 977.

EFFECTIVE DATE

Sec. 9. This Act shall become effective 30 days after the date of the enactment of this Act.

Approved December 20, 1975.

20 USC 971 note.

LEGISLATIVE HISTORY:

HOUSE REPORT No. 94-680 accompanying H. R. 7782 (Comm. on
        Education and Labor).
SENATE REPORT No. 94-289 (Comm. on Labor and Public Welfare).
CONGRESSIONAL RECORD, Vol. 121 (1975):
        July 25, considered and passed Senate.
        Dec. 1, considered and passed House, amended, in lieu of
                H. R. 7782.
        Dec. 4, Senate concurred in House amendments.
WEEKLY COMPILATION OF PRESIDENTIAL DOCUMENTS, Vol. 11, No. 52:
        Dec. 20, Presidential statement.

B. 22 U.S.C. § 2549, Immunity from Seizure Statute

(a) Agreements; Presidential determination; publication in Federal Register

Whenever any work of art or other object of cultural significance is imported into the United States from any foreign country, pursuant to an agreement entered into between the foreign owner or custodian thereof and the United States or one or more cultural or educational institutions within the United States providing for the temporary exhibition or display thereof within the United States at any cultural exhibition, assembly, activity, or festival administered, operated, or sponsored, without profit, by any such cultural or educational institution, no court of the United States, any State, the District of Columbia, or any territory or possession of the United States may issue or enforce any judicial process, or enter any judgment, decree, or order, for the purpose or having the effect of depriving such institution, or any carrier engaged in transporting such work or object within the United States, of custody or control of such object if before the importation of such object the President or his designee has determined that such object is of cultural significance and that the temporary exhibition or display thereof within the United States is in the national interest, and a notice to that effect has been published in the Federal Register.

(b) Intervention of United States attorney in pending judicial proceedings

If in any judicial proceeding in any such court any such process, judgment, decree, or order is sought, issued, or entered, the United States attorney for the judicial district within which such proceeding is pending shall be entitled as of right to intervene as a party to that proceeding, and upon request made by either the institution adversely affected, or upon direction by the Attorney General if the United States is adversely affected, shall apply to such court for the denial, quashing, or vacating thereof.

(c) Enforcement of agreements and obligations of carriers under transportation contracts

Nothing contained in this section shall preclude (1) any judicial action for or in aid of the enforcement of the terms of any such agreement or the enforcement of the obligation of any carrier under any contract for the transportation of any such object of cultural significance; or (2) the institution or prosecution by or on behalf of any such institution or the United States of any action for or in aid of the fulfillment of any obligation assumed by such institution or the United States pursuant to any such agreement.

(Pub. L. 89-259, Oct. 19, 1965, 79 Stat. 985.)

Section was not enacted as a part of the Mutual Educational and Cultural Exchange Act of 1961, which comprises this chapter.

EXECUTIVE ORDER NO. 11312

Ex. Ord. No. 11312, Oct. 14, 1966, 31 F.R. 13415, which related to the delegation of functions to the Secretary of State, was revoked by Ex. Ord. No. 12047, Mar. 27, 1978, 43 F.R. 13359, set out as a note below.

EX. ORD. NO. 12047. IMPORTED OBJECTS OF CULTURAL SIGNIFICANCE

Ex. Ord. No. 12047, Mar. 27, 1978, 43 F.R. 13359, as amended by Ex. Ord. No. 12388, Oct. 14, 1982, 47 F.R. 46245, provided:

By virtue of the authority vested in me by the Act of October 19, 1965, entitled "An Act to render immune from seizure under judicial process certain objects of cultural significance imported into the United States for temporary display or exhibition, and for other purposes" (79 Stat. 985, 22 U.S.C. 2459), and as President of the United States of America, it is hereby ordered as follows:

SECTION 1. The Director of the United States Information Agency is designated and empowered to perform the functions conferred upon the President by the above-mentioned Act and shall be deemed to be authorized, without the approval, ratification, or other action of the President, (1) to determine that any work of art or other object to be imported into the United States within the meaning of the Act is of cultural significance, (2) to determine that the temporary exhibition or display of any such work of art or other object in the United States is in the national interest, and (3) to cause public notices of the determinations referred to above to be published in the Federal Register.

SEC. 2. The Director of the United States Information Agency, in carrying out this Order, shall consult with the Secretary of State with respect to the determination of national interest, and may consult with the Secretary of the Smithsonian Institution, the Director of the National Gallery of Art, and with such other officers and agencies of the Government as may be appropriate, with respect to the determination of cultural significance.

SEC. 3. The Director of the United States Information Agency is authorized to delegate within the Agency the functions conferred upon him by this Order.

SEC. 4. Executive Order No. 11312 of October 14, 1966 is revoked.

SEC. 5. Any order, regulation, determination or other action which was in effect pursuant to the provisions of Executive Order No. 11312 shall remain in effect until changed pursuant to the authority provided in this Order.

SEC. 6. This Order shall be effective on April 1, 1978.

SECTION REFERRED TO IN OTHER SECTIONS

This section is referred to in section 2611 of title 19.

C. Title III of Public Law 97-466, Convention on Cultural Property Implementation Act

Convention on
Cultural
Property
Implementation
Act.
19 USC 2601
note.

TITLE III—IMPLEMENTATION OF CONVENTION ON CULTURAL PROPERTY

SEC. 301. SHORT TITLE.

This title may be cited as the "Convention on Cultural Property Implementation Act".

19 USC 2601.

SEC. 302. DEFINITIONS.

For purposes of this title—

(1) The term "agreement" includes any amendment to, or extension of, any agreement under this title that enters into force with respect to the United States.

(2) The term "archaeological or ethnological material of the State Party" means—

(A) any object of archaeological interest;

(B) any object of ethnological interest; or

(C) any fragment or part of any object referred to in subparagraph (A) or (B);

which was first discovered within, and is subject to export control by, the State Party. For purposes of this paragraph—

(i) no object may be considered to be an object of archaeological interest unless such object—

(I) is of cultural significance;

(II) is at least two hundred and fifty years old; and

(III) was normally discovered as a result of scientific excavation, clandestine or accidental digging, or exploration on land or under water; and

(ii) no object may be considered to be an object of ethnological interest unless such object is—

(I) the product of a tribal or nonindustrial society, and

(II) important to the cultural heritage of a people because of its distinctive characteristics, comparative rarity, or its contribution to the knowledge of the origins, development, or history of that people.

(3) The term "Committee" means the Cultural Property Advisory Committee established under section 206.

Ante, p. 2349. (4) The term "consignee" means a consignee as defined in section 483 of the Tariff Act of 1930 (19 U.S.C. 1483).

(5) The term "Convention" means the Convention on the means of prohibiting and preventing the illicit import, export, and transfer of ownership of cultural property adopted by the General Conference of the United Nations Educational, Scientific, and Cultural Organization at its sixteenth session.

(6) The term "cultural property" includes articles described in article 1 (a) through (k) of the Convention whether or not any such article is specifically designated as such by any State Party for the purposes of such article.

(7) The term "designated archaeological or ethnological material" means any archaeological or ethnological material of the State Party which—

(A) is—
(i) covered by an agreement under this title that enters into force with respect to the United States, or
(ii) subject to emergency action under section 304, and
(B) is listed by regulation under section 305.

(8) The term "Secretary" means the Secretary of the Treasury or his delegate.

(9) The term "State Party" means any nation which has ratified, accepted, or acceded to the Convention.

(10) The term "United States" includes the several States, the District of Columbia, and any territory or area the foreign relations for which the United States is responsible.

(11) The term "United States citizen" means—
(A) any individual who is a citizen or national of the United States;
(B) any corporation, partnership, association, or other legal entity organized or existing under the laws of the United States or any State; or
(C) any department, agency, or entity of the Federal Government or of any government of any State.

SEC. 303. AGREEMENTS TO IMPLEMENT ARTICLE 9 OF THE CONVENTION.

19 USC 2602.

(a) AGREEMENT AUTHORITY.—
(1) IN GENERAL.—If the President determines, after request is made to the United States under article 9 of the Convention by any State Party—
(A) that the cultural patrimony of the State Party is in jeopardy from the pillage of archaeological or ethnological materials of the State Party;
(B) that the State Party has taken measures consistent with the Convention to protect its cultural patrimony;
(C) that—
(i) the application of the import restrictions set forth in section 307 with respect to archaeological or ethnological material of the State Party, if applied in concert with similar restrictions implemented, or to be implemented within a reasonable period of time, by those nations (whether or not State Parties) individually having a significant import trade in such material, would be of substantial benefit in deterring a serious situation of pillage, and
(ii) remedies less drastic than the application of the restrictions set forth in such section are not available; and
(D) that the application of the import restrictions set forth in section 307 in the particular circumstances is consistent with the general interest of the international community in the interchange of cultural property among nations for scientific, cultural, and educational purposes;
the President may, subject to the provisions of this title, take the actions described in paragraph (2).

(2) AUTHORITY OF PRESIDENT.—For purposes of paragraph (1), the President may enter into—
(A) a bilateral agreement with the State Party to apply the import restrictions set forth in section 307 to the archaeological or ethnological material of the State Party the pillage of which is creating the jeopardy to the cultural

patrimony of the State Party found to exist under paragraph (1)(A); or

(B) a multilateral agreement with the State Party and with one or more other nations (whether or not a State Party) under which the United States will apply such restrictions, and the other nations will apply similar restrictions, with respect to such material.

(3) REQUESTS.—A request made to the United States under article 9 of the Convention by a State Party must be accompanied by a written statement of the facts known to the State Party that relate to those matters with respect to which determinations must be made under subparagraphs (A) through (D) of paragraph (1).

(4) IMPLEMENTATION.—In implementing this subsection, the President should endeavor to obtain the commitment of the State Party concerned to permit the exhange of its archaeological and ethnological materials under circumstances in which such exchange does not jeopardize its cultural patrimony.

(b) EFFECTIVE PERIOD.—The President may not enter into any agreement under subsection (a) which has an effective period beyond the close of the five-year period beginning on the date on which such agreement enters into force with respect to the United States.

(c) RESTRICTIONS ON ENTERING INTO AGREEMENTS.—

(1) IN GENERAL.—The President may not enter into a bilateral or multilateral agreement authorized by subsection (a) unless the application of the import restrictions set forth in section 307 with respect to archaeological or ethnological material of the State Party making a request to the United States under article 9 of the Convention will be applied in concert with similar restrictions implemented, or to be implemented, by those nations (whether or not State Parties) individually having a significant import trade in such material.

(2) EXCEPTION TO RESTRICTIONS.—Notwithstanding paragraph (1), the President may enter into an agreement if he determines that a nation individually having a significant import trade in such material is not implementing, or is not likely to implement, similar restrictions, but—

(A) such restrictions are not essential to deter a serious situation of pillage, and

(B) the application of the import restrictions set forth in section 307 in concert with similar restrictions implemented, or to be implemented, by other nations (whether or not State Parties) individually having a significant import trade in such material would be of substantial benefit in deterring a serious situation of pillage.

(d) SUSPENSION OF IMPORT RESTRICTIONS UNDER AGREEMENTS.—If, after an agreement enters into force with respect to the United States, the President determines that a number of parties to the agreement (other than parties described in subsection (c)(2)) having significant import trade in the archaeological and ethnological material covered by the agreement—

(1) have not implemented within a reasonable period of time import restrictions that are similar to those set forth in section 307, or

(2) are not implementing such restrictions satisfactorily with the result that no substantial benefit in deterring a serious situation of pillage in the State Party concerned is being obtained,

the President shall suspend the implementation of the import restrictions under section 307 until such time as the nations take appropriate corrective action.

(e) EXTENSION OF AGREEMENTS.—The President may extend any agreement that enters into force with respect to the United States for additional periods of not more than five years each if the President determines that—

(1) the factors referred to in subsection (a)(1) which justified the entering into of the agreement still pertain, and

(2) no cause for suspension under subsection (d) exists.

(f) PROCEDURES.—If any request described in subsection (a) is made by a State Party, or if the President proposes to extend any agreement under subsection (e), the President shall—

(1) publish notification of the request or proposal in the Federal Register;

Publication in Federal Register. Submittal to Committee.

(2) submit to the Committee such information regarding the request or proposal (including, if applicable, information from the State Party with respect to the implementation of emergency action under section 304) as is appropriate to enable the Committee to carry out its duties under section 306(f); and

(3) consider, in taking action on the request or proposal, the views and recommendations contained in any Committee report—

(A) required under section 306(f) (1) or (2), and

(B) submitted to the President before the close of the one-hundred-and-fifty-day period beginning on the day on which the President submitted information on the request or proposal to the Committee under paragraph (2).

(g) INFORMATION ON PRESIDENTIAL ACTION.—

(1) IN GENERAL.—In any case in which the President—

Report to Congress.

(A) enters into or extends an agreement pursuant to subsection (a) or (e), or

(B) applies import restrictions under section 204, the President shall, promptly after taking such action, submit a report to the Congress.

(2) REPORT.—The report under paragraph (1) shall contain—

(A) a description of such action (including the text of any agreement entered into),

(B) the differences (if any) between such action and the views and recommendations contained in any Committee report which the President was required to consider, and

(C) the reasons for any such difference.

(3) INFORMATION RELATING TO COMMITTEE RECOMMENDA-TIONS.—If any Committee report required to be considered by the President recommends that an agreement be entered into, but no such agreement is entered into, the President shall submit to the Congress a report which contains the reasons why such agreement was not entered into.

Report to Congress.

SEC. 304. EMERGENCY IMPLEMENTATION OF IMPORT RESTRICTIONS.

19 USC 2603.

(a) EMERGENCY CONDITION DEFINED.—For purposes of this section, the term "emergency condition" means, with respect to any archaeological or ethnological material of any State Party, that such material is—

(1) a newly discovered type of material which is of importance for the understanding of the history of mankind and is in jeopardy from pillage, dismantling, dispersal, or fragmentation;

(2) identifiable as coming from any site recognized to be of

high cultural significance if such site is in jeopardy from pillage, dismantling, dispersal, or fragmentation which is, or threatens to be, of crisis proportions; or

(3) a part of the remains of a particular culture or civilization, the record of which is in jeopardy from pillage, dismantling, dispersal, or fragmentation which is, or threatens to be, of crisis proportions;

and application of the import restrictions set forth in section 307 on a temporary basis would, in whole or in part, reduce the incentive for such pillage, dismantling, dispersal or fragmentation.

(b) PRESIDENTIAL ACTION.—Subject to subsection (c), if the President determines that an emergency condition applies with respect to any archaeological or ethnological material of any State Party, the President may apply the import restrictions set forth in section 307 with respect to such material.

(c) LIMITATIONS.—

(1) The President may not implement this section with respect to the archaeological or ethnological materials of any State Party unless the State Party has made a request described in section 303(a) to the United States and has supplied information which supports a determination that an emergency condition exists.

Report.

(2) In taking action under subsection (b) with respect to any State Party, the President shall consider the views and recommendations contained in the Committee report required under section 306(f)(3) if the report is submitted to the President before the close of the ninety-day period beginning on the day on which the President submitted information to the Committee under section 303(f)(2) on the request of the State Party under section 303(a).

Extension.

(3) No import restrictions set forth in section 307 may be applied under this section to the archaeological or ethnological materials of any State Party for more than five years after the date on which the request of a State Party under section 303(a) is made to the United States. This period may be extended by the President for three more years if the President determines that the emergency condition continues to apply with respect to the archaeological or ethnological material. However, before taking such action, the President shall request and consider, if received within ninety days, a report of the Committee setting forth its recommendations, together with the reasons therefor, as to whether such import restrictions shall be extended.

Report.

(4) The import restrictions under this section may continue to apply in whole or in part, if before their expiration under paragraph (3), there has entered into force with respect to the archaeological or ethnological materials an agreement under section 203 or an agreement with a State Party to which the Senate has given its advice and consent to ratification. Such import restrictions may continue to apply for the duration of the agreement.

19 USC 2604.

SEC. 305. DESIGNATION OF MATERIALS COVERED BY AGREEMENTS OR EMERGENCY ACTIONS.

After any agreement enters into force under section 303, or emergency action is taken under section 304, the Secretary, after consultation with the Director of the United States Information Agency, shall by regulation promulgate (and when appropriate shall revise) a list of the archaeological or ethnological material of the State Party covered by the agreement or by such action. The

Secretary may list such material by type or other appropriate classification, but each listing made under this section shall be sufficiently specific and precise to insure that (1) the import restrictions under section 307 are applied only to the archeological and ethnological material covered by the agreement or emergency action; and (2) fair notice is given to importers and other persons as to what material is subject to such restrictions.

SEC. 306. CULTURAL PROPERTY ADVISORY COMMITTEE.

19 USC 2605.

(a) ESTABLISHMENT.—There is established the Cultural Property Advisory Committee.

(b) MEMBERSHIP.—

(1) The Committee shall be composed of eleven members appointed by the President as follows:

(A) Two members representing the interests of museums.

(B) Three members who shall be experts in the fields of archaeology, anthropology, ethnology, or related areas.

(C) Three members who shall be experts in the international sale of archaeological, ethnological, and other cultural property.

(D) Three members who shall represent the interest of the general public.

(2) Appointments made under paragraph (1) shall be made in such a manner so as to insure—

(A) fair representation of the various interests of the public sectors and the private sectors in the international exchange of archaeological and ethnological materials, and

(B) that within such sectors, fair representation is accorded to the interests of regional and local institutions and museums.

(3)(A) Members of the Committee shall be appointed for terms of two years and may be reappointed for 1 or more terms.

(B) A vacancy in the Commission shall be filled in the same manner in which the original appointment was made.

(c) EXPENSES.—The members of the Committee shall be reimbursed for actual expenses incurred in the performance of duties for the Committee.

(d) TRANSACTION OF BUSINESS.—Six of the members of the Committee shall constitute a quorum. All decisions of the Committee shall be by majority vote of the members present and voting.

(e) STAFF AND ADMINISTRATION.—

(1) The Director of the United States Information Agency shall make available to the Committee such administrative and technical support services and assistance as it may reasonably require to carry out its activities. Upon the request of the Committee, the head of any other Federal agency may detail to the Committee, on a reimbursable basis, any of the personnel of such agency to assist the Committee in carrying out its functions, and provide such information and assistance as the Committee may reasonably require to carry out its activities.

(2) The Committee shall meet at the call of the Director of the United States Information Agency, or when a majority of its members request a meeting in writing.

(f) REPORTS BY COMMITTEE.—

(1) The Commitee shall, with respect to each request of a State Party referred to in section 303(a), undertake an investigation and review with respect to matters referred to in section 303(a)(1) as they relate to the State Party or the request and

shall prepare a report setting forth—

    (A) the results of such investigation and review;

    (B) its findings as to the nations individually having a significant import trade in the relevant material; and

    (C) its recommendation, together with the reasons therefor, as to whether an agreement should be entered into under section 303(a) with respect to the State Party.

(2) The Committee shall, with respect to each agreement proposed to be extended by the President under section 303(e), prepare a report setting forth its recommendations together with the reasons therefor, as to whether or not the agreement should be extended.

(3) The Committee shall in each case in which the Committee finds that an emergency condition under section 304 exists prepare a report setting forth its recommendations, together with the reasons therefor, as to whether emergency action under section 304 should be implemented. If any State Party indicates in its request under section 303(a) that an emergency condition exists and the Committee finds that such a condition does not exist, the Committee shall prepare a report setting forth the reasons for such finding.

(4) Any report prepared by the Committee which recommends the entering into or the extension of any agreement under section 303 or the implementation of emergency action under section 304 shall set forth—

    (A) such terms and conditions which it considers necessary and appropriate to include within such agreement, or apply with respect to such implementation, for purposes of carrying out the intent of the Convention; and

    (B) such archaeological or ethnological material of the State Party, specified by type or such other classification as the Committee deems appropriate, which should be covered by such agreement or action.

(5) If any member of the Committee disagrees with respect to any matter in any report prepared under this subsection, such member may prepare a statement setting forth the reasons for such disagreement and such statement shall be appended to, and considered a part of, the report.

(6) The Committee shall submit to the Congress and the President a copy of each report prepared by it under this subsection.

(g) COMMITTEE REVIEW.—

(1) IN GENERAL.—The Committee shall undertake a continuing review of the effectiveness of agreements under section 303 that have entered into force with respect to the United States, and of emergency action implemented under section 304.

(2) ACTION BY COMMITTEE.—If the Committee finds, as a result of such review, that—

    (A) cause exists for suspending, under section 303(d), the import restrictions imposed under an agreement;

    (B) any agreement or emergency action is not achieving the purposes for which entered into or implemented; or

    (C) changes are required to this title in order to implement fully the obligations of the United States under the Convention;

Report to Congress.

the Committee may submit a report to the Congress and the President setting forth its recommendations for suspending such import restrictions or for improving the effectiveness of any such agreement or emergency action or this title.

(h) FEDERAL ADVISORY COMMITTEE ACT.—The provisions of the Federal Advisory Committee Act (Public Law 92–463; 5 U.S.C. Appendix I) shall apply to the Committee except that the requirements of subsections (a) and (b) of section 10 and section 11 of such Act (relating to open meetings, public notice, public participation, and public availability of documents) shall not apply to the Committee, whenever and to the extent it is determined by the President or his designee that the disclosure of matters involved in the Committee's proceedings would compromise the Government's negotiating objectives or bargaining positions on the negotiations of any agreement authorized by this title.

5 USC app.

(i) CONFIDENTIAL INFORMATION.—

(1) IN GENERAL.—Any information (including trade secrets and commercial or financial information which is privileged or confidential) submitted in confidence by the private sector to officers or employees of the United States or to the Committee in connection with the responsibilities of the Committee shall not be disclosed to any person other than to—

(A) officers and employees of the United States designated by the Director of the United States Information Agency;

(B) members of the Committee on Ways and Means of the House of Representatives and the Committee on Finance of the Senate who are designated by the chairman of either such Committee and members of the staff of either such Committee designated by the chairman for use in connection with negotiation of agreements or other activities authorized by this title; and

(C) the Committee established under this title.

(2) GOVERNMENTAL INFORMATION.—Information submitted in confidence by officers or employees of the United States to the Committee shall not be disclosed other than in accordance with rules issued by the Director of the United States Information Agency, after consultation with the Committee. Such rules shall define the categories of information which require restricted or confidential handling by such Committee considering the extent to which public disclosure of such information can reasonably be expected to prejudice the interests of the United States. Such rules shall, to the maximum extent feasible, permit meaningful consultations by Committee members with persons affected by proposed agreements authorized by this title.

(j) NO AUTHORITY TO NEGOTIATE.—Nothing contained in this section shall be construed to authorize or to permit any individual (not otherwise authorized or permitted) to participate directly in any negotiation of any agreement authorized by this title.

SEC. 307. IMPORT RESTRICTIONS.

19 USC 2606.

(a) DOCUMENTATION OF LAWFUL EXPORTATION.—No designated archaeological or ethnological material that is exported (whether or not such exportation is to the United States) from the State Party after the designation of such material under section 305 may be imported into the United States unless the State Party issues a certification or other documentation which certifies that such exportation was not in violation of the laws of the State Party.

(b) CUSTOMS ACTION IN ABSENCE OF DOCUMENTATION.—If the consignee of any designated archaeological or ethnological material is unable to present to the customs officer concerned at the time of making entry of such material—

(1) the certificate or other documentation of the State Party required under subsection (a); or

(2) satisfactory evidence that such material was exported from the State Party—

(A) not less than ten years before the date of such entry and that neither the person for whose account the material is imported (or any related person) contracted for or acquired an interest, directly or indirectly, in such material more than one year before that date of entry, or

(B) on or before the date on which such material was designated under section 305,

the customs officer concerned shall refuse to release the material from customs custody and send it to a bonded warehouse or store to be held at the risk and expense of the consignee, notwithstanding any other provision of law, until such documentation or evidence is filed with such officer. If such documentation or evidence is not presented within ninety days after the date on which such material is refused release from customs custody, or such longer period as may be allowed by the Secretary for good cause shown, the material shall be subject to seizure and forfeiture. The presentation of such documentation or evidence shall not bar subsequent action under section 310.

(c) DEFINITION OF SATISFACTORY EVIDENCE.—The term "satisfactory evidence" means—

(1) for purposes of subsection (b)(2)(A)—

(A) one or more declarations under oath by the importer, or the person for whose account the material is imported, stating that, to the best of his knowledge—

(i) the material was exported from the State Party not less than ten years before the date of entry into the United States, and

(ii) neither such importer or person (or any related person) contracted for or acquired an interest, directly or indirectly, in such material more than one year before the date of entry of the material; and

(B) a statement provided by the consignor, or person who sold the material to the importer, which states the date, or, if not known, his belief, that the material was exported from the State Party not less than ten years before the date of entry into the United States, and the reasons on which the statement is based; and

(2) for purposes of subsection (b)(2)(B)—

(A) one or more declarations under oath by the importer or the person for whose account the material is to be imported, stating that, to the best of his knowledge, the material was exported from the State Party on or before the date such material was designated under section 305, and

(B) a statement by the consignor or person who sold the material to the importer which states the date, or if not known, his belief, that the material was exported from the State Party on or before the date such material was designated under section 305, and the reasons on which the statement is based.

Seizure and forfeiture. (margin note)

(d) RELATED PERSONS.—For purposes of subsections (b) and (c), a person shall be treated as a related person to an importer, or to a person for whose account material is imported, if such person—

(1) is a member of the same family as the importer or person of account, including, but not limited to, membership as a brother or sister (whether by whole or half blood), spouse, ancestor, or lineal descendant;

(2) is a partner or associate with the importer or person of account in any partnership, association, or other venture; or

(3) is a corporation or other legal entity in which the importer or person of account directly or indirectly owns, controls, or holds power to vote 20 percent or more of the outstanding voting stock or shares in the entity.

SEC. 308. STOLEN CULTURAL PROPERTY.

19 USC 2607.

No article of cultural property documented as appertaining to the inventory of a museum or religious or secular public monument or similar institution in any State Party which is stolen from such institution after the effective date of this title, or after the date of entry into force of the Convention for the State Party, whichever date is later, may be imported into the United States.

SEC. 309. TEMPORARY DISPOSITION OF MATERIALS AND ARTICLES SUBJECT TO TITLE.

19 USC 2608.

Pending a final determination as to whether any archaeological or ethnological material, or any article of cultural property, has been imported into the United States in violation of section 307 or section 308, the Secretary shall, upon application by any museum or other cultural or scientific institution in the United States which is open to the public, permit such material or article to be retained at such institution if he finds that—

(1) sufficient safeguards will be taken by the institution for the protection of such material or article; and

(2) sufficient bond is posted by the institution to ensure its return to the Secretary.

SEC. 310. SEIZURE AND FORFEITURE.

19 USC 2609

(a) IN GENERAL.—Any designated archaeological or ethnological material or article of cultural property, as the case may be, which is imported into the United States in violation of section 307 or section 308 shall be subject to seizure and forfeiture. All provisions of law relating to seizure, forfeiture, and condemnation for violation of the customs laws shall apply to seizures and forfeitures incurred, or alleged to have been incurred, under this title, insofar as such provisions of law are applicable to, and not inconsistent with, the provisions of this title.

(b) ARCHAEOLOGICAL AND ETHNOLOGICAL MATERIAL.—Any designated archaeological or ethnological material which is imported into the United States in violation of section 307 and which is forfeited to the United States under this title shall—

(1) first be offered for return to the State Party;

(2) if not returned to the State Party, be returned to a claimant with respect to whom the material was forfeited if that claimant establishes—

(A) valid title to the material,

(B) that the claimant is a bona fide purchaser for value of the material; or

19 USC 2612.   **SEC. 313. REGULATIONS.**

The Secretary shall prescribe such rules and regulations as are necessary and appropriate to carry out the provisons of this title.

19 USC 2613.   **SEC. 314. ENFORCEMENT.**

In the customs territory of the United States, and in the Virgin Islands, the provisions of this title shall be enforced by appropriate customs officers. In any other territory or area within the United States, but not within such customs territory or the Virgin Islands, such provisions shall be enforced by such persons as may be designated by the President.

19 USC 2601
note.
Publication in
Federal
Register.

SEC. 315. EFFECTIVE DATE.

(a) IN GENERAL.—This title shall take effect on the ninetieth day after the date of the enactment of this Act or on any date which the President shall prescribe and publish in the Federal Register, if such date is—

(1) before such ninetieth day and after such date of enactment; and

(2) after the initial membership of the Committee is appointed.

(b) EXCEPTION.—Notwithstanding subsection (a), the members of the Committee may be appointed in the manner provided for in section 306 at any time after the date of the enactment of this Act.

Approved January 12, 1983.

LEGISLATIVE HISTORY—H.R. 4566:

HOUSE REPORTS: No. 97-257 (Comm. on Ways and Means) and No. 97-989 (Comm. of Conference).
SENATE REPORT No. 97-564 (Comm. on Finance).
CONGRESSIONAL RECORD:
    Vol. 127 (1981): Oct. 13, considered and passed House.
    Vol. 128 (1982): Dec. 19, considered and passed Senate, amended.
              Dec. 21, House agreed to conference report.
              Dec. 22, Senate agreed to conference report.

D. Convention on the means of prohibiting and preventing the illicit import, export and transfer of ownership of cultural property

adopted by the General Conference at its sixteenth session,
Paris, 14 November 1970

Having decided, at its fifteenth session, that this question should be made
the subject of an international convention.
Adopts this Convention on the fourteenth day of November 1970.

The General Conference of the United Nations Educational, Scientific and
Cultural Organization, meeting in Paris from 12 October to 14 November
1970, at its sixteenth session,

Recalling the importance of the provisions contained in the Declaration of
the Principles of International Cultural Co-operation, adopted by the
General Conference at its fourteenth session,

Considering that the interchange of cultural property among nations for
scientific, cultural and educational purposes increases the knowledge of
the civilization of Man, enriches the cultural life of all peoples and inspires
mutual respect and appreciation among nations,

Considering that cultural property constitutes one of the basic elements of
civilization and national culture, and that its true value can be appreciated
only in relation to the fullest possible information regarding its origin,
history and traditional setting,

Considering that it is incumbent upon every State to protect the cultural
property existing within its territory against the dangers of theft, clandestine excavation, and illicit export,

Considering that, to avert these dangers, it is essential for every State to
become increasingly alive to the moral obligations to respect its own
cultural heritage and that of all nations,

Considering that, as cultural institutions, museums, libraries and archives
should ensure that their collections are built up in accordance with univer-
sally recognized moral principles,

Considering that the illicit import, export and transfer of ownership of
cultural property is an obstacle to that understanding between nations
which it is part of Unesco's mission to promote by recommending to interested States, international conventions to this end,

Considering that the protection of cultural heritage can be effective only if
organized both nationally and internationally among States working in
close co-operation,

Considering that the Unesco General Conference adopted a Recommendation
to this effect in 1964,

Having before it further proposals on the means of prohibiting and preventing the illicit import, export and transfer of ownership of cultural property,
a question which is on the agenda for the session as item 19.

Article 1

For the purposes of this Convention, the term "cultural property" means
property which, on religious or secular grounds, is specifically designated by
each State as being of importance for archaeology, prehistory, history, literature, art or science and which belongs to the following categories:

(a) Rare collections and specimens of fauna, flora, minerals and anatomy,
and objects of palaeontological interest;

been illegally exported after entry into force of this Convention, in the States concerned. Whenever possible, to inform a State of origin Party to this Convention of an offer of such cultural property illegally removed from that State after the entry into force of this Convention in both States;

(b) (i)   to prohibit the import of cultural property stolen from a museum or a religious or secular public monument or similar institution in another State Party to this Convention after the entry into force of this Convention for the States concerned, provided that such property is documented as appertaining to the inventory of that institution;

   (ii)   at the request of the State Party of origin, to take appropriate steps to recover and return any such cultural property imported after the entry into force of this Convention in both States concerned, provided, however, that the requesting State shall pay just compensation to an innocent purchaser or to a person who has valid title to that property. Requests for recovery and return shall be made through diplomatic offices. The requesting Party shall furnish, at its expense, the documentation and other evidence necessary to establish its claim for recovery and return. The Parties shall impose no customs duties or other charges upon cultural property returned pursuant to this Article. All expenses incident to the return and delivery of the cultural property shall be borne by the requesting Party.

Article 8
The States Parties to this Convention undertake to impose penalities or administrative sanctions on any person responsible for infringing the prohibitions referred to under Articles 6 (b) and 7 (b) above.

Article 9
Any State Party to this Convention whose cultural patrimony is in jeopardy from pillage of archaeological or ethnological materials may call upon other States Parties who are affected. The States Parties to this Convention undertake, in these circumstances, to participate in a concerted international effort to determine and to carry out the necessary concrete measures, including the control of exports and imports and international commerce in the specific materials concerned. Pending agreement each State concerned shall take provisional measures to the extent feasible to prevent irremediable injury to the cultural heritage of the requesting State.

Article 10
The States Parties to this Convention undertake:
(a)   To restrict by education, information and vigilance, movement of cultural property illegally removed from any State Party to this Convention and, as appropriate for each country, oblige antique dealers, subject to penal or administrative sanctions, to maintain a register recording the origin of each item of cultural property, names and addresses of the supplier, description and price of each item sold and to inform the purchaser of the cultural property of the export prohibition to which such property may be subject;
(b)   to endeavour by educational means to create and develop in the public

mind a realization of the value of cultural property and the threat to the cultural heritage created by theft, clandestine excavations and illicit exports.

Article 11

The export and transfer of ownership of cultural property under compulsion arising directly or indirectly from the occupation of a country by a foreign power shall be regarded as illicit.

Article 12

The States Parties to this Convention shall respect the cultural heritage within the territories for the international relations of which they are responsible, and shall take all appropriate measures to prohibit and prevent the illicit import, export and transfer of ownership of cultural property in such territories.

Article 13

The States Parties to this Convention also undertake, consistent with the laws of each State:
(a) To prevent by all appropriate means transfers of ownership of cultural property likely to promote the illicit import or export of such property;
(b) to ensure that their competent services cooperate in facilitating the earliest possible restitution of illicitly exported cultural property to its rightful owner;
(c) to admit actions for recovery of lost or stolen items of cultural property brought by or on behalf of the rightful owners;
(d) to recognize the indefeasible right of each State Party to this Convention to classify and declare certain cultural property as inalienable which should therefore *ipso facto* not be exported, and to facilitate recovery of such property by the State concerned in cases where it has been exported.

Article 14

In order to prevent illicit export and to meet the obligations arising from the implementation of this Convention, each State Party to the Convention should, as far as it is able, provide the national services responsible for the protection of its cultural heritage with an adequate budget and, if necessary, should set up a fund for this purpose.

Article 15

Nothing in this Convention shall prevent States Parties thereto from concluding special agreements among themselves or from continuing to implement agreements already concluded regarding the restitution of cultural property removed, whatever the reason, from its territory of origin, before the entry into force of this Convention for the States concerned.

Article 16

The States Parties to this Convention shall in their periodic reports submitted to the General Conference of the United Nations Educational, Scientific and Cultural Organization on dates and in a manner to be determined by it, give information on the legislative and administrative provisions which they have adopted and other action which they have taken for the application of this Convention, together with details of the experience acquired in this field.

IN FAITH WHEREOF we have appended our signatures this seventeenth day of November 1970.

The President of the General Conference
ATILIO DELL'ORO MAINI

The Director-General
RENE MAHEU

Certified copy
   Paris,

*Director, Office of International
Standards and Legal Affairs,
United Nations Educational,
Scientific and Cultural Organization*

Glossary and Explanation of Footnote Citations

Below is a glossary of frequently cited references followed by an explanation of the sequence used in citing articles, books, cases and other reference material.

Glossary

Commonly cited references

Compilations of statutes and regulations

Publications marked by an asterisk are published by the U. S. Government Printing Office in Washington, D. C.

Am. Jur. 2d = *American Jurisprudence Second* (a general legal encyclopedia)

C.J.S. = *Corpus Juris Secundum* (a general legal encyclopedia)

*C.F.R. = *Code of Federal Regulations* (a subject-matter/agency-matter compilation of federal regulations published by the federal government)

*Cong. Rec. = *Congressional Record* (daily record of U.S. congressional actions)

*Fed. Reg. = *Federal Register* (the daily publication of the federal government which contains new and proposed federal regulations and notices of other current federal agency business)

*Stat. = *Statutes at Large* (a chronological compilation of U. S. statutes)

*U.S.C. = *United States Code* (the official publication of U.S. statutes organized by subject matter)

Case reporter names:

Cases:

Regional reporters of state court decisions, which follow, are published by the West Company, St. Paul, Minnesota. The "2d" after the initial(s) of the reporter means "second series." In addition, many states have their own reporter system for decisions. The titles of these reporter systems usually contain the state's name.

A. = *Atlantic Reporter*

N.E. = *North Eastern Reporter*

N.W. = *North Western Reporter*

P. = *Pacific Reporter*

S. = *Southern Reporter*

S.E. = *South Eastern Reporter*

S.W. = *South Western Reporter*

Reporters of decisions made by United States (federal) courts are published by the U.S. Government Printing Office.

F. = *Federal Reporter* (reports decisions of U.S. Courts of Appeals)

F. Supp. = *Federal Supplement* (reports decisions of the Federal District courts)

U.S. = *Supreme Court Reporter* (reports decisions of the U.S. Supreme Court)

Code of Federal Regulations. Washington, D.C.: U.S. Government Printing Office, 1983.

Cohen, Felix S. *Handbook of Federal Indian Law*. U.S. Solicitor for the Department of the Interior. Washington, D.C.: Government Printing Office, 1945.

Congressional Record. Washington, D.C.: U.S. Government Printing Office.

Corbin, Arthur Linton. *Corbin on Contracts*. St. Paul, Minn.: West Publishing Co., 1952.

Corning Museum of Glass. *The Corning Flood: Museum Under Water*. Edited by John H. Martin and Charleen K. Edwards. Corning, N.Y.: Corning Museum of Glass, 1977.

Corpus Juris Secundum. St. Paul, Minn.: West Publishing Co. 1936–.

Deloria, Vine., Jr., and Clifford M. Lytle. *American Indians, American Justice*. Austin, Tex.: University of Texas Press, 1983.

Dudley, Dorothy H., and Irma Bezold Wilkinson, and others. *Museum Registration Methods*. Washington, D.C.: American Association of Museums, 1979.

Duffy, Robert E. *Art Law: Representing Artists, Dealers and Collectors*. New York: Practising Law Institute, 1977.

Feilden, Bernard M. *Conservation of Historic Buildings*. Boston: Butterworth Scientific, 1982.

Feldman, Franklin, and Stephen E. Weil, eds. *Art Works: Law, Policy, Practice*. New York: Practising Law Institute, 1974.

Fennelly, Lawrence J. *Museum, Archive and Library Security*. Boston: Butterworth, 1983.

Fremont-Smith, Marion R. *Foundations and Government, State and Federal Law and Supervision*. New York: Russell Sage Foundation, 1965.

Galloway, Joseph M. *The Unrelated Business Income Tax*. New York: Wiley, 1982.

Goldberg, Steven S., *Taxation of Charitable Giving*. Tax Law and Practice: Practice Handbook Series, No. 5. New York: Practising Law Institue, 1973.

Guide to the Management of Recent Mammal Collections. See Williams, Stephen L., Ren'e Lauback, and Hugh H. Genownys.

Handbook for Museum Curators. London: Museums Association (a serial publication last published in 1965).

Hopkins, Bruce R. *Charity Under Siege: Government Regulation of Fund-Raising*. New York: Wiley, 1980.

International Committee on Museum Security. *Museum Security Survey*. Edited by Diana Menkes. Paris: International Council of Museums, 1981.

Johnson, E. Verner, and Joanne C. Horgan. *Museum Collection Storage*. Paris: UNESCO, 1979.

Keck, Caroline, and others. *A Primer on Museum Security*. Cooperstown, N.Y.: New York State Historical Association, 1966.

Kenney, Alice P. *Access to the Past: Museum Programs and Handicapped Visitors*. Nashville, Tenn.: American Association for State and Local History, 1980.

Law of Trusts. See Scott, Austin Wakeman.

Legal Problems of Museum Administration. See American Law Institute-American Bar Association.

Lewis, Ralph H. *Manual for Museums*. National Park Service, U.S. Department of the Interior. Washington, D.C.: Government Printing Office, 1976.

Martin, John H. See Corning Museum of Glass.

McGimsey, Charles Robert, III. *Public Archeology*. New York: Seminar Press, 1972.

Menkes, Diana. See International Committee on Museum Security.

Merryman, John Henry, and Albert E. Elsen. *Law, Ethics, and the Visual Arts*. New York: Matthew Bender, 1979–.

Metropolitan Museum of Art. *Museums and the Disabled*. New York: Metropolitan Museum of Art, 1979.

Meyer, Karl Ernest. *The Plundered Past*. New York: Atheneum, 1973.

Mill, John Stuart. *Dissertations and Discussions*. Vol. 1. Boston: Little, Brown and Co. 1864.

Moore, John Bassett. *A Digest of International Law*. Washington, D.C.: Government Printing Office, 1906.

Morris, John. *Managing the Library Fire Risk*. 2d ed. Berkeley, Calif.: University of California, 1979.

Museum Ethics. See American Association of Museums.

Nason, John William. *Trustees and the Future of Foundations*. New York: Council on Foundations, 1977.

National Trust for Historic Preservation in the United States. *A Guide to State Programs*. Washington, D.C.: National Trust for Historic Preservation, 1972.

Nauert, Patricia, and Caroline M. Black. *Fine Arts Insurance: A Handbook for Art Museums*. Savannah, Ga.: Association of Art Museum Directors (distributed by the American Association of Museums, Washington, D.C.), 1979.

O'Keefe, P. J. See Prott, Lyndel V.

Pfeffer, Irving, and Daniel Herrick (eds.). *Risk Management Manual for Museums*. New York: Association of Art Museum Directors, 1974–.

Prott, Lyndel V., and P. J. O'Keefe. *Law and the Cultural Heritage*. Abingdon, Oxon, England: Professional Books, 1984–.

Professional Practices in Art Museums. See Association of Art Museum Directors.

Prosser, William Lloyd. *Handbook of the Law of Torts*. 4th ed. St. Paul, Minn.: West Publishing Co., 1971.

Reese, Rosemary S., comp. *Care and Conservation of Collections*. Edited by Frederic L. Rath, Jr. and Merrilyn Rogers O'Connell. Vol. 2. *A Bibliography on Historical Organization Practices*. Nashville, Tenn.: American Association of State and Local History, 1977.

Restatement of the Law. See American Law Institute.

Reusing Old Buildings: Preservation Law and the Development Process. Study materials and papers prepared for a conference co-sponsored by the Conservation Foundation, National Trust for Historic Preservation, American Bar Association—Section of Urban, State, and Local Government Law, in cooperation with the National Association of Home Builders, *et al*. Washington, D.C.: The Conservation Foundation, 1982.

Scott, Austin Wakeman. *The Law of Trusts*. 3rd ed. Boston: Little, Brown, 1967.

Smithsonian Institution [Snider, Harold]. *Museums and Handicapped Students: Guidelines for Educators*. Washington, D.C.: Smithsonian Institution, 1977.

Snider, Harold. See Smithsonian Institution.

Statutes at Large. Washington, D.C.: U.S. Government Printing Office.

Steiner, Charles. See Metropolitan Museum of Art.

Story, Joseph. *Commentaries on the Laws of Bailments*. 8th ed. Boston: Little, Brown and Co., 1870.

Thomson, Garry. *The Museum Environment*. Boston: Butterworth, 1978.

Tillotson, Robert C. *Museum Security*. Translated by Martha de Molke. Paris: International Council of Museums, 1977.